This one is for
la brujita.

By G. W. Robinette

Did Lin Zexu Make Morphine? Vols. I, II (2008)

Why Drug Wars Fail, Vol. I (2012)

Translated by G. W. Robinette

The General History of Drugs, Vol. I (2010)
by Antonio Escohotado

WEEDING
CANNABIS FIELDS

or: How <u>Not</u> to Weigh a Witch

A work of pure fiction by

G. W. Robinette

GRAFFITI MILITANTE PRESS
Valparaiso, Chile
2014

Acknowledgments

Hashish was sold in small shops in Ceuta and Melilla under Franco; some of his best legions were Moroccan. After the death of *Il Caudillo* (though the legislature forbade it) the Spanish Supreme Court established the right of personal use for all drugs. But the *Guardia Civil* (the former dictator's secret police, who attempted a *coup d'etat* in 1982) continued to machete the small gardens of *cultivadores*. Prosecutors indicted these hobbyists not for possession but for trafficking, demanding years in prison, their only evidence being the gross weight of the seized plants. Each case turned upon this magic number.

Fernanda de la Figuera, the activist and master grower (who established the right to home cultivation of cannabis in her own trial in the early 1990s), appeared in many of these proceedings as an expert witness for the defense. She helped inexperienced judges understand that kilos of wet plant were not grams of dried flowers. Her rapid-fire testimony and impressive command of the subject were invariably persuasive. Not a few growers today owe her their freedom.

In order to more accurately determine this ratio of smokable bud to freshly harvested flora, she sponsored a measurement program for the plants grown at the A.R.S.E.C.A. Research Centre, near Malaga. During a number of growing seasons, harvests and post-harvest processing in the first decade of the 2000s, I was able to track plants from seed to *keiki* to growth spurt to sexual differentiation to first bud to attacks of *gusanos* and *plagas* to ripe *colas* and through the subsequent stages of harvest, drying, manicuring and curing.

Throughout this invaluable apprenticeship, she challenged my *gringo* values and beliefs. Indeed, the ideas and preliminary statistics presented here first appeared in *Cañamo*, in an article by Fernanda de la

Figuera entitled, "*El Número Mágico.*" They are used by permission. In every sense, this book would not exist without her. The errors belong to me alone.

G. W. Robinette
2014

Figure 1.
Fernanda de la Figuera.

Preface

As drug wars fail (*all* drug wars fail), the legal argument shifts from none to some, from Just Say No to How Much is Enough. Mere possession no longer convicts. So mere quantity must.

But like witchcraft, trafficking is a crime dark and difficult to prove. A willing seller files no taxes. A willing buyer keeps no receipts. No witness observes this private transaction. No victim complains of harm. There is no evidence *of* a crime; instead, the evidence *is* the crime.

The defendant's own property must be tortured until it testifies against her and confesses her guilt. Plastic baggies may seal her fate. A kitchen scale may tip the balance against her.

Yet far more important than these *indicios* of modern witchcraft will always be the sheer quantity of the offending substance. A conscientious judge will literally and electronically weigh the evidence, an inanimate object (though clearly one possessed by the devil), in order to sieve out the nefarious *traficante* from the innocent backyard gardener.

The drug warriors know this too. The drug war is their rice bowl. It pays off their mortgages and finances their doughnuts, lap dances and alcoholism. Inflating the amount of dried flowers obtainable from a given plant is simple personal and institutional self-interest. Hence the fraudulent yield/density study, *Cannabis Fields*.

Well and truly humorous is that this DEA study generates data that contradicts its own fore-ordained conclusions. The drug warriors again demonstrate uncanny ignorance of plant biology. However, I was also surprised to learn that it had taken in some of the less sceptical activists. Damning the study in as few words as possible: *the data simply does not support the conclusions that either side wishes to draw.*

This book will make everyone unhappy. Well, *pox vobiscum*. Chapters 1-12 deconstruct *Cannabis Fields*. Appendix A and B have copies of a similar study. Appendix C presents data from a Spanish cannabis club and questions some of the assumptions, both legal and philosophical, behind this search for a magic number that can more accurately weigh witches.

Lost in Austin
January 2014

Figure 2.
The Hexsenwaag at Oudewater.

Introduction

*Therefore ... one accused of being a witch ought never
to be folly [sic] acquitted and set free ...
inasmuch as the proof of such crimes is
so obscure and so difficult that not one
witch in a million would be accused
or punished if the procedures were
governed by the ordinary rules ....*
Jean Bodin (1530 – 1596)[1]

The Ignorant Inquisitor. The famous French jurist and witchfinder was complaining because it was not enough that a suspected witch should have in her dwelling cannabis, hashish, poppies, opium or belladonna. These plants and their simple extracts could be characterized as innocuous or even medicinal when found in the homes of doctors, respectable herbalists, ecclesiastics, nobles or, of course, magistrates and counselors to the court.[2] Possession alone of what were then known as *diabolic* herbs could not secure conviction.

---

[1] Burr, George L., ed. Translations and Reprints from the Original Sources of European History, vol. III, no. 4. Philadelphia, PA: Department of History of the University of Pennsylvania, 1912, pp. 5-6; *C'est pourquoi celui qui est atteint & accusé d'etre Sorcier, ne doit jamas etre envoyé absoubs à pur & à plain .... D'autant que la preuve de telles meschácetez est si cachee & si difficile, qu'il n'y auroit personne accusé n'y puny d'un million de Sorciers qu'il y a, si les parties estoient reglees en procez ordinaire par faute de preuve ... (J. Bodin. De la Démonomanie des Sorciers, l. iv, ch. v. Paris: Chez Jacques du Puys Librairie Juré, 1580, pp. 217-218, www.archive.org, //gallica.bnf.fr (1598), pp. 473-474).*

[2] "Por supuesto ... en el domicilio de un eclesiástico, un magistrado o un noble se entendía justificada. ... [L]as mismas plantas, los mismos brebajes y los mismos untos pueden presentarse

To distinguish the good *hausfrau* from the bad witch, a responsible and conscientious inquisitor required more reliable and trustworthy indications (*indicios*), like a confession obtained through torture or the possession of banned books, though nothing showed up in court so often as prohibited ointments, potions, salves or home remedies.[3] To be sure other signs (*señales*) would also do such as birthmarks, warts, points on the body insensitive to the prick of a needle or one nipple too many.[4]

Among the many bizarre indications of witchcraft was that a suspect should exhibit a "weight not in proportion to her size."[5] The thinking behind this criterion grew out of the well-known-by-all fact that witches flew upon brooms and therefore had to be much lighter than they appeared. Theologians argued over this application of impeccable legal logic to a patently false premise. Toward the end of the Middle Ages some even correctly attributed these reports of communal magical flight to the use of entheogenic herbs.[6]

---

también como cosas perfectamente inocuas, saludables e incluso imprescindibles. Eso explica ... tanto las solanaceas como el opio y el cáñamo sean empleados por médicos y boticarios respetables ... (Escohotado, pp. 295 – 296)."

[3] *"Puede, pues, afirmarse que si bien hay varios «indicios» recurrentes de brujeria, como la posesion de ciertos libros ... ninguno tiene la continuidad y solidez de los «untos y potages» como prueba"* (Escohotado, p. 281).

[4] *"Por «señales» de filiación satánica se entendía prácticamente cualquier característica no muy habitual, como manchas o taras anatómicas congénitas, puntos insensibles al contacto de una aguja, incluso verrugas en ciertos casos. A falta de otras pruebas, una mujer que tenía un pezón de más fue condenada ..."* (Escohotado, p. 281, ftnt 24, quoting Huxley, 1970, p. 126).

[5] *"Uno era el peso, pues si cierta persona pesaba poco, o simplemente tenía un peso no congruente con su volumen la jurisprudencia tenía resuelto que era signo de brujería"* (Escohotado, p. 311).

[6] The Catholic Church repressed and persecuted these ancient ceremonies that often included an ointment of solanaceas (datura, mandragora, for example) applied to the sensitive mucous membranes of the vagina with a broomstick (see Escohotado, pp. 277-280).

The Corrupt Weighmaster.   While scholars debated, thousands of women from all across Europe voted with their feet. They traveled many hundreds of miles to be weighed at an official witch-weighing balance (*hexsenwaag*, in Dutch).   One of the most popular at Oudewater, Holland issued an official "Certificate of Weighing" (*Certificaet van Weginghe*) which could acquit a woman of the charge of witchcraft if her weight corresponded to the proportions of her body.[7]

But first this required an accurate appraisal by the weighmaster. He estimated her weight beforehand, a practice still popular at rural county fairs for judging livestock.   An overestimation by eye would convict any hapless woman who could not pay on the side.   "Masters of the Weighhouses ... were often corrupt and would declare a woman too light in exchange for a couple of ducats."[8]   Oudewater, for example, supposedly received its right to weigh witches in 1545 from the invading Spanish Emperor Charles V when the weighmaster of a neighboring town was found to be corrupt.[9]

Five hundred years later the Inquisition is condemned for the madness that it was. The witch balance at Oudewater is only a popular tourist destination in the summer. The weighmaster has even received a complaint from a self-confessed witch who argued strongly *against* her newly obtained certificate of innocence.

Need versus Greed.   Today it is the cultivator of cannabis who must endure the medieval trial by balance. Some cannabis might be respectable for medicinal reasons or even for personal use in a few progressive US states or countries. But too much clearly augurs a legally dangerous if not downright diabolic possession for the defendant. The new witch finders hack down her plants, weigh

---

[7] See www.hexsenwaag.nl, www.oudewater.nl, www.holland.com, //rechtsgeschie denis.wordpress.com/2013/08/19/weighing-the-witches-at-oudewater.

[8] Ibid.

[9] Ibid.

the dead wet flora and solemnly present this number in court. Instead of weighing the witch, they now weigh her garden.

So how much is too much? The answer hinges philosophically on the difference between necessity and desire. Legally, it turns upon the biological relationship between plants and their dried flowers.

But often plants are sensitive to how closely they are grown together. The weight of flower, leaf, stalk or seed (and the ratio of one weight to another) varies not only with the cultivar but with the amount of space in which the plant is allowed to grow. To discover some general rule one has to grow the same plant both closer together and farther apart from its neighbors. Hence, the yield/density study.

This kind of study is common in academia and commercial agriculture. It's purpose usually is to identify the density that produces the maximum yield for a given variety. That it should be sponsored by the DEA, not usually thought of as an educational or mercenary institution, suggests a less than eleemosynary motive. It also heralds the beginning of the end of the war on cannabis. When activists grow the plant, and the DEA grows the plant, the war is over: the plant has won.

Yield/Density Studies.   Many plants depend

largely on temperature, solar radiation, moisture and soil fertility for their growth and nutritional requirements. A thick population crop may have limitations in the maximum availability of these factors. It is, therefore, necessary to determine the optimum density of plant population per unit area for obtaining maximum yields.[10]

---

[10] Baloch, A. W., et al. "Optimum Plant Density for High Yield in Rice (*Oryza sativa* L.)," *Asian Journal of Plant Sciences*, Volume 1, Number 1: 2002, pp. 25-27.

INTRODUCTION

Not only rice[11] but safflower (*Carthamis tinctorius* L.),[12] soybeans,[13] wheat and flax,[14] canola,[15] corn,[16] Douglas fir,[17] and hemp,[18] all exhibit this property that density affects yield. A good yield/density study typically will grow the same plant at different densities; some will be grown closer to their neighbors and others will have more space in which to

---

[11] Bozorgi, Hamid Reza et al. "Effect of Plant Density on Yield and Yield Components of Rice," *World Applied Sciences Journal*, 12 (11): 2011, pp. 2053-2057; Lin, X. Q. et al. "Effect of plant density and nitrogen fertilizer rates on grain yield and nitrogen uptake of hybrid rice (*Oryza sativa* L.)," Journal of Agricultural Biotechnology and Sustainable Development, Vol. 1 (2): November 2009, pp. 44-53.

[12] Zarei, Gholamreza et al. "Effect of Planting Density on Yield and Yield Components of Safflower Cultivars in Spring Planting," *World Academy of Science, Engineering and Technology* 60: 2011, pp. 135-137.

[13] Hosseini, N. Majnoun et al. "Effect of Plant Population Density on Yield and Yield Components of Eight Isolines of cv. Clark (*Glycine max* L.)," *J. Agric. Sci. Technol.*, Vol. 3: 2001, pp. 131-139; Rahman, M. M. and M. M. Hossain. "Plant Density Effects on Growth, Yield and Yield Components of Two Soybean Varieties under Equidistant Planting Arrangement," *Asian Journal of Plant Sciences*, Vol. 10 (5): 2011, pp. 278-286.

[14] Deng, Jianming et al. "Models and tests of optimal density and maximal yield for crop plants," *PNAS*, www. pnas.org/cgi/doi/10.1073/pnas.1210955109.

[15] Naseri, Rahim et al. "Study on effects of different plant density on seed yield, oil and protein content of four canola cultivars in western Iran," *International Journal of Agriculture and Crop Sciences*, vol. 4-2: 2012, pp. 70-78.

[16] Nik, Mohsen. Moussavi et al. "Effect of plant density on yield and yield components of corn hybrids (*Zea mays*)," *Scientific Research and Essays*, Vol. 6 (22): 7 October 2011, pp. 4821-4825; Kgasago, Hans. "Effect of planting dates and densities on yield and yield components of short and ultra-short growth period maize (*Zea mays* L.)," Department of Plant Production and Soil Science, University of Praetoria, 2006, pp. i-111.

[17] Reukema, Donald L. "The Yield and Density Aspect – Does Dense Spacing Really Produce the Most Volume," *Proceedings of the 1966 Annual Meeting of Western Reforestation Coordinating Committee*, Portland, Oregon, 1966.

[18] Van der Werf, Hayo M. G. "The effect of plant density on light interception in hemp (*Cannabis sativa* L.)," *Journal of the International Hemp Association*, 4(1): 1997, pp. 8-13.

expand.[19]   To control the density, extra rows of plants are grown around the plants from which they intend to take a sample.[20]   The sample is then taken at random.[21]

Cannabis and Density.   *Cannabis sativa* L. is one of those plants in which density affects yield. Grow cannabis close together with its neighbors and it grows up straight and tall and narrow, one central stalk with not many leaves, a few short branches near the top, and perhaps only a single bud at the apex. Industrial hemp is often grown in this fashion in hemp plantations in Canada, Holland, Hungary, Australia and Spain. Give each plant a square yard in which to grow and the plants spread out a little more. Give them two square yards or even three and the sativas especially will expand to fill these larger areas if they can.

Cannabis Fields began as a yield/density study. The original plan was to find some relationship between the weight or canopy of a freshly harvested plant and the weight of its dried flowers. Very quickly, however, it morphed into just another bit of doctored evidence to support an ideological crusade. Instead of allowing the science to dictate their conclusions, the inquisitors at the DEA have shown themselves to be only the latest avatars of the corrupt medieval weighmaster.

---

[19] See, for example, Baloch (2002), p. 25, where the authors grew rice at spacings of 20 x 20 cm, 22.5 x 22.5 cm and 25x25 cm or Bozorgi (2011), p. 2054, whose team chose spacings of 15 x 15, 20 x 20 and 25 x 25 cm; Van der Werf (1997), p. 8 used densities of 10, 30, 90, and 270 per meter squared.

[20] Van der Werf (1997) surrounded his experiment with a "3-m wide buffer of hemp" (p. 10); Zarei (2011) planted seven rows to each plot but measured only on the five central rows (p. 135); Rahman and Hossain (2011) excluded border plants (p. 280).

[21] Naseri (2012), p. 71; Hosseini (2001), p. 132.

Table of Contents

_____

TABLE OF CONTENTS

WEEDING
CANNABIS FIELDS
or: How <u>Not</u> to Weigh a Witch

All four of the figures in *Cannabis Fields* and two of the tables
are incorrect. The third table (Table 4) is pure invention. The DEA
fed the plants through a leaf shredder so the flowers were never
separated from the leaves. They zeroed the raw seed data to create the
sinsemilla, then added the missing seed to the stalk but reported it in
the leaf and bud. They grew the two largest plants by cutting all the
other plants around them early, then harvested these huge anomalies
last and used the measurements to skew the formulas. Their sample
was non-random. They planted in rows and harvested by columns.
They eliminated smaller plants from their sample and replaced them
with larger plants. Both neighbor and edge effects occurred. No
photographs were provided. There is good reason to doubt the
planting dates. All the plants would have fit together on a single
football field and could have been grown in a single season. Neither of
the putative lead authors, who signed their names to incorrectly
reported, retitled abstracts after twenty-five years, ever saw the plants
or wrote a single word of the study.

The report passed through at least two sets of hands: a bought-
off academic and an ambitious alcoholic. The academic wrote the
recipe which the alcoholic altered and chopped in two. Together the
hash they served up became *Cannabis Fields.*

First, Doctor Leonard Sly designed what should have been a
competent yield/density study. Plants were grown. Measurements
were taken. Data was collected. Results were tabulated. He wrote a
brief, simple report with one table and four figures. Figure 2 had a

single pie chart. Two formulas were developed. But the results of this preliminary report did not please his DEA overlords.

So Agent Lewis Lost decided to adapt and overcome the limitations of the study. Tables and figures were split and amended. Bud magically appeared from a shredded mass of green, leafy bits. Seeded plants became sinsemilla. Large plants replaced small. He inserted a different study with a different protocol (possibly of male plants) to divert attention from the original results. The text was partially rewritten and a completely new section, the Domestic Estimate, was added to produce what the DEA had long desired: scientific proof of a Poundaplant®. Lost was proud of his work and wanted to show it to others, mostly judges and juries.

But it wasn't that easy for the DEA bureaucracy to release what had previously been classified. So Agent Lost needed to do one more thing. He cut and shuffled the report twice, standard counter-intelligence procedure. One year became two, the dates were changed, plant numbers were erased, and the field data was deliberately disordered. He attempted to obscure when and where and how the plants were grown.

The purpose of *Cannabis Fields* is to imprison home growers of cannabis. It was written to provide evidence for the DEA's long-testified-to-in-court ratio of a pound of something dried and smokeable that could be harvested from every cannabis plant, a magic number that would convict almost anyone. But although Dr. Sly sold his petty soul, Agent Lost clearly flunked high school math and fell asleep in biology class.

Figure 3. Preparation.
The compost heap; turning the soil for the first time.

*Figure 4. A solution of ortiga
mixed with tobacco and garlic to be used
as a root tonic and bug dissuader.*

1
Some Liars Can't Figure

"The old saying is that 'figures will not lie,'
but a new saying is 'liars will figure.'
It is our duty ... to prevent the liar from figuring;
... to prevent him from perverting the truth,
in the interest of some theory he wants to establish.
We can only do this by being absolutely fair ourselves."
-- Carroll D. Wright (1840 – 1909)[1]

---

[1] First U.S. Commissioner of Labor, opening remarks given 25 June 1889 at the Seventh Annual Convention of Chiefs and Commissioners of the Bureaus of Labor Statisticians held at Hartford, Conn, <u>Joint Documents of the State of Michigan for the year 1889</u>, vol. III, Part I. Lansing, MI: Darius D. Thorp, State Binder and Printer, 1890, p. 311 (GB); www.quoteinvestigator.com; <u>The Encyclopaedia Britannica</u>, 11th ed., vol. XXVIII, Vetch to Zymotic Diseases. NY: The Encyclopaedia Britannica Company, 1911, p. 846, www.1911encyclopedia.org.

We begin our fictional tale of deconstruction with Table 1 of *Cannabis Fields* as reported on page three:

Table 1
Average Cannabis Yields at
Maturity for High Planting Densities

SPONSOR	YEAR	DENSITY	YIELD*	SEED STOCK
Univ. of MS	1985	9 ft. sq.	222 grams	Mexico
Univ. of MS	1986	9 ft. sq.	274 grams	Mexico
DEA	1990	18 ft. sq.	233 grams	Colombia
DEA	1991	9 ft. sq.	215 grams	Mexico

*Yield = oven dry yield of usable leaf and bud from mature 120 day or older plants.

Table 1.
Table 1 from Cannabis Fields.

A.   Too Many Kooks Roil the Froth

What's wrong with this table? The answer is almost everything. But even if you don't run the numbers, there is something glaringly odd about this collection of data. Why is the data under the column heading Density given in "ft. sq." while the corresponding entries under Yield are given in grams? This may seem like a trivial question. But pull on this one string and the rest of the study unravels.

1.   Mixed Metrics.   *Cannabis Fields* has a number of these kinds of curiosities. Not least is this mixed use of metric and English measurements. It's not that this can't be done, it is that it is generally not done, so it begs questions when it happens.

SOME LIARS CAN'T FIGURE

The plots were laid out in feet but the harvest is reported in the metric system, for instance. Table 4 gives its diameters in feet and its estimated yield [Leafnbud®] in grams. Figure 1 has its x-axis labelled "square feet of growing area" but its height/diameter ratios are calculated using data recorded in centimeters. This isn't so bad, but why measure in one system and report in the other, or for that matter, both?

This contrasts with Figure 3, graphing grams versus grams, and Figure 4, showing grams versus centimeters. The data in Attachment 1 consistently uses the metric system to report weights and heights and diameters. But Tables 1 and 2 and Figure 1 in the body of the report inconsistently mix English areas with metric weights and Table 4 mixes English diameters with metric weights.

Why do Table 1 and Table 2 report their yield [Leafnbud®] in grams? One cannabis activist has converted the data to ounces in his booklet, *Cannabis Fields and Postage*. Though his calculations are correct, the data he calculates from is incorrect and thus, so are his results. In a completely related matter, why do Table 1 and Table 2 use the quaint "ft. sq." to report their "Density"? It is not nitpicking to observe that this column heading should really be labelled "Square Feet of Growing Area Per Plant." Density is defined as the number of plants per any given unit of area. It is generally given as a number per meters squared, as in Attachment 1. Notice that as the density increases, the alloted growing area for each plant decreases, and vice versa.

Now there are three possibilities for this. One, perhaps the author attempts to confuse us. He just wants to make it difficult for us to calculate. Which would be odd in a supposedly scientific paper dedicated to reporting supposedly scientific results which normally use the metric system. Two, the author is incompetent. But anyone who can design a yield/density study and do the necessary calculations would probably be familiar with the metric system. Alternatively, three, the mixed metrics are the product of at least two different people, one who understood the metric system and another who did not.

2.   A Designing Doctor.   The first pair of hands to touch *Cannabis Fields* belongs to an academic, one Dr. Leonard Sly. His loyalty, his morals, his ability to question, had clearly been purchased some time ago. This ethically-challenged professor knew ahead of time what the DEA meant to do with his report.

The reason *Cannabis Fields* masquerades as a yield/density study is that the good doctor designed it to be just that. He chose five different densities: 0.15, 0.21, 0.31, 0.62, and 1.23. These numbers correspond, respectively, to plot dimensions of 2.4 by 2.7, 1.8 by 2.7, 1.8 by 1.8, 0.9 by 1.8, and 0.9 by 0.9 meters per plant. For the five different densities, he laid out ten plots. Each plot contained roughly but not exactly 100 plants. His design called for a sample space of 950 plants (not counting edge rows), from which 38 mature plants could be selected, or four percent, in order to arrive at a statistically meaningful result. There was one plot of 0.15 (2.4 by 2.7 meters), three plots of 0.21 (1.8 by 2.7 meters), one plot of 0.31 (1.8 by 1.8 meters), three plots of 0.62 (0.91 by 1.8 meters), and two plots of density 1.23 (0.9 by 0.9 meters).

The reason for using three plots (not one) for two of the densities is that the design of the study also called for checking to see if planting date had any effect on the yield [Leafnbud®] of the plants. (It didn't.) So each of the three plots of the 0.21 density and each of the three plots of the 0.62 density were planted on staggered dates, probably a week or two apart. Why did he use two plots of density 1.23 (0.9 by 0.9 meters)? I don't know. We'll do the field layout in Chapter 8.

Afterwards, he did the basic calculations and drew up a first set of tables and figures to illustrate his conclusions. He reported his results using the metric system. The data set in the original Attachment 1 (now lost) was his work. Figures 3 and 4 are entirely his as is the correlation matrix. The only reason they are wrong is because the plants he used to calculate them from have been replaced by others.

SOME LIARS CAN'T FIGURE

3.   Lost in Place.   At this point the study passed out of the hands of the academic and into the hands of the alcoholic, Agent Lewis Lost, aka the Liar. He wasn't very happy with the good doctor's limited results. So he changed them.

In this sense, *Cannabis Fields* is very much a palimpsest. The original writing of Dr. Sly has been partially effaced to make room for the later contributions of Agent Lost. Yet traces of the original report remain underneath.

Lew's a good ol' boy. But he is certainly not the brightest Christmas bulb in the box. From the parts he added, it's clear that he likes to use large words incorrectly, make unjustified *pronunciamientos* with perfect certainty, and espouse his anti-cannabis ideology. No doubt he has never felt he has ever been properly appreciated for his true genius. His secret wish may be that once in his life someone will actually believe that he knows what he is talking about.

Lewis decided he could alter the morally dubious professor's original report to achieve the DEA's holy grail: [Trumpets! Ta-da!] a Poundaplant®!   DEA agents have testified to this fictitious achievement in courts of law for decades. It's catchy, onomatopoeic and easy to remember even with a hangover. [Can a grower obtain a pound of dried flowers from a single cannabis plant? I have seen better than two pounds. But will you do this on average? Unlikely.]

But bullet-headed Lewis can't use the metric system. He doesn't understand it. He is also unclear on the concept of density. Density is not given in "foot square." He should have converted grams to ounces if he wanted to use English measurements or used density instead of square feet if he wanted to use metrics. But all that would have required work.

So he reports yield [Leafnbud®] in grams and density in "ft. sq." This is, of course, an abbreviation for "foot square." And "foot square" is a colloquialism, often found in the South, for square feet. You can almost hear the accent dripping off the magnolias. I spent part of my misbegotten youth there.

B.   Correcting Table 1

But once we understand there were at least two authors of *Cannabis Fields* and not just one (one who can handle the metric system and one who cannot), this helps us decipher what Lewis changed and what he left alone of Professor Sly's original report. Table 1 and Table 2, for example, have both been altered by Lewis the Liar.

Lewis's purpose, of course, is Poundaplant®. For this he needs large plants. He calls attention in the first line of the report to one of the two largest plants in the entire field (both deliberately manufactured anomalies), plant number 103.01 with a dry yield [Leafnbud®] of 2308.4 grams.

For Lewis, small plants are the anomalies: "The similarity of [the smaller] plant yields contained in Table 1 is remarkable ... (page 3)." Their shape is odd: "The noticeably high [height/diameter] ratio for the 9 foot square planting density confirms that this plant canopy shape is different than all of the other observations which had relatively large amounts of space in which to grow (page 3)." Larger plants from the low density plots are normal: "The additional space allows the plant to assume a natural canopy shape ... (page 3)." High density is different; low density is normal. High density is unnatural; low density is natural. Small yields are bad; large yields are good.

Never acknowledged is that the other domestic US growers of cannabis might not necessarily want large plants. Most home gardeners have limited space in which to grow. Larger plants are also more difficult to hide and tend to attract rippers, cops and the DEA. They require more water and more maintenance. They are a complete bother to clean by hand during a late season attack of *gusanos*, requiring a step-ladder and a long reach. Further, larger plants do not necessarily produce the highest quality cannabis in terms of taste, high, pain relief, or interest. So home cultivators often have limited interest in growing extra large plants in their gardens.

SOME LIARS CAN'T FIGURE

1.   Picking Cherries.   Now Lewis just needs the data to prove that large plants are good and small plants are bad. Since the data won't demonstrate his preconceived ideas, he discards what he doesn't like. The introduction to Table 1, on page two, reads: "Table 1 depicts the average yield for *all* mature (120 days or older) cannabis plants using a dense planting pattern of either 9 square feet per plant or 18 square feet per plant (page 2, italics added)."

All?   The third entry in Table 1 ignores that statement completely. Lewis only includes the Colombian. Deliberately not included are the two mature (145 day old) plants from plot F in Attachment 1, also with density 0.62 (18 square feet of growing area per plant). Why were these two plants not invited to the party? And what of the plot labelled H, also of density 0.62? Were there no mature plants from this plot? Instead, only one immature plant and no mature plants are reported in Attachment 1.

Contrast that with plots A, B, and C with density 0.21 which together have 34 plants listed in Attachment 1, nine of them mature. Plots E, F and H of density 0.62 have only 9 plants in Attachment 1, just five of them mature. Plots with larger plants dominate the data; plots with smaller plants go unreported. Much of the data that could have been used to construct an honest Table 1, with the yields from *all* the mature plants is missing. Clearly, he must have been unhappy with the yield [Leafnbud®] from all the 0.62 density plants. So he decided to use only the Colombian. You can get any answer you want if you cherry-pick your data.

The three mature Colombian plants have an average yield [Leafnbud®] of 233.17 grams. Three plants isn't really enough to pretend you have any kind of a statistically viable average but Lewis doesn't know this. We can recalculate the figure for *all* the 0.62 density plots by adding the extra two mature plants from plot F to the three mature from plot E. Together, they sum to 1770.8 which divided by 5 gives an average of 354.16 grams. This is considerably more than the 233 grams reported from the 0.62 density Colombian alone.

Lewis has inserted only the Colombian and cut out almost all of the data from the other two 0.62 density plots. He only refers to them once in the body of the paper, on page two. You can see this insertion better in the earlier Linda Smith version (see Appendix 2) where this entry is not properly indented under the category headings, kind of an obvious giveaway that someone stuck something in there at the last minute. Reporting only the Colombian violates the stated protocol for Table 1 to include all the data from all the mature plants.

Here's what Lewis started with for his new Table 1:

Lewis's Proto-Table 1
Average Cannabis Yields
[Leafnbud®] at Maturity for High Planting Densities

SPONSOR	YEAR	DENSITY	YIELD*	SEED STOCK
DEA	1990	0.62	354.16	Col/Hyb/Jam
DEA	1991	1.23	214.61	Mexican

Table 2.
What Lewis Started with for Table 1.

Here's his new table after he eliminated the data that did not fit:

Lewis's Proto-Table 1 (Beta)
Average Cannabis Yields
[Leafnbud®] at Maturity for High Planting Densities

SPONSOR	YEAR	DENSITY	YIELD*	SEED STOCK
DEA	1990	0.62	233.17	Colombia
DEA	1991	1.23	214.61	Mexican

Table 3.
What Lewis got for Table 1 after eliminating the data he didn't like.

CANNABIS YIELDS: ATTACHMENT 2
1985-86 YIELD DATA, UNIVERSITY OF MISSISSIPPI

UNIVERSITY OF MISSISSIPPI 1985 YIELD STUDY DATA

Table 1. Statistics for the Production of Marijuana from Plants of different Age.

Week	Plant #	WET WEIGHT(s) Whole Plant	Stalk/Stems	leaves	DRY WEIGHT(s) Stalk/Stems	leaves	% of dry leaves to dry WP²	% of dry leaves to wet WP²	% of dry stalk/stem to wet WP²	% of Dry plant to wet WP²	% of Wet leaves to wet WP²	% of Wet stalk/stem to wet WP²	% of dry leaves to wet leaves	Budget (cm)
12	1	328	182	146	82	53.5	39	16	25	41	45	56	37	180
13	2	1309.7	702	607.7	380	130.5	26	10	29	39	46	54	21	231
14	3	1055	657	398	282	158.1	36	15	28	42	38	62	40	269
15	4	2163	1197	966	622	372.5	37	17	29	46	45	55	39	286
16	5	2222	1518	704	704	241.0	25	11	33	43	68	68	34	224
17	6	2268	1533	735	726	268.2	25	12	36	48	68	67	36	281
18	7	1972	1331	641	823	221.5	25	11	33	44	68	67	35	300
19	8	1724	1278	446	655	171.4	20	10	39	49	33	74	38	328
20	9	3472	2535	937	668	388.7	24	11	35	46	26	73	41	359
21	10	2164	1661	503	854	217.6	20	10	39	50	23	77	43	358
Average		1867.77	1259.4	608.37	630.9	222.37	27.7	12.3	32.6	44.8	34.7	65.4	36.5	273.6

WP² = Whole plant.

UNIVERSITY OF MISSISSIPPI 1986 YIELD STUDY DATA

Table 2. Statistics for the Production of Marijuana from Mature Plants.

Plant #	WET WEIGHT(s) Whole Plant	Stalk/Stems	leaves	DRY WEIGHT(s) Stalk/Stems	leaves	% of dry leaves to dry WP²	% of dry leaves to wet WP²	% of dry stalk/stem to wet WP²	% of Dry plant to wet WP²	% of Wet leaves to wet WP²	% of Wet stalk/stem to wet WP²	% of dry leaves to wet leaves	Budget (cm)
1	3869	2635	1261	1456	709	33	11	37	56	52	68	36	249
2	2680	1620	1060	688	361	34	16	26	39	40	61	34	231
3	1712	1200	512	620	181	23	11	36	47	50	70	35	213
4	2133	1292	861	680	289	30	14	32	45	39	61	34	216
5	1730	1218	512	570	171	23	10	33	43	30	70	33	221
6	2344	1314	1030	621	319	34	14	27	40	44	56	31	221
7	2283	1541	742	810	140	15	6	36	43	33	68	19	257
8	2231	1418	813	734	280	28	13	33	46	36	64	34	224
9	1168	808	360	400	130	25	11	34	45	36	69	36	224
10	1376	965	411	540	157	23	11	39	51	30	70	38	244
Avg.	2155.3	1401.1	754.2	711.9	273.7	26.8	12.2	33.3	45.5	34.5	65.7	35	220

Table 4.
Tables 1 and 2, Attachment 2, from a similar study.

2.   **Table 1, Attachment 2.**   Now Lew needs some
more data to fill out his new Table 1. So, he bravely imports it from
another study with a different protocol, one purportedly done in 1985
and 1986, this data reported separately in Attachment 2. Naturally, he
does it badly.

First, on the basis only of form, these two studies should never
have been combined. Nothing in Attachment 2 suggests that the
plants grown for that study were limited in their growing space.
Density as a column heading nowhere appears. No protocol is
recorded describing how the plants were grown, whether there were
outer rows or neighbor effects, the size of the plots, or even whether
density was a factor that was controlled in any way. The only place
their quantity of growing area is reported is in Table 1. Lewis gives
them each "9 ft. sq." and we are expected to take him at his word. In
fact, we have no write up at all of this earlier study. Like *Cannabis Fields*
it remains unpublished and has not been peer reviewed.

Second, on the basis of content, the nagging detail that no seed
was recorded for any of the plants from this other study we are not
supposed to notice. And that this earlier study divides the plants into
two parts only, "Stalk/Stems" and "leaves," we are also supposed to
overlook. That the data in Attachment 2 taken by itself only accurately
describes *male* plants is of no importance. That these "leaves" in
Attachment 2 are somehow transformed into yield [Leafnbud®] in
Table 1 is something else, like the little man behind the curtain
furiously pulling his levers and switches, we should pay no attention to.

Notwithstanding these objections, in his haste Lewis brings the
numbers over without thinking. Table 1, Attachment 2 records the
yield [leaves] from the 1985 [male] plants as averaging 222 grams. In
fact, the average of the dry weights of the leaves from the ten 1985
plants recorded in Table 1, Attachment 2 is indeed listed as 222.37
somethings. The 7 hundredths is completely spurious.

But in his hurry to construct his new Table 1 on page three,
Lewis again violates the declared protocol. Only dry yield [Leafnbud®]

from "mature 120 day or older plants" can be considered for inclusion. The male plants [no seed, no flowers] listed in Table 1, Attachment 2 for the year 1985 are ordered by the week in which they were harvested. But only 120 day or older plants are suitable for being included in Table 1. Logically, only the last four plants, from weeks 18, 19, 20 and 21, should have made it into Lewis's Table 1. Sum them and you get 999.2 somethings. Divide this by four and you have 249.8 somethings not 222.3 grams.

3.   Table 2, Attachment 2.   This now calls into question the 1986 data in Attachment 2. Notice that the form for Table 2, Attachment 2, is clearly a copy of the form for Table 1, Attachment 2 except for the missing first column, "Week." All the other columns are exactly the same, in exactly the same order, except that the columns in the 1986 data are effectively shifted to the left one column width in comparison to the 1985 column data.

In other words, to produce it Lewis just needs a pair of scissors and a photocopier. To get the 1986 data he cuts off the "Week" column and photocopies the remaining columns shifted to the left by one column. He retitles his new data, removing "Plants of Different Age" and adding "Mature Plants" instead. To throw off suspicion he lists the data for the 1986 plants in reverse order, from largest to smallest.

Two clues suggest this was lazy Lewis's method: First, the superscript "1" is added to "WP" six times in the column headings for the 1985 data. The accompanying footnote below Table 1, Attachment 2 explains that the WP with a superscript "1" means "Whole plant." The same superscript appears also six times in the 1986 data but no explanatory footnote is provided. This suggests that the same footnote was meant to be applied to a single table of male plant data, not two different tables. Second, and more tellingly, the word "Average" in the top table of Attachment 2 has been abbreviated "Avg." in the bottom table. Without the "Week" column in the bottom table there is now not enough room to write out the whole word. In the 1985 data, the word "Average" stretches across the first two columns, the "Week" column and the "Plant #" columns. Without the "Week" column, the 1986 data does not permit that luxury. Hence, the necessary abbreviation, "Avg."

It's clear, just from the numbers given for the 1986 plants, that they had more space in which to grow. The 1985 plants show an average closer to the 1.23 density and the 1986 plants an average closer to the 0.62 density. We certainly can't assume the densities as given in the body of *Cannabis Fields* for this earlier study are correct as Lewis gives them because this is not at all substantiated in the data itself.

Let's irrationally assume the top four columns of the 1986 data actually represent weeks 18, 19, 20, and 21 of ten other male plants. We notice that generally these ten plants tend to be somewhat heavier than the ten in the upper table of Attachment 2. Which suggests the density was lower as well. Together these four weigh 1540 somethings. Divided by four they average 385 somethings.

At this point we can construct a corrected version of Lewis's Table 1, that is, what he should have reported had he brought over the numbers correctly from the so-called 1985 and 1986 data:

Table 1 (Corrected)
Average Cannabis Yields
[Leafnbud®] at Maturity for High Planting Densities

SPONSOR	YEAR	DENSITY	YIELD*	SEED STOCK
UM	1985	1.23	249.80	Mexican
UM	1986	0.62	385.00	Mexican
DEA	1990	0.62	354.16	Col/Hyb/Jam
DEA	1991	1.23	214.61	Mexican

Table 5.
Table 1 of Cannabis Fields, Corrected.

C.   Correcting Table 2

Here is what Lewis reports for Table 2 on page three of *Cannabis Fields*:

Table 2
Average Cannabis Yields at
Maturity for Low Planting Densities

SPONSOR	YEAR*	DENSITY	YIELD	SEED STOCK
DEA-A	1990	81 ft. sq.	777 grams	Mexican
DEA-B	1990	81 ft. sq.	936 grams	Mexican
DEA-C	1990	81 ft. sq.	640 grams	Mexican
DEA	1991	72 ft. sq.	1015 grams	Mexican
DEA	1991	36 ft. sq.	860 grams	Mexican

*Seedlings for the 1990 measurement program were planted at two week intervals: DEA-A was planted on 4/17, DEA-B was planted on 5/8, and DEA-C was planted on 5/17. The 1991 plantings were made during the first week of June.

Table 6.
Table 2 from Cannabis Fields.

As an aside, the footnote to Table 2 is not to be trusted. More than likely this footnote originally identified the planting date of all the plots. The dates reported are *not* at two week intervals. From 4/17 to 5/8 is three weeks; from 5/8 to 5/17 is a week and two days. Though *Cannabis Fields* is foremost a yield/density study, the designer intended to vary the planting date as well. So three plots of the 0.21 density (1.8 by 2.7 meters), labelled DEA-A, DEA-B, and DEA-C were planted on different dates. But there were also three plots of the 0.62 density (0.91 by 1.8 square meters per plant). Presumably these were varied by planting date as well, or else why grow so many plots in the first place?

Planting these six plots a week apart, not two, would have used up the last two weeks of April and most of the month of May. It is also deeply suspicious to have given specific dates for the three plots of the 0.21 density, said nothing about the planting dates of the 0.62 density, and then blithely reported that the rest (the 0.15, 0.31, and 1.23) were planted "during the first week of June."

The description for Table 2 on page 3 reads: "Table 2 displays the yields for cannabis at maturity for identical seed stocks at three low planting densities and for different planting dates and years." The three densities he is talking about are 0.15, 0.21, and 0.31. But the 0.21 density has been split into three parts, giving it extra emphasis.

We can recalculate the yield for that density by summing the mature plant yields and taking an average for plots A, B, and C. If we do, Lewis's proto-Table 2 initially looked something like this:

Lewis's Proto-Table 2
Average Cannabis Yields
[Leafnbud®] at Maturity for Low Planting Densities

SPONSOR	YEAR	DENSITY	YIELD	SEED STOCK
DEA	1991	0.15	1013.70	Mexican
DEA	1990	0.21	751.42	Mexican
DEA	1991	0.31	860.06	Mexican

Table 7.
What Lewis started with for his Table 2.

Lewis then splits the 0.21 density into three separate plots, reporting the yields for DEA plots A, B, and C individually. Plots A and B have too few mature plants to get a statistically meaningful average, only three plants and two respectively. Somewhere between seven and nine is what you might expect to see per density had the plants been chosen evenly distributed by density.

Next, he moves these three new entries (all with the same density). He splits it because he needs data he does not have and wants to emphasize the larger plants. He moves it because it would look out of place if he reported the real number.

He reports the density in his new Table 2 for each of the plots A, B, and C incorrectly. It should have been 0.20 as reported in the data in Attachment 1 (which would be one plant per 1.8 times 2.7 meters, or 1 divided by 4.86 square meters, or .2057613 or actually 0.21 with proper rounding). Instead he gives them each 81 "ft. sq."

Too bad Lewis the Liar can't figure. Because 1.8 meters is two yards, or six feet. And 2.7 meters is three yards, or nine feet. And six times nine is not eighty-one, but fifty-four square feet.

We can create a corrected Table 2:

Table 2 (Corrected)
Average Cannabis Yields
[Leafnbud®] at Maturity for Low Planting Densities

SPONSOR	YEAR	SQ. FT.	YIELD	SEED STOCK
DEA	1991	72	1013.70	Mexican
DEA-A	1990	54	776.87	Mexican
DEA-B	1990	54	935.45	Mexican
DEA-C	1990	54	640.33	Mexican
DEA	1991	36	860.06	Mexican

Table 8.
Table 2 from Cannabis Fields, Corrected.

So why does Lewis deliberately misreport the square feet of growing area per plant for three of the plots as 81 "ft. sq." when the correct number of square feet of growing area per plant was 54? Good question. The answer will have to wait until Chapter Two when we consider Figure 1.

D.   The Ancestral Mensa

It should be clear by now that Lewis's two tables were derived from a single table, an ancestor table, the progenitor of Table 1 and Table 2, one we can label Table I ("Table Eye"). References to it still remain in the earlier Linda Smith version of the report under the section entitled "Yield [Leafnbud®] Results" on pages two and three: "Table I depicts the average yield for all mature (120 grow days or older) cannabis plants ... (page 2)" and "The similarity of plant yields contained in Table I ... (page 3)."

The original Table I was put together by Doctor Sly. Like so many harmless academics, he enjoyed using Roman numerals to lend his tables and figures a bit of *gravitas*. The Is have been changed to 1s in the Konrad version (see Appendix 1) of the report.

Now, I could be wrong, so let's consider three other possibilities. One, am I making too much out of what could very well be a mere typo? I mean, it is easy to type an 'I' in place of a '1' and in the subsequent Konrad version this disparity has disappeared. I might accept this argument. But please explain why it appears twice? Two, alternatively, maybe the unknown author just couldn't make up his mind which he wanted to use, Roman numerals or integers. In which case, this is the first yield/density study he has ever written? Surely, he has a standard form for these things. Three, maybe the secretary decided to clean up the study, taking it upon herself to change the numerals for integers. But somehow I don't think any jealous academic is going to give away the power to rewrite his papers so easily.

Another way you can tell that Table 1 and Table 2 were once one original table is by the asterisks on the column headings. Table 1 has an asterisk on the column heading "YIELD" [Leafnbud®]. This refers to the footnote below Table 1: "*Yield [Leafnbud®] = oven dry weight of usable leaf and bud from mature 120 day or older plants." Table 2 has no such asterisk but it is clear that the same thing is meant to be true for its column heading "YIELD" [Leafnbud®] as well.

Similarly, Table 2 has an asterisk next to its column heading, "YEAR." Again, this refers to a footnote below Table 2: "*Seedlings for the 1990 measurement program were planted at two week intervals: DEA-A was planted on 4/17, DEA-B was planted on 5/8, and DEA-C was planted on 5/17. The 1991 plantings were made during the first week of June." But again, clearly this is meant to refer to the 1990 and 1991 plots listed in Table 1 as well. This follows Lewis's *modus operandi* for splitting the data in Attachment 2 into two tables but not repeating the footnote in the second table.

But beyond the confusion over Roman numerals and asterisks, a table comparing yield with density is what you would expect to find presented first in a standard yield/density study. Since there were five densities, you would expect to find five entries, one for each of the different plot densities grown in (according to *Cannabis Fields*) the years 1990 and 1991. It's the first thing you would want to know. How does the yield [Leafnbud®] vary when the plants are grown closer together or farther apart? The original yield/density table, that is, Table I, would have listed the average yield [Leafnbud®] of the mature plants for each of the five different densities from low to high. A mature plant is defined to be a plant that had been growing for at least 120 days.

Since the original Table I is missing, I've recreated it as best I could from the data included in Attachment 1. The data (what we have of it) shows gradation, not a sudden and decisive split between high and low density plantings. There was no reason to split it into two tables to begin with, except a transparently absurd ideology. I hope this gives some idea of what the original Table I might have looked like:

Table I
Average Cannabis Yields
[Leafnbud®] at Maturity

SPONSOR	YEAR†	DENSITY	YIELD*	SEED STOCK
DEA	1991	0.15	1013.70	Mexican
DEA	1990	0.21	751.42	Mexican
DEA	1991	0.31	860.06	Mexican
DEA	1990	0.62	354.16	Col/Hyb/Jam
DEA	1991	1.23	214.61	Mexican

*YIELD = grams of oven dry yield [Leafnbud®] from mature (120 grow days or older) plants.

†Seedlings for the 1990 measurement program were planted at two week intervals: DEA-A was planted on 4/17, DEA-B was planted on 5/8, and DEA-C was planted on 5/17. The 1991 plantings were made during the first week of June.

Table 9.
The Missing Table I.

Table I shows a standard gradation of yield as the density increases. It is what you would have found with many plants. Given a chance to expand, they will. Grown in competition with one another, their yield will be limited also.

But Lewis doesn't want to see that. He doesn't want small plants. He wants large plants. Biology be damned! So Lewis (no doubt after having imbibed a rather alcoholic magic potion) cut what was originally a single Table I into two tables, Table 1 for high density and Table 2 for low density. The distinction is completely artificial.

SOME LIARS CAN'T FIGURE

E.   Discussion

Cannabis Fields began as a yield/density study.   It quickly became corrupted.   Large plants replaced small.   It's purpose is to produce a Poundaplant®.

A competent academic designed a standard yield/density study. Then an ideological alcoholic altered it.   In the process, he committed a number of errors.

Table 1 and Table 2 are obviously derived from an original yield/density table, Table I.   The data, what we have of it, shows a normal gradation of yield as the density varies.   Splitting the data into two tables, one of "high" density and one of "low" density serves no purpose.

The first two entries in Table 1 come from a separate study with a different protocol that did not control for density.   That study, whose data is listed in Attachment 2, records only "leaves" not yield [Leafnbud®].   The first entry mechanically repeats the average of all ten (male) plants from 1985, regardless of age; but the four mature plants with 120 or greater grow days average 249.8 grams, not 222.3. The second entry repeats the sum for ten more (male) plants from 1986, but the form for Table 2, Attachment 2, has obviously been derived from Table 1, Attachment 2; the plants are heavier and probably had larger space in which to grow; they are listed in reverse order and show more similarities to the 0.62 density than any other; the average of the top four is 385 grams, not 274.

As well, so much of Table 2 is also simply wrong.   The first three entries are from the same density and should have been, and originally were, reported as a single density in the original Table I.   The first two plots have only three and two mature plants, respectively, so any "average" is statistically meaningless.   Once again, the densities are reported not in plants per unit area but as what should have been labelled "square feet of growing area per plant."   The density for the first three entries is reported as "81 ft. sq." but in fact, those plots had 54 square feet of growing area per plant.

Arithmetic is not Lewis's strong suit. He sure can lie, though. And you have to give him D for determination. Even more amusing is that Lewis's tremulous lie has reverberated through the net, on website after website. Even those who should know better accept his errors and authoritatively propagate them as fact. So in a way, I guess Lewis got his wish.

Figure 5.
Seed Selection.

Figure 6.
Fernanda wishes each seed un buen viaje.

2
Some Figures Will Lie

Big Dave: But we had supply. The Japs were eatin' bugs and grubs and thistles. Anyway ... we bust off the beach and we find Arnie Bragg, this kid, missing on recon. The Japs had eaten the son of a bitch. ... So what do I say, honey? What do I say when I don't like dinner? ... Arnie Bragg? Again?
The Man Who Wasn't There (2002)[1]

---

[1] Directed by Joel Coen. Produced by Ethan Coen. Distributed by Universal Pictures.

Which brings us to Figure 1. We have recreated in Chapter 1 what Dr. Sly's original yield/density table looked like (the long lost Table I), pasted back together from the scraps Lewis left us in Table 1 and Table 2. But another question begs to be asked: Why is this information not presented in graphic form?

Cannabis Fields began as a yield/density study. It was designed to answer the question: How does yield [Leafnbud®] vary as cannabis plants are grown closer together or farther apart from one another? A graph would help us understand this information better than a simple listing of the data set in a table.

But there is no discussion of what should have been the central theme of the paper. The omission is striking. So striking is it, that Lewis feels the need to add a line on pages three and four to try to explain why this information is not there: "The significance of the relationship between planting density and plant yield [Leafnbud®] will be discussed later in this paper." Except for Figure 3, it never is.

Instead, the focus of the paper shifts from yield/density to height/diameter ratios to canopy/density and then to canopy/yield, in spite of the fact that none of the latter three are as accurate in predicting yield as density. Figure 1 shows height over diameter ratios: "The height-diameter graph of Figure 1 shows that planting density is a significant factor affecting plant canopy shape, which in turn affects plant yield (page three)." But if you want to predict yield, why not go there directly from density rather than going around Robin Hood's barn through flawed and inaccurate canopy measurements?

The reason is to support Lewis's cut-from-whole-cloth Table 4, comparing canopy estimates by the DEA's state eradication program coordinators. (No doubt these bureaucrats were out in the field carefully measuring each and every plant seized with a tape measure delineated in feet.) So where is the yield versus growing area graph?

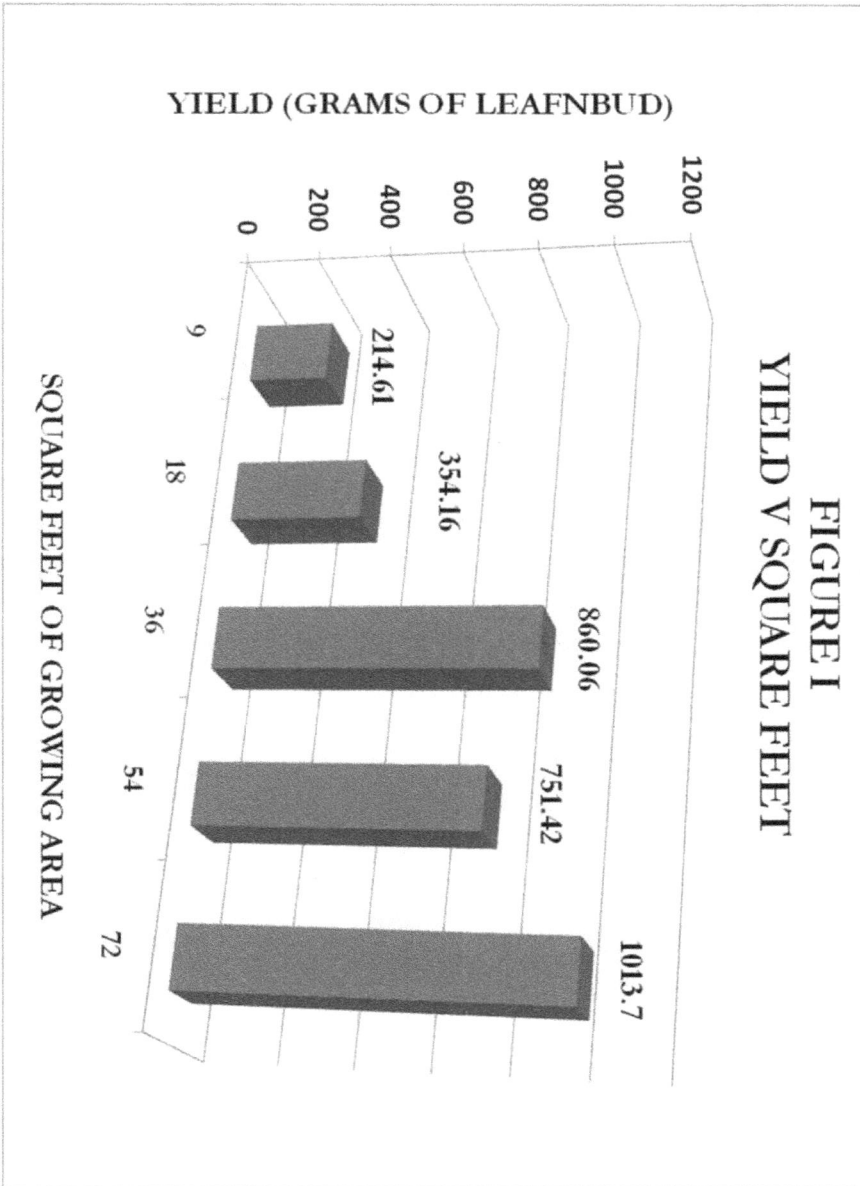

Figure 7.
The Missing Figure I: as Yield v Square Feet Column Graph.

A.   The Figure That Wasn't There

This missing figure (call it Figure I) should have accompanied the missing Table I. Figure I would have compared the average yield [Leafnbud®] to the average growing space for each plant. There are a number of ways to view this data.

1.   Leafnbud v Square Feet.   In honor of Lewis's mixed metrics, let's look at how the yield [Leafnbud®] varies as the square feet of growing area per plant increases or decreases. We have graphed it first as a three-dimensional column graph in Figure 7. It has ascending values along the x-axis toward the right, opposite to what Lewis has done with his Figure 1.

Second, what kind of x-y relationship is there between the yield and the square feet of growing area? This is, after all, one of the most important things you might want to know about in a yield/square feet of growing area study. Microsoft's Excel (2007) which allows you to try various formulas to see which one produces the curve of best fit (CBF).

We can try five different curves, an exponential, linear, logarithmic, polynomial and power series to see which one fits the data best. The R-squared tells us how well the curve fits the data. It is usually written as a number between zero and one. A low value means it does not fit very well. A high value, a value closer to one, means it fits the data very well.

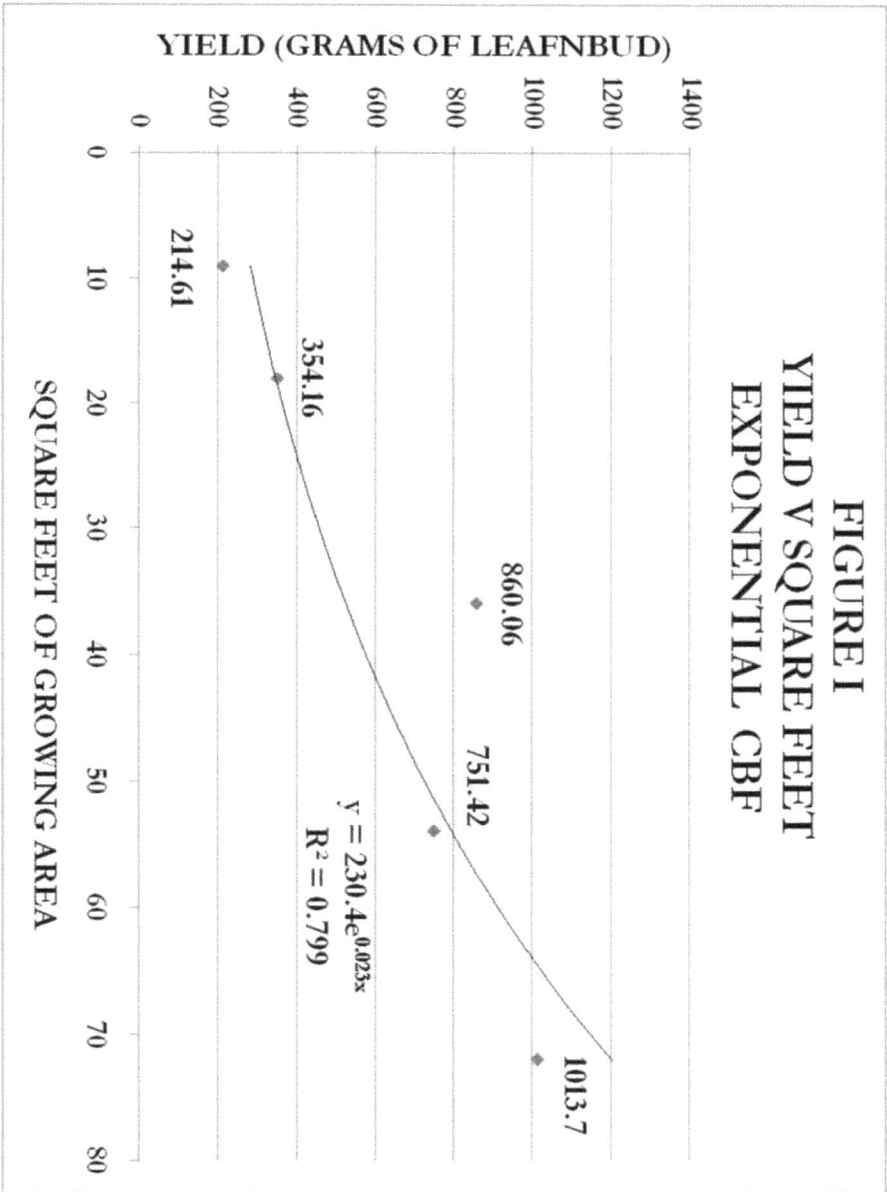

Figure 8.
The Missing Figure I: as Yield v Square Feet, Exponential CBF.

51

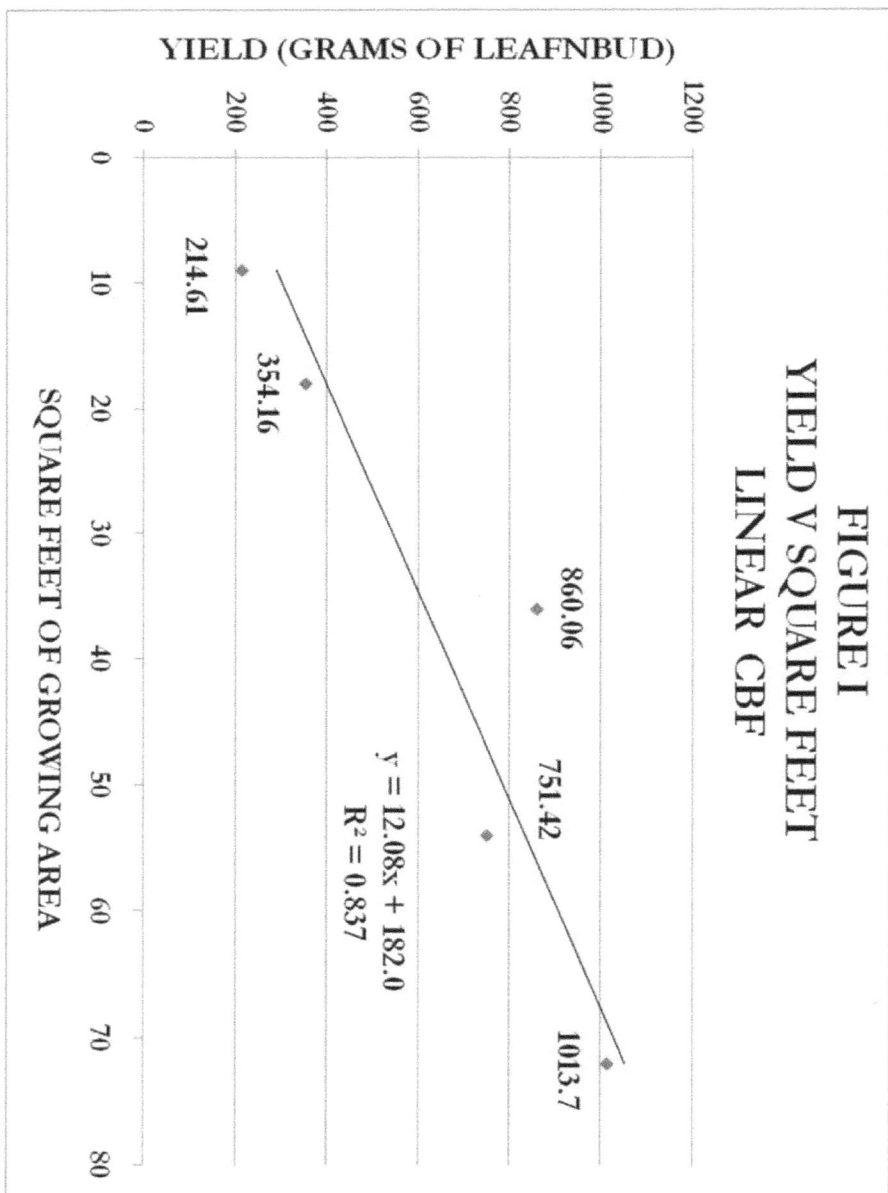

Figure 9.
The Missing Figure I: as Yield v Square Feet, Linear CBF.

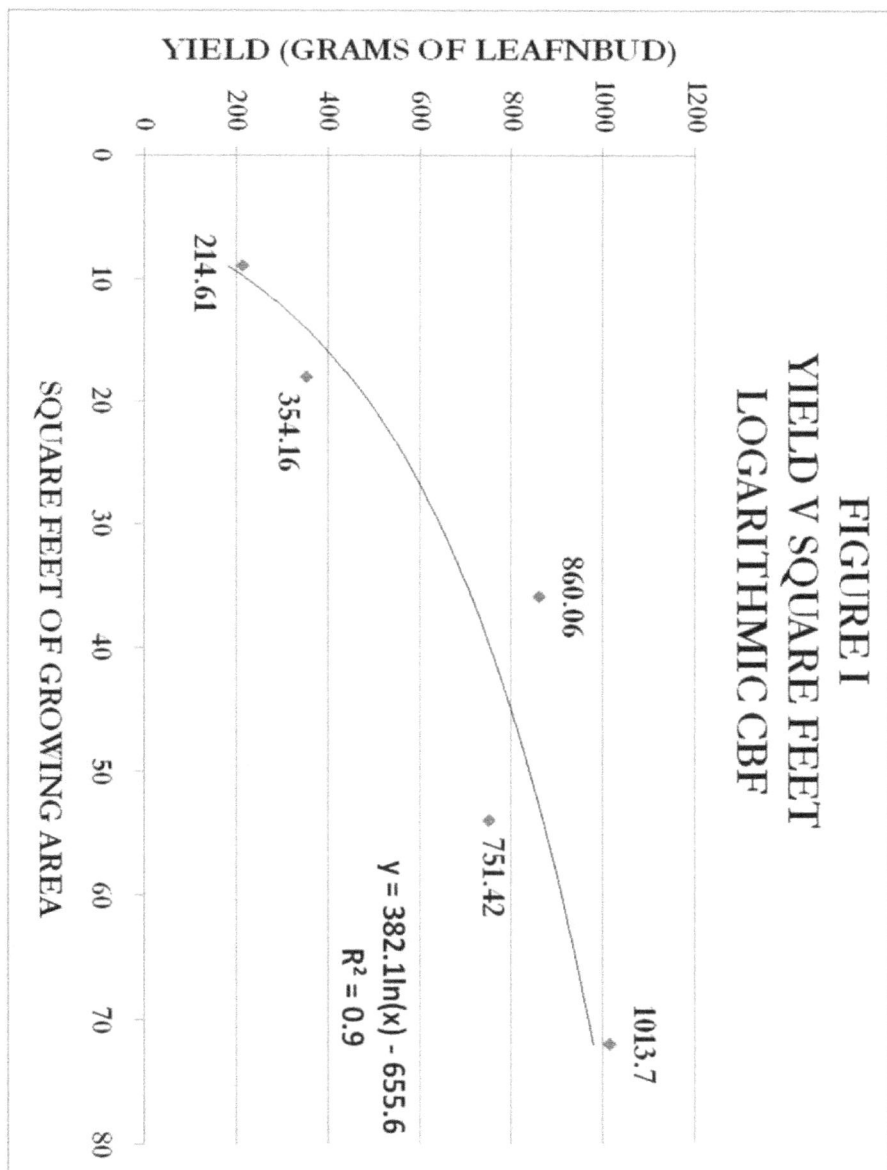

Figure 10.
The Missing Figure I: as Yield v Square Feet, Logarithmic CBF.

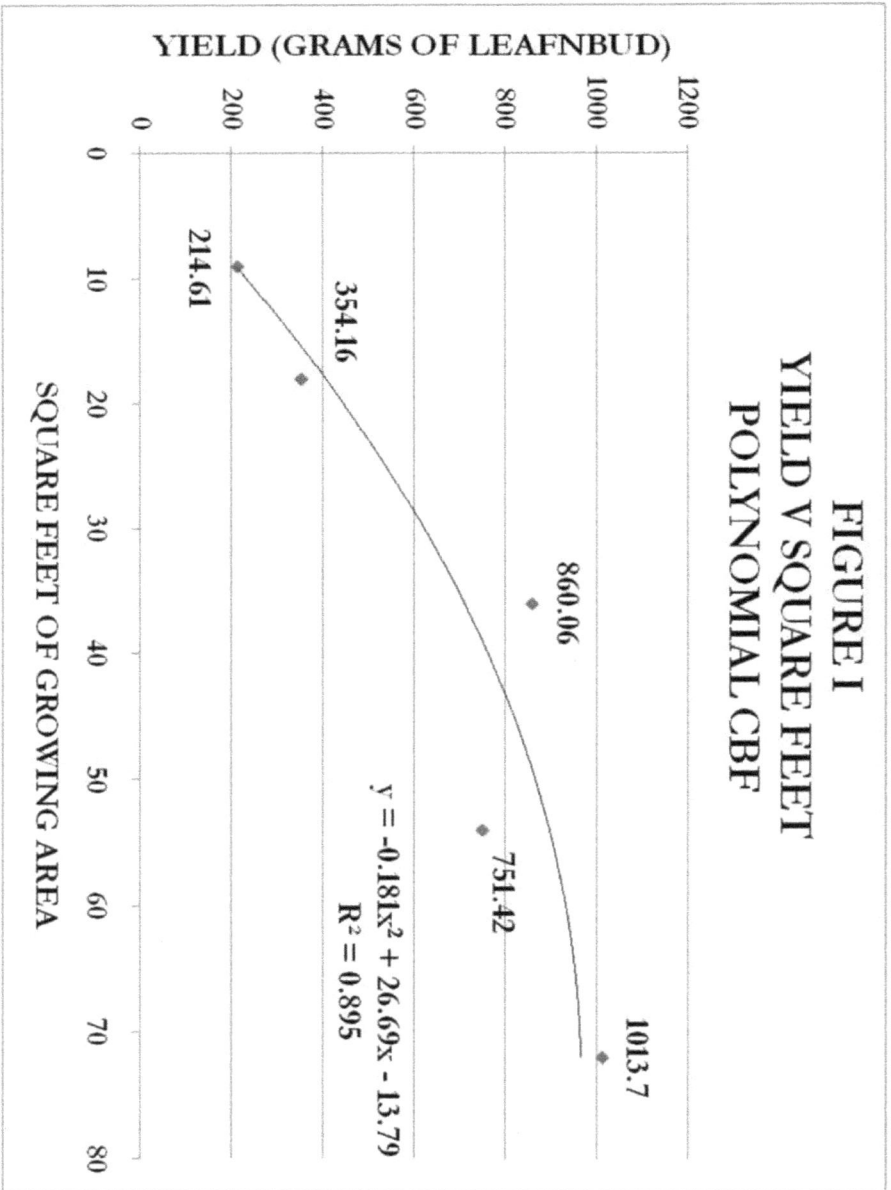

FIGURE I
YIELD V SQUARE FEET
POLYNOMIAL CBF

YIELD (GRAMS OF LEAFNBUD)

SQUARE FEET OF GROWING AREA

214.61

354.16

860.06

751.42

1013.7

$y = -0.181x^2 + 26.69x - 13.79$
$R^2 = 0.895$

Figure 11.
The Missing Figure I: as Yield v Square Feet, Polynomial CBF.

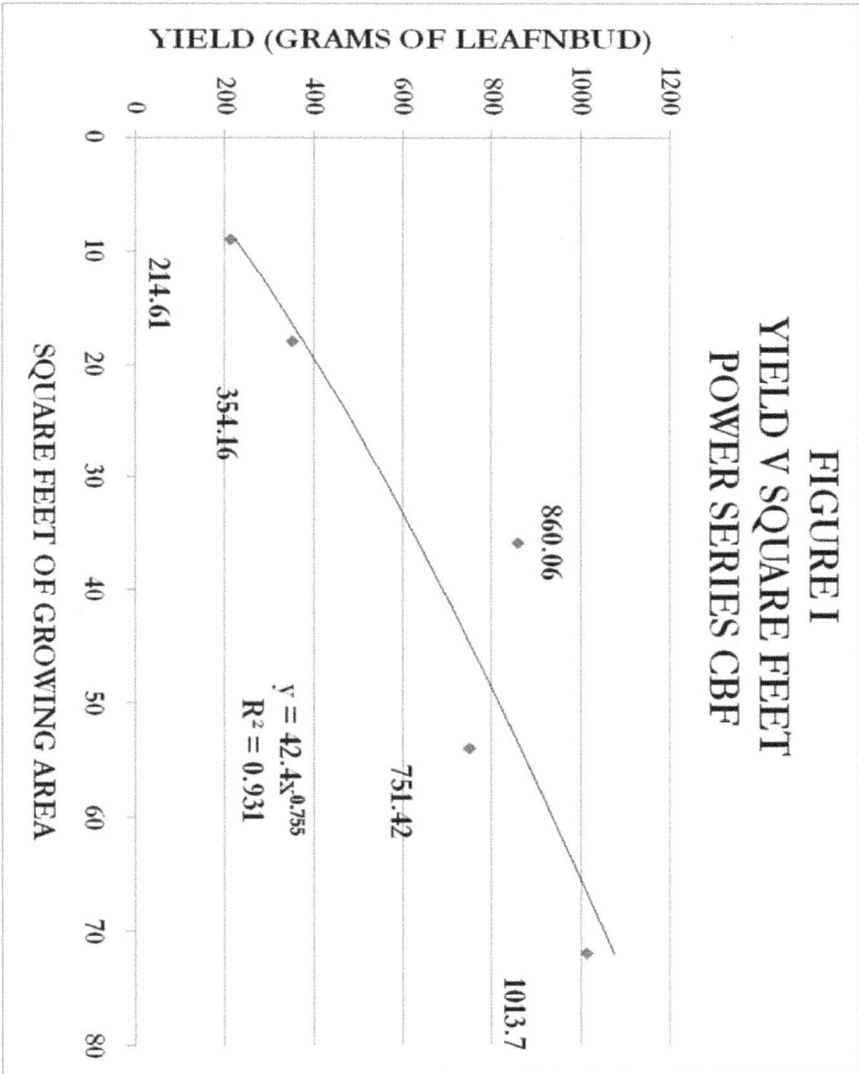

Figure 12.
The Missing Figure I: as Yield v Square Feet, Power Series CBF.

The R-squared of the power series curve is higher than the other four.

2. **LNB v SF w/o Anomalies.** It is important to note the presence of the two anomalies in the data set of the 38 mature plants (those with 120 or more grow days). In Chapter 8, once we recreate how the plants were laid out in the field in which they were grown, it will become clear the way these two supersized plants from the beginning deliberately violated the study protocol.

Cannabis Fields calls attention to them twice, the first time (as already noted) in the first paragraph of the paper: "can be up to 2.3 kilograms (5.1 pounds)." (Yes, Lewis, it is possible to grow large plants. But large plants of course do not always produce the best herb. In fact, the better flowers frequently come from the smaller or more modest plants.) The second time these plants are referenced occurs on page 4: "However, two plants, identification numbers 107.01 and 103.01 in the 1991 low planting density plots, had extremely high yields [Leafnbud®] in comparison to neighboring plants."

And the data does show the yields [in Leafnbud®] that are described in the body of the paper on page 4: "The dry weight yield [Leafnbud®] for plant 107.01 was 2,086.9 grams (4.6 pounds) and plant 103.01 yielded [in Leafnbud®] 2,308.4 grams (5.1 pounds)." These are two oversized results. Plant 107.01 comes from the plot of Mexican in 1991 where each plant had nearly-three-yards by three yards of growing space (2.4 meters by 2.7 meters). It's nearest competitor (plant 109.12) with the same space had roughly half that yield [Leafnbud®], with 1155.1 grams. Plant 103.01 was grown in the 1991 Mexican plot in which each plant had two yards by two yards (1.8 meters by 1.8 meters) in which to grow. It's nearest competitor was 104.17 which had by comparison roughly only a third (813.3 grams) as much yield [Leafnbud®].

It's important to recognize that plants of this magnitude tend to skew the data. Now it is one thing to include anomalies in your data set. If you are going to include them, it is only fair to notice them, as was done twice in the paper. But the anomalies will wreck the curve.

We can correct for this by eliminating these two anomalies and recalculate the averages for the two plots. We can view the data for the remaining 36 mature plants (minus the anomalies), first as a column graph and second as x-y scattergraphs.

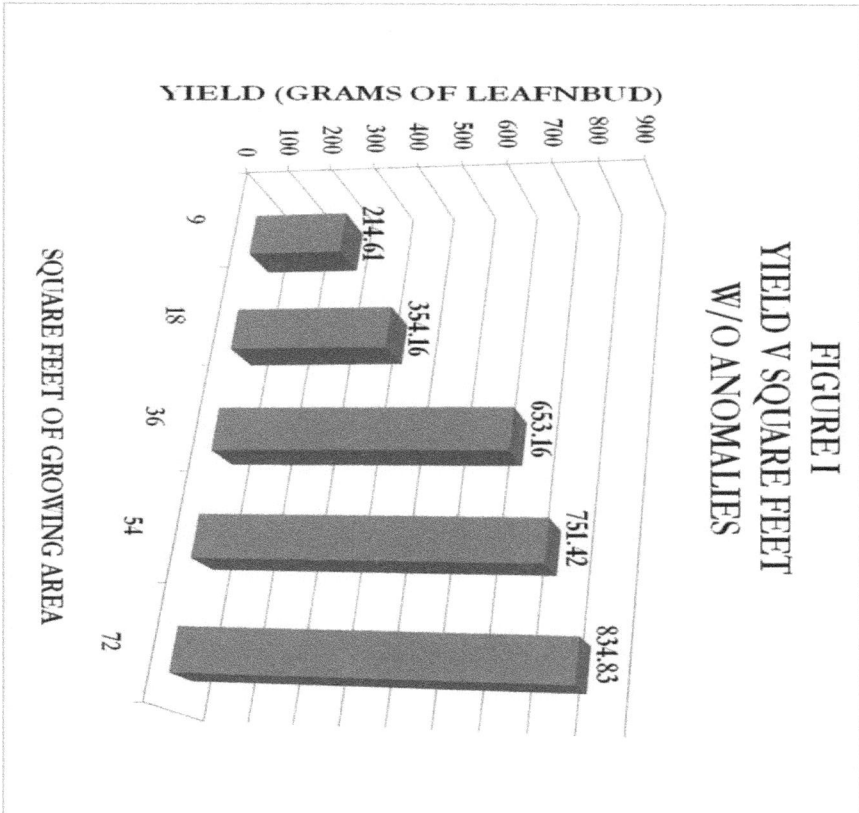

Figure 13.
The Missing Figure I: as Yield v SF w/o Anomalies, Column Graph.

Notice that the values begin to approach a smooth continuum.
Next, let's try some scattergraphs:

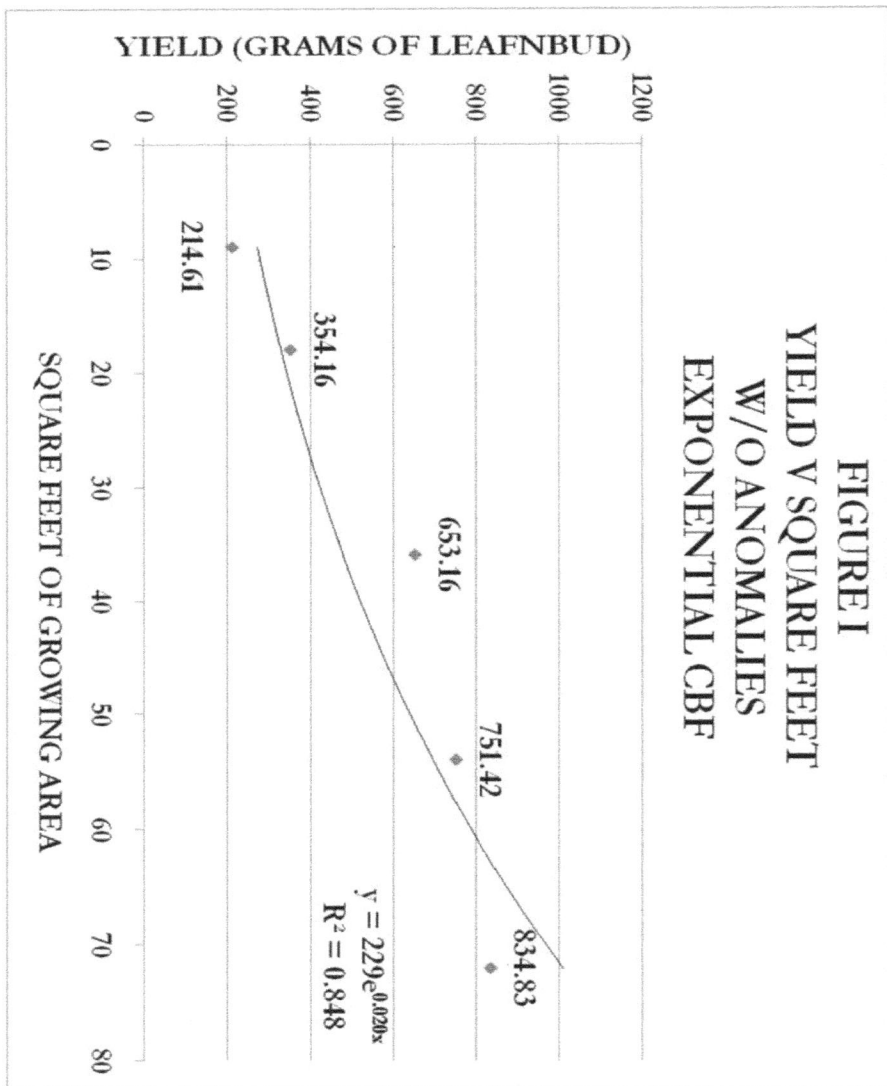

Figure 14.
The Missing Figure I: as Yield v SF w/o Anomalies, Exponential CBF.

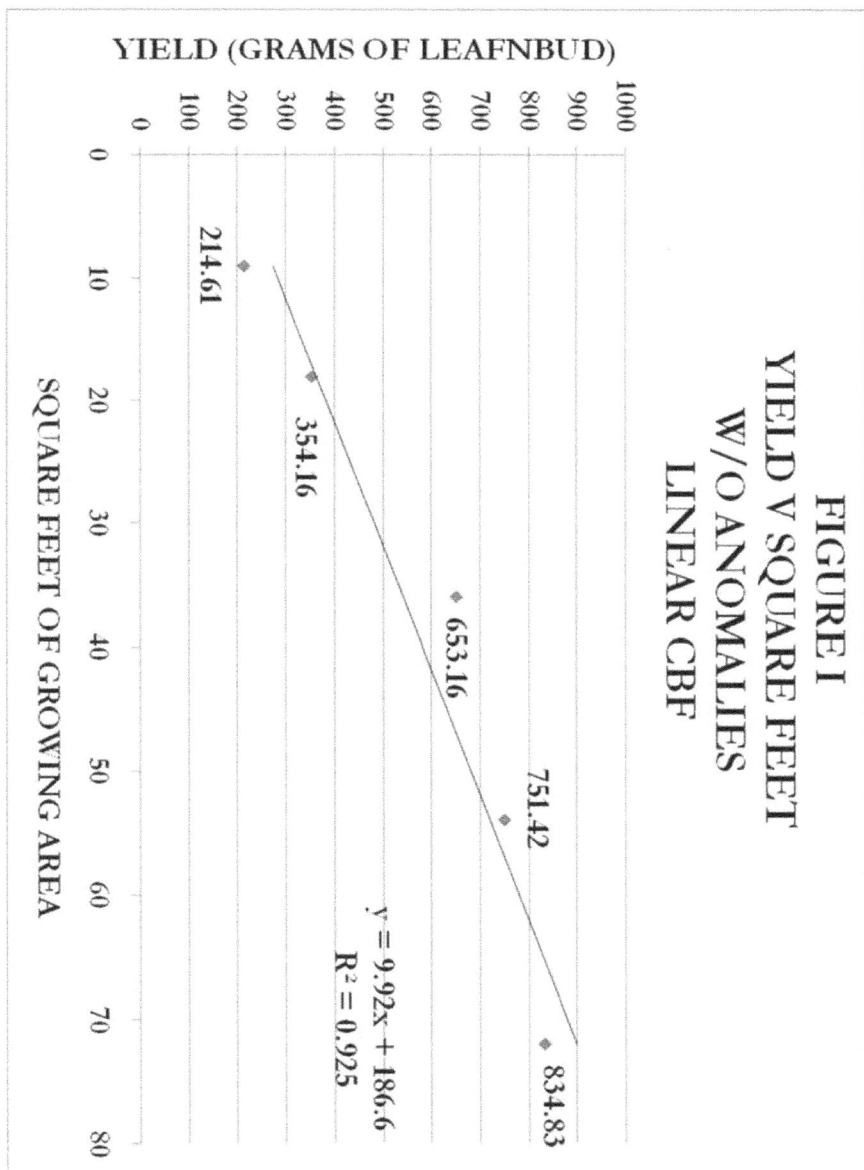

Figure 15.
The Missing Figure I: as Yield v SF w/o Anomalies, Linear CBF.

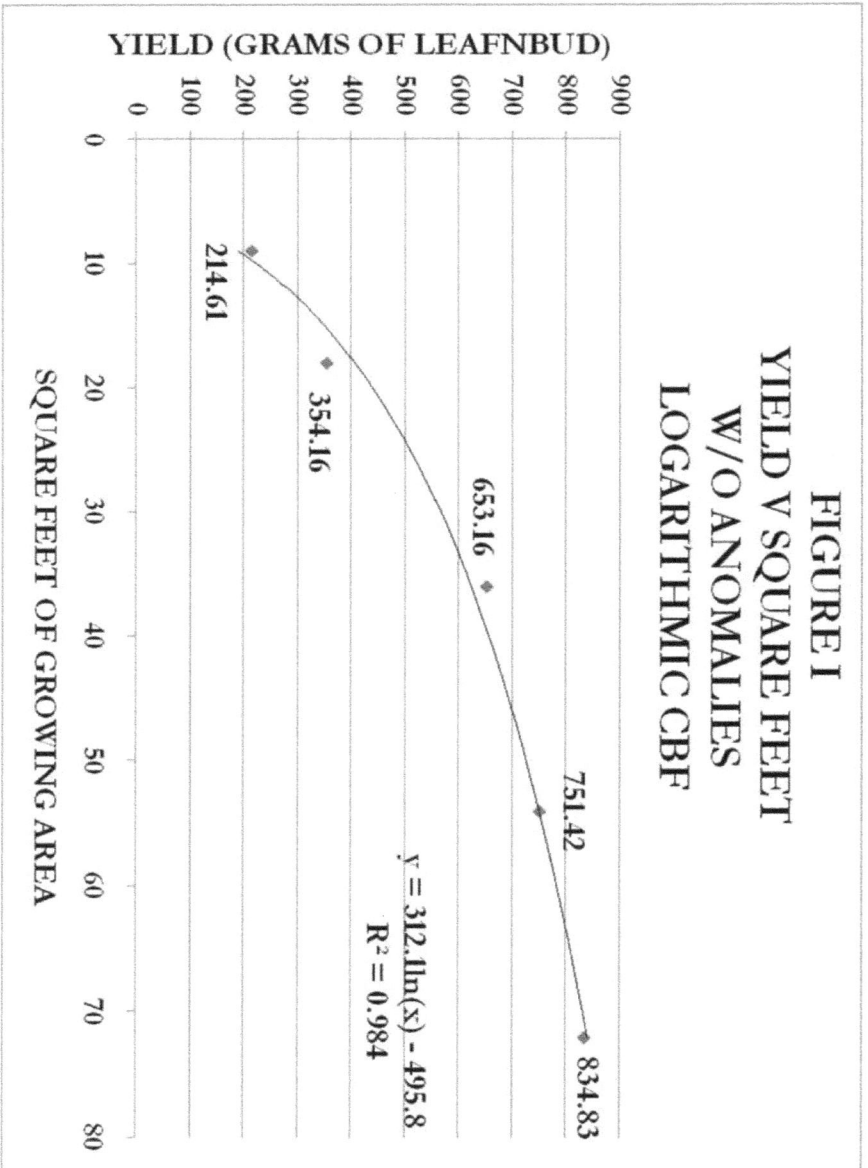

Figure 16.
The Missing Figure I: as Yield v SF w/o Anomalies, Logarithmic CBF.

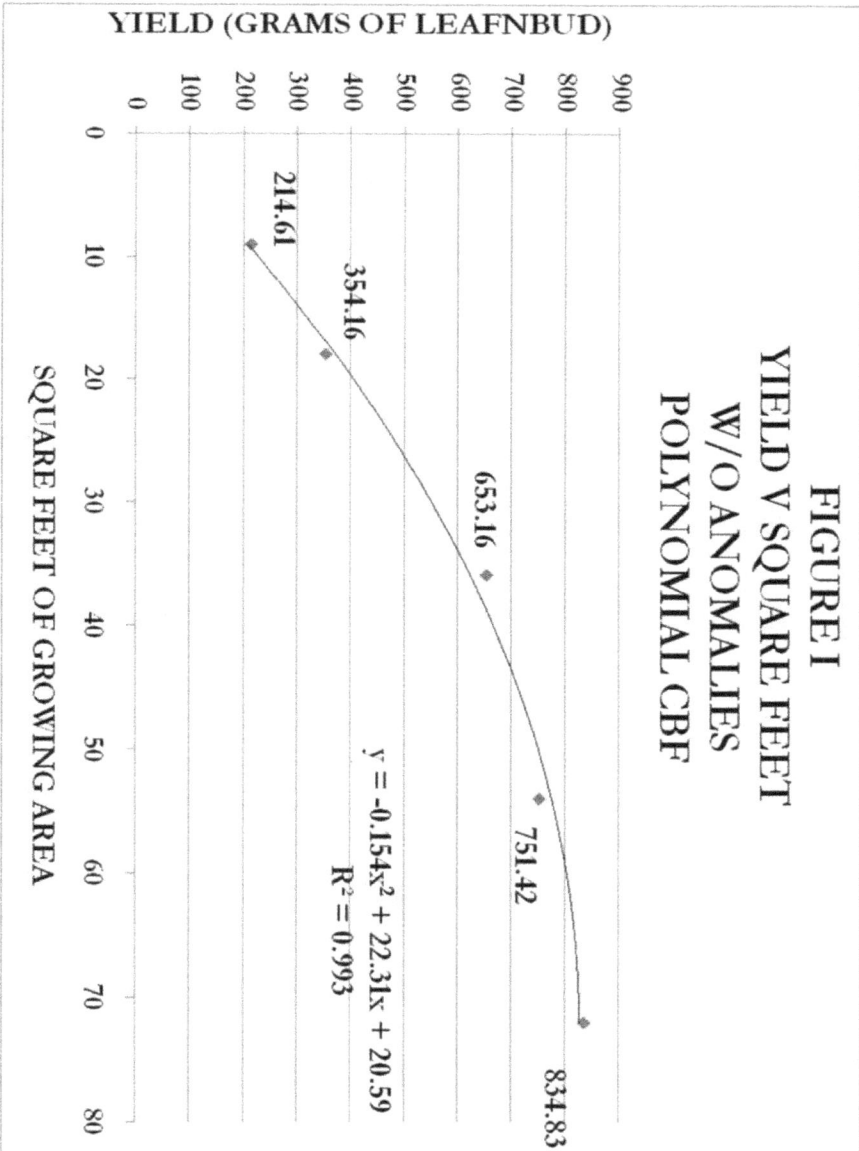

YIELD (GRAMS OF LEAFNBUD)

FIGURE I
YIELD V SQUARE FEET
W/O ANOMALIES
POLYNOMIAL CBF

SQUARE FEET OF GROWING AREA

214.61

354.16

653.16

751.42

834.83

$y = -0.154x^2 + 22.31x + 20.59$
$R^2 = 0.993$

Figure 17.
The Missing Figure I: as Yield v SF w/o Anomalies, Polynomial CBF.

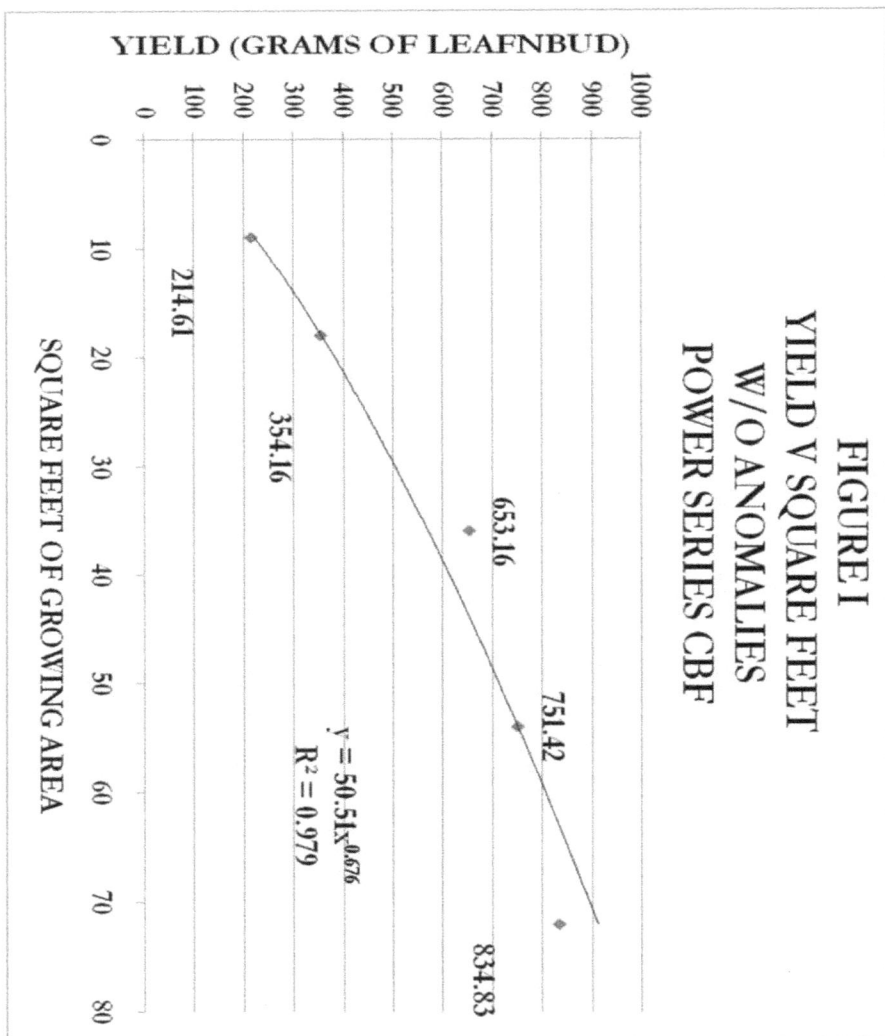

Figure 18.
The Missing Figure I: as Yield v SF w/o Anomalies, Power Series CBF.

Without the presence of the anomalies distorting the data set, the curves generally fit much better, with the polynomial providing the curve of best fit.

3. **LNB v Density.** Now let's graph the
yield [Leafnbud®] as it is usually done, versus the density:

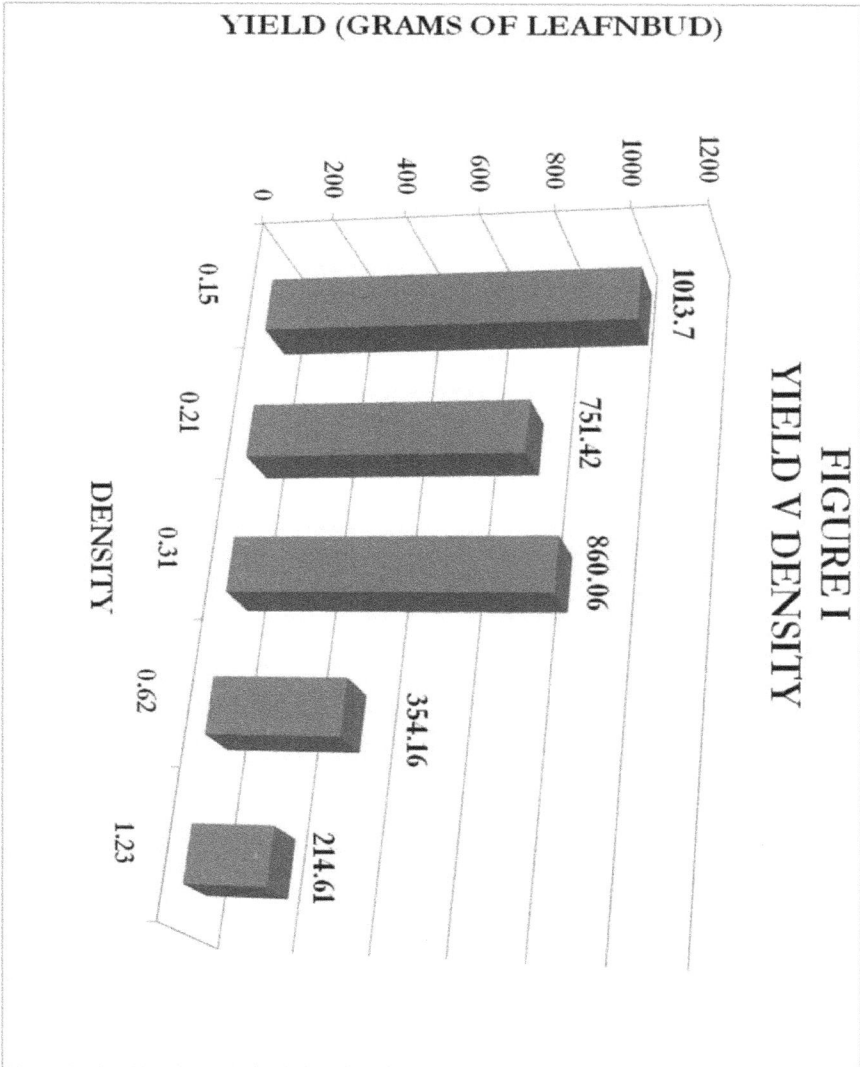

Figure 19.
The Missing Figure I: as Yield v Density Column Graph.

Again, let's examine their x-y curves:

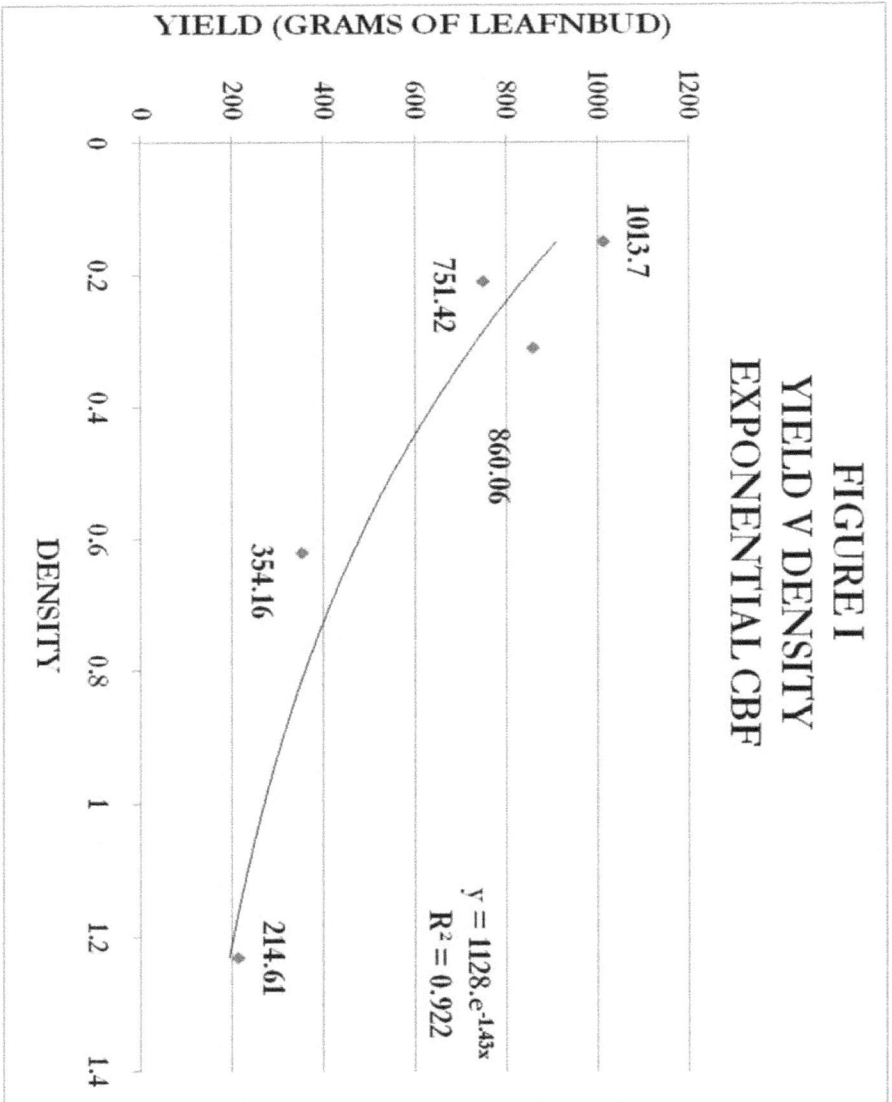

FIGURE I
YIELD V DENSITY
EXPONENTIAL CBF

$y = 1128.e^{-1.43x}$
$R^2 = 0.922$

YIELD (GRAMS OF LEAFNBUD)

DENSITY

1013.7

751.42

860.06

354.16

214.61

Figure 20.
The Missing Figure I: as Yield v Density, Exponential CBF.

64

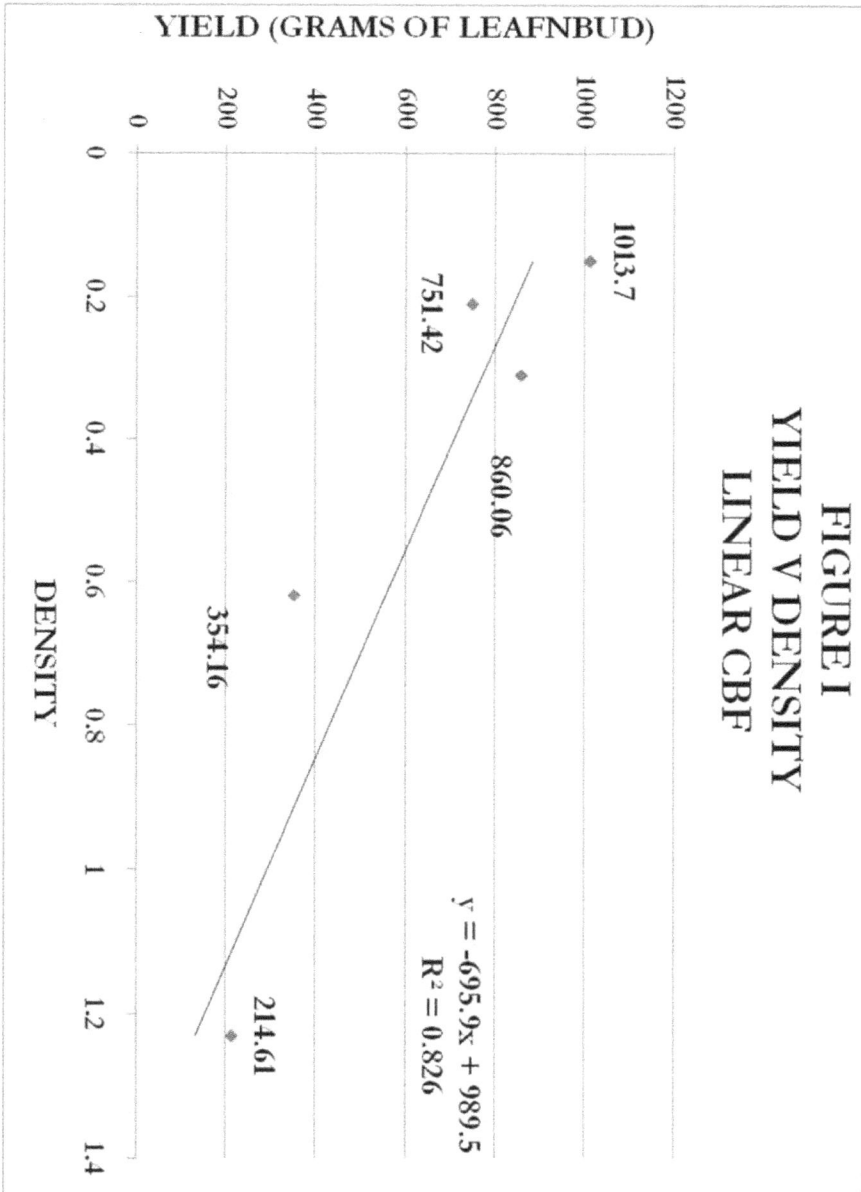

Figure 21.
The Missing Figure I: as Yield v Density, Linear CBF.

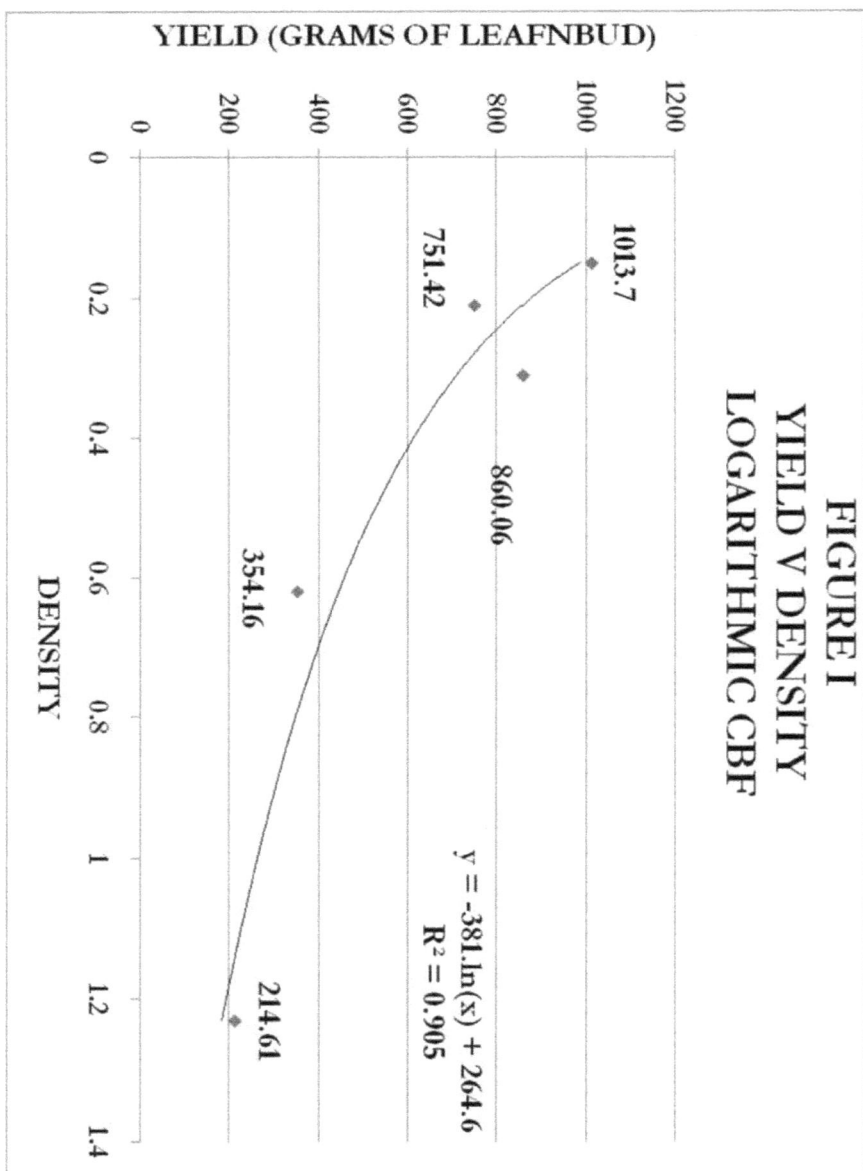

Figure 22.
The Missing Figure I: as Yield v Density, Logarithmic CBF.

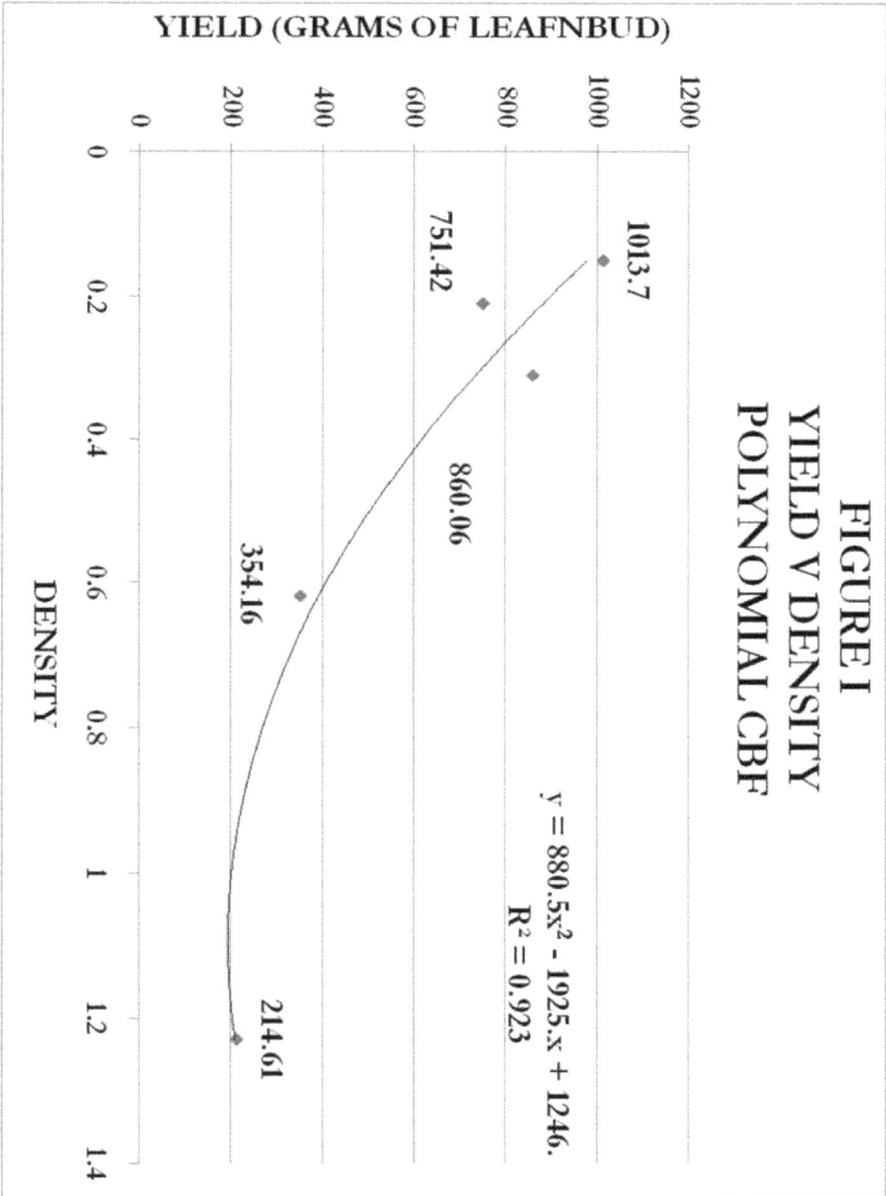

FIGURE I
YIELD V DENSITY
POLYNOMIAL CBF

y = 880.5x² - 1925.x + 1246.
R² = 0.923

Figure 23.
The Missing Figure I: as Yield v Density, Polynomial CBF.

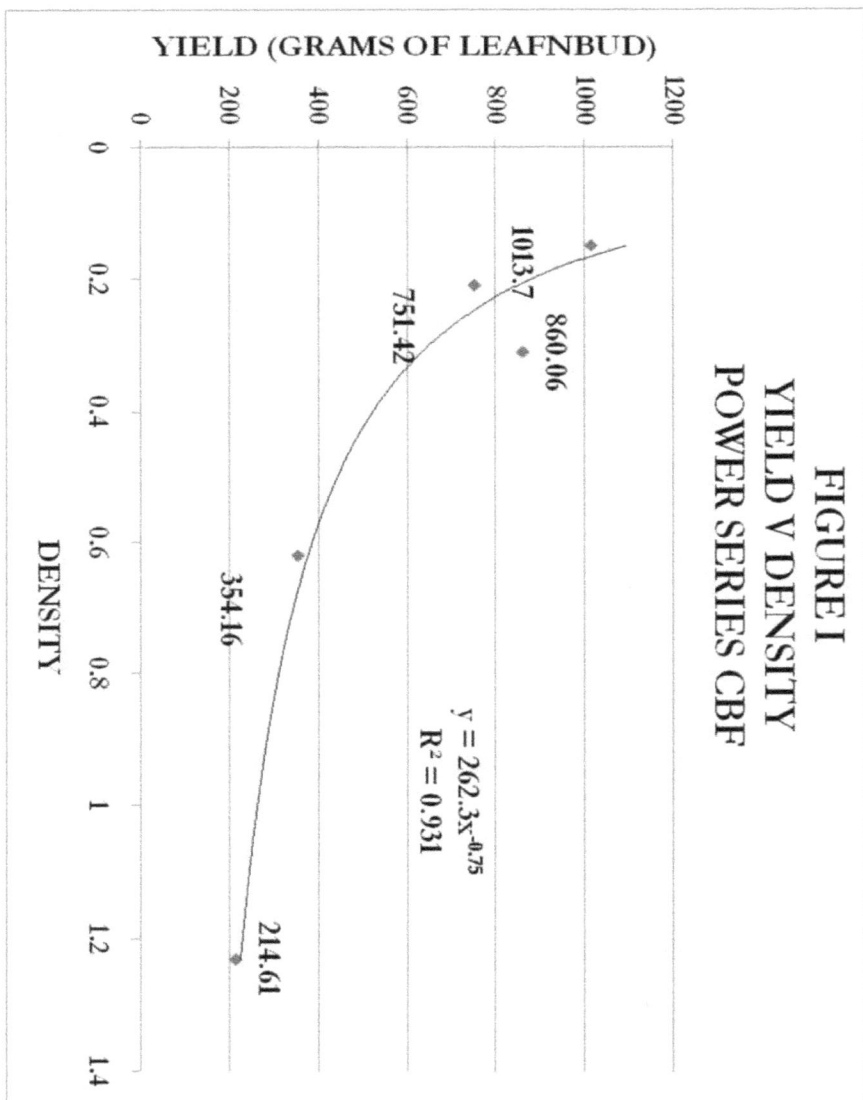

FIGURE I
YIELD V DENSITY
POWER SERIES CBF

YIELD (GRAMS OF LEAFNBUD)

DENSITY

$y = 262.3x^{-0.75}$
$R^2 = 0.931$

1013.7

860.06

751.42

354.16

214.61

Figure 24.
The Missing Figure I: as Yield v Density, Power Series CBF.

With the anomalies, the power series curve fits best.

68

4. **LNB v Density w/o Anomalies.** This time we'll take out the anomalies:

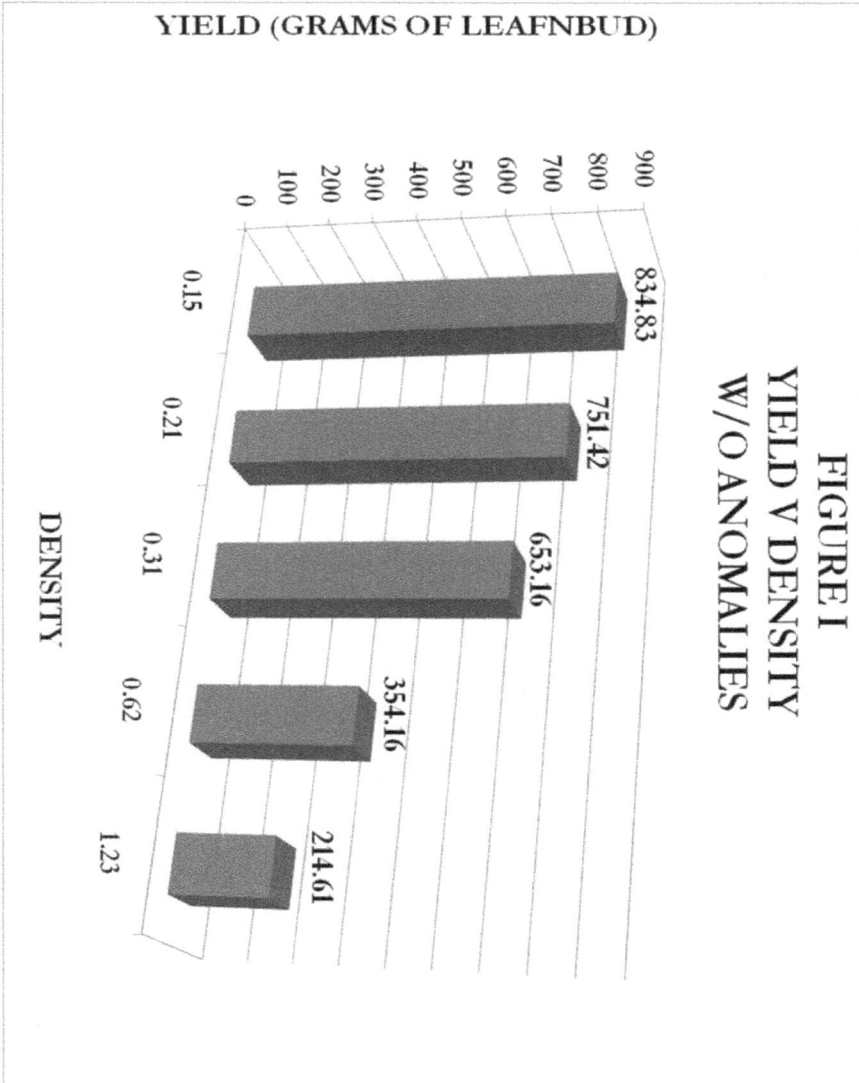

Figure 25.
The Missing Figure I: as Yield v Density w/o Anomalies, Column Graph.

Here are the scattergraphs:

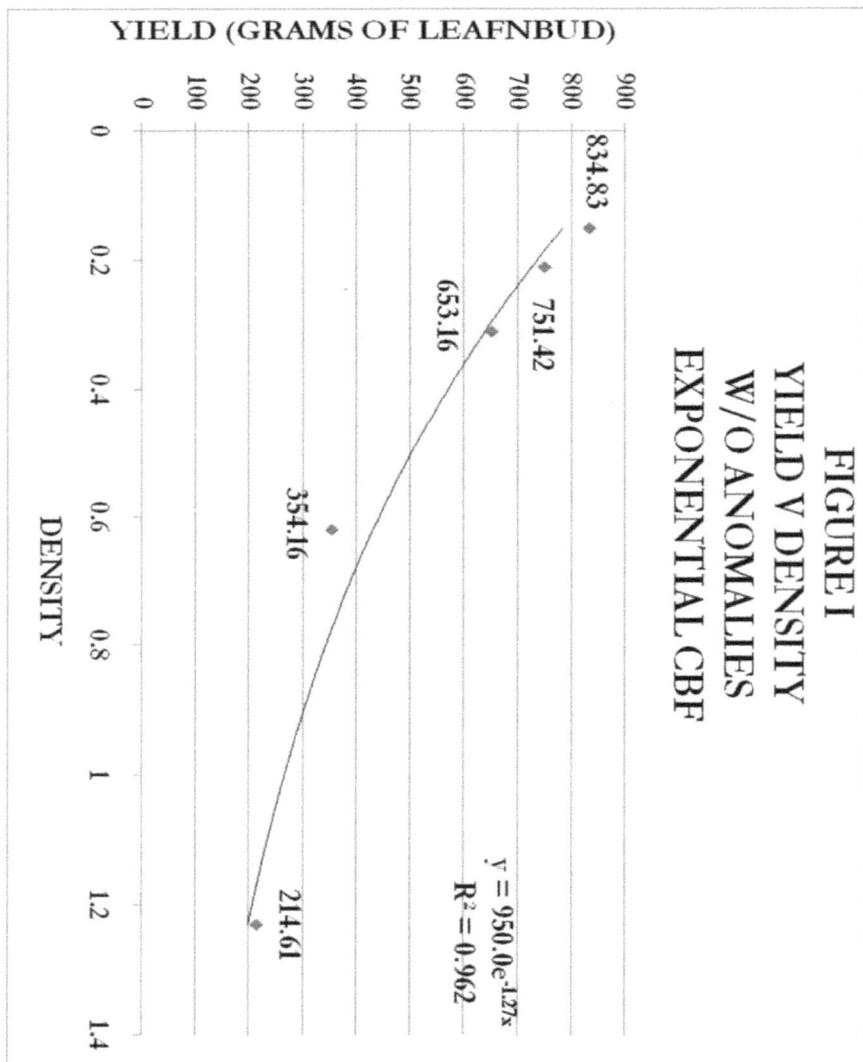

Figure 26.
The Missing Figure I: as Yield v Density w/o Anomalies, Exponential CBF.

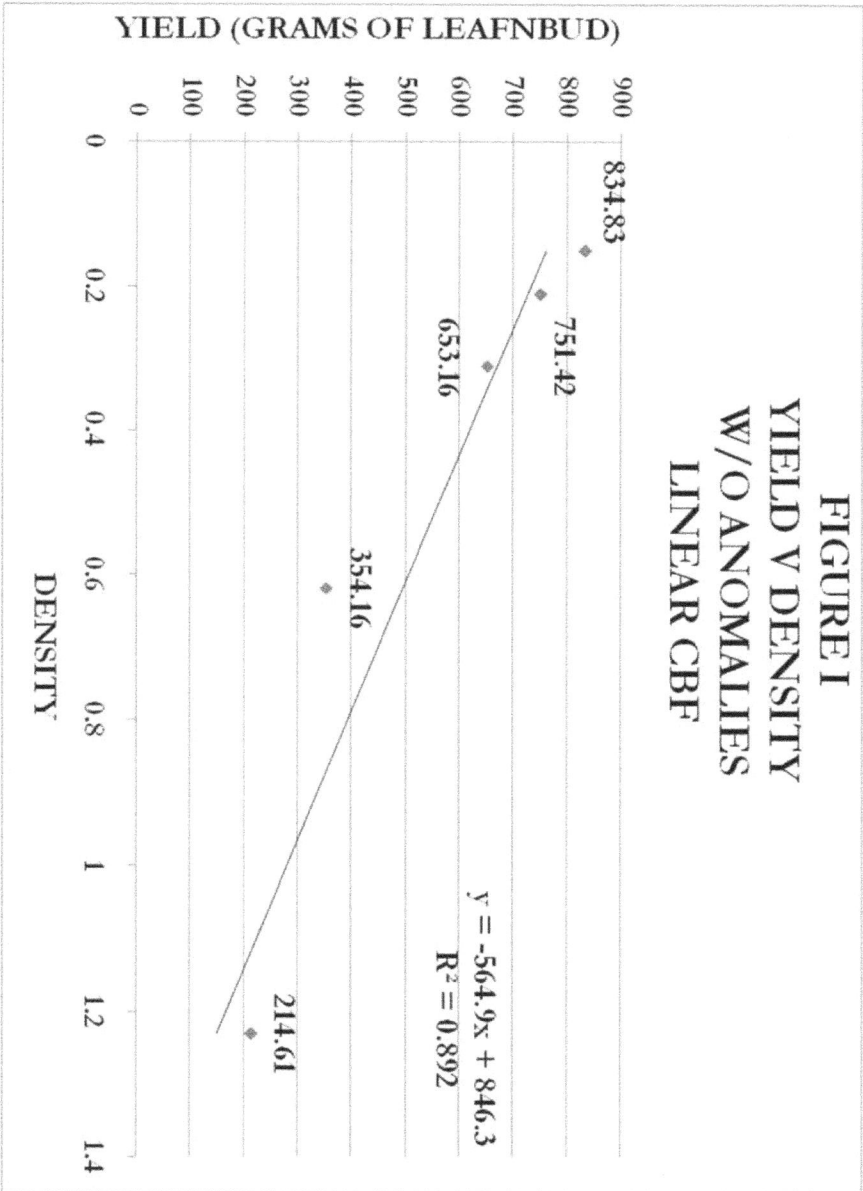

Figure 27.
The Missing Figure I: as Yield v Density w/o Anomalies, Linear CBF.

71

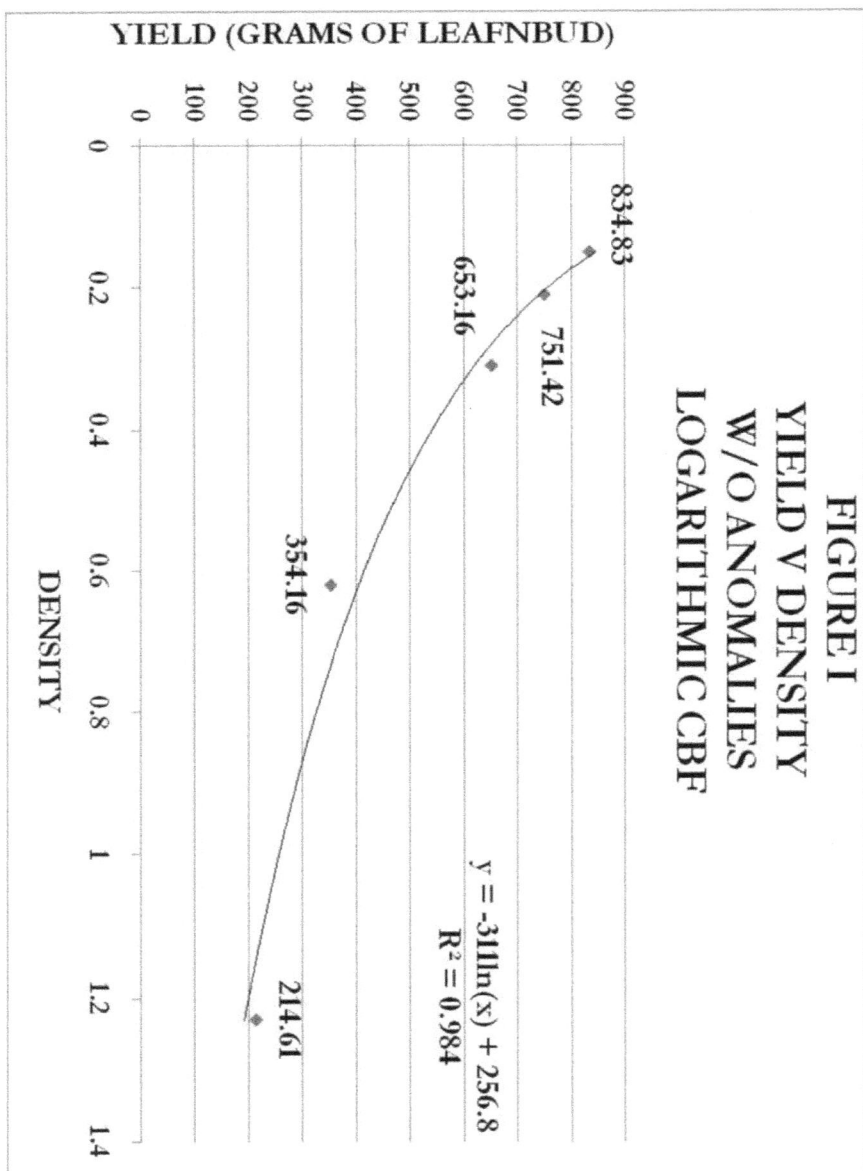

Figure 28.
The Missing Figure I: as Yield v Density w/o Anomalies, Logarithmic CBF.

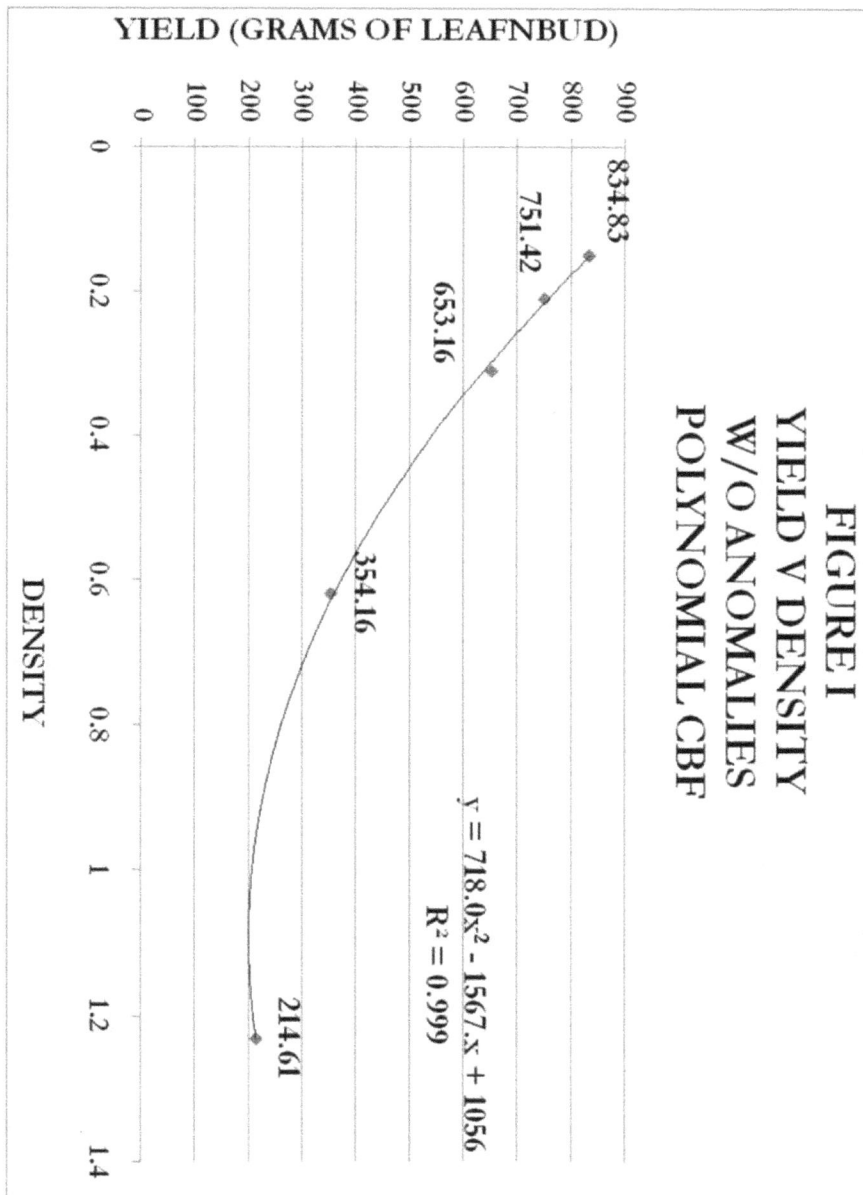

Figure 29.
The Missing Figure I: as Yield v Density w/o Anomalies, Polynomial CBF.

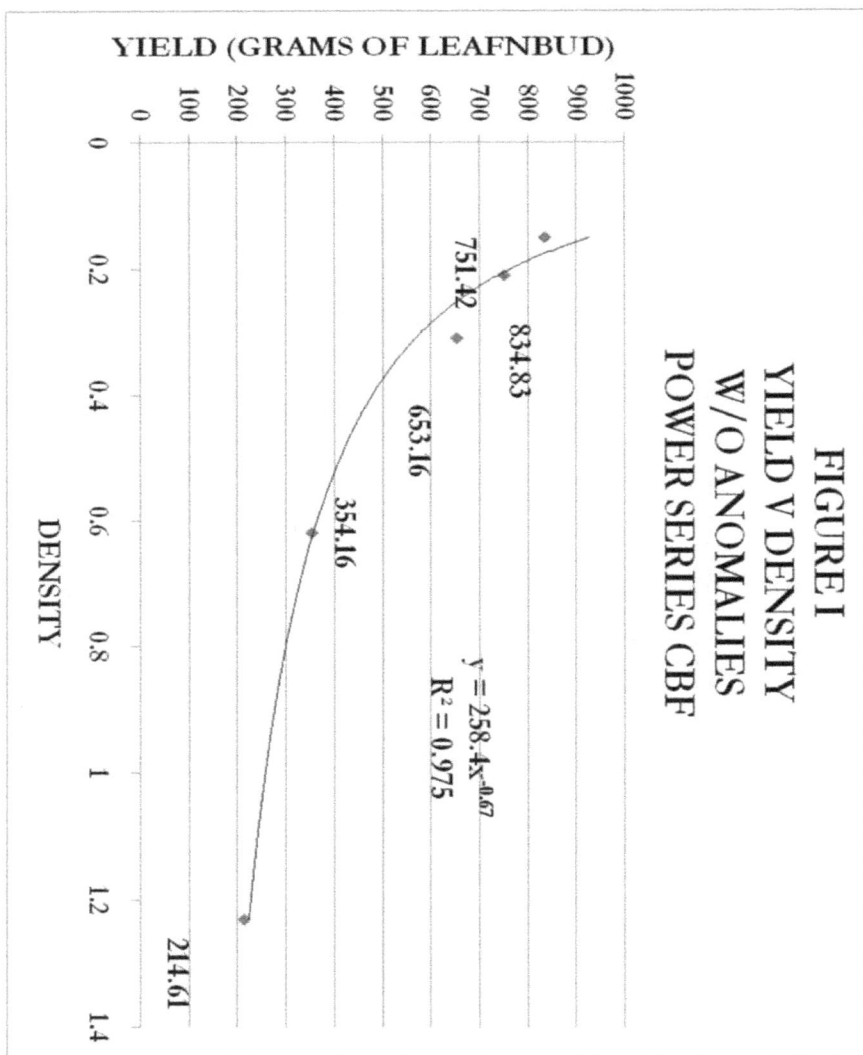

Figure 30.
The Missing Figure I: as Yield v Density w/o Anomalies, Power Series CBF.

Here, without the anomalies, the polynomial equation provides the best fit, with an R-squared of .999, a remarkable result.

B.   Lewis's Figure 1

So Figure 1 on page 4 should have been a graphic illustration of the original Table I. We would have liked to see a visual depiction of how yield [Leafnbud®] varied with the density. It's what you would have expected in a yield/density study.

1.   Figure 1, Faked.   Instead we are treated to a height/diameter ratio versus square feet graph:

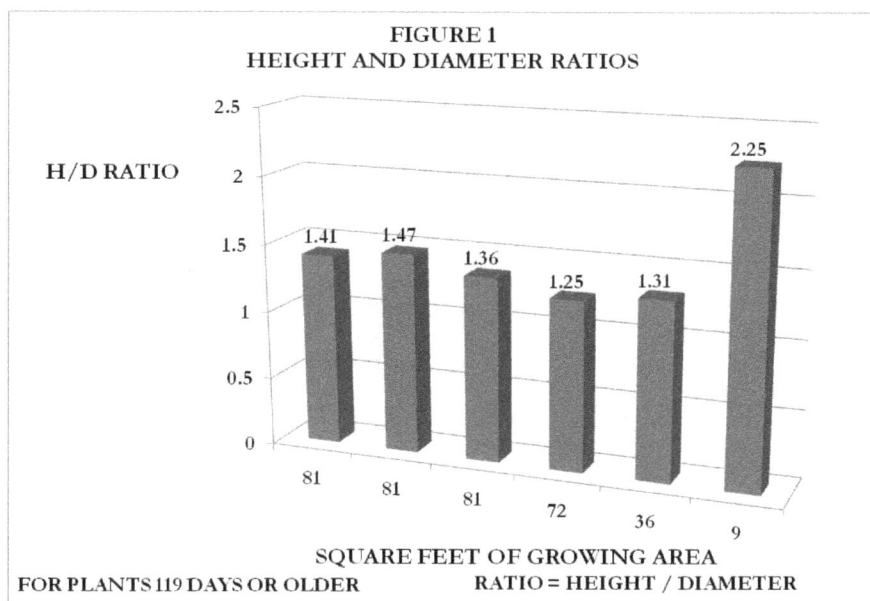

Figure 31. Figure 1 from Cannabis Fields.

The numbers on Lewis's x-axis descend instead of ascend when read from left to right. Normally, the point where the x-axis and y-axis meet is considered zero. All numbers emanate from the zero point, ascending upward on the y-axis and to the right on the x-axis. This is mere convention but it is nearly universal convention.

Lewis also repeats the mistakes found in his newly manufactured Table 2. For example, his 81 square feet of growing area for the first three columns in Figure 1, the three plots A, B, and C, shows up again; it should be 54. The height/diameter ratios make it clear that these three plots are meant.

Lewis the Liar doesn't understand that every alteration he makes in Dr. Sly's original paper betrays its origins. He would have done better to have simply created his own new figures and tables instead of trying to adapt the ones in the original report. But he's not that smart. He makes the mistake that all liars make, which is to try to tell a lie that alters the truth as little as possible.

2. Figure 1, Corrected. Here's what Figure 1 would look like if Lewis had reported the growing area for the three plots A, B, and C properly as 54 square feet:

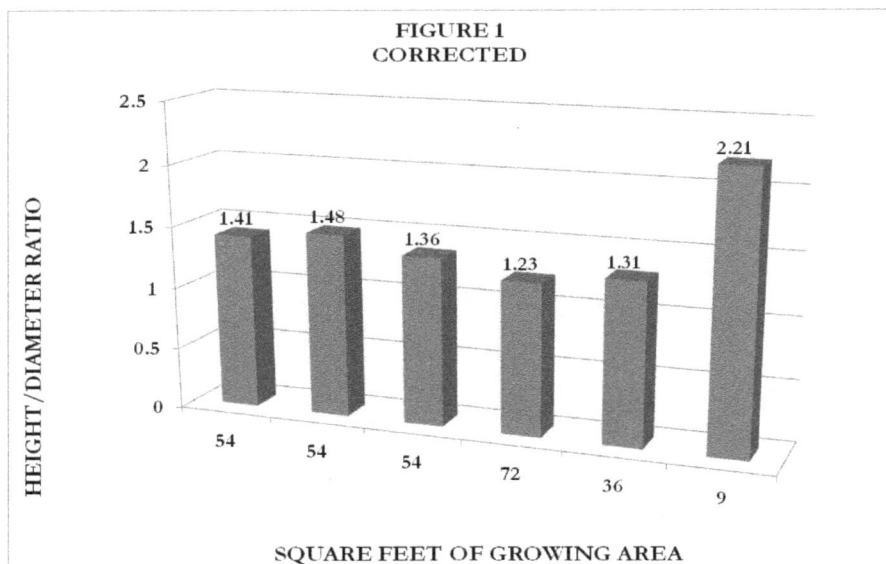

Figure 32. Figure 1 from Cannabis Fields, Corrected.

Notice that the horizontal axis in this corrected Figure 1 is somewhat suspicious. The x-axis increases from left to right to 72 and then falls off suddenly to 9. Listing the square feet of growing area correctly for the A, B, and C plots as 54 square feet throws off the graph. It is more than likely this is the reason Lewis changed the numbers in the first place. In other words, instead of an inability to multiply correctly, this may be a misrepresentation that began in Figure 1 and propagated itself back to Table 2.

It should also now be obvious that the original title for the x-axis of the original Figure 1, the one drawn up by Professor Sly, read Density not Square Feet of Growing Area. Why? Because then the five densities would have ascended from left to right as 0.15, 0.21, 0.31, 0.62, and 1.23. Remember, as density rises, square feet of growing area falls.

3.   Height/Diameter Ratio v SF.   We can recalculate ratios for each of the five densities versus square feet:

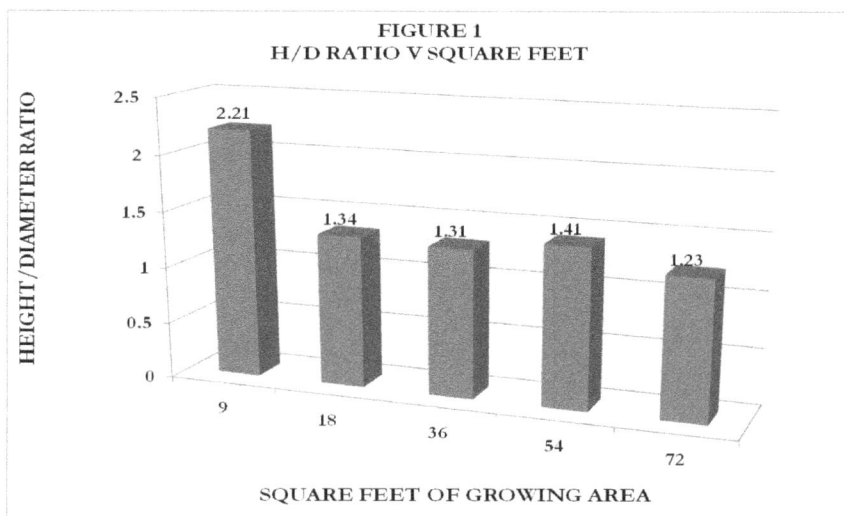

Figure 33. H/D Ratios v Square Feet, Recalculated.

4. H/D v Density.

Or we can present the ratios compared to density:

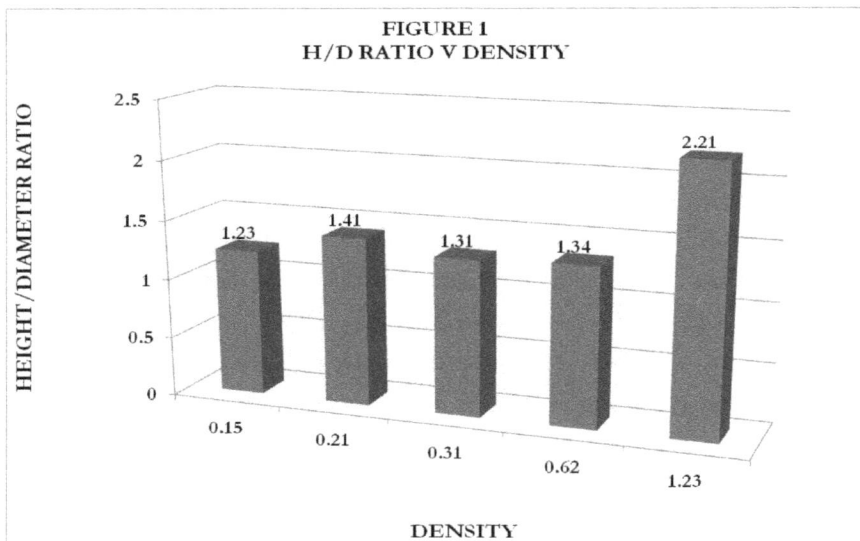

FIGURE 1
H/D RATIO V DENSITY

Figure 34. H/D Ratios v Density, Recalculated.

Now it's much easier to see what Lewis did with Sly's original Figure 1. This was probably the original column graph comparing the density to the height/diameter ratios for each of the five different densities in the 1990-1991 study. We can compare this chart with the one Lewis put together.

The introduction to Figure 1 on page 3 admits that he has been manipulating and cherry-picking the data: "Figure 1 presents *select* plant height-diameter ratios ... [italics added]." Ah, that lovely word "select." It has connotations of "prime, grade A, those truly worthy of inclusion" or it can denote, "I left out all the data that didn't agree with the conclusion I was looking for." In this case, it's the latter.

Not only is the 1985 and 1986 data missing (both lack diameter measurements), so is all the data from the plants with 18 square feet of growing area (density 0.62), that is, from plots E, the Colombian, as well as plots F and H. At least some of it was good enough for Table 1, but none of it is worthy of Figure 1. Once this data has been excised, it's a neat job to pretend one of the densities is bad: "The noticeably high ratio from the 9 foot square planting density confirms that this plant canopy shape is different than all of the other observations which had relatively large amount of space in which to grow." Which is as pathetic as the bad cop's trick of placing the tall suspect that he wants to convict in a line-up with midgets.

Next, the plants with 54 square feet of growing area (density 0.21) have been cut into three pieces and moved one column to the left. (Why does he move them? I really don't know. He could have left them in place. It still would have looked strange.) Lewis doesn't understand density so he labels his columns by square feet. But if he reports his three new columns correctly as having 54 square feet, the horizontal axis, already descending to the right instead of ascending, would look well and truly bizarre as we showed in the previous column graph, Figure 1 Corrected. So he just picks a number out of a hat, hey let's use 81, no one will ever know.

Finally, he adds to the bottom of his faked Figure 1, the description: "For plants 119 days or older." This is another oddity. The write up on page 3 tells us the data for this column graph come from the "planting densities used in 1990 and 1991." So why not use the original designation of 120 days from Table 1?

The definition of "mature" keeps changing. (As we shall see later, it will continue to do so.) There are no 119 day old plants in the data given from 1990 and 1991. I do not know why Lewis has done this. It is pointless. The only rationale I can suggest is that his alteration of Figure 1 itself evolved and perhaps at one point he was toying with the idea of including certain plants from the weekly totals of the male plants from the two tables in Attachment 2 which would have included two 17 week old (17 time 7 is 119) plants, but then he thought better of it because it was just too much work.

His purpose with Figure 1 is the same as it was with Tables 1 and 2, which is to decry the smaller yielding plants as not natural and as different while extolling the larger yielding plants as normal. He also wants to divert your attention from yield versus density to plant canopy shape versus density. The reason for this, of course, is that it is the less accurate formula for computing dry weight yield [Leafnbud®] from canopy diameter, not the more accurate formula using the freshly harvested plant weight, that he wishes to use to get his Poundaplant® in the tacked on section, the Domestic Estimate.

Lewis now tries his best to baffle us with bullshit: "The height-diameter graph of Figure 1 shows that planting density is a significant factor affecting plant canopy shape which in turn affects plant yield (page 3)." So why not simply use a direct calculation from density to yield [Leafnbud®]? But we've already answered that. Lewis's answer: "The significance of the relationship between planting density and plant yield will be discussed later in this paper (pages 3, 4)." No, it won't.

Are height to diameter ratios interesting? Of course. If you multiply the height by the diameter of the plant, effectively you are producing the area of the rectangle that encloses the silhouette of the plant. Multiplying by the reciprocal of the diameter does nothing but compress the data into a smaller range. If you did height by diameter squared, you'd have the volume of the imaginary box that enclosed the plant just before you harvested it. If you did height time pi times one half the diameter squared, you'd have the cylinder that enclosed it. But again, the only reason to include this would be to emphasize canopy as a predictive variable over fresh weight or density, even though canopy is inherently less accurate.

5.   H/D v Density w/o Anomalies.   Just for fun, it might be useful to look at what the original graph of height/diameter ratio versus density would have looked like if we remove the two anomalies from the data set:

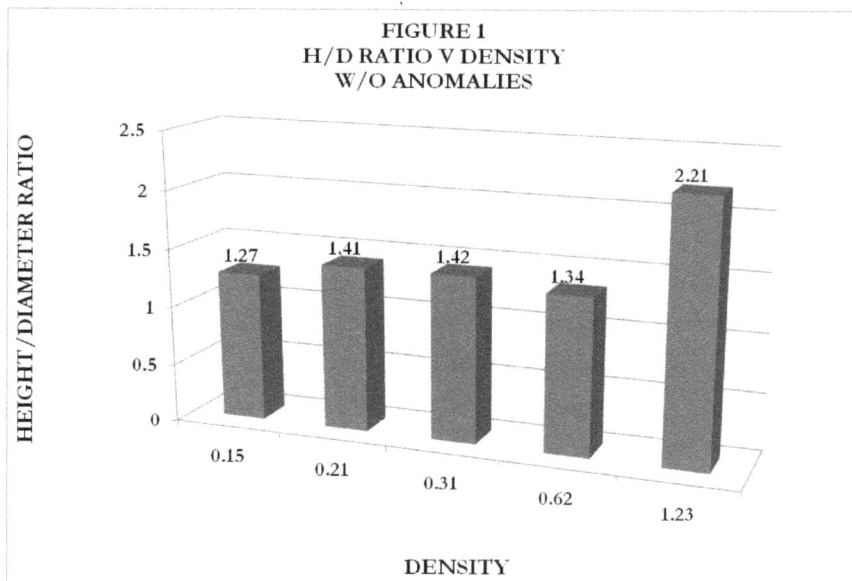

FIGURE 1
H/D RATIO V DENSITY
W/O ANOMALIES

Figure 35. H/D Ratios v Density w/o Anomalies.

With this you begin to appreciate the effect of the lack of data in Attachment 1 for the 0.62 density plots. If these plots had been reported properly, we might have seen a number that would have come close to splitting the difference between the 0.31 and 1.23 densities. We will never know.

C.   Discussion

Cannabis Fields began as a yield/density study. We should have seen a Figure I to go with our Table I.   The focus should have been on the average yield [Leafnbud®] obtainable as the density varied. Since it has gone missing, we have graphed it against square feet and against density, both with and without the anomalies. A polynomial curve of best fit when applied to the yield [Leafnbud®] graphed against density without the anomalies gives an R-squared of .999.

Instead, we are treated to a height/diameter ratio versus square feet graph for Figure 1. But Figure 1 has deliberately misrepresented the square feet per plant for three of its densities as 81 when the correct answer is 54. Further, much of the data that should have been there has been removed, especially the data concerning the 0.62 density (18 square feet per plant). As well, the definition of mature changes from 120 or more grow days to 119 or more. The purpose of the graph is to distract our attention away from how the yield varies with changes in density, to condemn small plants as unnatural, to focus on large plants and to promote a less accurate canopy formula. All this will attempt to justify the DEA's favorite estimate of a Poundaplant®. All of this is served up on a plate and the reader is expected to chow down, to which one can only retort: "Arnie Bragg? Again?"

Figure 36. First Growth.
Previous page: Day 13, 2004;
a simple greenhouse.
Above: Plantitas, 2 June 2008.

3
Where's the Bud?

"Many of the principal advocates of UFO abduction seem to want the validation of science without submitting to its rigorous standards of evidence. ... Precisely because of human fallibility, extraordinary claims require extraordinary evidence."

-- Carl Sagan (1934 – 1996)[1]

---

[1] Astronomer and populizer of science. From "Interview," posted 02.27.96 on *NOVA*, "Carl Sagan on Alien Abduction," www.pbs.org. See also, "Encyclopedia Galactica," *COSMOS*, episode 12, aired 14 Dec 1980, 1:24 minutes in, *PBS*.

$\mathbf{T}$he corollary to the first part of the quotation is that lack of evidence does not allow one to draw *any* conclusions. The corollary to the second part of the quotation is that even mild claims should have *some* evidence to support them. *Cannabis Fields* says bud was separated from leaf. The pie charts in Figure 2 (page 5) are drawn to illustrate this separation. They even give percentages. But the data in Attachment 1 doesn't show this. So where's the bud?

A.   What Lewis Says

Lewis claims that the plants were "separated into *four* component parts – stem/branches, leaves, female flowering tops, commonly known as buds or colas, and seed (page 2, italics added)," not three. Lewis claims that the flowers were separated from the leaf for each plant. Figure 2 on page 5 shows two pie charts, one for the sinsemilla and one for the ratios of the weights of the non-sinsemilla oven dried cannabis components. Each of the pie charts has lines drawn indicating the individual separation not only of seed and stalk/branch but also of bud from leaf.

The pie charts in Figure 2 will become important later. On pages 9 and 10, the stated percentages in Figure 2 will be used to calculate both Yield Adjustment Factors and the Domestic Estimate. But anyone can make claims, change a three to a four and add extra lines to pie charts.

We will examine the claims regarding the bottom pie chart of Figure 2 in the next chapter when we look at the sinsemilla. On the following page is the top pie chart from Figure 2 of *Cannabis Fields* (page 5) indicating the different percentages of each component of a mature nonsinsemilla plant:

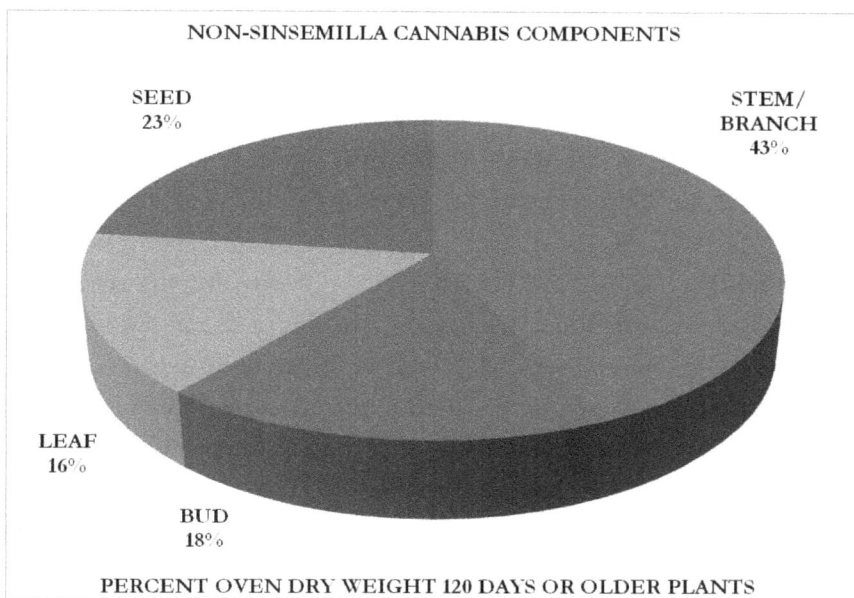

Figure 37.
The top pie chart of Figure 2, drawn by Dr. Sly and altered by Lewis.

B.   What the Data Shows

But there is no bud in the data. Attachment 1 (from which the conclusions in the body of the paper are supposed to be derived) gives no separate weights for the female flowers nor for the leaves. The pie charts on page five separate them. The paper claims they were separated. Yet the data says nothing about them.

This may not be apparent to those who have only given the study a cursory reading. *If* fertilized female cannabis plants were grown to maturity (no photographs are provided), those plants must have (given the biological facts) produced stalk and branch, seed, leaf, and flowers. But we are not given any separate weights for the flowers.

Nor do we have any separate weights for the leaf. This contrasts with separate weights explicitly provided for Stem (stalk and denuded branches) and Seed. Instead of separate weights for leaf and separate weights for flowers, the only numbers we are given in Attachment 1 are for Yield Fresh and Yield Dry. This oddity begs two questions: a) Why are separate weights provided for only two parts of the plant? and, b) What is meant by this term, Yield?

1.   Yield?   Normally, the term yield when applied to agriculture means the specific part or parts of the plant desired by the farmer. For the cultivators of recreational or medicinal cannabis, these are the dried female flowers. Even Lewis the Liar admits this: "The bud structure is highly desired by illicit growers because it contains the highest number of THC producing glands (page 9)." But not even Lewis will make the claim: "The *leaf* structure is highly desired by illicit growers because ...."

In *Cannabis Fields*, yield means both leaf *and* bud [Leafnbud®], though it can also mean leaf by itself. Table 1 (page 3) reports a yield for plants from the 1985-1986 University of Mississippi study. But the data in Attachment 2 divides each plant into only two parts: Stalk/Stems and leaves. The word yield does not appear in Attachment 2. The numbers in Table 1 of Attachment 2 (222 and 274, respectively) are rounded from the dry weights of leaves (column 7, 1985, column 6, 1986, Attachment 2). More evidence that yield can mean leaf by itself comes from a statement on page 9 describing the "estimated yield of a male plant in early August ...." Male plants produce no bud, no female flowers. This yield can only have consisted of leaf.

Even more evidence comes from a yield that is reported from immature plants, either male or female. *Cannabis Fields* reports a yield from 30, 36, 55, 56, 64, 65, 82 and 83 day old plants in plots A, B, and C from 1990 and the three different plots labeled only Mexican Variety from 1991. But even Dr. Sly admits: "The crop cycle consists of two stages. The first stage is the vegetative stage which is characterized by a 30 to 90 day period of vigorous growth of sexually undifferentiated plants (page 8)." The yield from these less than 90 day old plants can only have consisted of leaf. As well, Table 1 includes a yield from what are called leaves in Attachment 2 from 12 week (84 day) old plants.

2.   Usable?   So the yield in *Cannabis Fields* is leaf and bud [Leafnbud®] or merely leaf by itself, essentially the green, leafy bits, as distinguished from the woody parts (stalk and branches) or the small, oval, hard things (seed). To try to justify this odd system of nomenclature, the ethically-challenged professor has added usable to yield: "to predict usable yield (page 1)," "oven dry weight of usable yield (page 3)," "usable oven dry weight material (leaf and bud) in a mature cannabis plant (page 4)," "and estimate of usable dry weight material (page 6)," "Usable yield is then calculated using the percentages of bud and leaf (page 7)," and "usable material in the illicit market (page 8)."

But the addition of the adjective usable adds nothing. Which part of the plant is not usable? The outer part of the stalk can be used to start fires in the winter or composted for next year's crop. The fiber within the stalk can be woven into rope or linen. The seed can be eaten or replanted or used to make oil.

Which part of the yield is not usable? Usable for what? In fact, the only reason to use usable is to hide the fact that some parts of the plant are not being reported individually. Lewis and I went to different high schools together. His mother and my mother were both mothers living in different cities together.

Are we to suppose that both leaf and bud are usable for the same thing? Which would be what? Smoking? The DEA continues to maintain that cannabis aficionados enjoy smoking leaf which they obtain from that huge illicit market for the highly desired Leafnbud®? This conveniently allows them to roughly double or even triple the quantity of evidence used to convict a home grower at trial, in the same way they used to weigh the plants they seized with the dirt and roots attached.

The dried female flowers are smoked. Leaf is almost always simply trimmed and composted. You *can* smoke leaf. *You* can smoke leaf. But you won't do it more than once. You *can* soak leaf, either bud leaf or shade leaf, in alcohol or oil, to make useful topical rubs. You can do the same with the dried, cleaned roots. You *can* run bud leaf through an icewater extractor, but you won't get more than one or two percent by weight of a not particular interesting hashish for all your considerable time and trouble and expense. You can extract from bud leaf roughly the same percentage of sticky, gooey hash oil using butane. (Google the word *bleve* before you do this indoors over a gas stove, please.) You *can* soak bud leaf in butter and cook with it to make brownies, quite nice ones depending on the flowers from which they were obtained. But experienced growers quickly learn that sow's ears don't make silk purses.

Leaves and flowers are different parts of a plant. Why have they been combined into one category while stalk and seed are reported separately? The word usable attempts to justify, not clarify, this odd nomenclature. In its latest incarnation, *Cannabis Fields* has returned as an abstract entitled "Biomass Field Studies of Field Cultivated Cannabis sativa L. Plants." Here, yield is no longer Leafnbud® but has become a rather more trendy usable biomass. But the stalk and branches cannot be ground up to become usable biomass? Once again there is an attempt to both obscure and justify the reason for not reporting the leaf and bud separately.

3.   The Great Trimming Party.   The data in Attachment 1 disputes both the separation claim and the pie charts that depict said separation. The data lists individual weights for Stem and Seed, both Fresh and Dry. But the individual weights for bud or leaf are nowhere to be found. The data in Attachment 1 (which is what, finally, we have to go by) shows that the plants were only separated into *three* component parts: stalk and branches, seed, and an undifferentiated biomass of Leafnbud® covertly disguised as yield. At the very least, the amusing pie charts in Figure 2 cannot be justified by the data submitted. So, let us repeat the mantra, where's the bud?

Now one of two things is true. We are asked to believe that the bud was separated from the leaf when the plant was freshly cut, that the bud and the leaf were then weighed separately, that these weights were carefully recorded, that each was baked in an oven for two days, that each was reweighed separately, that these new weights were carefully recorded, and finally that this raw data so painstakingly gathered was then thrown away in the trash.

The 38 mature (> or = 120 days old) plants weighed collectively when harvested 185,948.7 grams. They produced a dry mass in Leafnbud® of 24,441.5 grams or roughly 24 kilos. Anyone who has actually trimmed 38 large plants, clipping the large shade leaves, snipping the bud leaves and carefully manicuring the buds, will know just how much work is involved (remember, these are the dark ages and mechanical trimmers had not hit the market yet).

Did the DEA hire a trimming crew from Humboldt County and fly them to Mississippi for this task? What kind of salve did the trimmers use for their tired, aching hands? Having so labor intensively gathered this raw data, the separate weights for the bud and the separate weights for the leaf, which would have been so useful in court, the DEA then threw these raw numbers away?

4.   **How to Make Leafnbud®.**   Or ... the plants were unceremoniously fed through a leaf shredder. The leaf shredder indiscriminately mangled the leaf and bud together, allowing the seeds to fall through a screen at the bottom, while out the back emerged a stripped and thrashed stalk with its bare branches still quivering. This method has the advantage of requiring much less labor and much less time.

With this alternative explanation, no bud was separated from any leaf. The plant was separated into *three* component parts only: stalk/branch, seed and Leafnbud®. Lewis the Liar then added the extra lines to the pie charts in Figure 2, and changed what had been a 'three' in the body of the paper to a 'four.'

Why? Obviously, a judge attempting to determine how much dried bud can be derived from a given green plant can't really use a large, undifferentiated mass of leaf mixed in with bud to come to any realistic conclusion. The leaf and bud together certainly establish an upper bound. You could say that the amount of bud per plant would probably be something less than the amount of leaf and bud combined. But what you can't say is how much bud there was and this is exactly what the judge requires. The ever resourceful Lewis overcame this difficult obstacle by altering a word and drawing a line on two pie charts. Lewis likes his lies simple. Lewis needed bud and by gosh, Lewis was going to get his bud.

You can believe what you wish. You are entitled to your own beliefs but you are not entitled to your own facts. Even mild claims require some evidence to support them. No facts suggest the plants were separated into *four* component parts. No facts suggest the leaf was separated from the bud. No facts suggest that bud makes up this percentage of a plant's weight or that leaf makes up that much. The conclusions in *Cannabis Fields* regarding the stated plant separation methodology or the separate percentages of dried leaf or dried bud per given dried plant in Figure 2 simply cannot be derived from the data.

I have redrawn *from the data* in Attachment 1 what the top pie chart in Figure 2 should look like. There were 21 non-sinsemilla (seeded) plants in the 1990-1991 plots with greater than or equal to 120 grow days, and hence, by the original definition, were mature. Once you recalculate the percentages from the data, it becomes clear that the original data set of Attachment 1 no longer exists.

92

Here's what the top pie chart of Figure 2 looks like when you redraw it from the data:

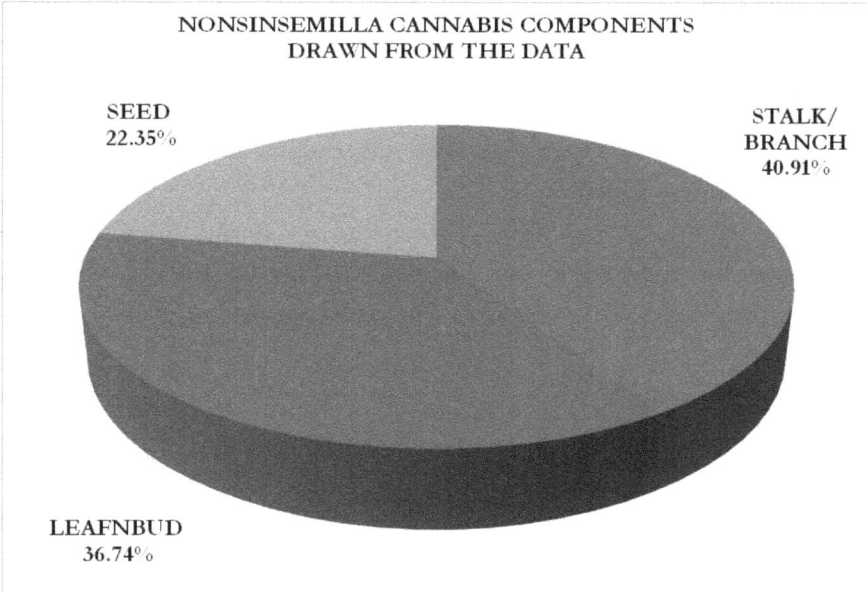

Figure 38.
The top pie chart of Figure 2, redrawn from the data in Attachment 1.

You could argue a rounding error by which 22.35% seed became 23%. But the top pie chart in Figure 2 on page five shows 43% for Stem/Branches while the real number is a tad under 41%, 40.91% rounded to two decimal places. Added together, Lewis's Leaf at 16% and Bud at 18% come to only 34% while the data gives a shade under 37%, 36.74% to two places rounded, as the correct figure for the combined and shredded Leafnbud®. The only thing we can conclude is that after the upper pie chart was drawn, some of the plants were removed and others added to take their place.

C.   Discussion

The top pie chart of Figure 2 supposes that the non-sinsemilla plants were separated into four parts but the data shows they were only separated into three: seed, stalk/branch, and Leafnbud®.   Like the Red Queen, the anonymous authors of *Cannabis Fields* want words to mean just what they want them to mean.   Yield means leaf and bud, but sometimes leaf alone.   Usable means useful for completely different purposes together.

So where is the bud?   Either the good old boys down in Mississippi had themselves one heck of a trimming party or they fed the plants through a leaf shredder. The data supports the latter.

Figure 39. Transplanting.
Previous page: Spacing out the keikis;
filling the holes with potting soil.
Above: Fernanda introduces each
plant to the garden.

4
What Sinsemilla?

"Yet Clare's sharp questions must I shun;
Must separate Constance from the Nun —
O, what a tangled web we weave,
When first we practise to deceive!"
-- Sir Walter Scott (1771 – 1832)[1]

---

[1] Marmion: A Tale of Flodden Field in Six Cantos, ed. Michael Macmillan. London: Macmillan and Company, Ltd., 1899 (GB), p. 157, Canto VI, Stanza 17. See also www.gutenberg.org.

Not only was there no separation of bud from leaf, neither was there any sinsemilla. Yet the bottom pie chart of Figure 2 on page five assures us there were unseeded plants and even gives us an average of the percentages for their component parts:

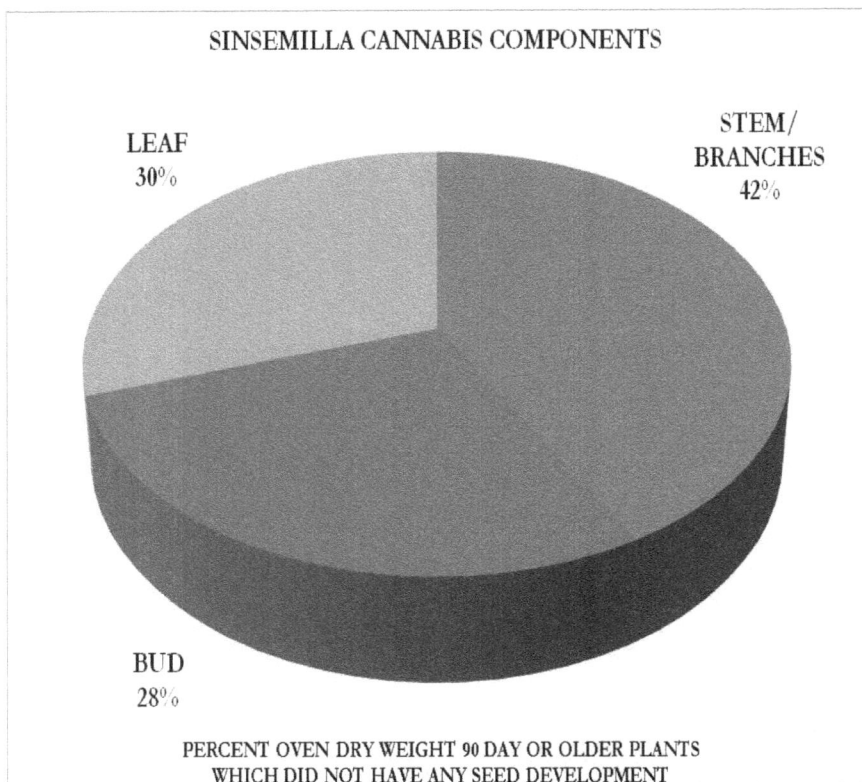

SINSEMILLA CANNABIS COMPONENTS

STEM/
BRANCHES
42%

LEAF
30%

BUD
28%

PERCENT OVEN DRY WEIGHT 90 DAY OR OLDER PLANTS
WHICH DID NOT HAVE ANY SEED DEVELOPMENT

Figure 40.
The Bottom Pie Chart in Figure 2, page 5, from Cannabis Fields.

We have already seen in the previous chapter that the individual percentages for leaf and for bud are not supported by the data. Instead, the best the data can give us is a melange of ground up, green, leafy bits known affectionately as Leafnbud®. But how in the world could the DEA have produced any sinsemilla?

WHAT SINSEMILLA?

A.   Miracle at Yoknapatawpha

The DEA grew sinsemilla plants without trying. Indeed, they deliberately allowed male plants to mature and produce pollen in the midst of closely spaced plots of mixed female and male plants. We know this because they admit it: "However, no attempt was made to cultivate unfertilized female plants, commonly known as 'sinsemilla' (page 1)."

Confirmation, as noted in Chapter 3, comes from a statement on page 9 which describes the "estimated yield of a male plant in early August." So, the DEA left the male plants in the field next to the female plants even though they were aware that "male plants form the stamens from which *huge* amounts of pollen are released (page 9, italics added)." At least one website pretends that the male plants were pulled. They weren't.

Yet there in Attachment 1 of *Cannabis Fields* are these long strings of zeroes, showing no seed, either fresh or dry, for unpollinated mature plants five months (153 days) old living in the midst of "huge amounts of pollen." What can we make of this phenomena? How can we explain this miracle? Have NIDA's "(t)rained scientists"[2] produced a genetically modified female plant that repels pollen?

Mortals work to achieve sinsemilla plants. Those not growing cannabis in what can only be described as Mississippi's enchanted Garden of Eden must observe their plants daily, inspecting each plant carefully for the first appearance of the males. Males can show up overnight. Male plants have to be pulled at the earliest possible moment. Failure to do this will guarantee that the females will become pollinated. Every serious, experienced grower in the real world has suffered through at least one failure to pull the males before they can release their pollen.

---

[2] Konrad, Kris. *Cannabis Fields and Postage*, page 9, saveacownow.org.

But not in Yoknapatawpha. There were ten plots. Each plot or cultivation area was large: "The planting of approximately 100 plants per cultivation area insured that there was a large and representative population from which plants were sampled (page 2)." Of those 100 plants, roughly 50 were male and 50 were female. Of the roughly 1000 plants in the ten plots, about 500 were male and about 500 female. All of the plots would have fit nicely on a single football field.

Bonus question for ten points extra credit, the Amana 4000 cubic foot refrigerator/freezer and the all-expenses-paid vacation to Hawaii: If you plant 1000 cannabis plants closely together and you do not pull the males at the earliest opportunity and you let the females mature, how many unseeded female plants do you expect to harvest? Ding, ding, ding, ding, ding-ding-ding ....

Time's up. Any answer other than zero defines you as an optimist who believes in faith-based farming. Perhaps you feel there is a deity who will protect all your females from the veritable whirlwinds of male pollen all around them. Clearly, such divine intervention occurred with the DEA plantations in 1990.

B. A Fickle Deity

Sadly, their deity forsake them the very next year. One of the biological curiosities of the plants grown by the DEA is that the mature female plants appear to be impossible to pollinate in 1990 and incredibly easy to pollinate in 1991. All the plants reported in 1990 have no seed data. All the plants except three in 1991 had seed.

Yet they claim to have followed the same methodology each time. In 1990 no male pollen reached the females planted right beside them. Wow! What extraordinary good luck! In 1991 the females were almost uniformly seeded. Oh no! What extraordinary bad luck! And all of this occurred with the exact same variety of Mexican.

WHAT SINSEMILLA?

Even more curious, it seems this deity the DEA prays to was incredibly selective in how she distributed the pollen. The Mexican Variety – 0.9m x 0.9m of 1991 is the only one to show both sinsemilla and non-sinsemilla plants in the same plot. Now, at this point two curious and completely unrelated facts suddenly become connected. First, the plant numbers for this same plot of Mexican are given in decimals, not integers. Second, the Methodology section assures us that "no plants on the *outer rows* were selected (page 2, italics added)." In yield/density studies, this repeats the standard protocol in which the rows of plants from which the sample is to be chosen are surrounded by extra rows so as to preserve the overall average density of the plot as plants are harvested during the season. Plants growing on outer rows will receive more sunlight, water, nutrients and so forth, and have a better chance to grow larger, warping the overall measurement of the plants in that density.

Obviously, outer rows suggests inner rows. And row upon row suggests columns. But we also have decimal plant numbers, two digits to the left and two to the right of the decimal point. Let's assume (see Chapter 8 for the results of such an assumption) that the decimal plant numbers refer to rows and columns. (They have to keep track of the plants somehow.) That suggests that the two digits to the left of the decimal indicate the row and the two digits to the right of the decimal indicate the column. (Okay, how would you do it?) Then plant number 87.17, using these totally outlandish and unwarranted assumptions, would indicate the seventeenth plant (column 17) in row eighty-seven. That particular plant was completely unseeded, pure sinsemilla, with zeroes in its columns for fresh and dry seed. Its near neighbor, one yard away, plant 87.19, produced 138.4 grams of dry seed.

But the DEA's pollen deity was even more selective than that. The twenty-third plant in row ninety-five, plant number 95.23, was pure sinsemilla while its diagonal neighbor, number 96.22, yielded 208.8 grams of dry seed. The latter had a diameter of 113 centimeters, exceeding its 0.9 meter plot. So, with even a gentle breeze its branches would almost have been touching the former which had a diameter of 99 centimeters. Such amazing work by this goddess, no doubt performed in the middle of a dark night with only the very finest, camel hair pollen brush.

C.   Appleseeds and Seedless Oranges

But wait, there's more! In spite of the phenomenal ability of this Deaity® to pollinate some plants and not others, her devotee Lewis the Liar figured she needed some help. So he decided to make his definition of mature for the sinsemilla plants rather more fluid than for the non-sinsemilla. In Figure 2 on page five he compares apples and oranges.

The top pie chart for the non-sinsemilla cannabis components of Figure 2 shows the "percent oven dry weight [for] 120 days or older plants." In contrast, the bottom pie chart in Figure 2 for the sinsemilla cannabis components shows the "percent oven dry weight [for] 90 day or older plants which did not have any seed development." We saw the definition of mature vary once before. It happened already in Figure 1, where it mysteriously changed from 120 day old plants to 119 day old plants, to no particular effect. Here in Figure 2, while a non-sinsemilla plant needs at least 120 grow days to be considered mature, a sinsemilla plant only needs 90. This alters the rules in the middle of the game.

But not just between sinsemilla and non-sinsemilla, as it also competes with previous calculations for the sinsemilla plants themselves. The components of the sinsemilla plants in Figure 2 are calculated using 90 day or older plants. This contradicts the protocol already used in Table 1 where yield [Leafnbud®] is calculated using only mature plants, that is, those with 120 or more grow days. On page 2, a mature plant is defined to be a plant that is 120 days or older: "Table 1 depicts the average yield for all mature (120 days or older) plants ...." Table 1 gives a figure for the dry yield [Leafnbud®] from the nine plants that are 120 days or older in the DEA 1991 plot with "9 ft. sq." of growing area (0.9 x 0.9 meters) as 215 grams (rounded up from 214.6).

But there is only one plot with both sinsemilla and non-sinsemilla plants. And only plants with 120 or more grow days, whether non-sinsemilla or sinsemilla, were included in the calculation for the average yield [Leafnbud®] of this plot. The seven plants aged 91 days old were not included even though they also have zeroed seed data, and so could be considered mature by the definition in the bottom pie chart of Figure 2.

As well the DEA plot of Colombian with "18 ft. sq." of growing area (0.91 x 1.8 meters), all of which is pure sinsemilla, lists a dry yield [Leafnbud®] of 233 grams (233.16) in Figure 1. But this was calculated only from the three plants with greater than or equal to 120 grow days, ignoring the other four plants which all have equal to or greater than 90 grow days and also have zeroed seed data. The yield [Leafnbud®] from the sinsemilla plants in plots A, B, and C is similarly calculated from 120 day or older plants, though they also have plants with 90 or more grow days without any seed data.

This new definition of mature also contradicts the protocol used in Figure 1, where the height/diameter ratios of the sinsemilla plants in plots A, B, and C are calculated from plants 120 days old or older. As noted earlier, there are no 119 day old plants from 1990 and 1991. There is a single 17 week old plant listed in the earlier 1985 study in Attachment 2 but it is not used in the calculation for height/diameter ratios in Figure 1.

This also contradicts experience and common sense. A ninety day old cannabis plant that shows no seed development is not sinsemilla any more than a sixty day old plant that shows no seed development. Plants develop at different rates. Some 90 day old plants have not yet exhibited their sex. Some plants put in dirt in April turn male in the middle of September. Sinsemilla means without seed.

Cutting a plant early doesn't give you a sinsemilla plant; it means you simply don't know whether or not the flowers, whenever they might have appeared, would have become pollinated and produced seed.

D.   The Liar's Dilemma

But why does Lewis the Liar feel the need to shift the definition of mature from 120 days or older to 90 days or older only for the sinsemilla plants and only for Figure 2?   Consider Lewis's problem. He wants to demonstrate to the judge and jury that he has scientific proof of a Poundaplant®. Unfortunately, he has data only for masses of wet Leafnbud®. He has to find bud where he has none. So, as we saw in Chapter 3, he adds some lines to a pie chart and declares he separated out bud from leaf though the data says he didn't.

But he has the same problem trying to find sinsemilla. Home growers attempt to cultivate seedless plants.   They aren't always successful but they try. Lewis has data only for seeded plants, which is what you would expect from large plantations of plants, one of every two of which is male, each male releasing "huge amounts of pollen." His results need to be relevant in court. He has to find sinsemilla and all he has is data from seeded plants. What's a poor (and lazy) DEA agent to do?

Solution? He zeroes the seed data! Plants with seed data are by definition non-sinsemilla. Plants without seed data are, by the same criterion, without seed, hence, sinsemilla. Pretty easy, eh?

Ah, but now Lewis has a second problem: Where can he put the missing seed?   He has to put it somewhere.   Otherwise the numbers won't add up.

The Plant Fresh and Plant Dry numbers are calculated, not observed. The weight of the whole plant, either wet or dry, is summed from the individual weights of its component parts, that is, the weights from the Stem, Yield [Leafnbud®], and Seed data, Fresh and Dry respectively. The freshly harvested plant was not weighed entire. Its weight was calculated by summing the weights of its three separate parts, taken when wet. Similarly the dried plant was not weighed entire; that weight is also the sum of the separate weights from the dry Stem, Yield [Leafnbud®], and Seed data.

(You know this if you have ever actually tried to weigh a whole plant, separate it into its component parts, weigh each part, then sum the weights to try to equal the original weight of the unseparated plant, essentially trying to put the plant back together again with a scale. I have a reasonable amount of money that says you cannot get the first weight to equal the second to the accuracy of a tenth of a gram. The weights never quite add up correctly. This is because, in the real world with real organic material, there are always losses at every stage of the process. Handling losses alone guarantee this. Some seed, bud or leaf always ends up on the drying room floor.)

So Lewis zeroes the Seed data in Attachment 1 to create his sinsemilla but this data still has to appear somewhere. Why? If you eliminate the Seed weights from the data set, the remaining Stem and Yield [Leafnbud®] weights will not add up to the Plant weights, either Dry or Fresh. He could have simply added the remaining Stem and Yield [Leafnbud®] weights together to get rather lighter sinsemilla plants. But he wants heavier plants not lighter ones so he can achieve his goal of a Poundaplant®.

He's only got two choices. He can't add it to the Yield [Leafnbud®] data. The formula in Figure 3 for the ratio between the fresh weight of a plant to its dry yield [Leafnbud®] has already been calculated by Professor Sly. Remember, Lewis can lie but he can't figure. As a result he has no choice. He is forced to add the seed data to the data for the stalk/branch. Am I making this up? I mean, the "NIDA field data has a solid scientific basis,"[3] right?

---

[3] Konrad, Kris. *Cannabis Fields and Postage*, page 9, saveacownow.org.

E.   Not Making This Up

Now, if Lewis did this, then the weights of the Stem (stalk and branch) of the sinsemilla plants should be roughly 20 percent or so heavier than the Stem of the non-sinsemilla plants, since seed makes up 22.35 percent of a seeded plant according to the upper pie chart in Figure 2, corrected and drawn from the data.

So let's check. First, we'll do the Stem Dry to Plant Dry ratio for the mature (120 or more grow days, the original definition) sinsemilla. There are 17 sinsemilla plants that fit this criteria. The Stem Dry data for the seventeen mature (120 grow days or older) sinsemilla plants sums to 14,711.5 grams. The Plant Dry data of the same seventeen adds to 23,727.8 grams. (Actually, the Plant Dry data in Attachment 1 as given adds to 23,730.2 grams. This is because there are three errors in the data for the mature (120 or more grow days) sinsemilla. Plant number 97.19 should have a Plant Dry weight of 259.2 grams, summed from the Stem Dry of 132.4 and the Yield Dry of 126.8, instead of the 261.2 grams listed. Plant number 41.00 should show 576.4 grams, not 576.5, and number 42.00 should read 883.2 grams, not 883.5 grams for its Plant Dry weight.)

Divide Stem Dry by Plant Dry, or 14,711.5 by 23,727.8, and you get a ratio of .6200111. This means 62.00% of a mature (by the original definition) sinsemilla plant in the DEA plots is stalk and branch, not the 42% reported in the bottom pie chart of Figure 2. It is in striking contrast to the 43% percentage of stalk and branch reported for the twenty-one mature seeded plants given in the top pie chart of Figure 2, which should actually be 40.91% if you draw it from the data.

So let's draw the pie chart for the component parts of a mature (> or = 120 grow days) sinsemilla plant as given by the data in Attachment 1:

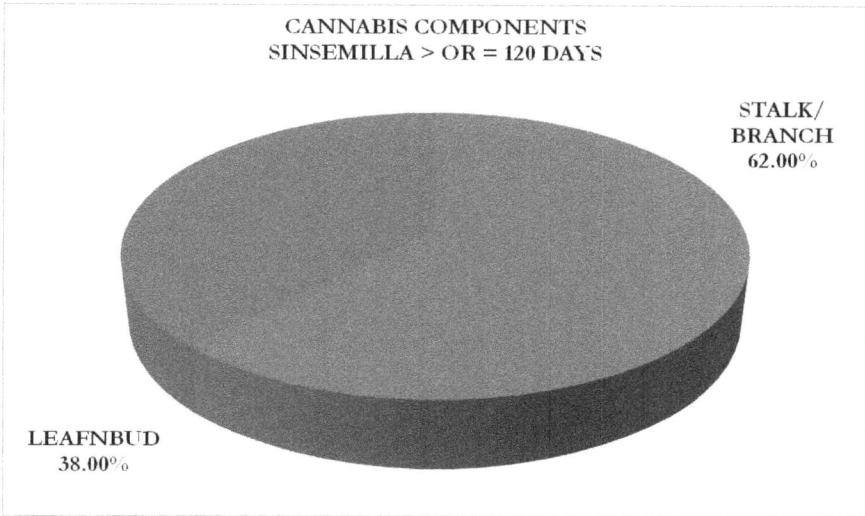

CANNABIS COMPONENTS
SINSEMILLA > OR = 120 DAYS

STALK/
BRANCH
62.00%

LEAFNBUD
38.00%

Figure 41.
The bottom pie chart of Figure 2, Cannabis Fields, drawn from the data.

We can check the individual ratios to make sure. The largest Stem Dry to Plant Dry ratio in the mature plants labeled as sinsemilla occurs in plant number 44.00 from the plot labeled Hybrid Variety – Plot F, 0.91 x 1.8 m Planting, 1990. The Stem Dry data for this plant is given as 1843.0 grams and the Plant Dry data is said to be 2654.2 grams. Divide 1843.0 by 2654.2 and we have .6943711, meaning stalk and branch make up 69.43711 percent of the total plant, calculated to five places without rounding, or roughly 69.44 percent to two places with rounding. The smallest ratio occurs in plant number 87.17 of the plot labeled Mexican Variety – 0.9 x 0.9 m Planting, 1991. The dry plant weighs 287.5 grams while the bare stalk and branches weigh 129.7 grams. Dividing the one by the other gives .4511304 according to my Chilean hand calculator, meaning the stalk and branches comprised some 45.11 percent of the total dry plant, the smallest ratio among the 17 mature sinsemilla plants (those that have equal to or greater than 120 grow days).

Compare the 62 percent average for the stalk and branch of the seventeen sinsemilla plants (mature defined to be 120 or more grow days) in Attachment 1 to the 40.91 percent average for the stalk and branch of the twenty-one non-sinsemilla plants (again, mature defined to be 120 or more grow days), as shown in Chapter 3:

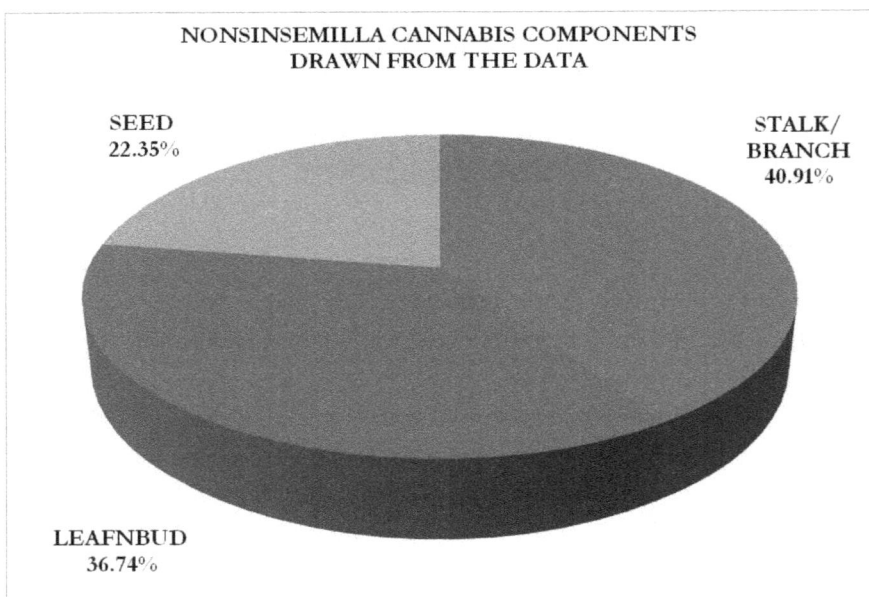

NONSINSEMILLA CANNABIS COMPONENTS
DRAWN FROM THE DATA

SEED
22.35%

STALK/
BRANCH
40.91%

LEAFNBUD
36.74%

Figure 42.
The top pie chart of Figure 2, Cannabis Fields, drawn from the data.

And now you see Lewis's problem. He wants to draw a pie chart showing the percentages of the component parts of a sinsemilla plant to go with the original pie chart showing the percentages of the component parts of a non-sinsemilla plant. But if he tells the truth, the stalk and branch for the sinsemilla plants will weigh considerably more than the stalk and branch of the non-sinsemilla plants. His Stem Dry

WHAT SINSEMILLA?

ratio for the sinsemilla betrays him by sharply contrasting with the Stem Dry ratio for the non-sinsemilla.

Why would the stalk and branches of a mature seeded plant weigh roughly 41% of total plant weight while the stalk and branches of a mature seedless plant weigh 62%? Since seed weighs more than flower, why would the stalk and branches of a sinsemilla plant bulk up to support less weight? And how would the plant do that in September and October when it is exiting its "vegetative stage (page 8)," when almost all of its growing has ceased and it has entered its "second stage, known as the flowering or fruiting period (page 8)"? Even assuming that a sinsemilla plant could reverse its own biological directive caused by the "reduction in day length (page 8)" and start growing new stalk and branch, how would the plant know until it was harvested whether it would ever become pollinated? Are the DEA plants psychic?

Hence, Lewis's need to change the definition of mature for his sinsemilla plants to include plants 90 days or older. He wants to hide the heavier stalk data from the sinsemilla plants within a larger mass of data in the hopes no one will notice. But even this won't help him.

If we sum the data for all forty-five plants that Lewis wishes to describe in Figure 2 as sinsemilla, we have a total dry plant of 44,329.2 grams and a total dry stalk and denuded branch of 24,136.1 grams for a ratio of 54.45% versus the 42% reported. Lewis has now conjured up out of thin air just for the bottom pie chart of Figure 2, and not for Table 1 or Figure 1, some twenty-eight newly coined sinsemilla plants with ages greater than or equal to 90 days and less than 120 days, all of which have zeroed seed data. Of course *all* the plants with ages less than 120 days have zeroed seed data.

So let's redraw the bottom pie chart of Figure 2, using the data given to us in Attachment 1, according to the new rules Lewis wants us to use, just for the sinsemilla:

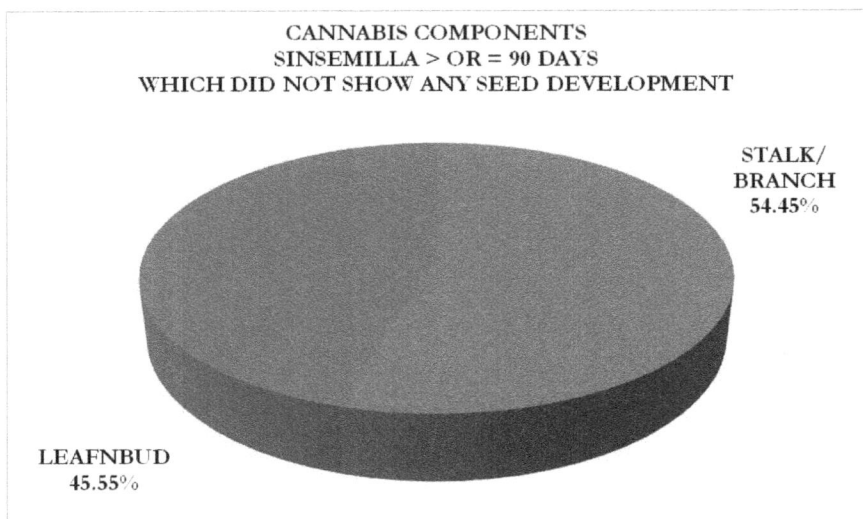

CANNABIS COMPONENTS
SINSEMILLA > OR = 90 DAYS
WHICH DID NOT SHOW ANY SEED DEVELOPMENT

STALK/
BRANCH
54.45%

LEAFNBUD
45.55%

Figure 43.
The bottom pie chart of Figure 2, CF, from the data using Lewis's rules.

Together these 28 new sinsemilla plants weighed dry some twenty kilos (20,601.4 grams). (Again, there was an error for the "Plant Dry" data for plant number 5.00 which should have read 165.5 grams, not the 166.2 listed.) The stalk and denuded branches of the 28 new sinsemilla weighed 9424.6 grams, for a ratio of 45.75%. The Stem Dry to Plant Dry ratios for these 28 even-newer-than-the-other sinsemilla plants range from the 91 day old plant, number 108.06 in the plot labeled Mexican Variety – 2.4 x 2.7 m Planting, 1991 with a Plant Dry of 1944.9 grams and a Stem Dry of 513.5 grams, or 26.40% stalk and branch, to the 111 day old plant, number 11.00 in the plot labeled Mexican Variety – Plot A, 1.8 x 2.7 m Planting, 1990 which weighed dry 2523.0 grams and whose dried stalk and branch weighed 1532.5 grams, for a ratio of 60.74%.

Could there have been plants between 90 and 120 days that had seed? We can track the change in stalk/branch percentages every 30 days to see where the destruction of data began, to see when the plants

110

younger than 120 days had seed that Lewis simply erased. First, let's take a look at the plants between 30 and 59 days old:

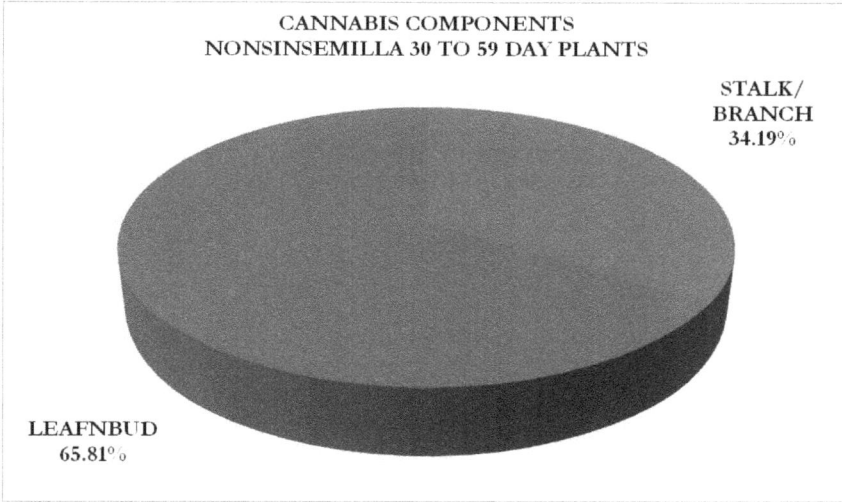

Figure 44. Day 30 to 59 nonsinsemilla components, from the data.

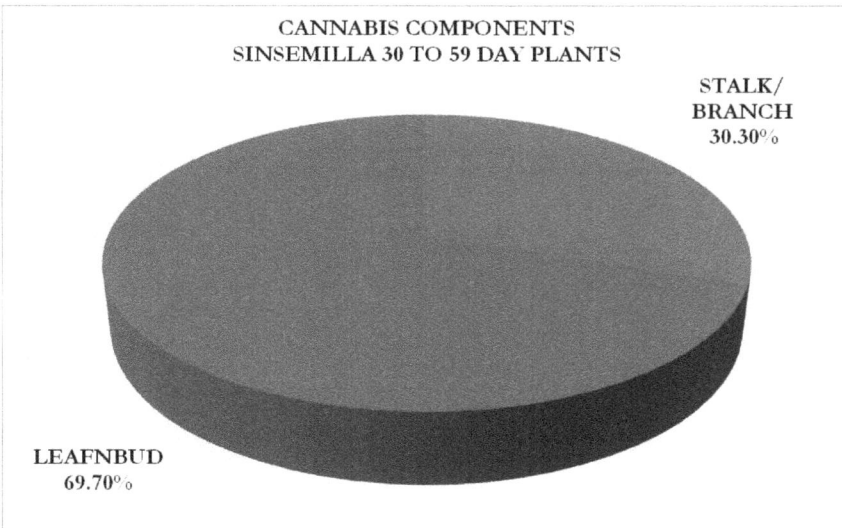

Figure 45. Day 30 to 59, sinsemilla components, from the data.

Notice that their ratios of Stalk/Branch and Leafnbud® are reasonably close to one another. We can also see that at this stage the plant is mostly green, leafy bits making up roughly two-thirds of the weight of the plant. This dovetails neatly with what can be observed in very young plants.

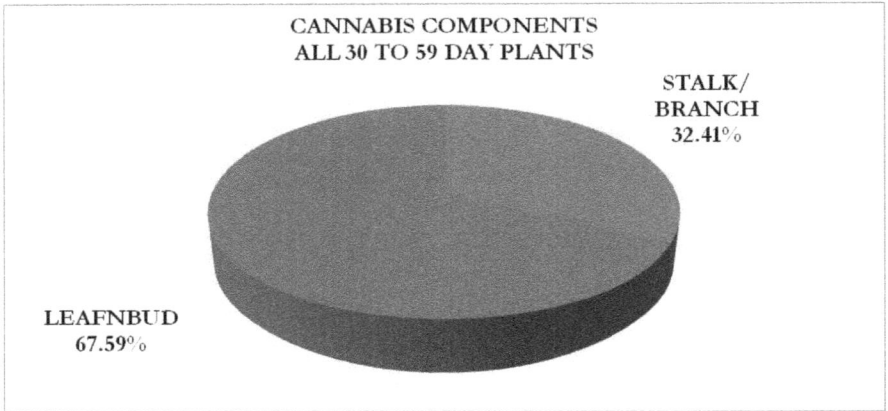

Figure 46. All 30 to 59 day old plant components.

A month later, the percentages have changed:

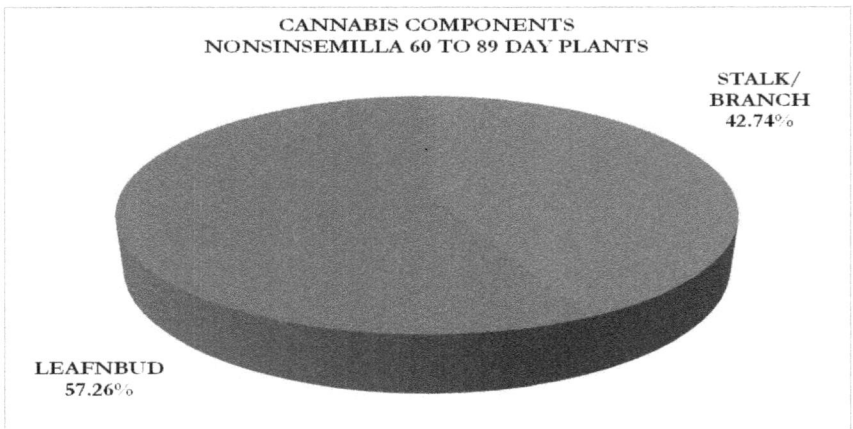

Figure 47. Day 60 to 89 nonsinsemilla components.

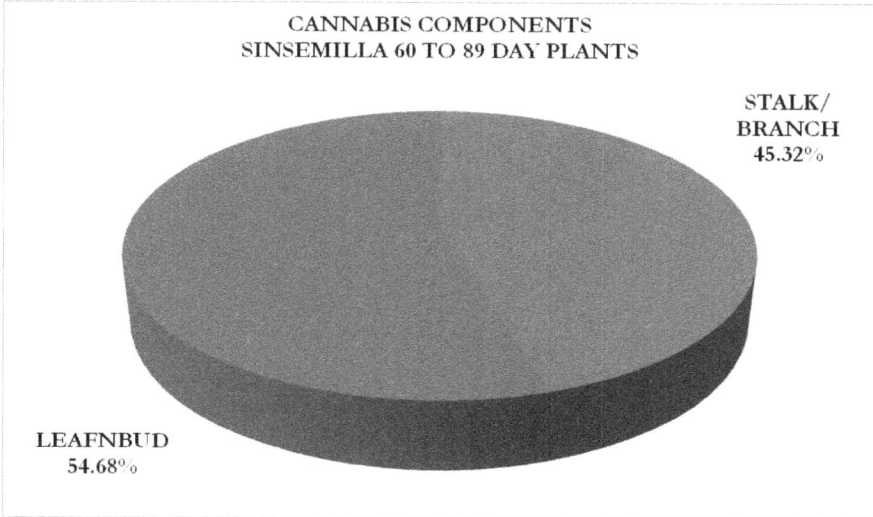

Figure 48. Day 60 to 89 sinsemilla components.

Taken together the plants of this age group show the following:

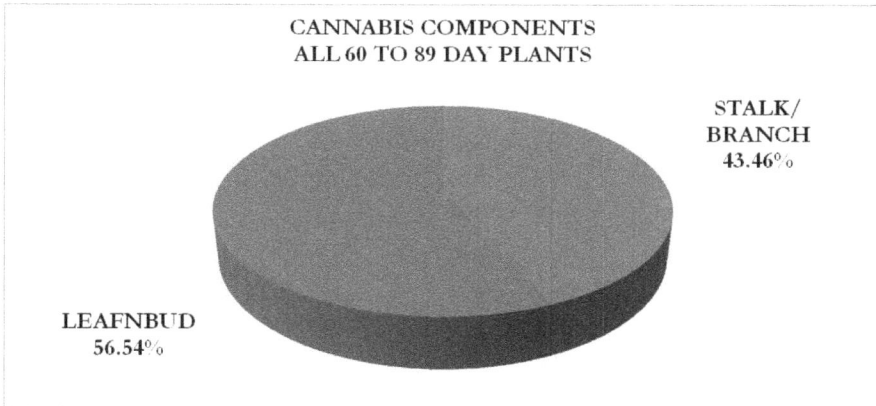

Figure 49. All 60 to 89 day old plant components.

These ratios are roughly what the mature plants will show. But a month later, the difference is dramatic:

113

CANNABIS COMPONENTS
NONSINSEMILLA 90 TO 119 DAY PLANTS

STALK/
BRANCH
40.03%

LEAFNBUD
59.97%

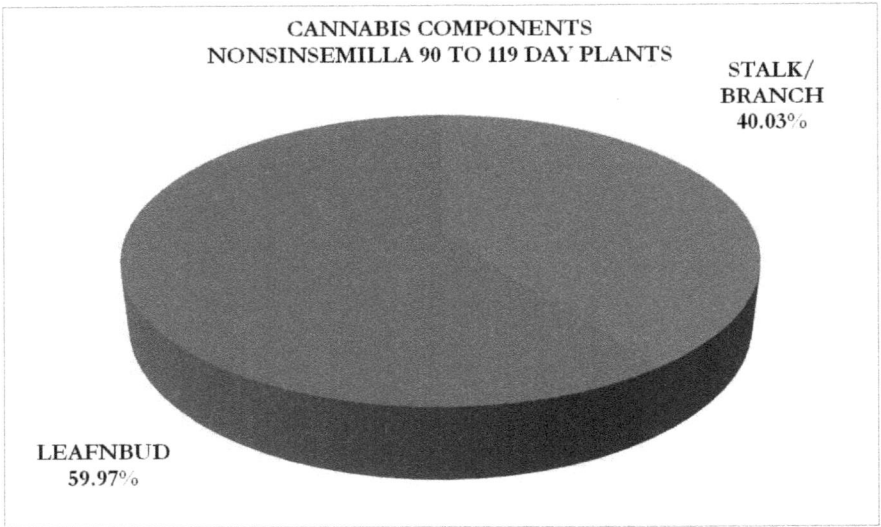

Figure 50. Day 90 to 119 nonsinsemilla components.

Compare these ratios to the sinsemilla plants of the same age:

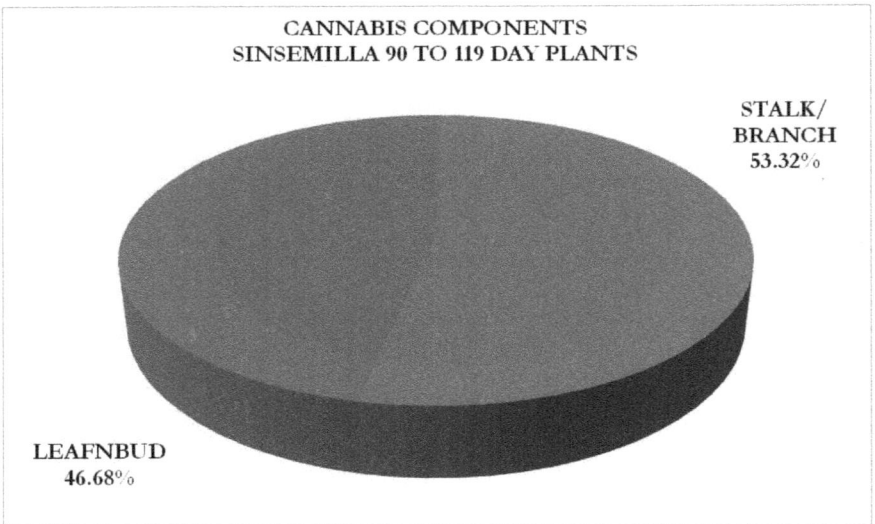

CANNABIS COMPONENTS
SINSEMILLA 90 TO 119 DAY PLANTS

STALK/
BRANCH
53.32%

LEAFNBUD
46.68%

Figure 51. Day 90 to 119 sinsemilla components.

So at least some of the so-called sinsemilla plants were producing seed at this stage and that seed was falling through the screen in the leaf shredder. Together, all the plants of this age group show:

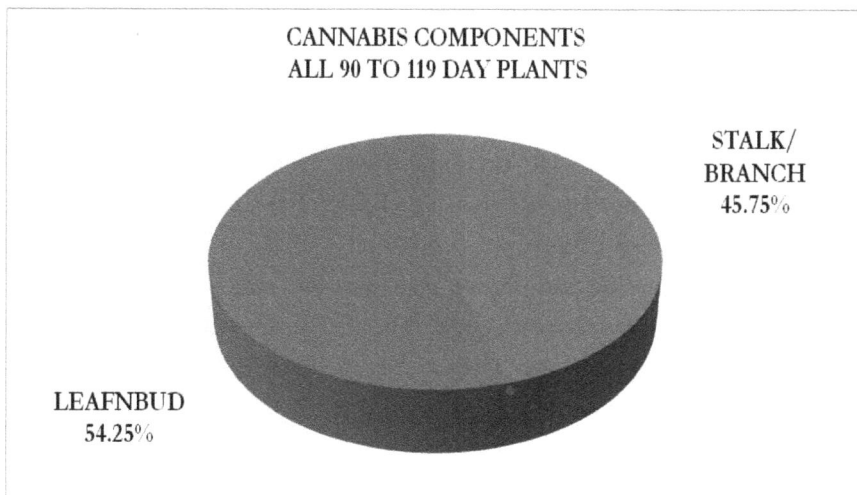

Figure 52. All 90 to 119 day old plant components.

F.   Discussion

Just as there was no separation of flowers from leaf because the plants were fed through a leaf-shredder, so there was no sinsemilla. [Is it possible to find seedless plants in a field of 1000 plants, 500 of which are male, without pulling the males? I have no data on this and neither does the DEA. Would you expect it?] The bottom pie chart of Figure 2 supposes there was but the data says not. The seed data for some of the seeded plants (there was no other kind) was erased, instantly creating new sinsemilla. This data was then added back to the data for stalk and branch in Attachment 1. This data shows that the percentage of stalk and branch in the so-called sinsemilla plants is some twenty percent higher than their non-sinsemilla cousins. Curiously, this percentage is then added to the Leafnbud® percentage in the bottom pie chart of Figure 2, evenly distributed, more or less, between nonexistent separate percentages for leaf and bud. The definition of mature in Figure 2 was then altered to try to hide this evidence in a larger mass of data.

Lewis's mom never taught him the poem with the line, "When first we practice to deceive." One silly lie leads to another. Sorry Lewis, you're not entitled to your own facts, good buddy. You got to give him credit though. He certainly went to a lot of trouble, even dancing the Mississippi shuffle to try to hide what he had done. Lewis can lie but he sure can't figure.

I guess what he did figure was that no one would bother to check his results. I guess he figured that everyone would just take the numbers in his pie charts on faith. And he's been right about that. Until now.

Figure 53. Early summer.
Previous page: Measuring, weeding
a field of cannabis.
Above: Irrigating.

118

5
The Magic Flout

Papageno: *I feed and train my chirping pets,*
I lay down traps and cast out nets,
I speak in fluent 'Pigeonese'
And charm the birds right off the trees.
-- *The Magic Flute* (2006)[1]

A.   Dr. Sly's Figure 3
B.   Figure 3 for All Plants
C.   All Plants w/o Anomalies
D.   Mature Plants Only
E.   Mature Plants w/o Anomalies
F.   Discussion

---

[1] Branagh, Kenneth, dir. Produced by Pierre-Olivier Bardet and Simon Moseley, distributed by Revolver Entertainment, Les Films du Losange, from imdb.com.

Figure 3 is also wrong but not because Lewis messed with it directly. He didn't know how. It is wrong because the data given in Attachment 1 does not yield the formula stated. This is because Dr. Sly calculated the formula from a previous set of plants. That data set was then altered by Lewis. He wanted only large plants so he cut out the data from many of the smaller plants. The real formula can be calculated from the data.

A.   Dr. Sly's Figure 3

The introduction to Figure 3 on page 6 reads: "Figure 3 depicts the linear relationship between plant fresh weight and yield dry weight." I cannot read well, either in the Konrad or Linda Smith version, the exact numbers for the R-squared or the N. I am just assuming they are nines and not eights or threes. The Linda Smith Figure 4 has N = 98.

Why is N in Figure 3 equal to 98? N is generally taken to be the number of plants used to construct the formula. One can only assume there were only 98 plants listed originally in Attachment 1. We know immediately the formula in Figure 3 cannot be drawn from Attachment 1 because N in Figure 3 does not equal to 102, the number of plants from which we have data recorded in Attachment 1.

Sometime after Dr. Sly calculated his formula the number of plants in Attachment 1 increased by four. Further, there is the statement on page six: "The predictive models developed are valid for *any sativa* variety plants *regardless of plant age or planting density* (italics added)." The words any and regardless suggest all of the plants were included for the graph in Figure 3. The word sativa is curiously uninstructive; it is not clear which varieties the author(s) wish to characterize as indica, so again we can only assume all plants are meant.

Here is what Dr. Sly drew, as near as I can determine:

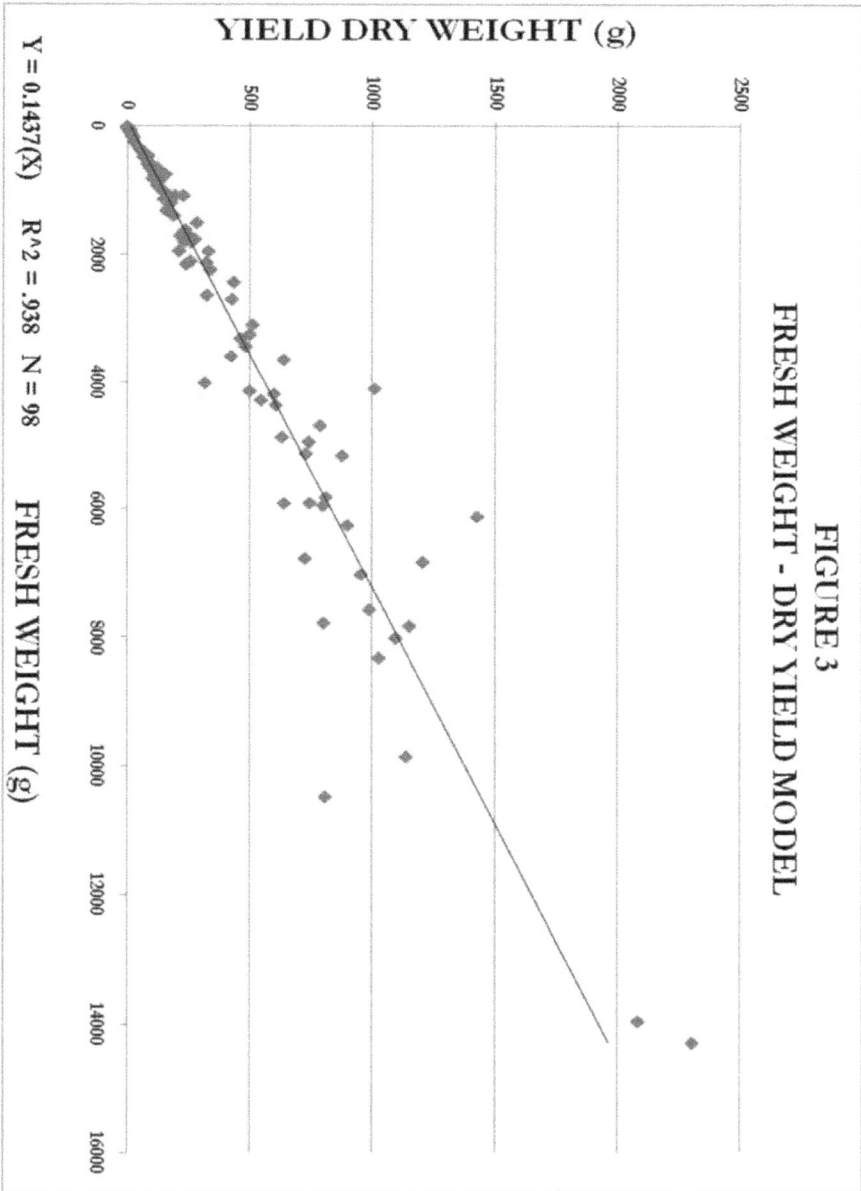

Figure 54.
Dr. Sly's Figure 3 from Cannabis Fields.

It could be argued that some subset of the 102 plants is meant but it is impossible to know which one. On page two, we read: "A very limited number of observations were made on the other major variety, 'indica.'" The names attached to the plots (Mexican, Colombian, Hybrid, and Jamaican) don't necessarily indicate which of the varieties are indica and which sativa. Also, as noted, "regardless of plant age or planting density" suggests the formula in Figure 3 was developed using all the plants. At any rate, we are left with the notion that $N = 98$, that there were ninety-eight original plants in the original sample, not 102 as there are today. I don't know which 98 plants were meant or even whether they exist in Attachment 1 anymore.

B.   Figure 3 for All Plants

We can calculate the ratio of grams of dried Leafnbud® to grams of freshly harvested plant using all 102 plants in Attachment 1. It's important to remember that these formulas will have less and less relevance to the quantity of dried flowers obtainable as the plants become younger and younger.

The sum of the fresh plant weights for all 102 plants is 273,401.9 grams. The sum of the dry Leafnbud® for all 102 plants is 38,950.3 grams. The ratio of dry Leafnbud® to fresh wet plant for all 102 plants is 0.1424653. In other words, assuming a strict linear relationship between the two, taking approximately 14.25 percent of the total weight of the freshly harvested plants would give you an estimate of the weight of the dried Leafnbud®, that highly sought after mix of ground up leaf and whatever flowers might have existed on the wet plant after the plant was fed through a leaf shredder and the seed and wood were removed.

We can graph Figure 3 from the data in Attachment 1. First, the x-y graphs of all the plants, anomalies included:

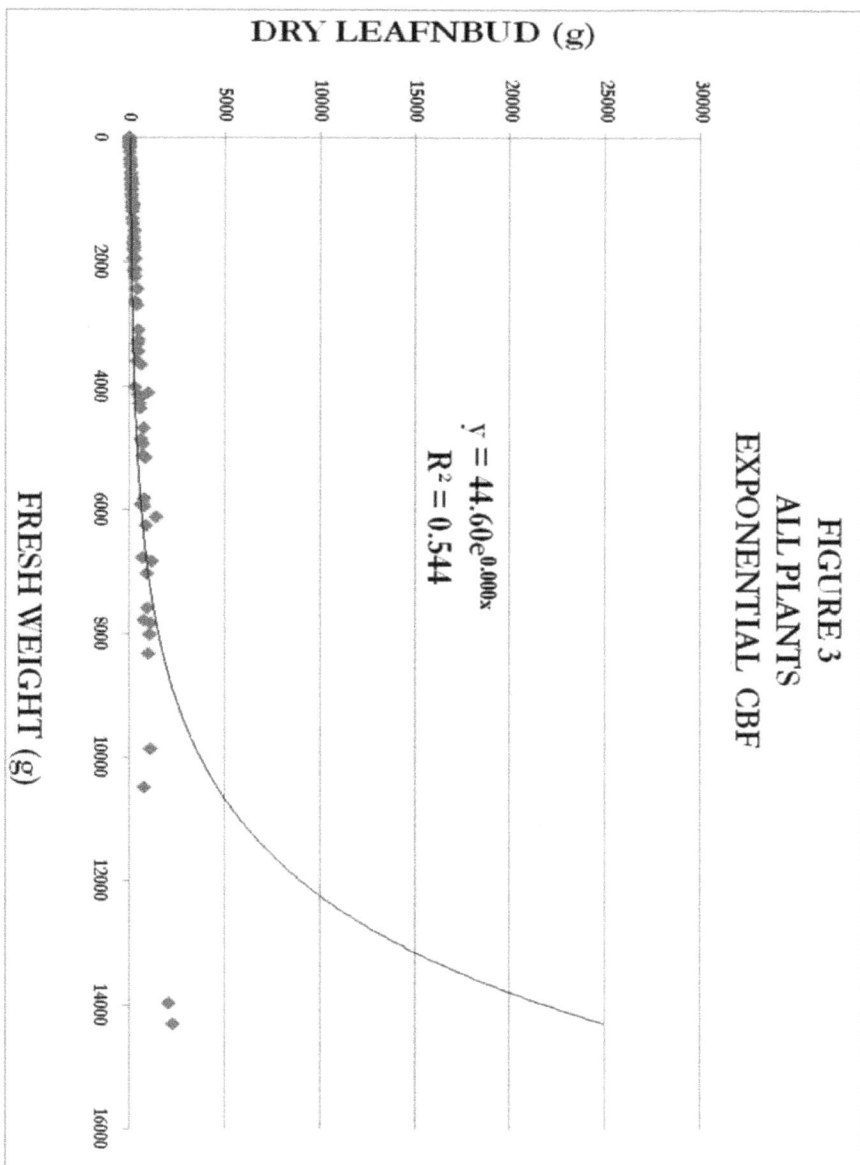

Figure 55.
All Plants, Exponential CBF.

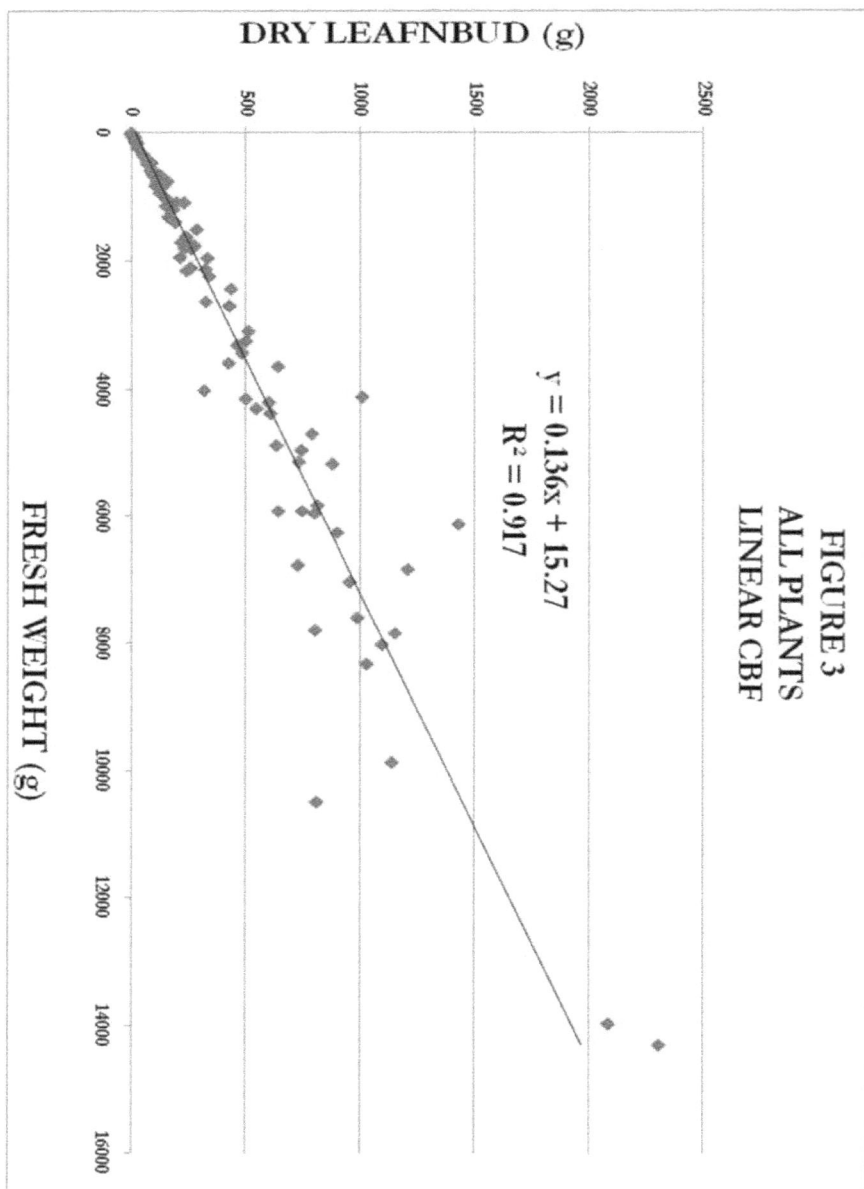

FIGURE 3
ALL PLANTS
LINEAR CBF

$y = 0.136x + 15.27$
$R^2 = 0.917$

Figure 56.
All Plants, Linear CBF.

124

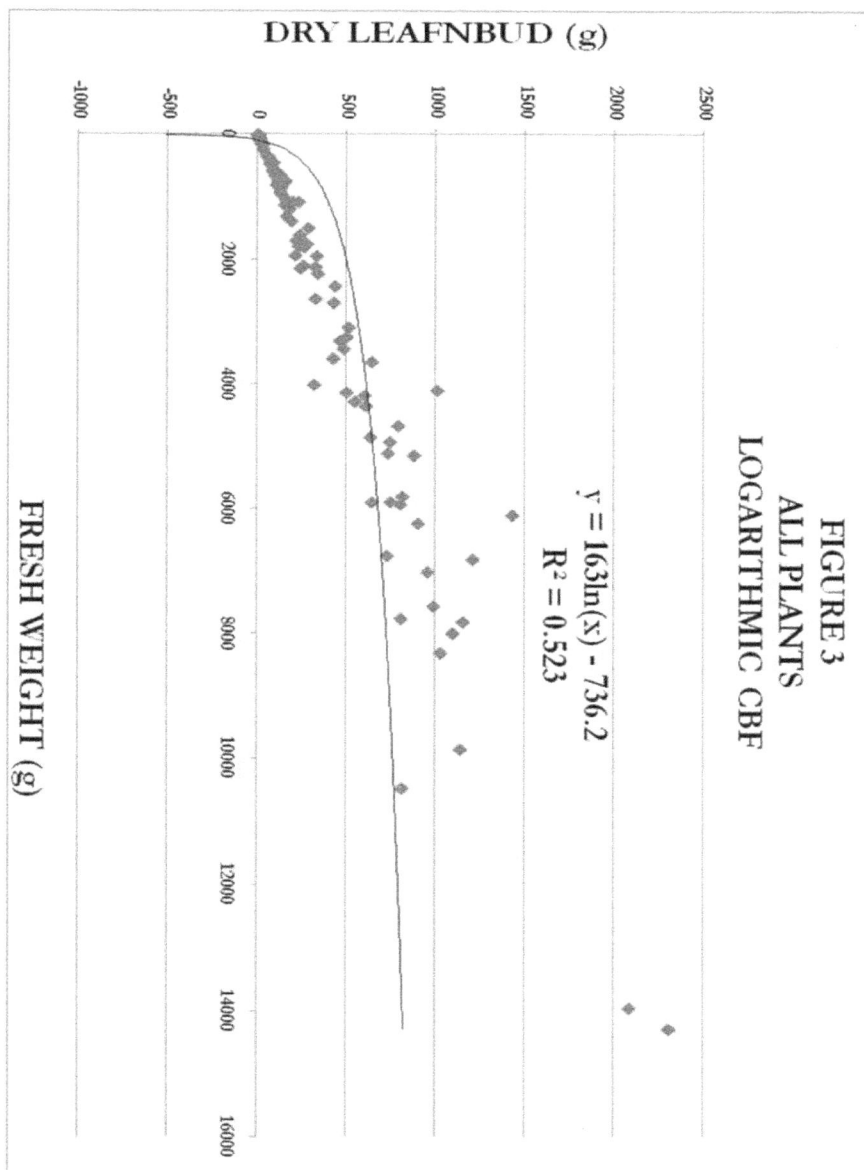

Figure 57.
All Plants, Logarithmic CBF.

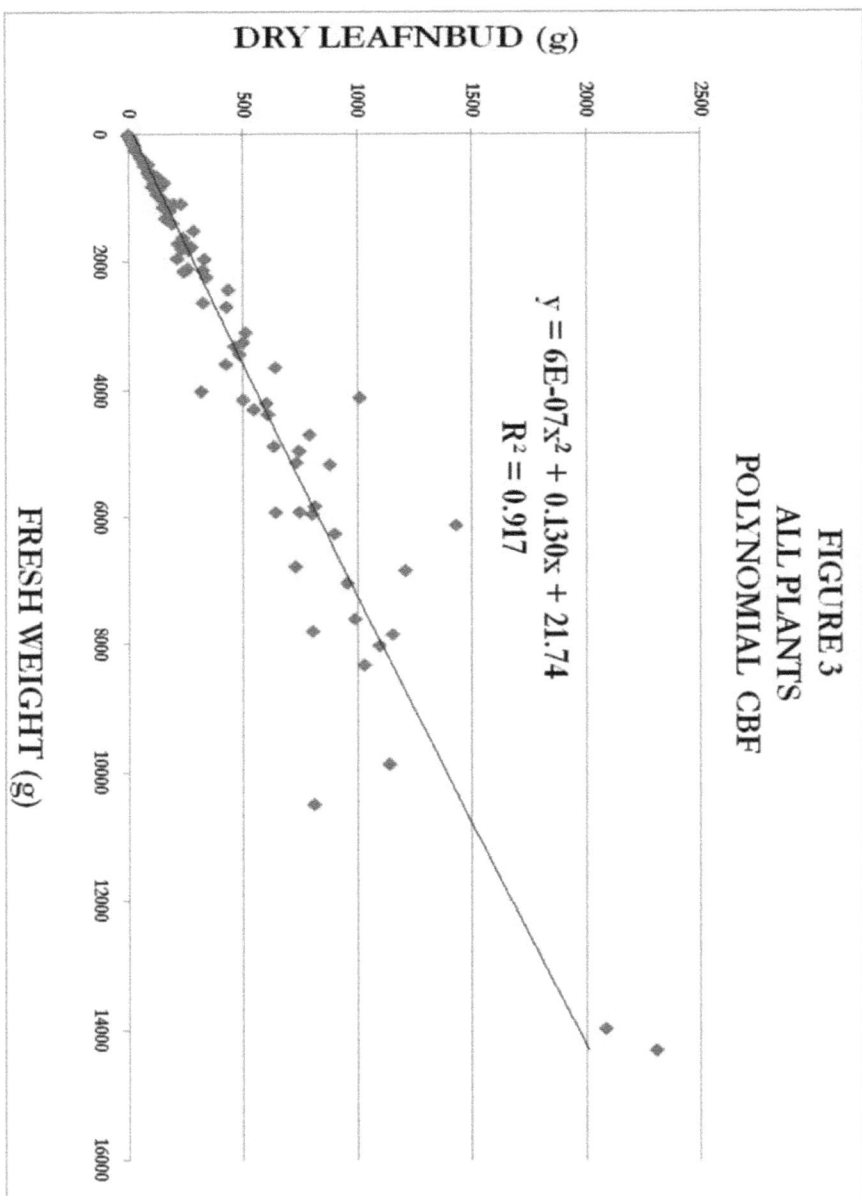

FIGURE 3
ALL PLANTS
POLYNOMIAL CBF

$$y = 6E\text{-}07x^2 + 0.130x + 21.74$$
$$R^2 = 0.917$$

DRY LEAFNBUD (g)

FRESH WEIGHT (g)

Figure 58.
All Plants, Polynomial CBF.

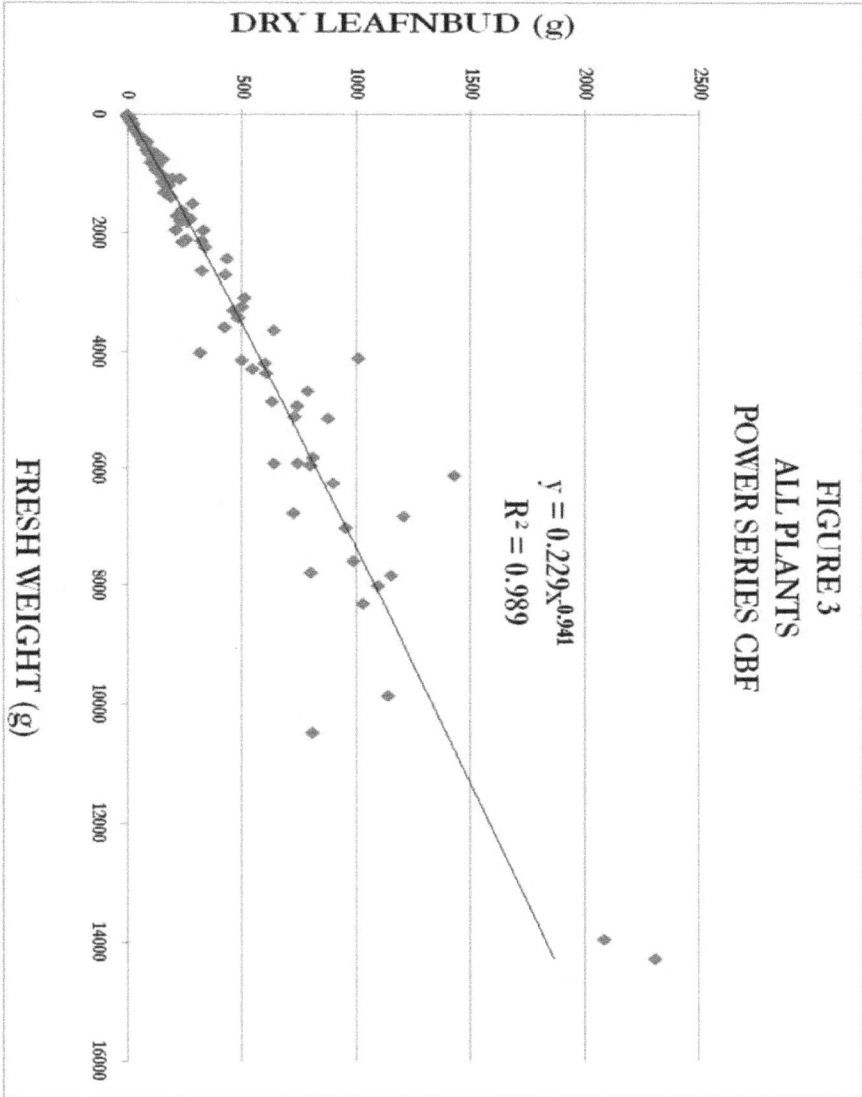

Figure 59. All Plants, Power Series CBF.

MS Excel returns nothing useful for the exponential CBF. The polynomial is near linear. The power series has an R-squared of 0.989.

C. All Plants w/o Anomalies

If we are going to calculate this ratio of dried Leafnbud® to fresh whole plant using all the plants regardless of age, we might at least remove the two anomalies from the data set:

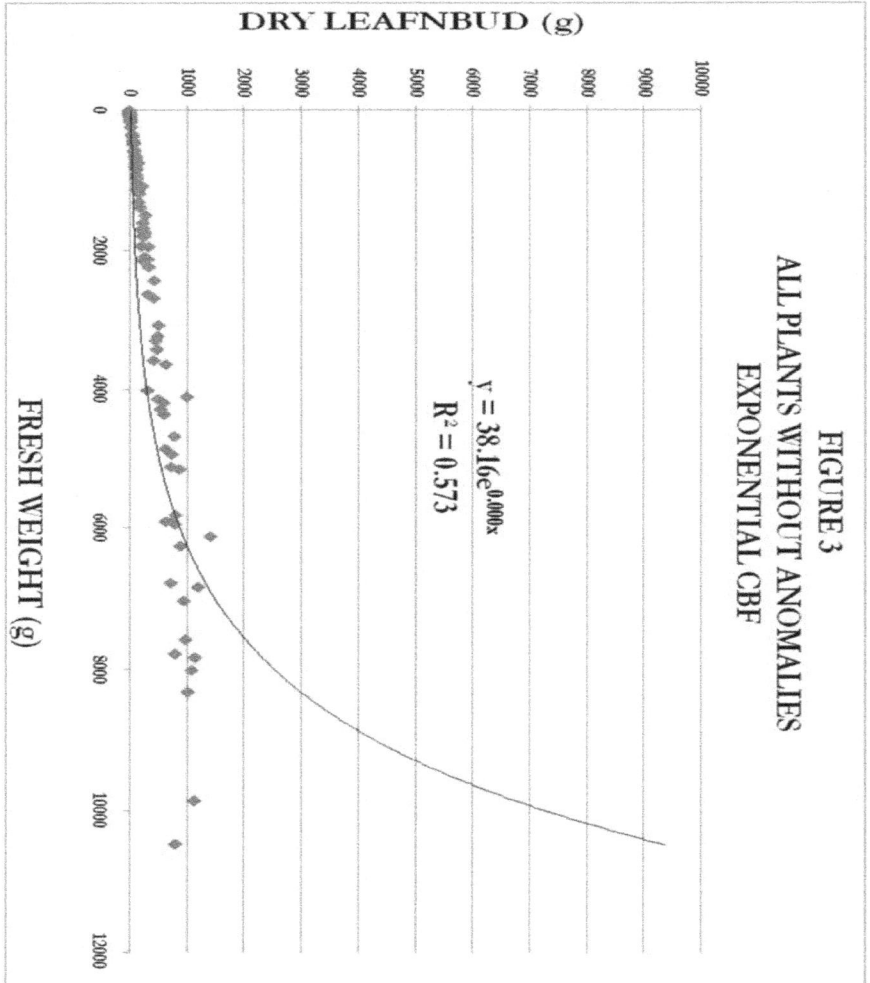

Figure 60.
All Plants w/o Anomalies, Exponential CBF.

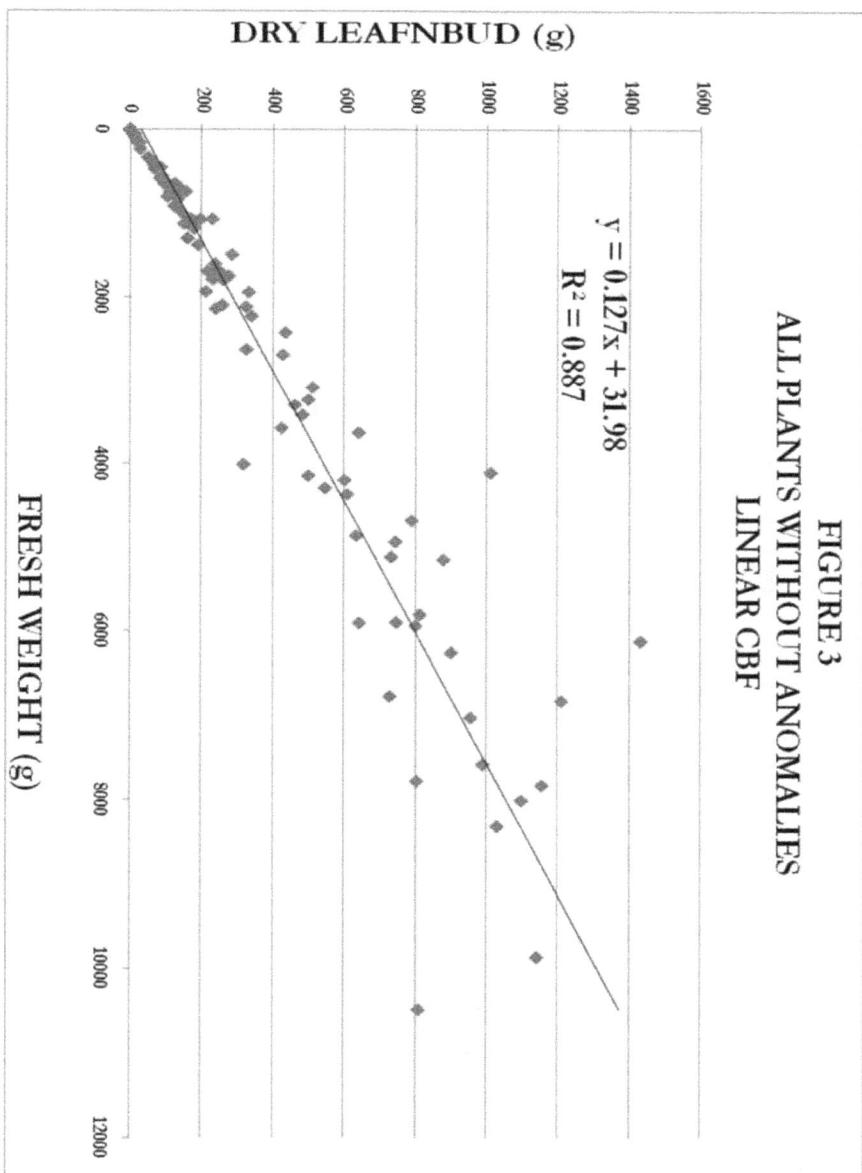

Figure 61.
All Plants w/o Anomalies, Linear CBF.

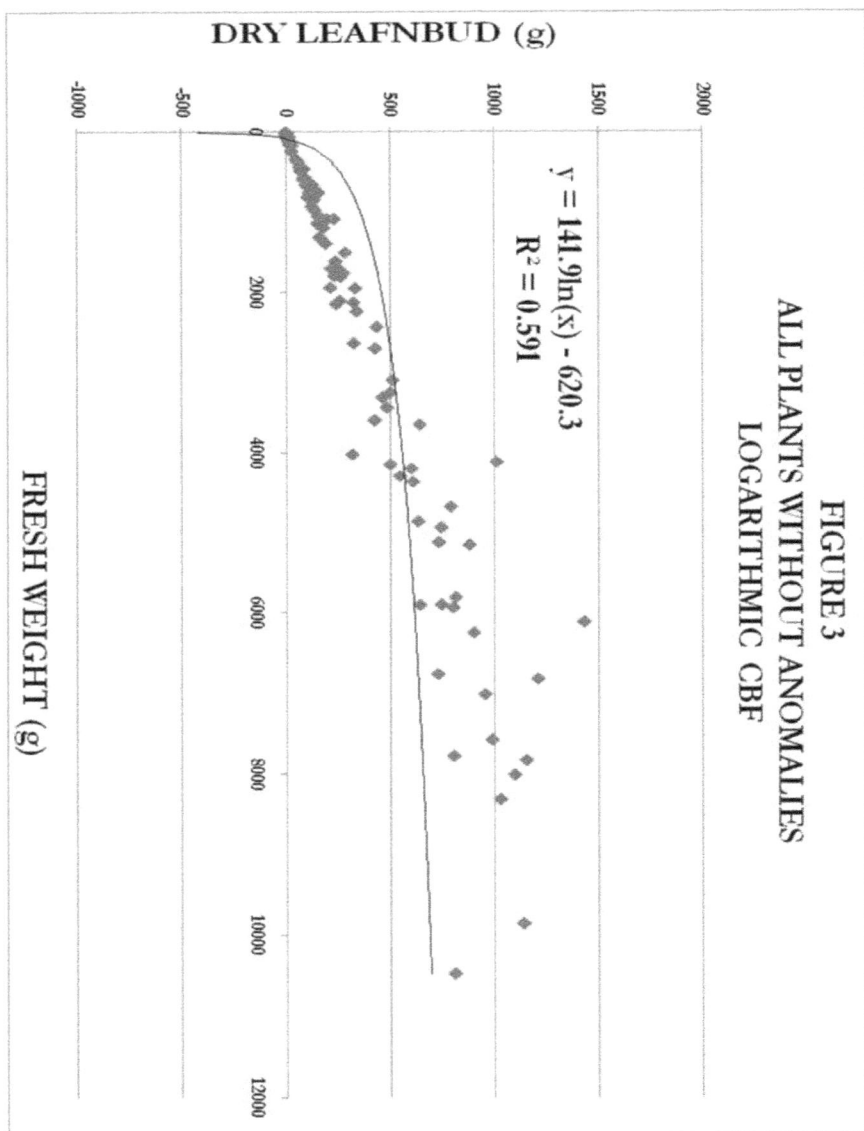

Figure 62.
All Plants w/o Anomalies, Logarithmic CBF.

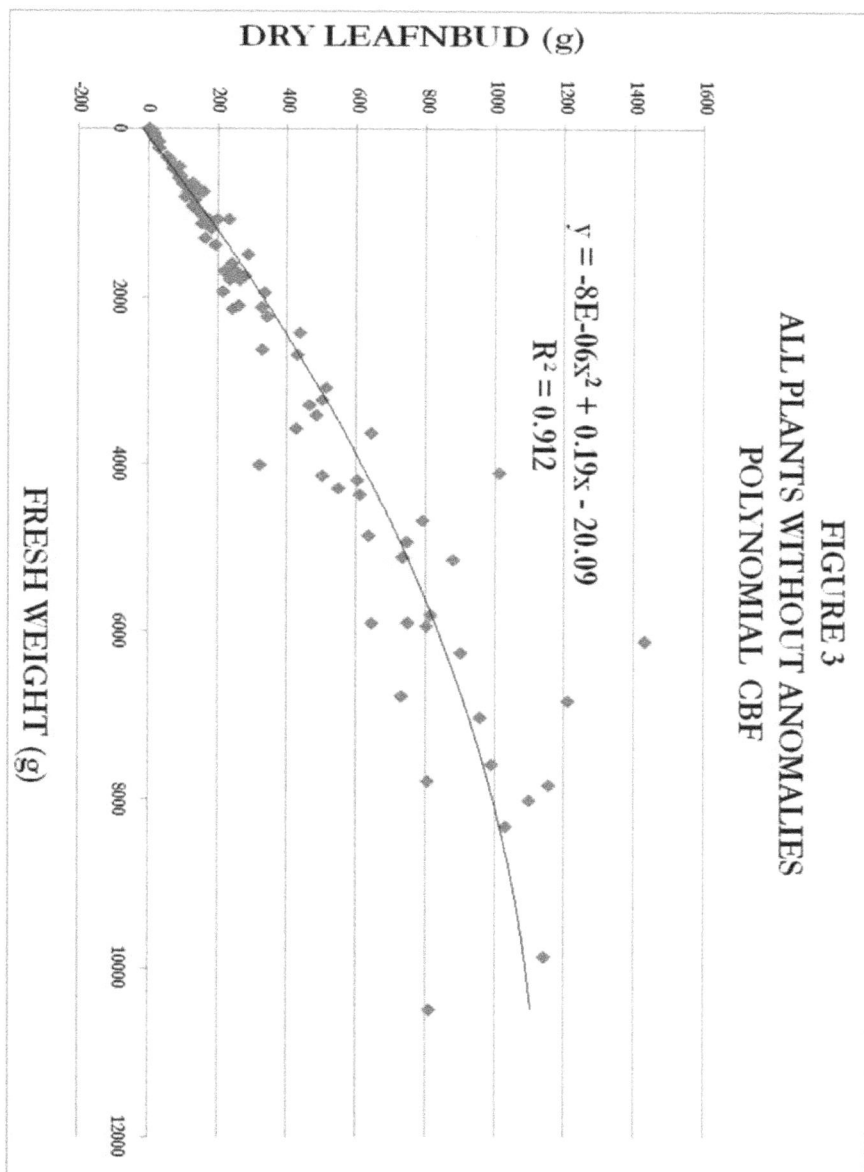

Figure 63.
All Plants w/o Anomalies, Polynomial CBF.

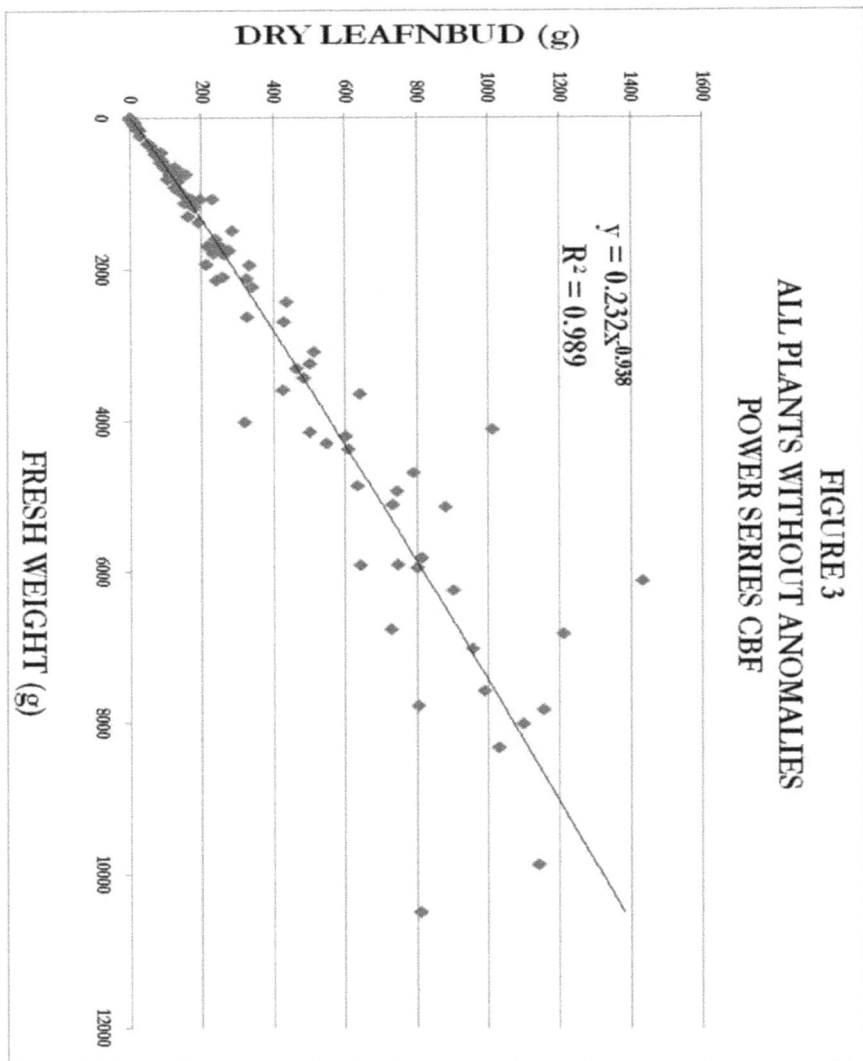

Figure 64.   All Plants w/o Anomalies, Power Series CBF.

Again, the exponential CBF is not useful.   The polynomial result is practically linear.   The power series curve fits best.

Without the two anomalies present, the fresh weight of the remaining 100 plants weighs altogether 245,154.3 grams and the dried Leafnbud® 34,555.0 grams. The ratio of the latter to the former is 0.140952. On average, then, assuming a linear distribution, multiplying the gross fresh weight of the freshly harvested plants times 14.10 percent would give a rough estimate of the dried Leafnbud® always assuming that the data from the younger plants has any relevance to this estimate whatsoever. Eventually this number needs to go before a judge who is trying to determine the quantity of dried flowers available on average from any given plant. How relevant is data from plants that, because of their age, clearly have no flowers?

D.   Mature Plants Only

Most prosecutions have evidence introduced of the gross weight of the freshly seized plants. Neither the police nor the DEA bother to record the canopy or height information. The only number introduced at trial is the total weight of the offending shrubbery. The legal question then becomes, how many grams of dry flowers are likely for that quantity of wet plant.

But most prosecutions also begin with plants that have been seized in the Fall. This is because they are easier to find than when those same plants were only a foot or so tall in the Spring. And the later the plants are cut, the more likely they are to have at least some flowers. None but the most ideologically driven would suppose it possible to extrapolate six months into the future from a seizure in the Spring of a given number of unsexed *keikis*.

How reasonable is it to ask, then, that this ratio of wet plant to dry flower should be based on *all* the plants in the data base? It is clear that plants with less than ninety grow days are very unlikely to have many flowers at all. Outdoor plants with less than sixty days are almost certain to have exactly zero flowers. We are assuming here outdoor plants grown from non-GMO, non-genetically bred seed.

So why wouldn't we want N to be 38, the number of mature plants (ones with 120 or more grow days)? Their x-y graphs are:

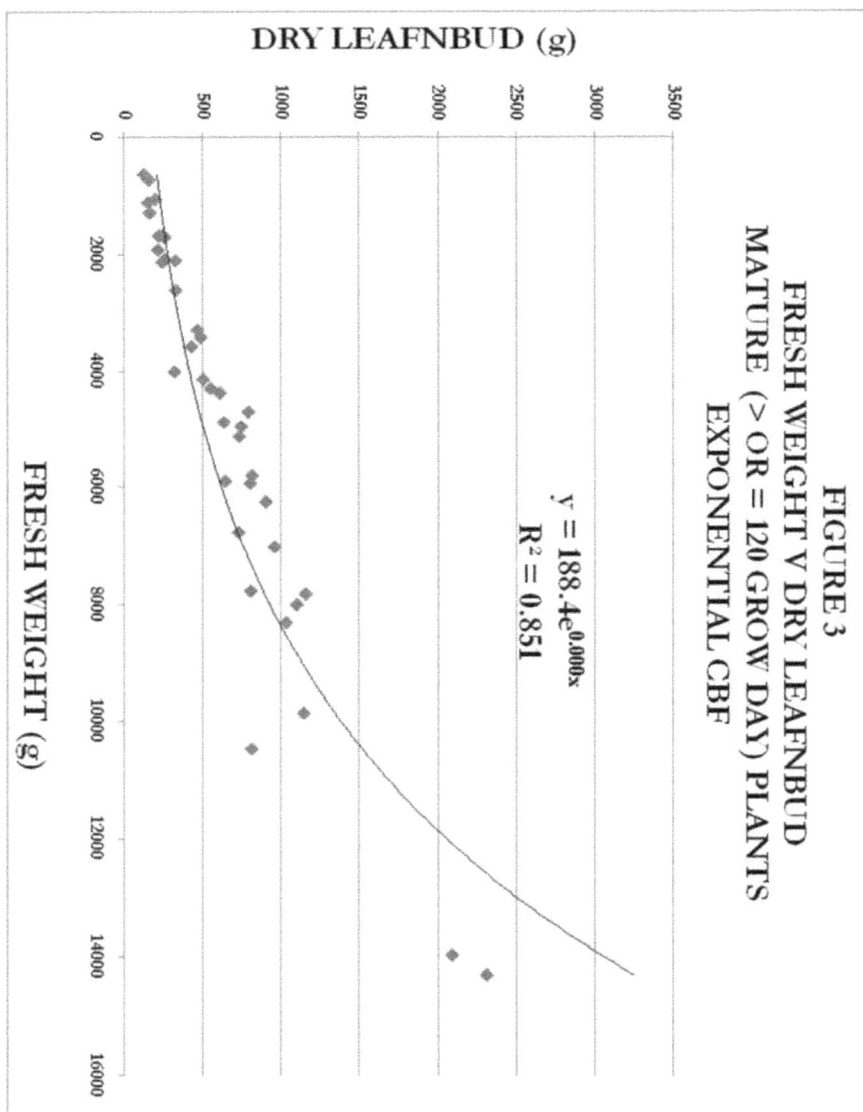

Figure 65.
Mature Plants Only, Exponential CBF.

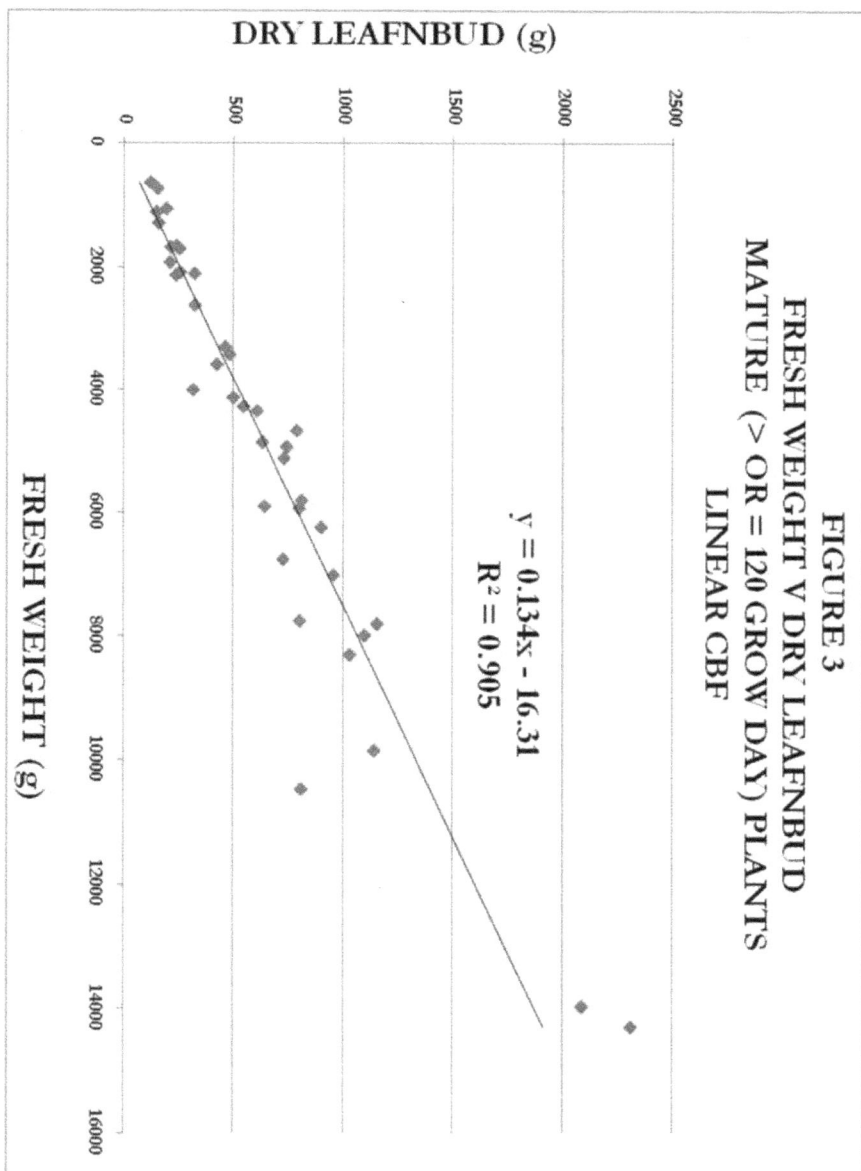

FIGURE 3
FRESH WEIGHT V DRY LEAFNBUD
MATURE (> OR = 120 GROW DAY) PLANTS
LINEAR CBF

$y = 0.134x - 16.31$
$R^2 = 0.905$

Figure 66.
Mature Plants Only, Linear CBF.

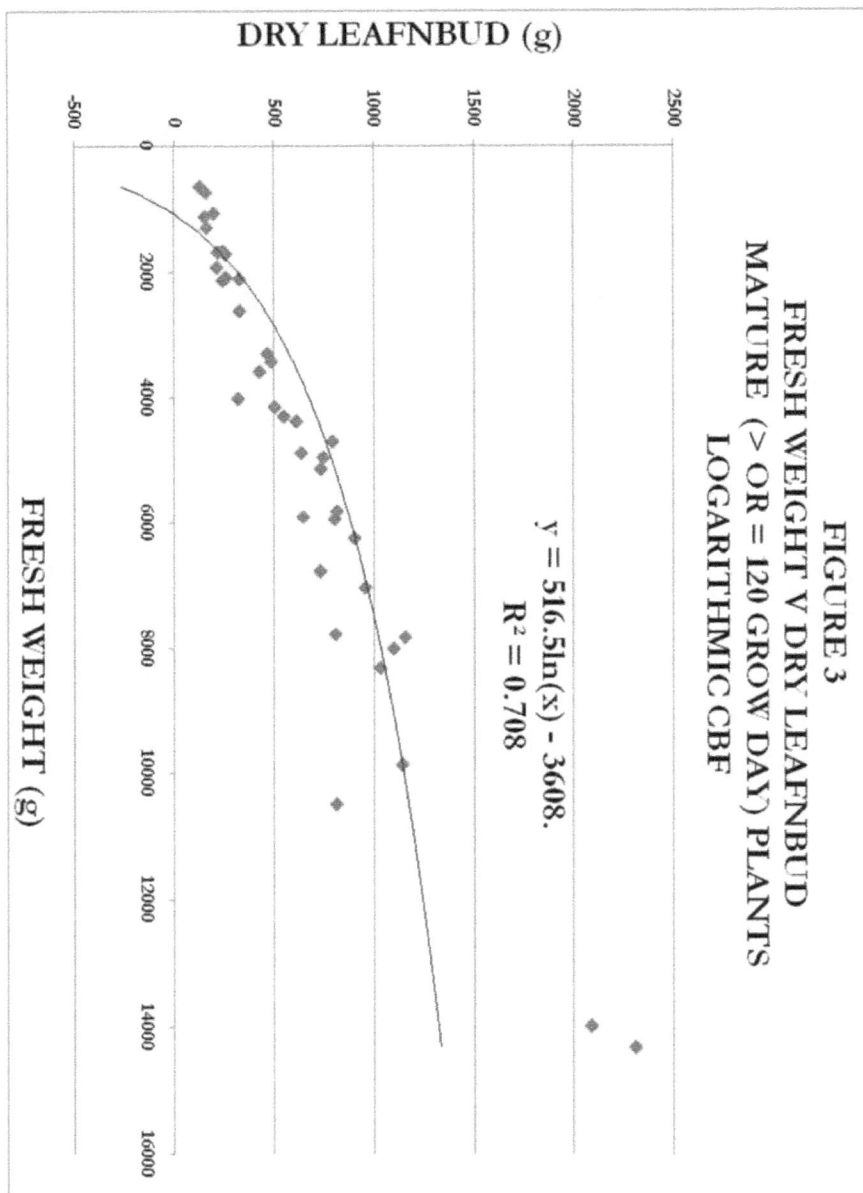

FIGURE 3
FRESH WEIGHT V DRY LEAFNBUD
MATURE (> OR = 120 GROW DAY) PLANTS
LOGARITHMIC CBF

$y = 516.5\ln(x) - 3608.$
$R^2 = 0.708$

Figure 67.
Mature Plants Only, Logarithmic CBF.

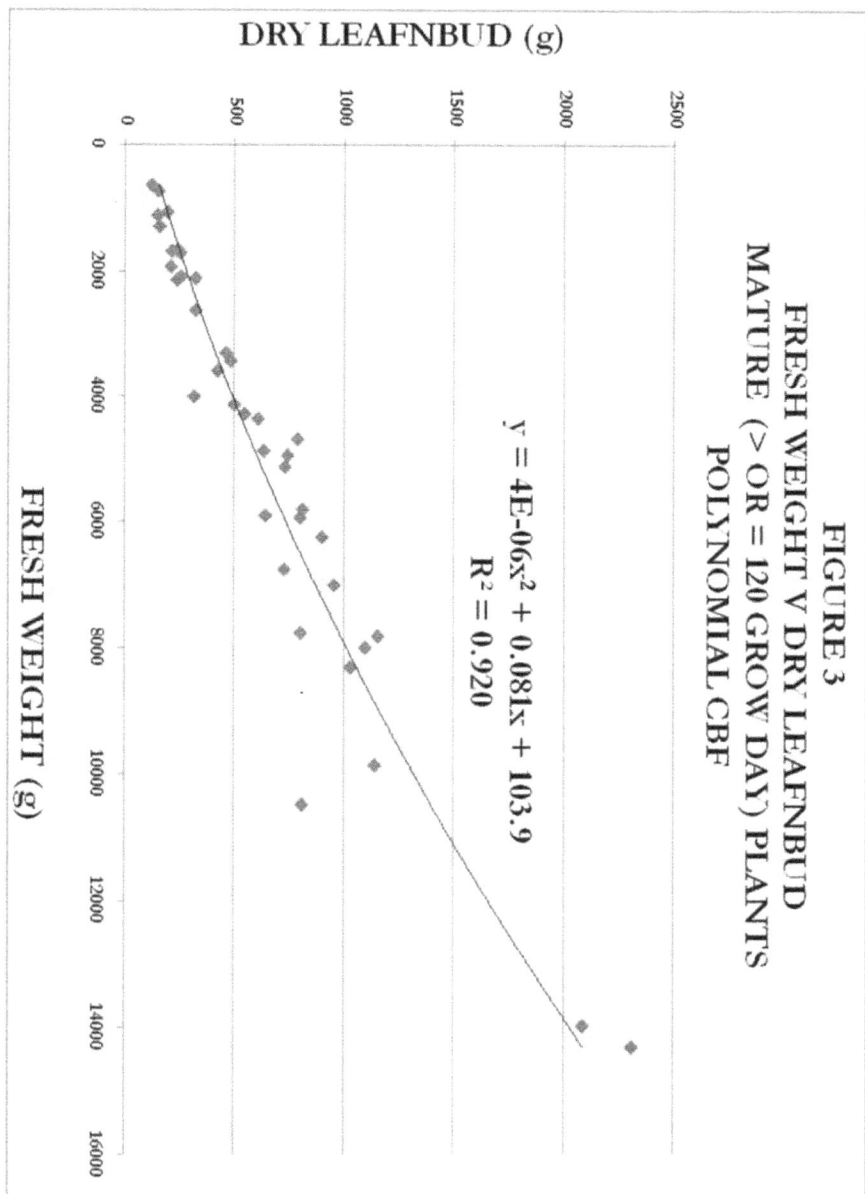

Figure 68.
Mature Plants Only, Polynomial CBF.

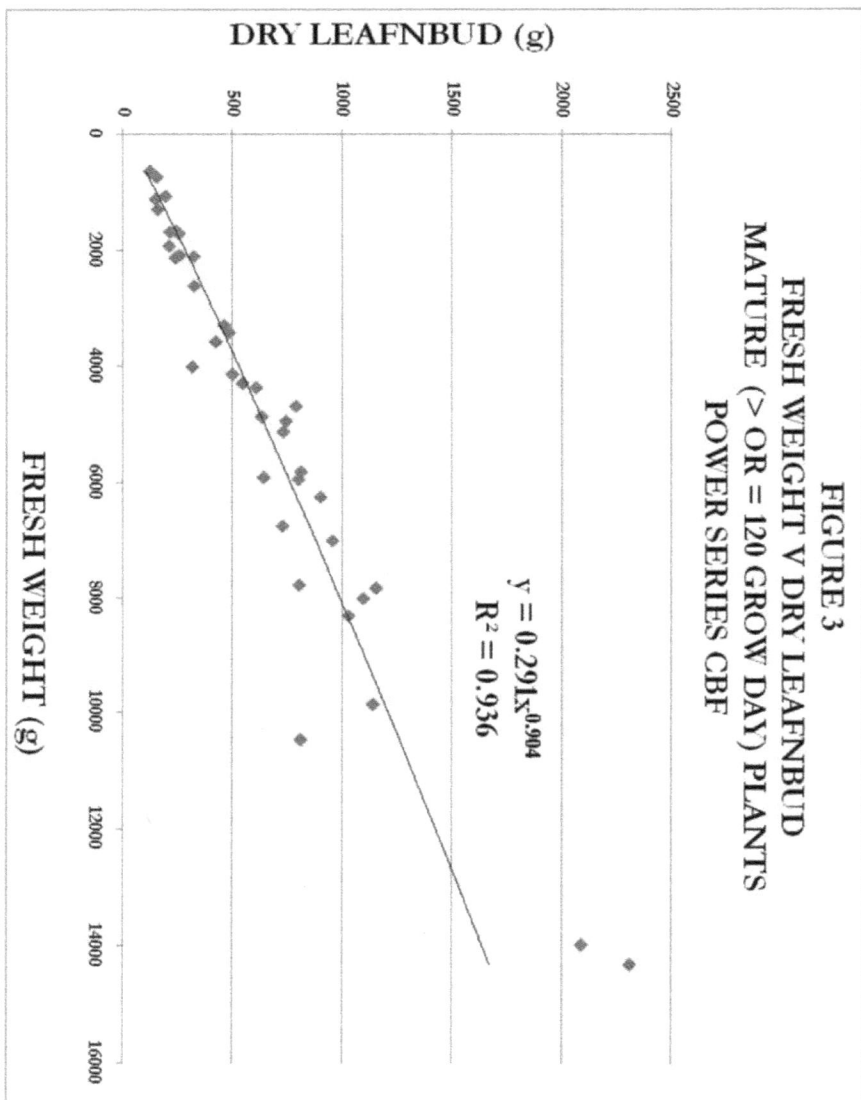

FIGURE 3
FRESH WEIGHT V DRY LEAFNBUD
MATURE (> OR = 120 GROW DAY) PLANTS
POWER SERIES CBF

$y = 0.291x^{0.904}$
$R^2 = 0.936$

Figure 69. Mature Plants Only, Power Series CBF.

The exponential CBF is scalar. The polynomial is close to linear. The power series curve fits best.

The 38 mature plants weighed wet, 185,958.9 grams. You won't get this result if you just add the numbers listed in Attachment 1. This is because three of the weights are incorrect. Remember that the data under the column heading Plant Fresh in Attachment 1 is calculated, not field. It is arrived at by summing the weights of the Stem Fresh, Yield [Leafnbud®] Fresh, and Seed Fresh data. But plant number 100.17 actually weighed 1721.9 grams, not 1721.8; plant number 102.12 actually weighed 3429.1 grams, not 3429.0; and plant number 109.11 actually weighed 7024.9 grams, not 7014.9.

The dry yield [Leafnbud®] for the 38 mature plants totaled 24,441.5 grams. Divide the dry yield [Leafnbud®] by the fresh plant and you get .1314349. Remember this is 13.14 percent by weight for dried Leafnbud®, not dried flowers. If you assume a linear relationship between Fresh Weight and Dried Leafnbud®, then the formula for finding the latter would be $Y = .1314 (X)$, where Y is the dried Leafnbud® and X is the weight of the freshly harvested plant. This is distinct from the formula $Y = .1437 (X)$ found at the bottom of Figure 3. This earlier formula was probably derived from the previous data set, the one with 98 plants. In other words, for whatever number of kilos of wet plant, take 13.14% of that number to estimate the grams of dried mashed up, mixed up melange of leaves and flowers on average for a female flowering plant with more than 120 grow days.

It makes more sense to calculate the ratio in Figure 3 using only mature plants than from plants that have only leaf and no flowers. Otherwise we might as well try to estimate the quantity of dried flowers possible for any given group of dry seeds. A particularly rabid prosecutor actually did this astronomical calculation in a particularly absurd trial that took place at the height of the drug war over possession of DEA-certified sterilized hemp seeds, some twenty-five pounds of them. The defense lawyer dryly asked that if this were really possible, why wasn't everyone making billions for an investment of only fifty dollars at a country feed store.

E.   Mature Plants w/o Anomalies

The two diamonds at the top right of the previous graphs are the anomalies. If we eliminate them we get the following x-y graphs:

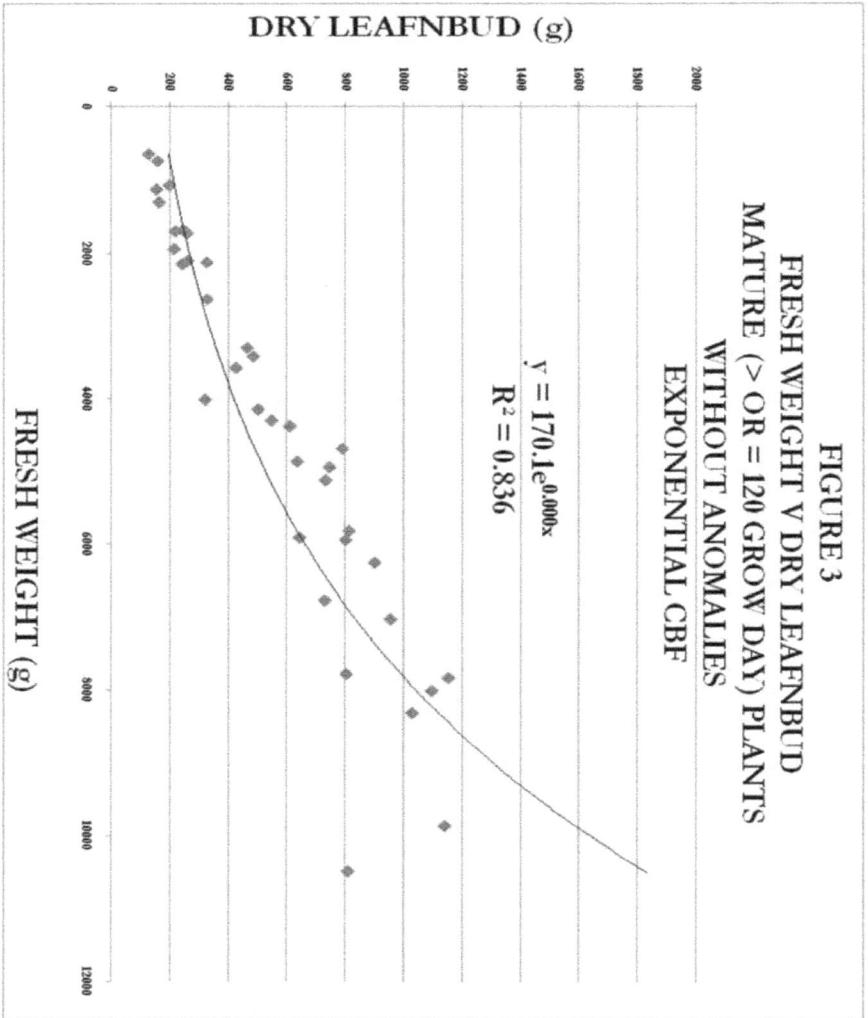

Figure 70.
Mature Plants w/o Anomalies, Exponential CBF.

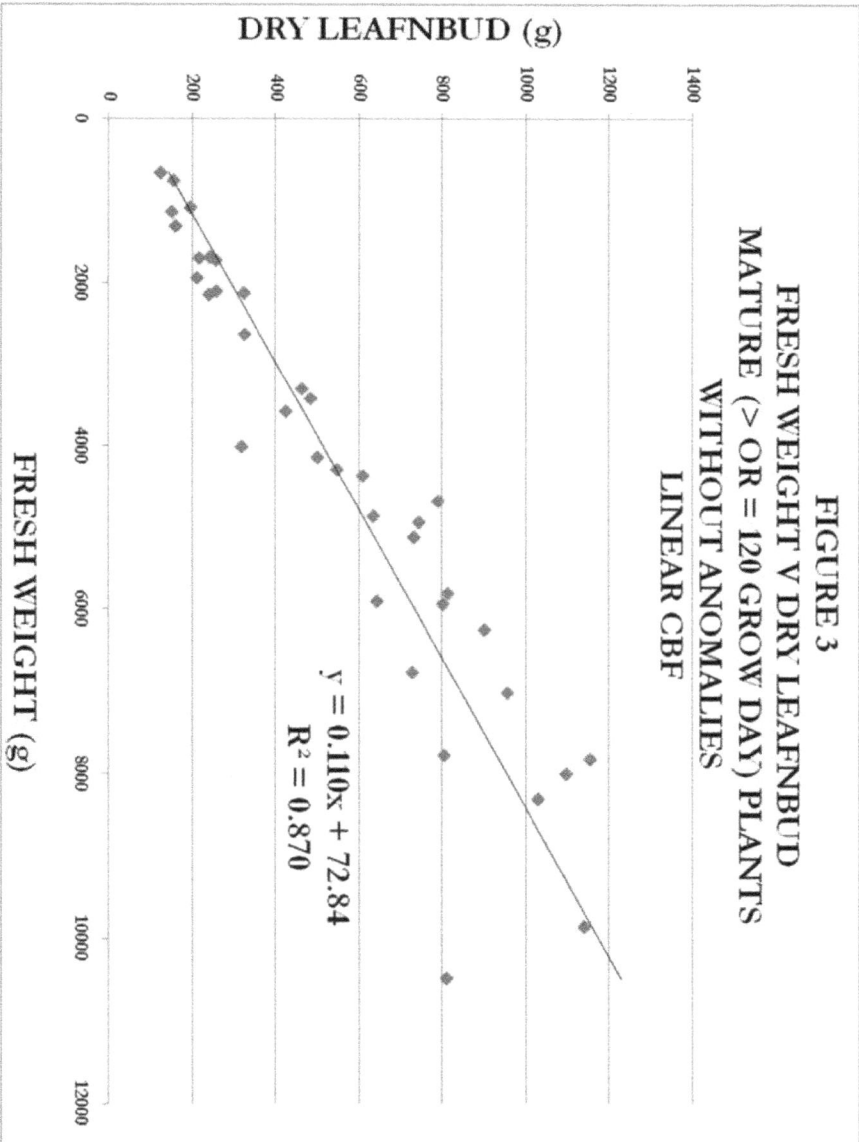

Figure 71.
Mature Plants w/o Anomalies, Linear CBF.

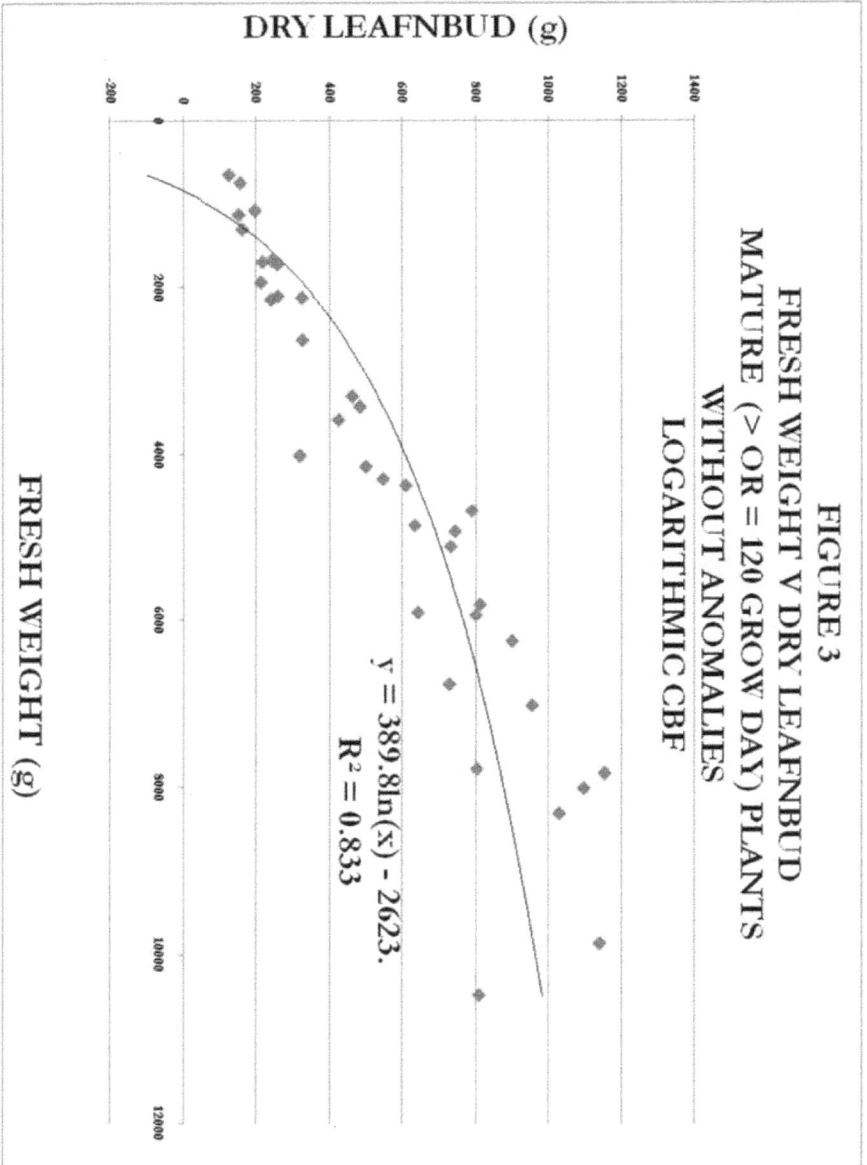

FIGURE 3
FRESH WEIGHT V DRY LEAFNBUD
MATURE (> OR = 120 GROW DAY) PLANTS
WITHOUT ANOMALIES
LOGARITHMIC CBF

$y = 389.8\ln(x) - 2623.$
$R^2 = 0.833$

DRY LEAFNBUD (g)

FRESH WEIGHT (g)

Figure 72.
Mature Plants w/o Anomalies, Logarithmic CBF.

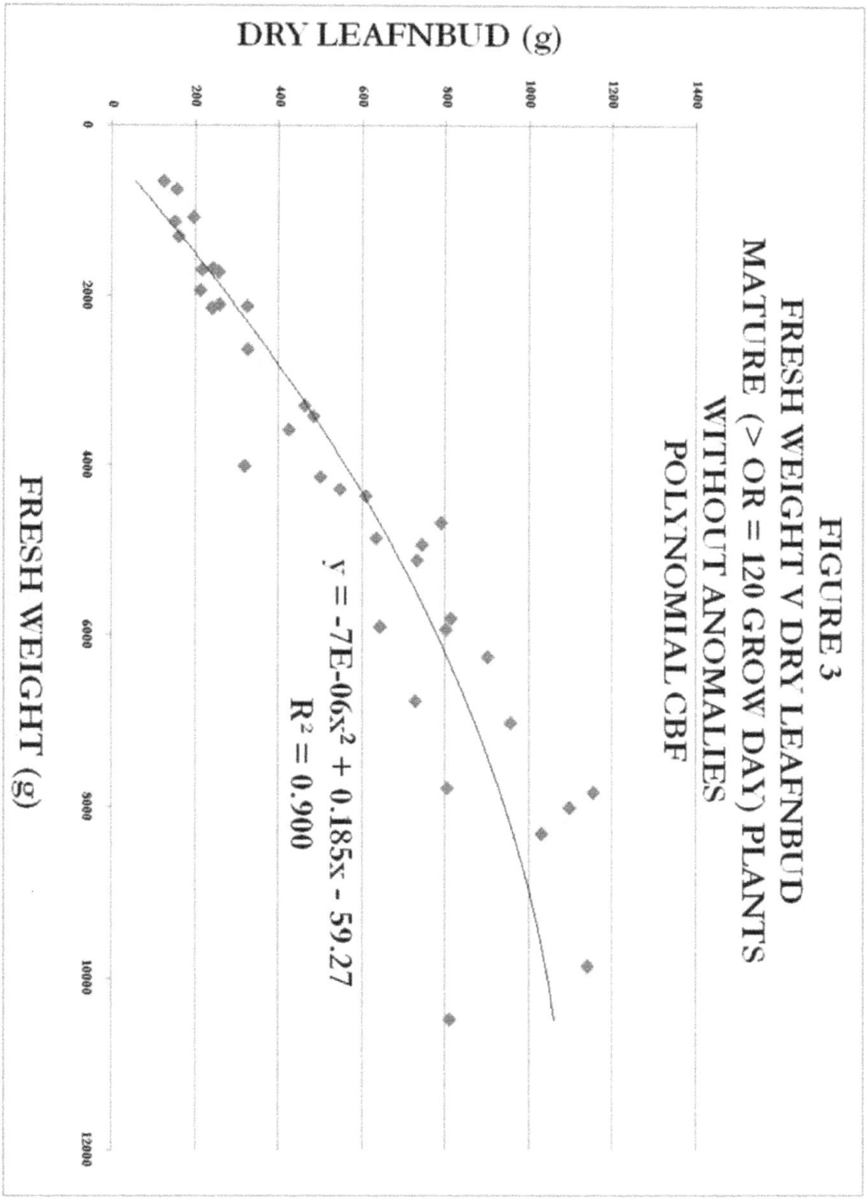

Figure 73.
Mature Plants w/o Anomalies, Polynomial CBF.

143

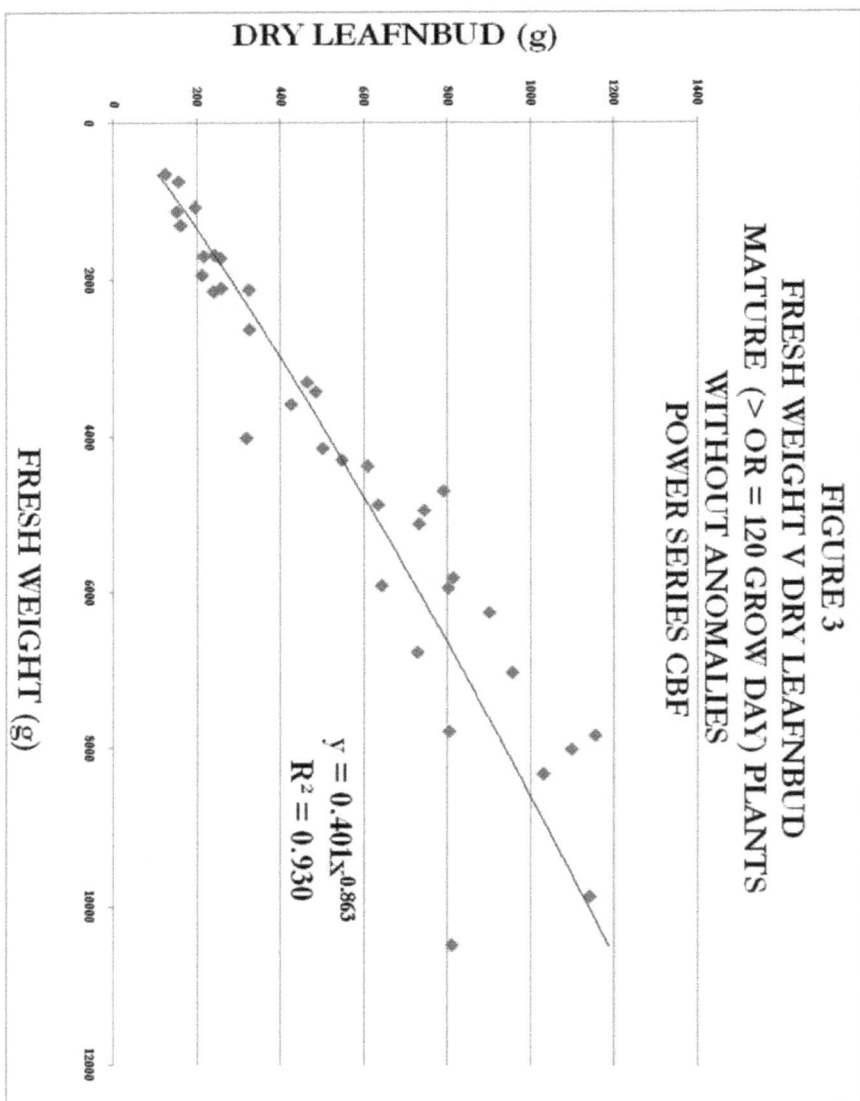

Figure 74. Mature Plants w/o Anomalies, Power Series CBF.

The exponetial is scalar, the polynomial linear and again, the power series fits best.

Without the two mature anomalies distorting the data set, the other 36 mature plants weigh fresh 157,711.3 grams and the dried Leafnbud® from those plants 20,046.2 grams for a ratio of 0.1271069. On average, multiplying the gross fresh weight of these plants by 12.71 percent would give you an estimate of the dried Leafnbud® from those plants, assuming a linear relationship between the two variables.

F.   Discussion

Figure 3 is Dr. Sly's graph of the fresh weight versus the yield [Leafnbud®]. The data in Attachment 1 does not support the conclusions he reached. But that is only because the original data has been replaced by a new set. Lewis added large plants and subtracted small ones but did not have the expertise to recalculate the formula.

Using the data in Attachment 1, we calculated the scattergraphs for all 102 plants using an exponential, linear, logarithmic, polynomial and power series curve of best fit for the fresh weight versus the dried Leafnbud®. We then removed the two obvious anomalies and plotted the same graphs again. This of course begs the question as to why we would want a ratio of dried flowers to whole plant for plants too young to have dried flowers. So we recalculated the plots for only the mature plants, the 38 with greater than or equal to 120 grow days. Then we removed the same two anomalies and did the same math for the 36 mature plants remaining in the set.

Does this tell us anything about the quantity of dried flowers there were? It does not. We graphed Leafnbud® versus fresh weight, not dried flowers versus fresh weight. There is no data in Attachment 1 for the separate weights of the dried flowers. Can we just estimate that the ratio of dried flowers to dried leaves is more or less 1?

Nothing in the data set allows us to do this. On September 1, most of the plant will be leaf, with hardly any flowers. On November 1, most of the plant will be flowers, with little leaf. Further, this ratio between leaf and flower will depend heavily on the grower. Some growers like to strip the shade leaves off at the first moment they turn color. Others leave them on. Some like to trim all the leaves off the plants in the garden, letting them fall to the dirt to become mulch. Others prefer to trim them indoors.

None of these ratios tell us anything about the percentage of dried flowers per kilo of law-flouting flora. Nor do they explain anything about sinsemilla plants. In fact, they don't give us much.

What can we use them for? They might give us an upper bound. Logically, the quantity of dried flowers mixed with leaves would probably be larger than the quantity of dried flowers alone.

What is this upper bound? It is difficult to use this information to compare to other plantations without making at least three assumptions. First, we have to assume that there weren't any other anomalies in the data set, and we know there was at least one. Second, we have to assume that the plants were chosen at random, and we know they were not. Third, we have to assume there was no obvious bias in the choice of the plants in the data set, and we know the DEA chose the largest plants they could find. Having made three completely unwarranted assumptions, we might be able to state that the ratio of dried flowers to wet plant is something quite a bit less than 12 percent on average.

Figure 75.
The plant doctor sexing.

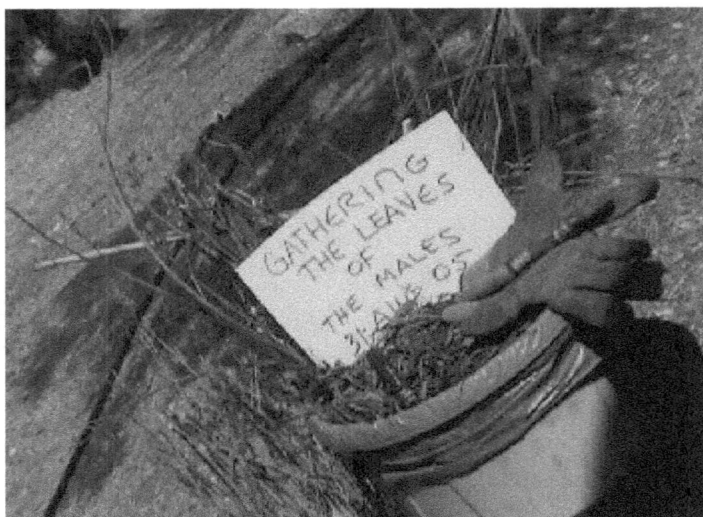

Figure 76.
Macho man; stripping the leaves.

148

6
Bending the Curve

*Dressmaker: Don't worry, Miss Bahmra. Our
designs will make even these little
mosquito bites look like
juicy, juicy mangos!*
-- Bend it Like Beckham (2002)[1]

A. **Dr. Sly's Version of Figure 4**
B. **Figure 4 for All Plants**
C. **All Plants w/o Anomalies**
D. **Mature Plants Only**
E. **Mature Plants w/o Anomalies**
F. **Calculating the Incalculable**
G. **Discussion**

---

[1] Chadha, Gurinder, dir. Produced by Gurinder Chadha and Deepak Nayare, distributed by Fox Searchlight Pictures, from www.imdb.com.

$\mathbf{F}$igure 4 is also incorrect for the same reasons Figure 3 is wrong. Lewis changed the plants so the formula no longer works. We can regraph it from the data in Attachment 1. First, Dr. S's version.

A.   Dr. Sly's Version of Figure 4

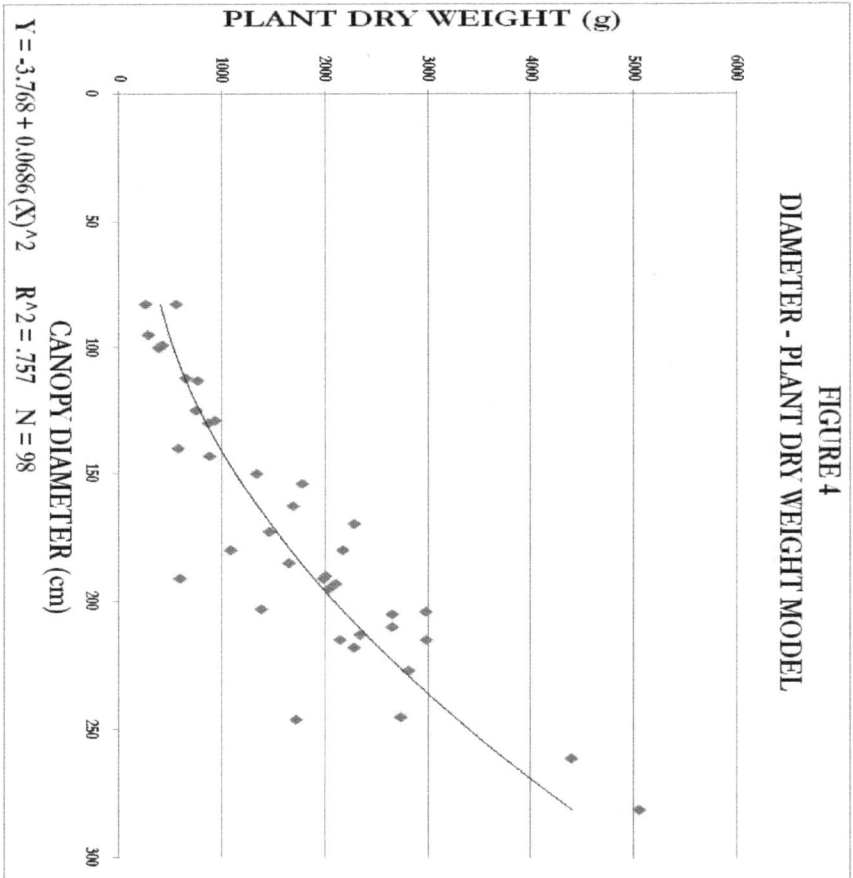

Figure 77.
Dr. Sly's Version of Figure 4.

He chooses a polynomial expression.

B.   Figure 4 for All Plants

The number of plants (N) is not 98, but 102. Page seven states: "Figure 4 depicts the curvilinear relationship between plant canopy diameter and the plant dry weight." The real x-y graphs are:

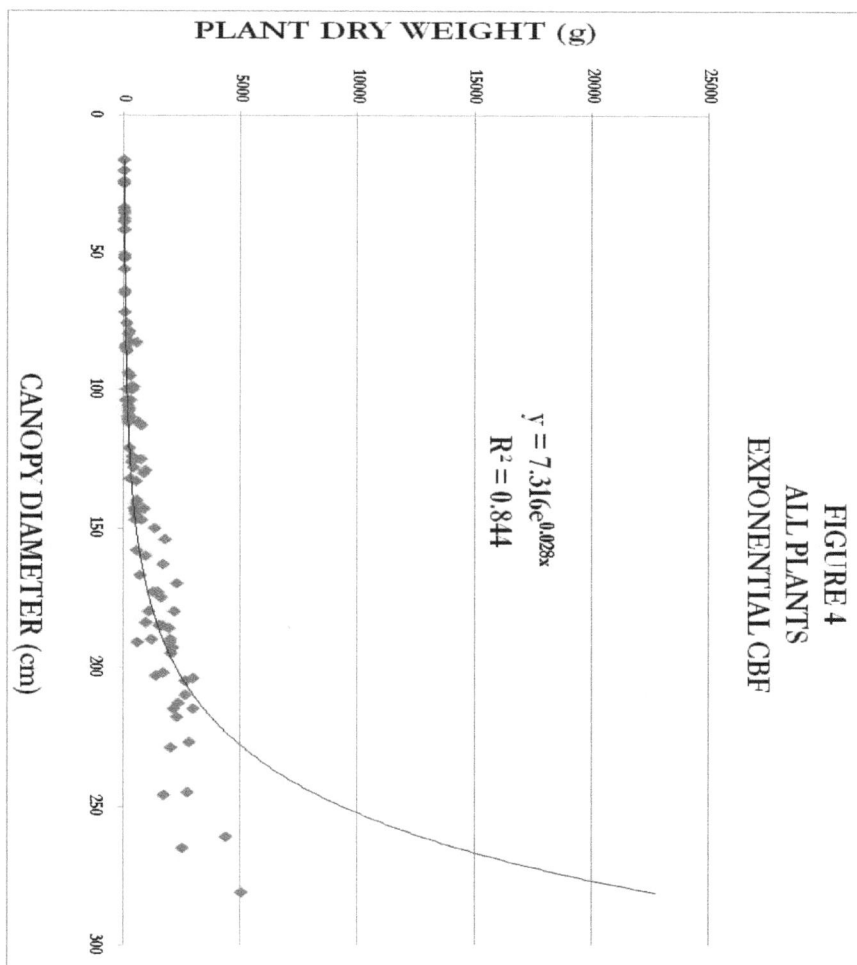

Figure 78.
All Plants, Exponential CBF.

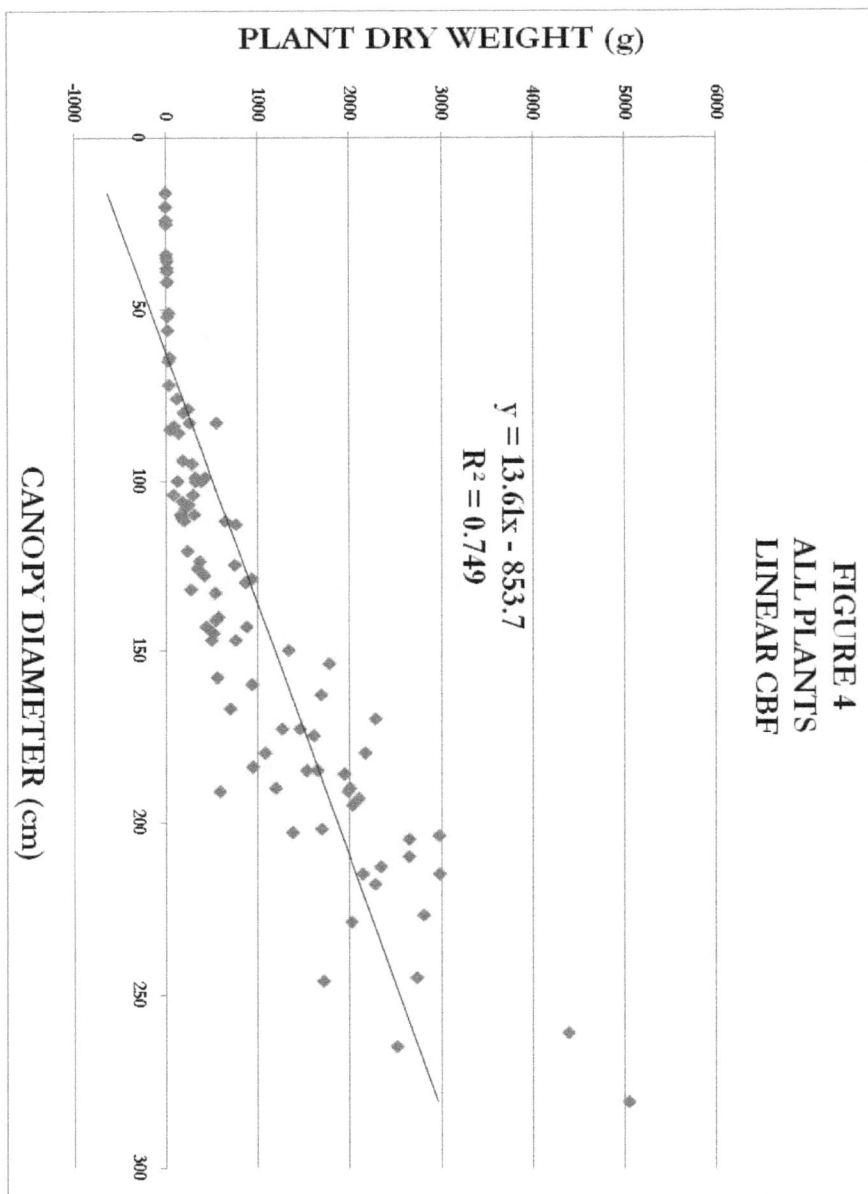

FIGURE 4
ALL PLANTS
LINEAR CBF

$$y = 13.61x - 853.7$$
$$R^2 = 0.749$$

Figure 79.
All Plants, Linear CBF.

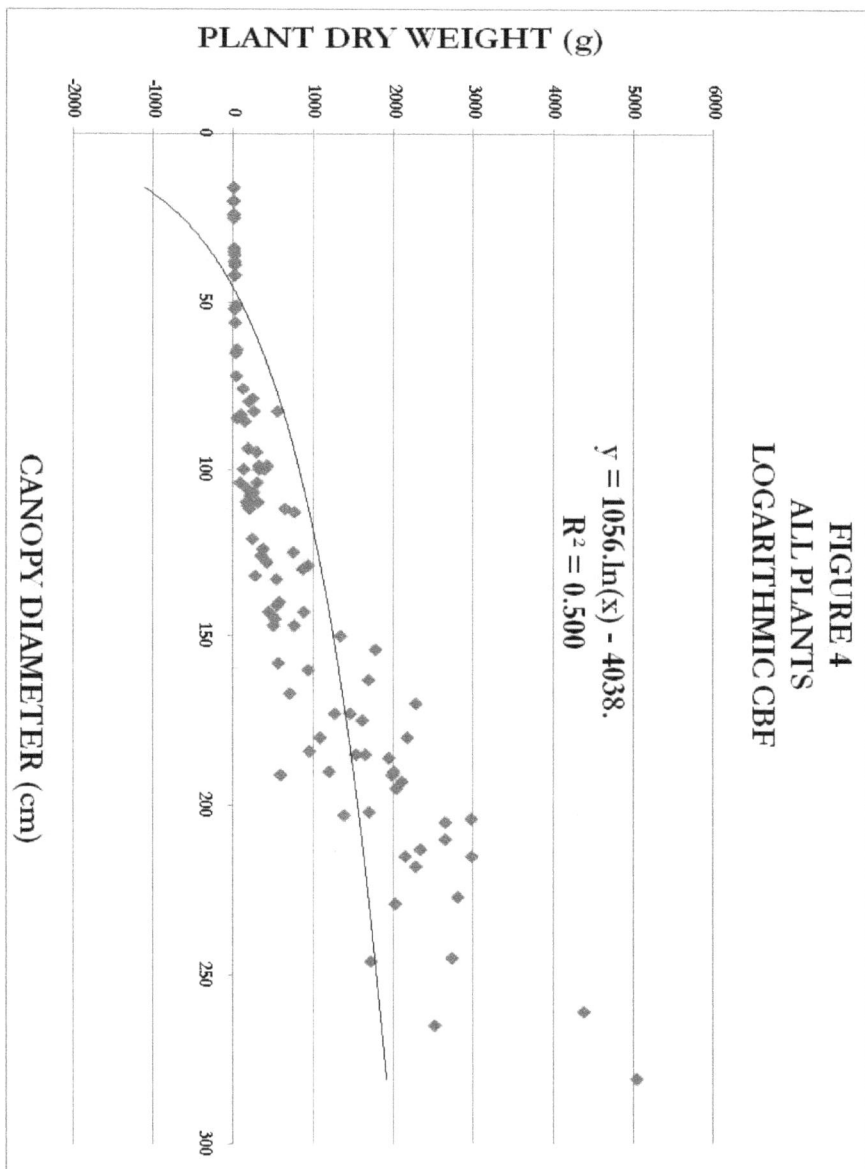

FIGURE 4
ALL PLANTS
LOGARITHMIC CBF

$y = 1056.\ln(x) - 4038.$
$R^2 = 0.500$

Figure 80.
All Plants, Logarithmic CBF.

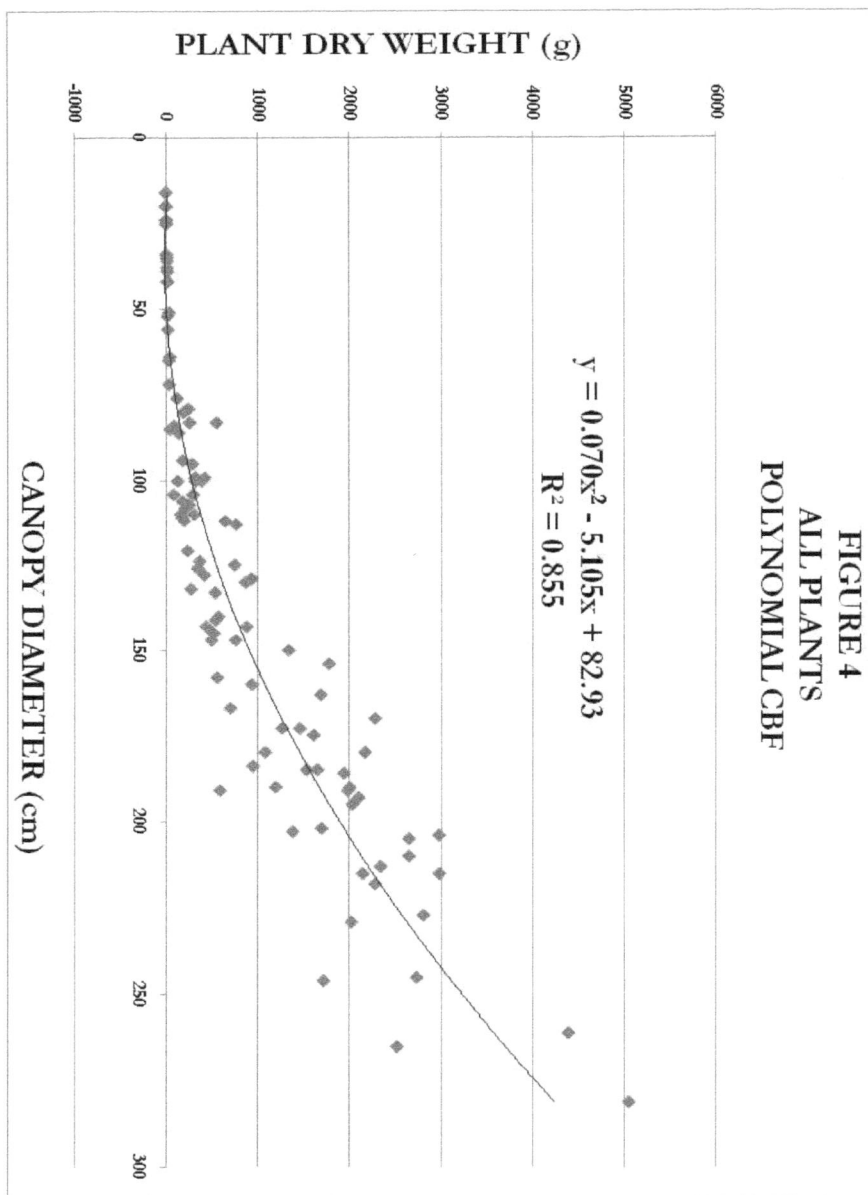

FIGURE 4
ALL PLANTS
POLYNOMIAL CBF

$$y = 0.070x^2 - 5.105x + 82.93$$
$$R^2 = 0.855$$

Figure 81.
All Plants, Polynomial CBF.

154

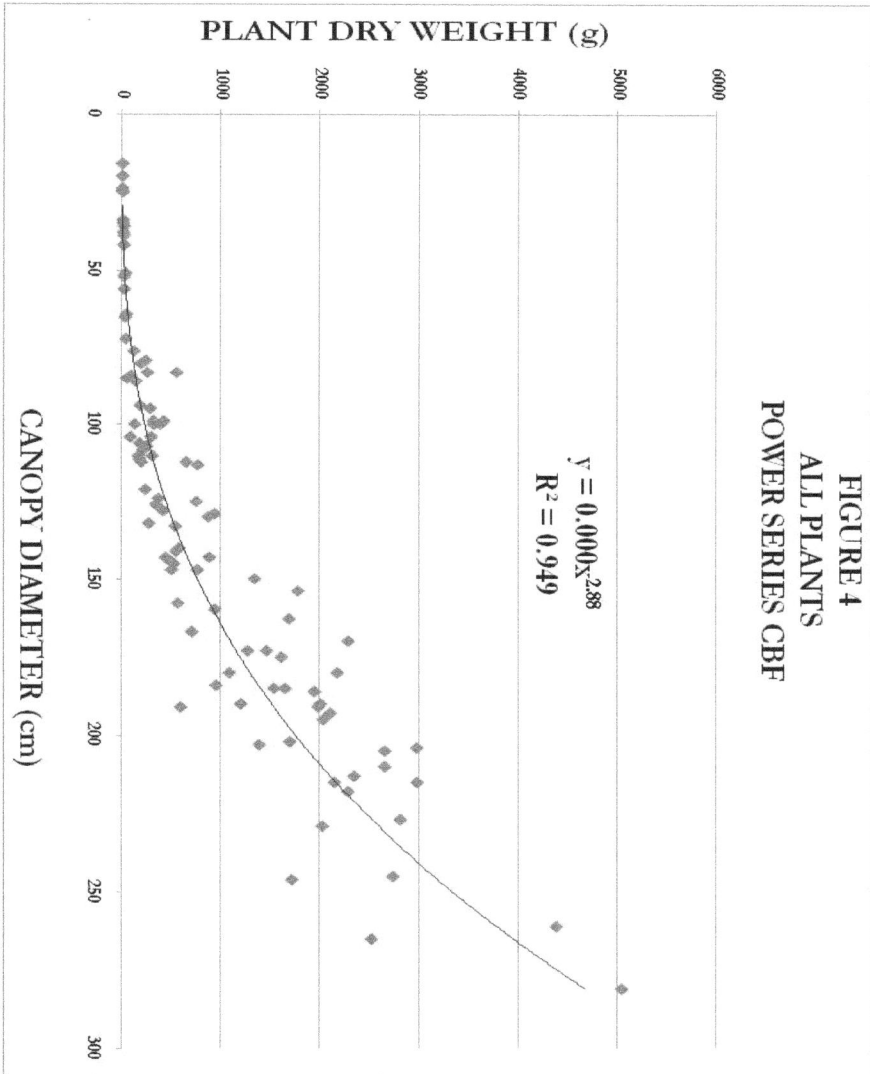

Figure 82.
All Plants, Power Series CBF.

The polynomial curve fits best. The power series formula returns zero, an artifact of the way MS Excel calculates and reports.

C.   All Plants w/o Anomalies

Without the two anomalies we have these x-y graphs:

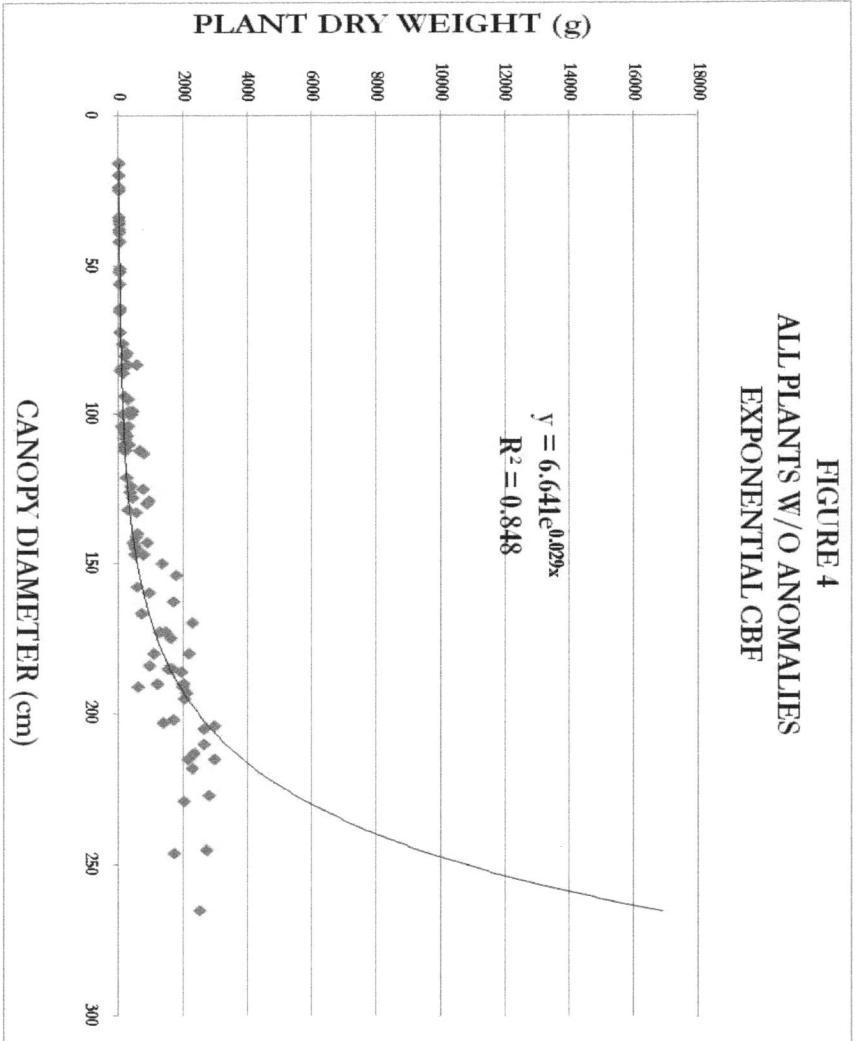

Figure 83.
All Plants w/o Anomalies, Exponential CBF.

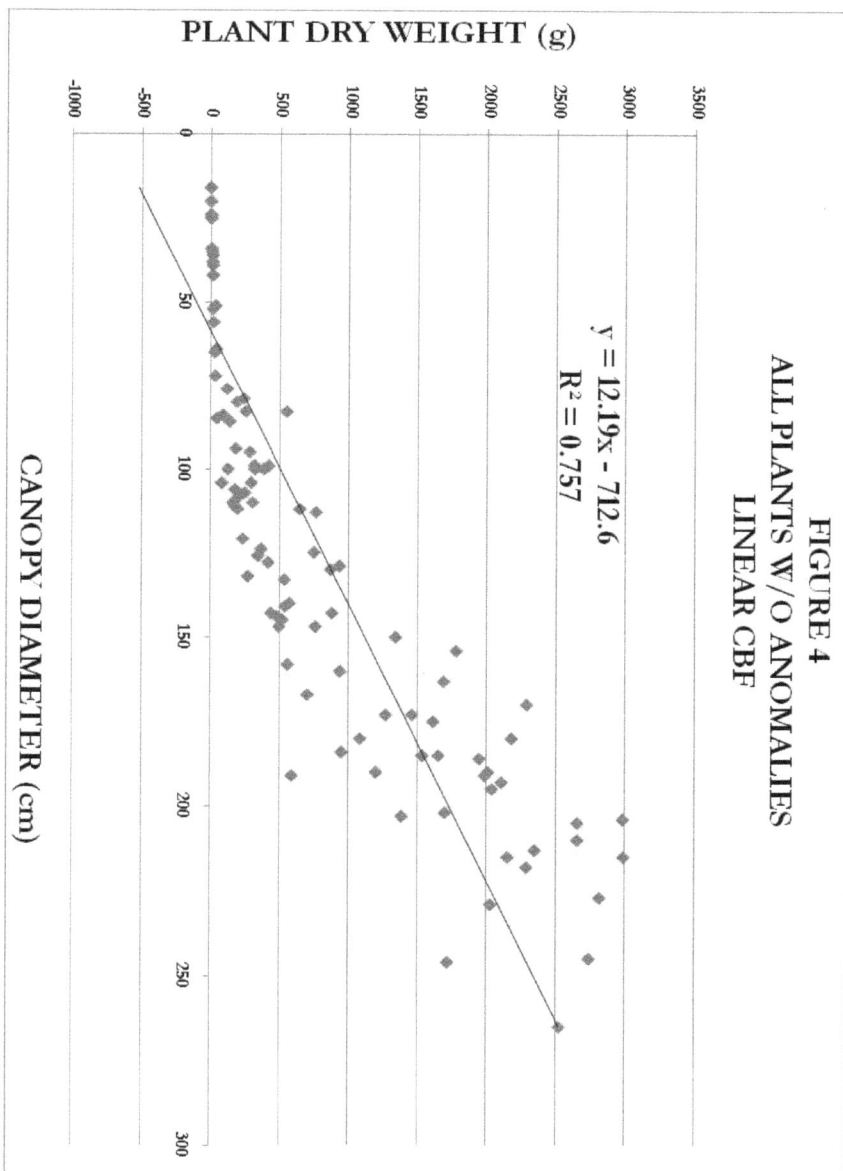

Figure 84.
All Plant w/o Anomalies, Linear CBF.

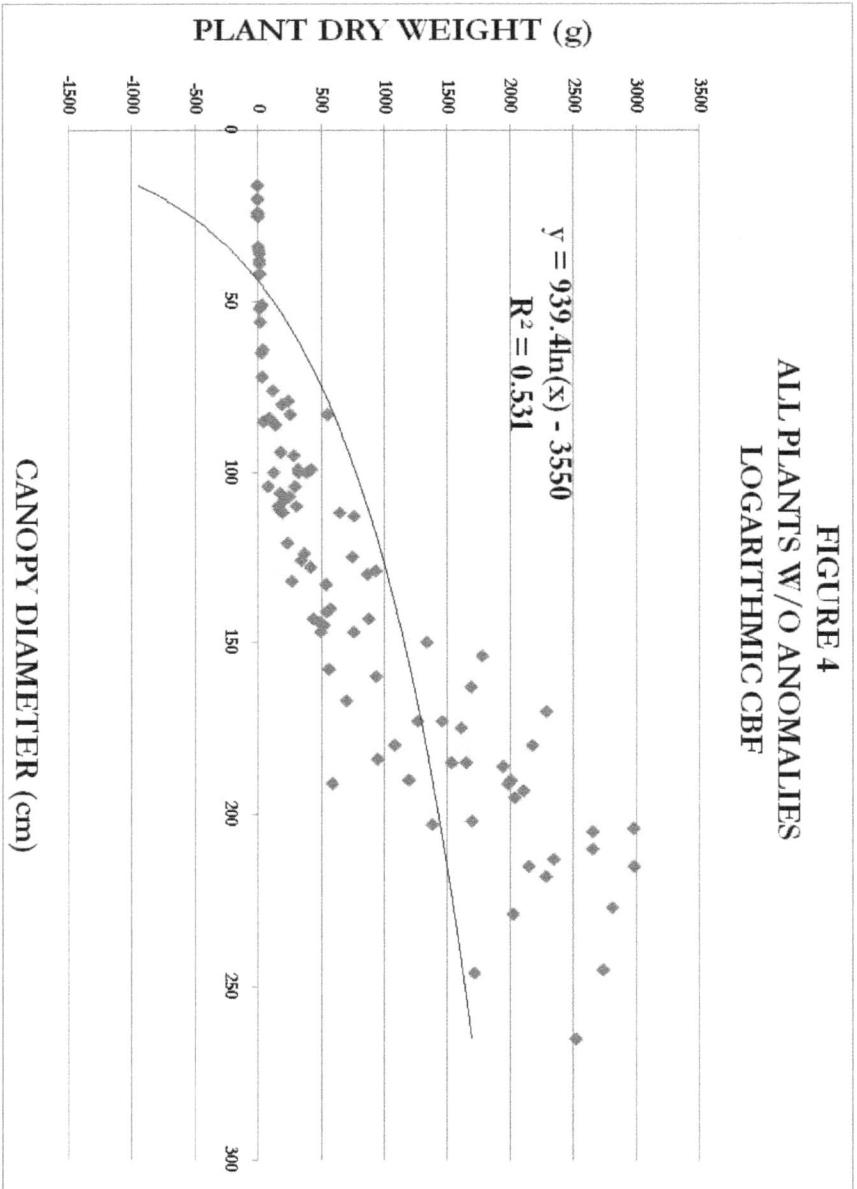

FIGURE 4
ALL PLANTS W/O ANOMALIES
LOGARITHMIC CBF

$y = 939.4\ln(x) - 3550$
$R^2 = 0.531$

PLANT DRY WEIGHT (g)

CANOPY DIAMETER (cm)

Figure 85.
All Plants w/o Anomalies, Logarithmic CBF.

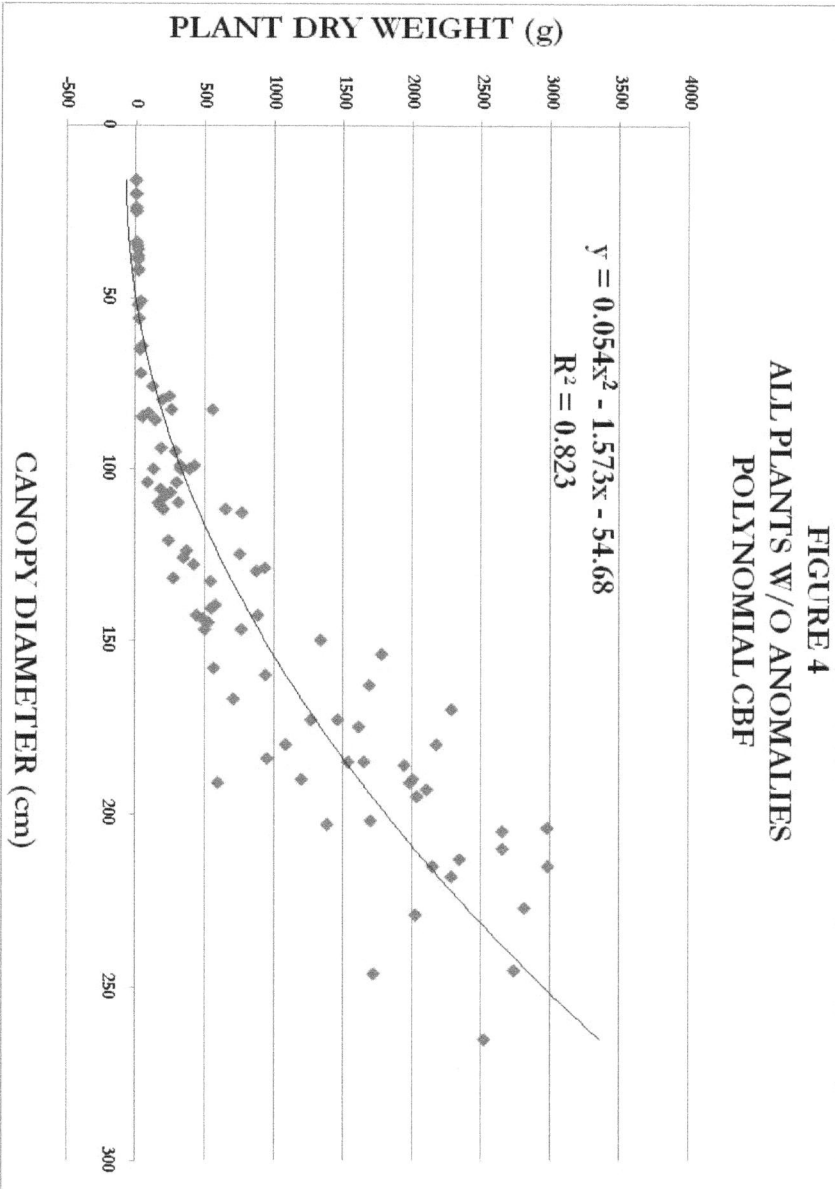

Figure 86.
All Plants w/o Anomalies, Polynomial CBF.

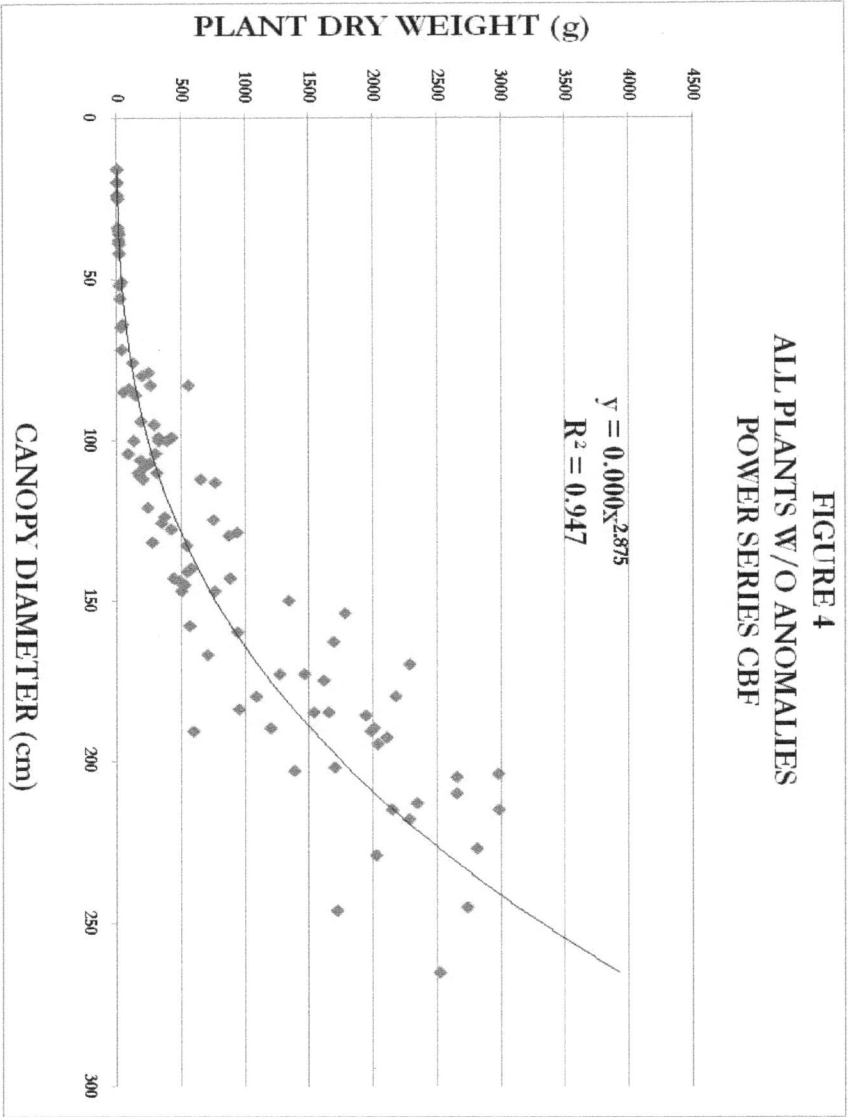

Figure 87.
All Plants w/o Anomalies, Power Series CBF.

The best fit is the exponential; the power series result is again zero.

D.   Mature Plants Only

The same arguments for using only mature plants apply to Figure 4 as they did with Figure 3. The x-y graphs from the data are:

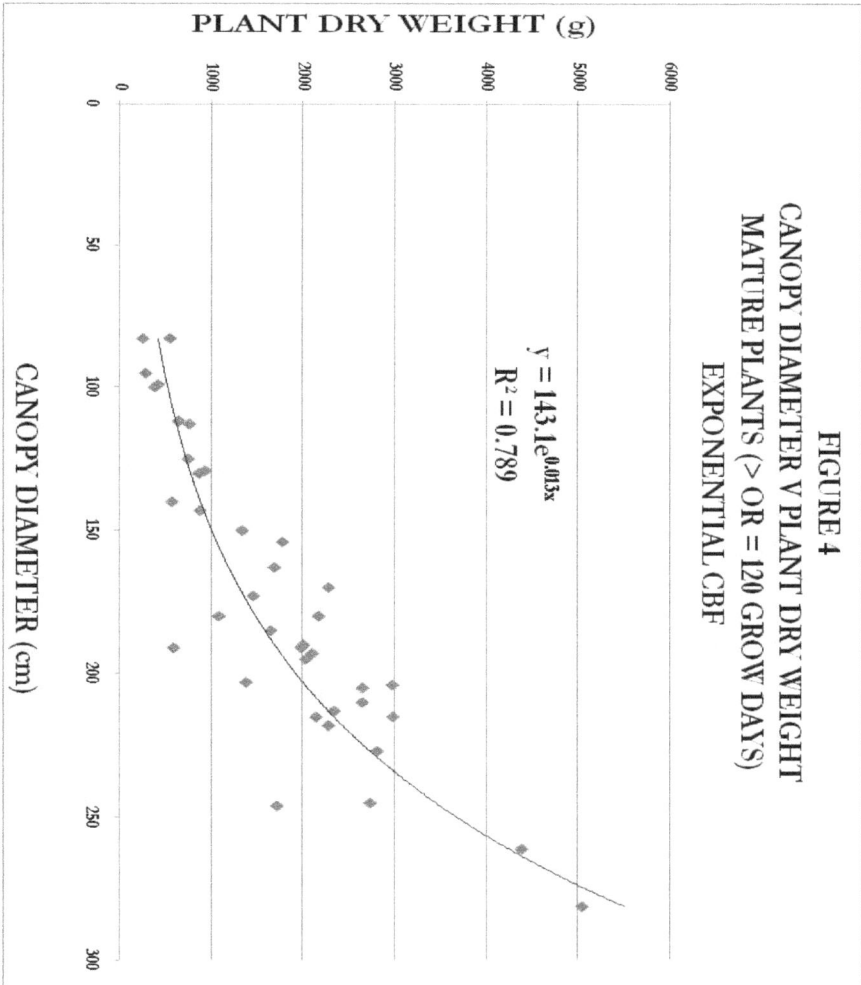

Figure 88.
Mature Plants Only, Exponential CBF.

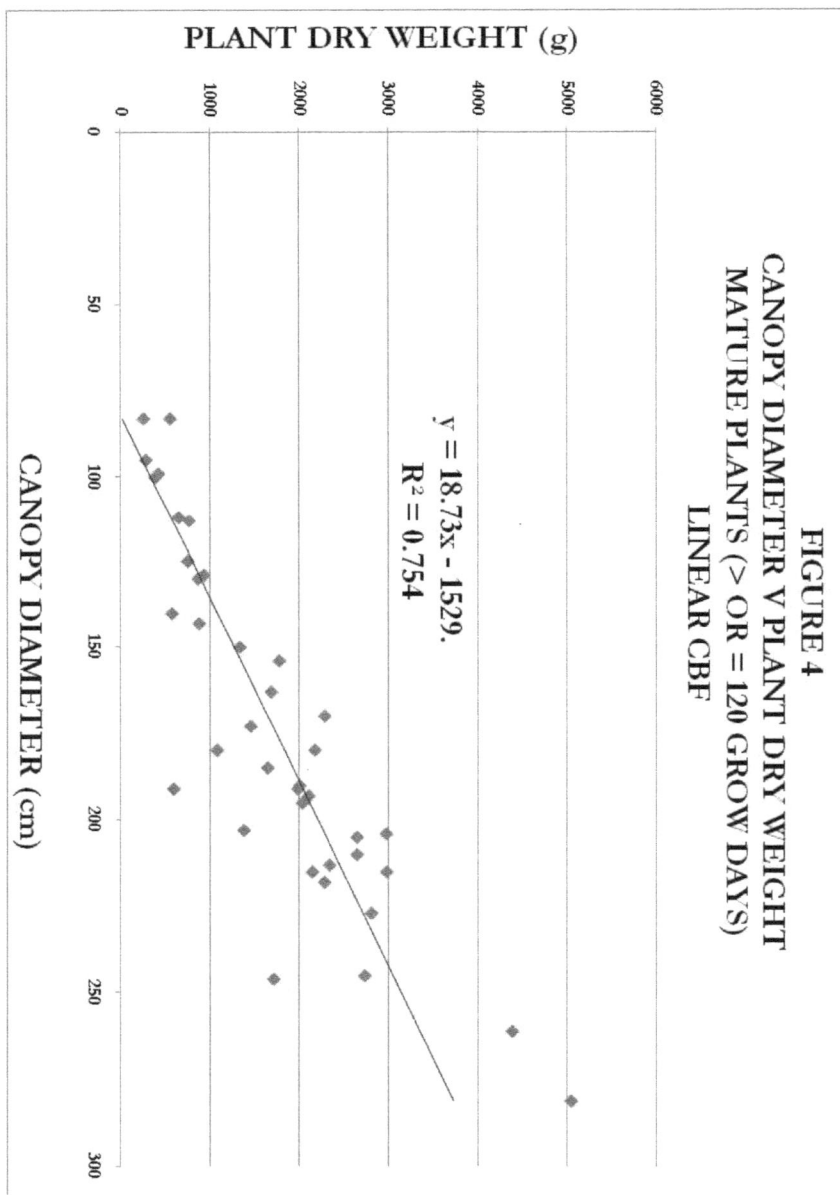

Figure 89.
Mature Plants Only, Linear CBF.

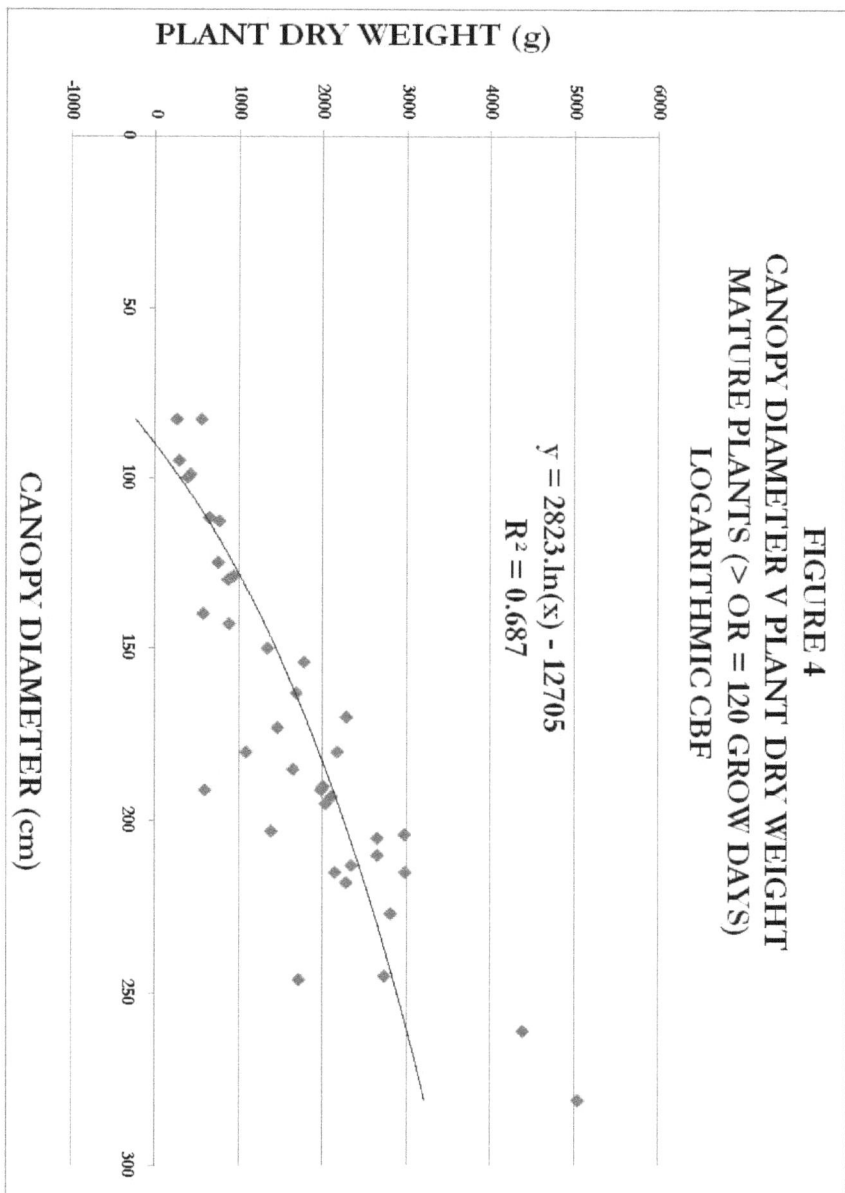

FIGURE 4
CANOPY DIAMETER V PLANT DRY WEIGHT
MATURE PLANTS (> OR = 120 GROW DAYS)
LOGARITHMIC CBF

$y = 2823.\ln(x) - 12705$
$R^2 = 0.687$

Figure 90.
Mature Plants Only, Logarithmic CBF.

163

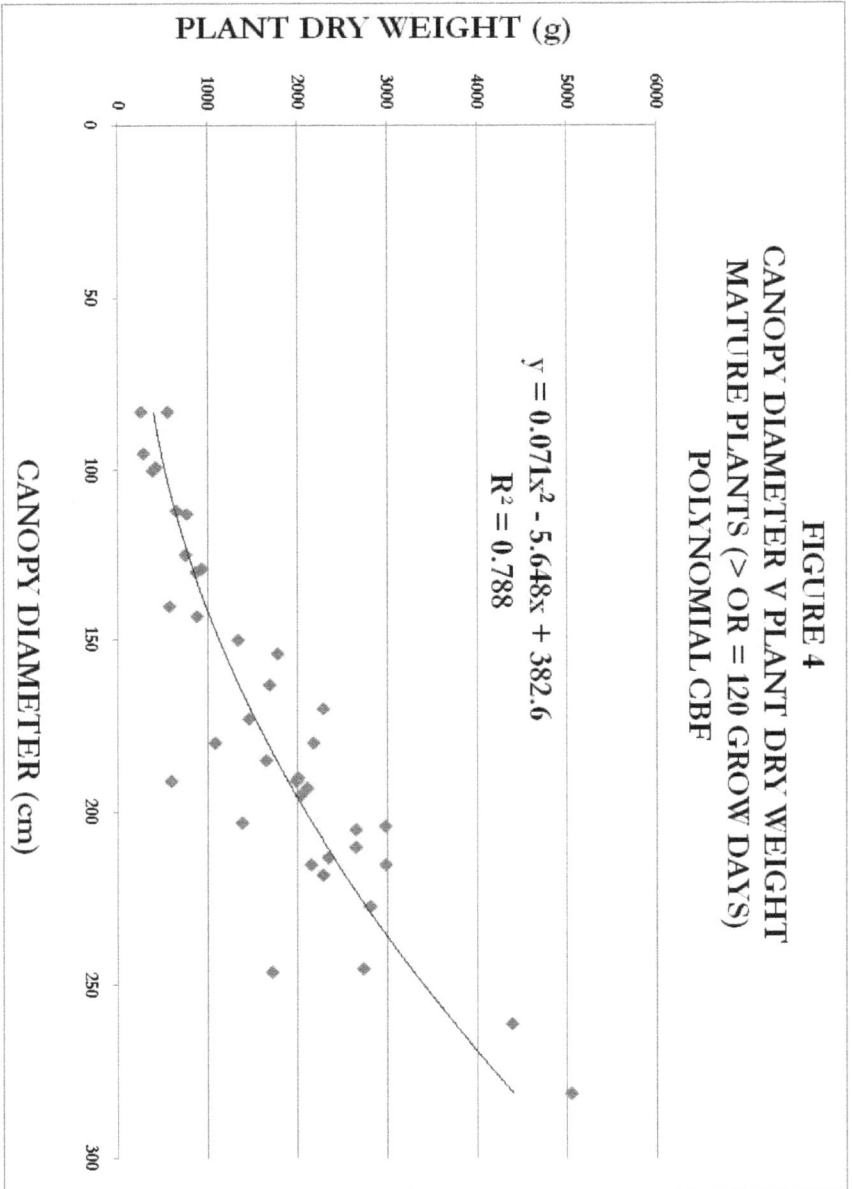

Figure 91.
Mature Plants Only, Polynomial CBF.

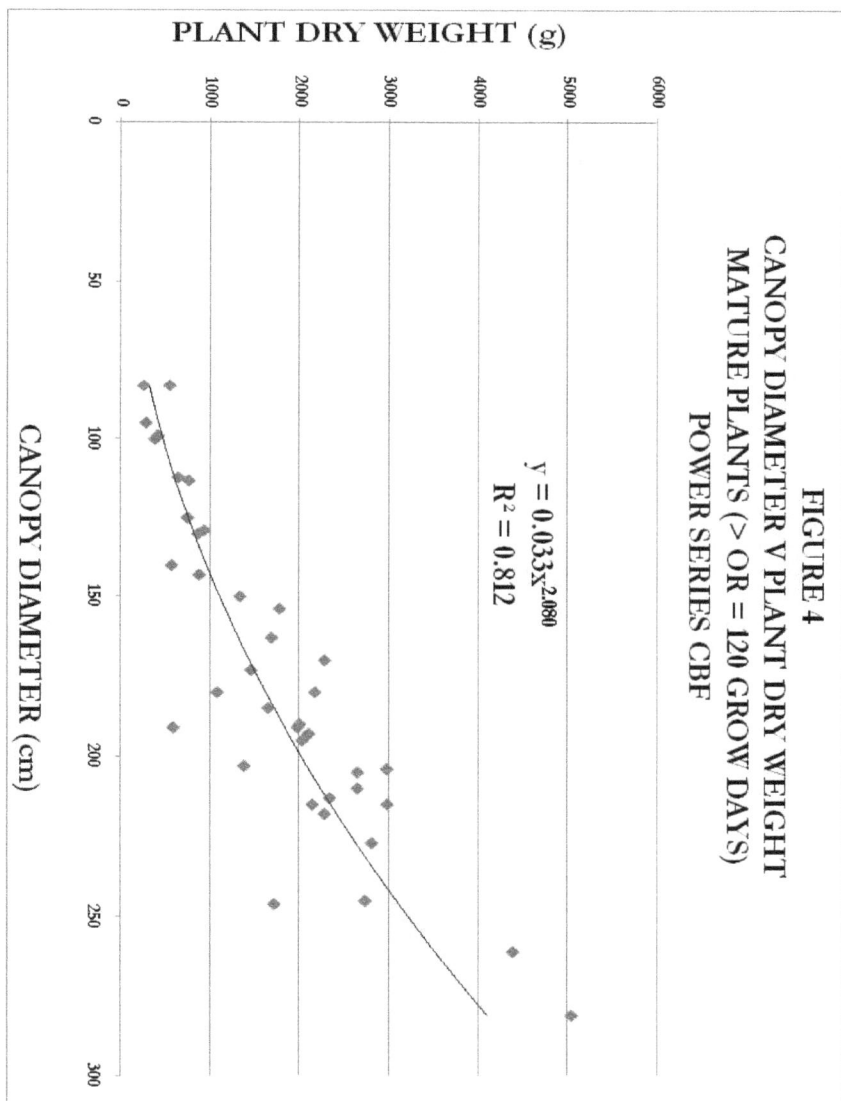

Figure 92.
Mature Plants Only, Power Series CBF.

The power series curve fits best.

E. Mature Plants w/o Anomalies

Or we can graph the mature plants without anomalies:

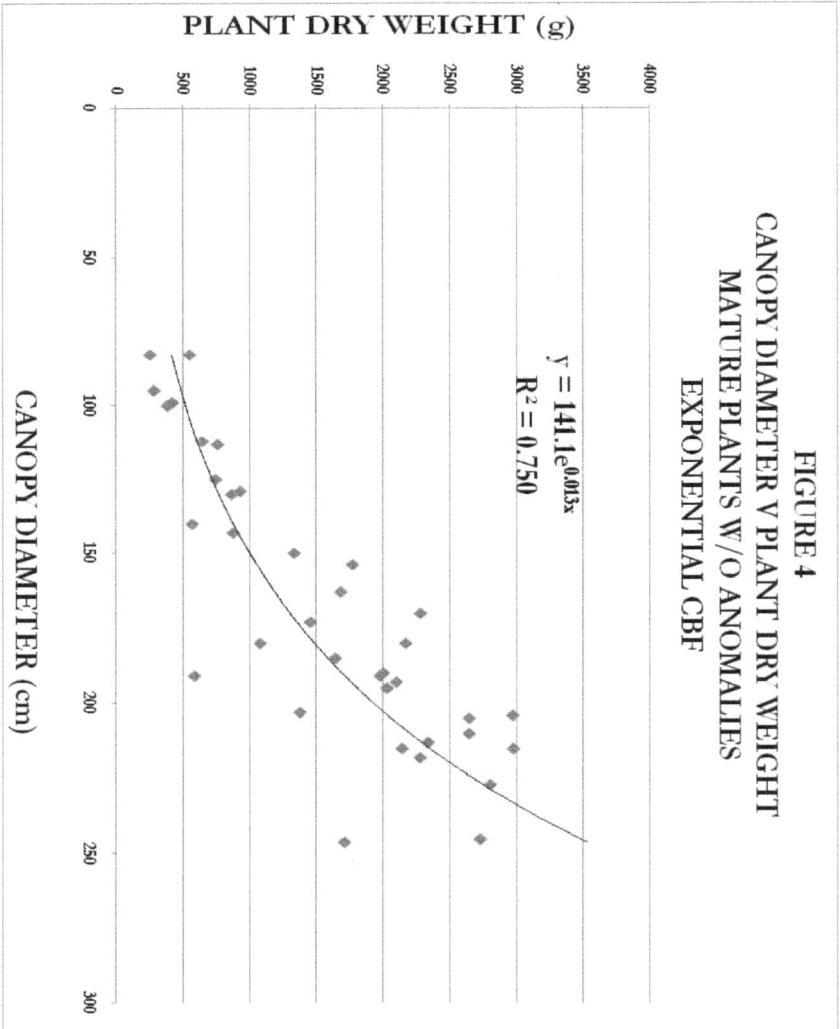

Figure 93.
Mature Plants w/o Anomalies, Exponential CBF.

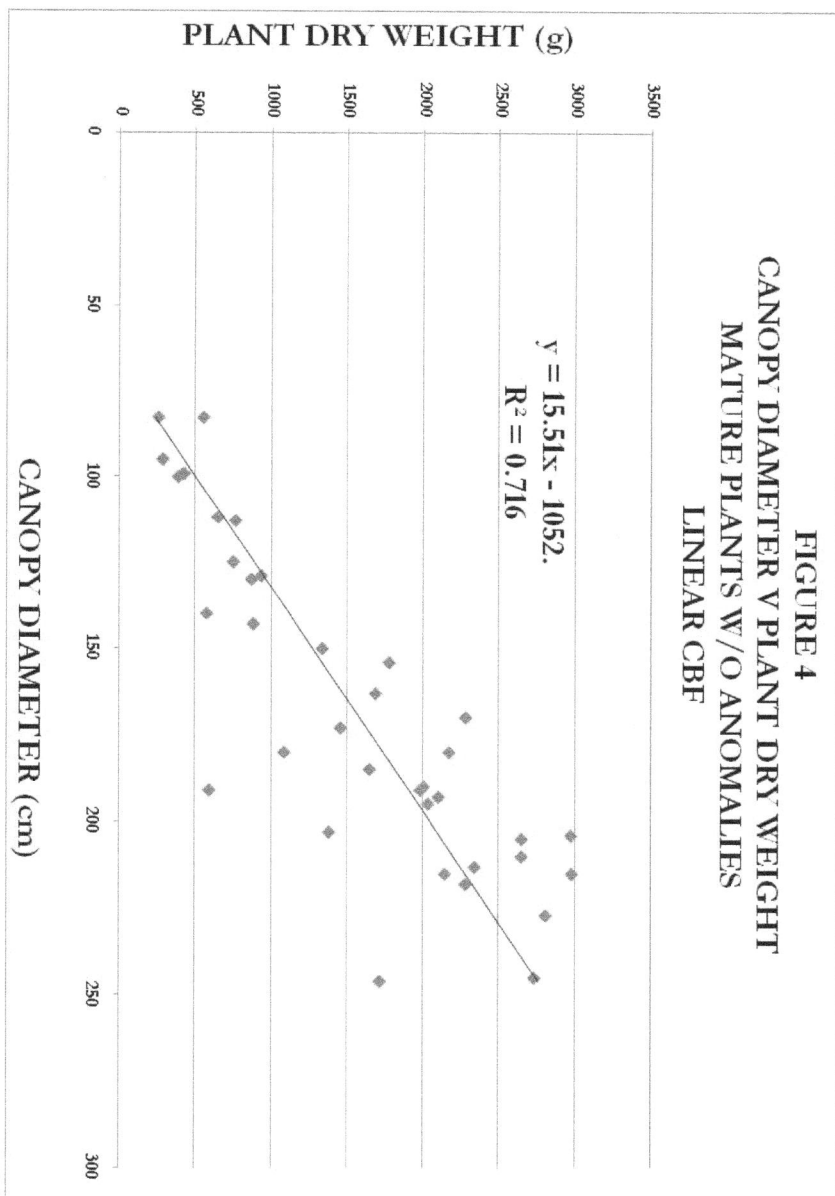

Figure 94.
Mature Plants w/o Anomalies, Linear CBF.

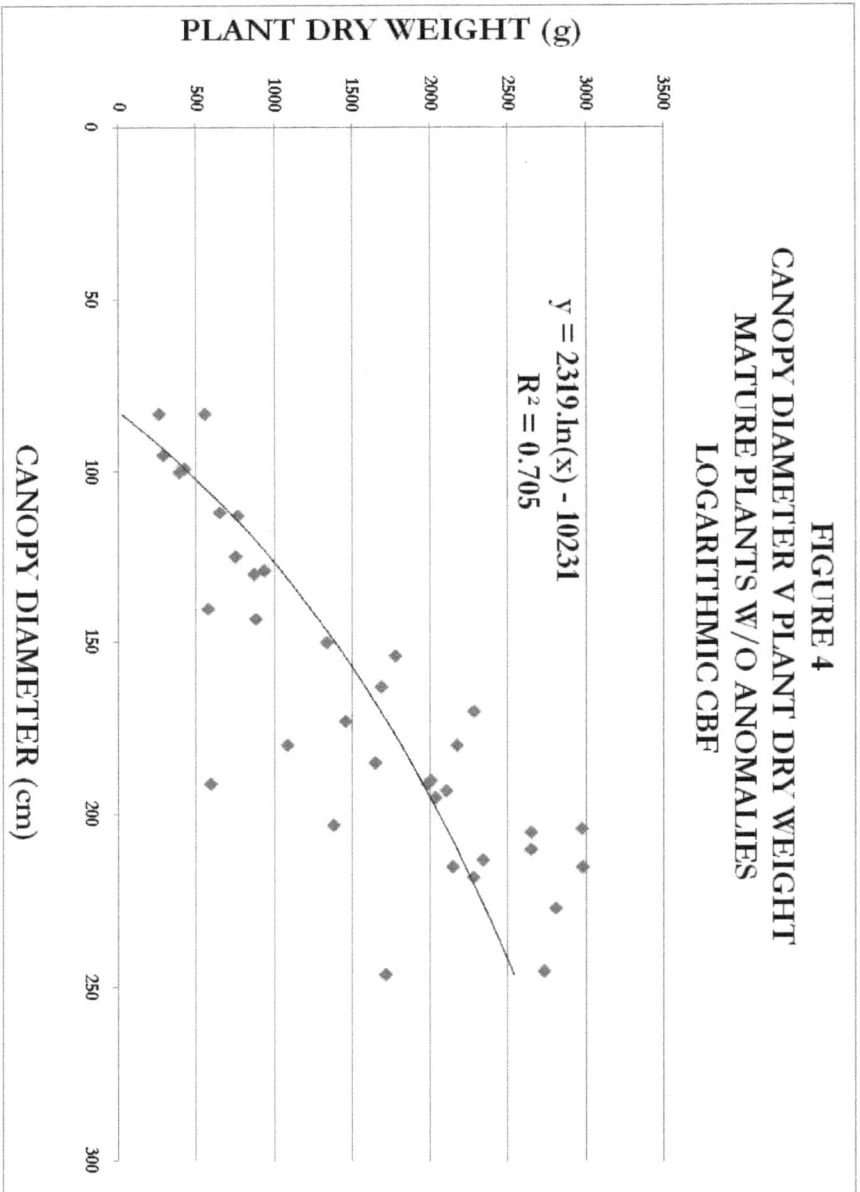

PLANT DRY WEIGHT (g)

FIGURE 4
CANOPY DIAMETER V PLANT DRY WEIGHT
MATURE PLANTS W/O ANOMALIES
LOGARITHMIC CBF

$y = 2319.\ln(x) - 10231$
$R^2 = 0.705$

CANOPY DIAMETER (cm)

Figure 95.
Mature Plants w/o Anomalies, Logarithmic CBF.

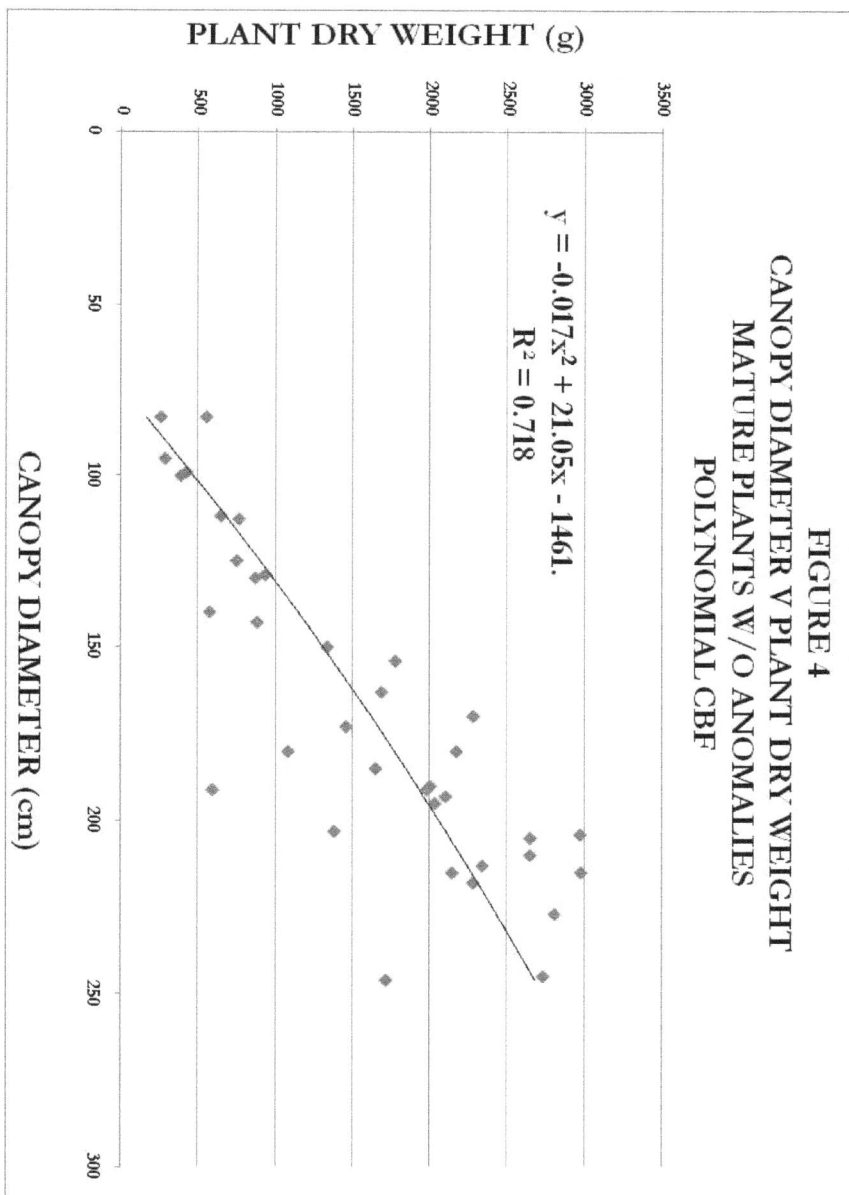

Figure 96.
Mature Plants w/o Anomalies, Polynomial CBF.

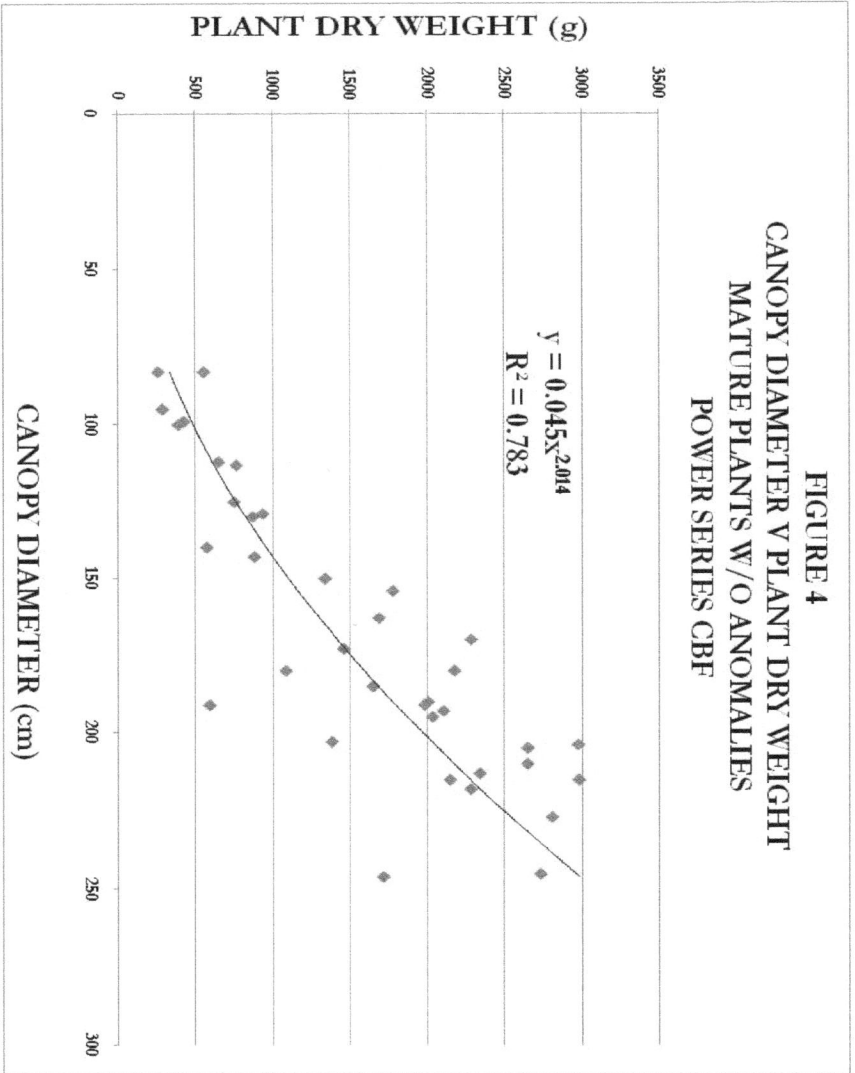

Figure 97.
Mature Plants w/o Anomalies, Power Series CBF.

F.   Calculating the Incalculable

Why use plant canopy formulas in place of yield/density or fresh weight/dried flower formulas? "The measurement of a plant canopy diameter is simpler than the measurement of the plant's fresh weight (page 7)." Which might be true considering the way they did it. First, they fed each plant through a leaf shredder, then separately weighed stalk and branch, seed, and Leafnbud®. After that they added back together the weights to find the plant weight, both fresh and dry.

But the simplest method of finding the plant's fresh weight is to cut it and hang it from an balance. This is much easier than trying to measure the canopy. The problems with canopy measurements in the field are twofold: a) when do you take the measurements, and b) how do you take the measurements. When is important, because after a rain storm for example, the branches tend to hang down to the ground, soaked with water. This extends their reach. How is the same problem. Branches, when dry, are springy and mobile. Do you stretch them, do you accept how the branches curve at that humidity?

Beyond these very real practical considerations, the stated method of calculating the plant diameter is guaranteed to produce larger results. Considering that the branches will stretch to find sunlight, it is possible to have a plant with long branches on one side and shorter on the other, depending on its neighbors or lack thereof. But the DEA's stated method of finding a diameter "is based upon measurement of the diameter of the plant at the broadest point in the canopy (page 7)." This guarantees you the largest diameter possible which will correlate much less well with the plant dry weight.

A better method is to take two diameter measurements, at right angles to one another and then average the two. This helps to reduce the effect of any one measurement that might be distorted because the plant might have longer branches on one side. The measurement of canopy is notoriously fluid in the field while the simple hanging of a plant from a balance is more straightforward.

But once you have a not very good estimate of plant dry weight, how does that help? The text on page seven continues: "Usable yield is then calculated using the percentages of bud and leaf described in Figure 2." But we know that usable yield is just a simple-minded way of saying Leafnbud®. We also know from Chapter 3 that there are no separate percentages of bud and leaf because the plants were put through a leaf shredder. All we could really calculate using this model is a very inaccurate method of finding how much Leafnbud® there might be for any given longest diameter of any given plant.

G.   Discussion

The calculations for Figure 4 are based on a data set that no longer exists. The real formulas can be calculated from the data present in Attachment 1, for all the plants, all plants without the anomalies, the mature plants only, and the mature plants only without the anomalies. Dr. Sly's formula is derived from diameters taken from all plants.   But the method of obtaining the diameter is also fundamentally flawed. By measuring the diameter at the broadest point in the canopy, they distort from the beginning the relationship with the plant dry weight. Better would be to take two diameter measurements at right angles to each other.

Even better would be to use the diameters of only the 38 mature plants, and better still only the diameters of the 36 mature plants, anomalies excluded. The reason is obvious. The purpose of using canopy measurements to obtain plant dry weight estimates is to eventually calculate the percentages of Leafnbud®. But only mature plants will have any flowers. By using the longest diameter, including the anomalies and stacking the data set with larger plants, the curve of best fit is certain to be bent, guaranteeing an equation that will give higher than true estimates of Leafnbud® per plant. It is these false estimates that will then generate (with the faked results of Figure 2) the mighty Poundaplant®.

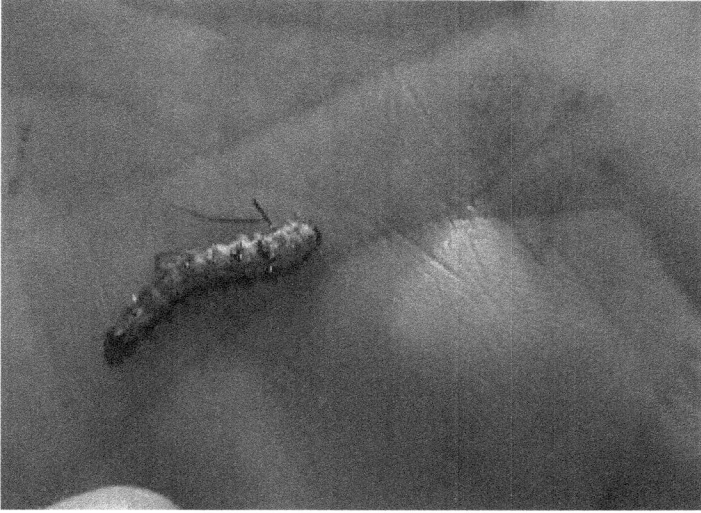

Figure 98.
The Conqueror Worm.

Figure 99.
Attack of the bichos.

7
A Glitch in the Matrix

Neo: Whoa. Déjà vu.
Trinity: What did you see?
Neo: A black cat went past us,
and then another that looked
just like it. ... What is it?
Trinity: A déjà vu is usually
a glitch in the Matrix. It happens
when they change something.
-- The Matrix (1999)[1]

---

[1] Wachowski Brothers, dirs. Produced by Joel Silver, distributed by Warner Brothers Pictures, from www.imdb.com.

The correlation matrix on the last page of Attachment 1 is also incorrect. This is not Lewis's fault. He didn't change a thing. But he should have.

A.   Dr. Sly's Correlation Matrix

Once Lewis the Liar changed the data set, he should have recalculated the correlation matrix for the new values. But he couldn't. Because he didn't know how. So he left the old one. As a result, it, like Figures 3 and 4, is also incorrect. This is the correlation matrix as calculated by Dr. S, from the last page of Attachment 1:

Correlation Matrix for Marijuana Plant Parameter Relationships, 1990-1991

	Days	Plant Density	Plant Height	Plant Diameter	Plant Fresh Weight	Plant Dry Weight	Plant Water	Stem Fresh Weight	Stem Dry Weight	Yield Fresh Weight	Yield Dry Weight	Seed Fresh Weight	Seed Dry Weight
Growth Days	1												
Plant Density	0.015	1											
Plant Height	0.846	0.009	1										
Plant Diameter	0.729	-0.315	0.83	1									
Plant Fresh Weight	0.628	-0.35	0.687	0.867	1								
Plant Dry Weight	0.66	-0.325	0.704	0.87	0.999	1							
Plant Water	-0.689	-0.245	-0.664	-0.476	-0.375	-0.47	1						
Stem Fresh Weight	0.638	-0.365	0.722	0.844	0.939	0.917	-0.337	1					
Stem Dry Weight	0.696	-0.336	0.746	0.853	0.943	0.945	-0.442	0.985	1				
Yield Fresh Weight	0.539	-0.334	0.609	0.824	0.962	0.932	-0.28	0.857	0.849	1			
Yield Dry Weight	0.562	-0.328	0.63	0.843	0.969	0.953	-0.358	0.853	0.862	0.99	1		
Seed fresh Weight	0.435	-0.155	0.396	0.528	0.66	0.728	-0.49	0.452	0.53	0.565	0.637	1	
Seed Dry Weight	0.446	-0.145	0.403	0.533	0.632	0.706	-0.527	0.43	0.511	0.538	0.604	0.94	1

CRITICAL VALUE (2-TAIL, P<0.05) = +/- .198; N=98

Figure 100. Dr. Sly's Correlation Matrix.

A GLITCH IN THE MATRIX

The values in the table are not correct. The only inference that can be drawn is that these values came from a different data set. As with Figure 3 and Figure 4, the number of plants (N) is equal to 98. Attachment 1 contains 102 not 98 plants.

The correlation is a number that describes how closely two variables are related. In this correlation matrix there are 13 variables for a total of 98 pairs of unique correlations. The top half of the table is not shown since it is a mirror image of the bottom half. A variable is always perfectly correlated with itself, hence the 1s along the diagonal.

The particular correlation used is the Pearson Product Moment Correlation. The formula is $r = N\Sigma xy - (\Sigma x)(\Sigma y) / \sqrt{(N\Sigma x^2 - (\Sigma x)^2)} (N\Sigma y^2 - (\Sigma y)^2)$, where r is the correlation, x and y are variables, N is the number of pairs of entries, Σxy is the sum of the products of the paired entries, Σx is the sum of the entries for variable x, Σy is the sum of the entries for variable y, Σx^2 is the sum of the squared entries for x, and Σy^2 is the sum of the squared entries for y. The correlation r will always be between -1.0 and +1.0.

Could the correlation have occurred by chance? For this you need to know the critical value, which is found in a statistics text. To look this up we need the significance level, commonly alpha = .05 meaning the odds are no more than 5 out of 100 that the relationship observed is due to chance. We also need the df or degrees of freedom which is N – 2. The two-tailed test means no particular hypothesis is supposed beforehand, either positive or negative.

At the bottom of the correlation matrix of Dr. S, one can read Critical Value (2-Tail P<0.05) = +/- .198 N = 98. This means that only the entries for Seed Fresh Weight versus Density (-0.155) and Seed Dry Weight versus Density (-0.145) were within the realm of chance. The df or degrees of freedom were 98 – 2 = 96.

B. The Correlation Matrix Reloaded

But this is what you get if you calculate a correlation matrix from all 102 plants listed in Attachment 1:

	Growth Days	Plant Density	Plant Height	Plant Diameter	Plant Fresh Weight	Plant Dry Weight	Plant Water	Stem Fresh Weight	Stem Dry Weight	Leafblood Fresh Weight	Leafblood Dry Weight	Seed Fresh Weight	Seed Dry Weight
Growth Days	1												
Plant Density	0.0214493	1											
Plant Height	0.050755	-0.0002948	1										
Plant Diameter	0.174453	-0.030362	0.021494	1									
Plant Fresh Weight	0.636935	-0.03336	0.0611032	0.0536638	1								
Plant Dry Weight	0.637446	-0.333342	0.0706034	0.0656666	0.056672	1							
Plant Water	-0.63215	-0.025446	-0.661014	-0.45730	0.34441	0.45139	1						
Stem Fresh Weight	0.669498	-0.13699	0.491231	0.83065	0.093716	0.091000	0.47733	1					
Stem Dry Weight	0.046369	-0.13707	0.336873	0.42473	0.94477	0.041454	0.191065	0.982162	1				
Leafblood Fresh Weight	0.531863	-0.327785	0.633236	0.539024	0.957331	0.944739	0.124102	0.650359	0.054044	1			
Leafblood Dry Weight	0.339613	-0.16204	0.397659	0.533008	0.638625	0.710867	0.405905	0.531738	0.549003	0.0982131	1		
Seed Fresh Weight	0.416008	-0.16204	0.397659	0.609010	0.6009146	0.080332	-0.389665	0.0534044	-0.478316	0.3132324	0.0583395	1	
Seed Dry Weight	0.475818	-0.015234	0.0441736	-0.15930633	0.383737	-0.490395	0.3460003	0.631499	0.094099				1

Figure 101. The Correlation Matrix, from the data.

The test is two-tailed, the significance level P is less than 0.05, the degrees of freedom are 100, and the critical value is .1946.[2]

---

[2] "Critical Values for Pearson's Correlation Coefficient," //capone.mtsu.edu/dkfuller/tables/correlationtable.pdf. See also www.gifted.uconn.edu and www.numeracy-bank.net.

C.   CM Reloaded w/o Anomalies

And this is what you get if you do the correlation matrix for the 100 plants in Attachment 1 excepting the anomalies:

	Growth Days	Plant Density	Plant Height	Plant Diameter	Plant Fresh Weight	Plant Dry Weight	Plant Water	Stem Fresh Weight	Stem Dry Weight	Leafblood Fresh Weight	Leafblood Dry Weight	Seed Fresh Weight	Seed Dry Weight
Growth Days	1												
Plant Density	0.073913	1											
Plant Height	0.3169794	0.013451	1										
Plant Diameter	0.334486	-0.297051	0.0535034	1									
Plant Fresh Weight	0.65325	-0.341543	0.7422358	0.650115	1								
Plant Dry Weight	0.6638078	-0.327984	-0.719908	0.0720359	0.0989026	1							
Plant Water	-0.632962	-0.203045	-0.662608	-0.460208	-0.176941	-0.506063	1						
Stem Fresh Weight	0.4233217	-0.319249	0.6896649	0.780072	0.954443	0.907439	-0.272642	1					
Stem Dry Weight	0.6897622	-0.306891	0.7310346	0.8230355	0.9590713	0.9452344	-0.4408667	0.979312	1				
Leafblood Fresh Weight	0.3602693	-0.3416	0.6666063	0.639129	0.9458367	0.91244	-0.294493	0.8666212	0.6535302	1			
Leafblood Dry Weight	0.3060945	-0.344721	0.771722	0.851217	0.9421633	0.940376	-0.1968304	0.857106	0.3812713	0.95496	1		
Seed Fresh Weight	0.4402319	-0.136724	0.4133968	0.4301343	0.4656291	0.3949766	-0.1357953	0.2723606	0.8498536	0.3172633	0.4452224	1	
Seed Dry Weight	0.466354	-0.12336	0.4091488	0.438506	0.451079	0.3728892	-0.0631404	0.36497	0.30164	0.440962	0.957278	0.957278	1

Figure 102. The CM, w/o the anomalies.

The test is two-tailed, P is less than 0.05, the degrees of freedom are 98, and the critical value is .1966.[3]

---

[3] "Critical Values for Pearson's Correlation Coefficient," //capone.mtsu.edu/dkfuller/tables/correlationtable.pdf.   See also www.gifted.uconn.edu and www.numeracy-bank.net.

D.   CM Revolutions Mature Plants

But why are we running the matrix for all the plants when what we really want to look at are the relationships for the mature plants. Mature is what it should be, those 38 plants with > or = 120 grow days:

	Growth Days	Plant Density	Plant Height	Plant Diameter	Plant Fresh Weight	Plant Dry Weight	Plant Water	Stem Fresh Weight	Stem Dry Weight	Leafmod Fresh Weight	Leafmod Dry Weight	Seed Fresh Weight	Seed Dry Weight
Growth Days	1												
Plant Density	-0.202034	1											
Plant Height	-0.00094	-0.34434	1										
Plant Diameter	0.2349599	-0.0804236	0.302721	1									
Plant Fresh Weight	0.177273	-0.653396	0.331424	0.351441	1								
Plant Dry Weight	0.08802346	-0.67366	0.344419	0.0884773	0.974436	1							
Plant Water	0.3746471	-0.356064	0.0021423	0.3041339	0.465837	0.2982166	1						
Stem Fresh Weight	0.3464031	-0.619833	0.3764438	0.127704	0.0840739	0.0805098	0.627839	1					
Stem Dry Weight	0.3894633	-0.69095	0.4445	0.086634	0.096657	0.07452	0.4639019	0.972372	1				
Leafmod Fresh Weight	0.1167131	-0.353723	0.2650979	0.71447	0.941351	0.41969	0.979365	0.623034	0.0825034	1			
Leafmod Dry Weight	0.07236	-0.350072	0.2721997	0.801787	0.0952096	0.0456253	0.3316636	0.1562063	0.1791101	0.1976615	1		
Seed Fresh Weight	-0.208415	-0.390015	0.154702	0.3290969	0.355676	0.1674467	0.744911		0.2170921	0.4734106	0.3981005	1	
Seed Dry Weight	-0.310864	-0.3390626	0.11368339	0.1233699	0.4968031	0.0627765	-0.300041	0.1043582				0.9919304	1

Figure 103. CM, Mature Plants Only.

The test is two-tailed, P<0.05, df = 36, and the critical value is .3202.[4]

---

[4] "Critical Values for Pearson's Correlation Coefficient," //capone.mtsu.edu/ dkfuller/tables/correlationtable.pdf.   See also www.gifted.uconn.edu and www. numeracy-bank.net.

E.   CM Revolutions w/o Anomalies

And here is the correlation matrix for the 36 mature plants without the anomalies:

	Growth Days	Density Plant	Height Plant	Diameter Plant	Fresh Plant Weight	Dry Plant Weight	Water Plant	Fresh Stem Weight	Dry Stem Weight	Fresh Leafhead Weight	Dry Leafhead Weight	Fresh Seed Weight	Dry Seed Weight
Growth Days	1												
Plant Density	-0.287395	1											
Plant Height	-0.000124	-0.35741	1										
Plant Diameter	0.368112	-0.836665	0.366433	1									
Plant Fresh Weight	0.257143	-0.708433	0.467324	0.90737	1								
Plant Dry Weight	0.121021	-0.76347	0.52763386	0.846669	0.961636	1							
Plant Water	0.567034	-0.133761	-0.001865	0.049722	0.478194	0.262086	1						
Stem Fresh Weight	0.369636	-0.61472	0.419579	0.685262	0.92904	0.823835	0.619703	1					
Stem Dry Weight	0.316383	-0.695636	0.521787	0.768124	0.958791	0.896164	0.477145	0.91970	1				
Leafhead Fresh Weight	0.260609	-0.664491	0.424505	0.71216	0.910579	0.913396	0.349867	0.890799	0.890109	1			
Leafhead Dry Weight	0.119394	-0.47365	0.479765	0.794866	0.931133	0.961816	0.412368	0.734438	0.841255	0.528262	1		
Seed Fresh Weight	-0.339774	-0.323802	0.22736	0.391295	0.29539	0.480982	-0.046828	0.057071	0.204709	0.161454	0.380732	1	
Seed Dry Weight	-0.57741	-0.300988	0.184013	0.381368	0.23961	0.448193	-0.449851	-0.008418	0.023072	0.0528622	0.476095	0.9937901	1

Figure 104.   CM, Mature w/o anomalies.

The test is two-tailed, P < 0.05, df = 34, and the critical value is .3291.[5]

---

[5] "Critical Values for Pearson's Correlation Coefficient," //capone.mtsu.edu/ dkfuller/tables/correlationtable.pdf.   See also www.gifted.uconn.edu and www. numeracy-bank.net.

F.   Discussion

By altering the data set, by changing the plants, taking out the smaller ones and replacing them with larger plants, Lewis caused the correlation matrix of Dr. Sly to become inaccurate. The real one can be calculated from the data set that exists, with N = 102 plants, not 98. Further, we can calculate the correlation matrix for the 100 plants in Attachment 1 without the anomalies.

But why are trying to find relationships between the variables for all the plants? What we could really use is the relationships for the variables for only the mature plants, those with 120 or more grow days. After all, this data is going to be used in court to try to convict a witch not for having seedlings but for having mature cannabis plants. So it is more useful to do the correlation matrix for the 38 mature plants. Better would be to do one for the 36 mature plants, excluding the deliberately cultivated anomalies.

It must be clear by now that the data set used to calculate Figure 3, Figure 4 and the correlation matrix has been replaced with another. That original set of data is no longer part of *Cannabis Fields*. Since we've seen this before, this is just déjà vu all over again.

Figure 105. Measuring #4, Espontanea, 2001.

Figure 106. Measuring #7, Warlock 00, 2001.

8
Field of Dreams

Terence Mann: Ray, people will come, Ray.
They'll come for reasons they can't even fathom.
... They'll arrive at your door as innocent as
children, longing for the past. Of course,
we won't mind if you look around, you'll say.
... This field, this game: it's a part of our past,
Ray. It reminds us of all that once was good
and it could be again.
-- Field of Dreams (1989)[1]

---

[1] Robinson, Phil Alden, dir.   Produced by Lawrence and Charles Gordon, distributed by Universal Pictures, from www.imdb.com.

Consider the problem of identifying the plants within the DEA plots. There were ten plots that we can label A through J (read on to see why). Each plot had roughly 100 plants: "The planting of approximately 100 plants per cultivation area ... (page 2)." So there were roughly 1000 plants to keep track of.

Why so many? The field needed a sample space of 950 plants so they could choose 38 mature plants, four percent of the sample, a statistically meaningful percentage. This does not count the edge rows needed to maintain the density of each plot.

A.   Edge Effects

The reason you plant outer rows around the rows from which you wish to choose your representative sample is to control the density. Dr. Sly's original protocol for the study is clear that this was intended: "[N]o plants on the outer rows were selected to avoid edge effects which could skew results because of an asymmetrical planting density (page 3)." This is standard for a yield/density study.

So each plot has inner rows from which you select (supposedly at random) the plants you are going to weigh and measure. The plants on the outer rows have more space on one side. So they will receive more sunlight, water, fertilizer and so on, on that side. The plants on the outer rows will probably grow larger, all other things being equal. If you choose to harvest, weigh and measure plants from the outer rows, you will skew the results for that density.

But that is theory. In practice some of the plots in *Cannabis Fields* did not have outer rows. In others, Lewis chose some of the plants for Attachment 1 from the outer rows. We'll see this when we do the lay out of the field.

B.   Neighbor Effects

Another way to control for density is to take into account what are called neighbor effects. If you choose to harvest the third plant in a row, then the second and the fourth plants are no longer eligible to be chosen. The protocol for *Cannabis Fields* acknowledges this on page 2: "If a particular plant was harvested for the measurement program, the neighboring plants were ineligible for future selection which avoided changing the planting density during the study." Again, this is standard operating procedure.

The reason for this is because you are harvesting the plants over a season of five months, every thirty days in this case. If you harvest one plant, you create a hole in the field. The plants neighboring this hole have less competition on that side. These neighbor plants then have access to more sunlight, more water, nutrients, and so forth on that side. Generally, this will result in these becoming larger plants than they otherwise would have been had they continued to be surrounded by other plants. Thirty days later, during the next cutting, these larger plants, if chosen, will skew the results for that density.

Was this part of the protocol followed? Not really. It will become clear when we lay out the field that Lewis chose plants growing next to empty spaces, spaces where plants had been harvested in previous cuttings. These neighbor plants would have been larger than the others in the density. Once again the results were skewed toward the larger plants.

C.   Selection Bias

The original design called for random selection. There are a number of methods of selecting plants at random. A computer program can select them. Or one might choose the third plant in the first row, the fifth plant in the second row and so forth. The selection is random so as not to introduce bias into the study.

When the bias of the investigator is introduced into the study, there can no longer be the claim of trying to find an average plant. Non-random selection alone dooms a study like this to claim that its results are generally applicable to other plantations. Instead, what occurs is an N = 1 study, which is what-some-people-found-when-some-people-planted-some-plants. N = 1 studies are useful and a lot of them together can point to an interesting result. But alone a single N = 1 study doesn't allow you to generalize to other gardens. It doesn't allow you to state that in general a cannabis plant will be this large or have this percent of that or to say much of anything at all.

The selection in *Cannabis Fields* was non-random. We know this because they admit it: "The selection of plants was based upon a determination of their representative physical size, shape, and overall vigor characteristics. The selection process captured the diversity of plant size by including cannabis plants ranging from the larger to the smaller plant specimens (page 2)." This is pseudo-intellectual bullshit for: "We just chose the plants we wanted, basically the largest ones we could find."

But why go to all the time and trouble to grow plants in different plots with different densities in the first place if you are simply going to choose the plants you like? Why go to the bother of growing edge rows to maintain constant plot density? Why go to the expense of planting large hundred-plant-or-so plots in the first place? Why not simply report that you grew a bunch of large plants and be done with it?

The purpose of controlling for density is to find an average plant, not big plants, not small ones, but a representative sample. Non-random selection defeats this purpose. Without random selection, just choosing the plants you like for your own biased personal reasons, you have the appearance but not the substance of a yield/density study.

D.   The Anomalies

If you cut down *all* the plants around a particular plant at the beginning of the study, then come back at the end to cut this lonely plant at the very end of the season, you produce the same effect as growing a single oak tree in a cow pasture. It spreads out in all directions and grows much larger than it would have had it been constrained in a forest with other trees.

This is what happened with the anomalies, plants numbered 107.01 and 103.01. The latter is referred to in the first sentence of the report: "(T)he usable dry weight yield [Leafnbud®] for female cannabis plants can be up to 2.3 kilograms (5.1 pounds)." As noted previously, plant number 103.01 does show that it had a yield [Leafnbud®] of 2308.4 grams. Does it not seem strange to anyone that a supposedly scientific study leads off with the anomalies?

Both anomalies are noted in the body of the report on page 4: "However, two plants, identification numbers 107.01 and 103.01 in the 1991 low planting density plots, had extremely high yields [Leafnbud®] in comparison to neighboring plants. The dry weight yield [Leafnbud®] for plant 107.01 was 2,086.9 grams (4.6 pounds) and plant 103.01 yielded [in Leafnbud®] 2,308.4 grams (5.1 pounds)."

An explanation is demanded for these two anomalies. An explanation is given, partly fact and partly faith-based: "These two plants were located in a low area. *It is believed* that the natural slope of the land caused these plants to receive additional water and possibly additional fertilizer through run on water. The significance of these yields [of Leafnbud®]is that they demonstrate that certain agronomic practices can produce higher average yields [of Leafnbud®] than those reported in Table 2 (page 4, italics added)."

Higher than those reported in Table 2? But in fact the data for Table 2 *includes* the data from these two anomalies. It is one thing to note the anomalies in a data set; all data sets have them. It is another to highlight them in the lead sentence in the paper. An even deeper circle of hell awaits you if you include them in your calculations since they tend to skew your results, unless of course you want the results skewed, in this case toward larger plants. Keep descending if you need to pretend that you don't really know how they occurred, as in, *"It is believed ...."* Did the author of those words not see these two plants? But the bottomless pit of eternal damnation is reserved for those who create the anomalies in the first place, lie about them afterwards and then go on to use them to skew the results anyway.

When we draw the field and the plots, it will become clear that the plants were planted in rows and cut by columns. But this excepts the two anomalies which were left standing alone on the edge of the field for the entire growing season. In other words the anomalies were manufactured. They happened by design, not accident. The DEA deliberately grew these large plants to skew the results for their non-random sample of mostly larger plants so as to be sure they could arrive at a Poundaplant®.

FIELD OF DREAMS

E.   The Identification Numbers

Which brings us back to the plant identification numbers. All of the i.d. numbers are decimal, even when they don't need to be. The data set given in Attachment 1 begins with data from the plots A, B, and C from 1990. These plants have decimal identification numbers but zeroes to the right of the decimal point. They are listed in numeric order. Clearly, one could just as simply use integers to number them. Why use decimals? Why 1.00, 2.00, and 3.00, not simply 1, 2, and 3?

Then suddenly Attachment 1 lists the data from what appear to be three plots from 1991. These three plots follow the same protocol in their subject headings for the 1990 plots except their plot letters have been removed and a different year has been added. The 1991 plant index numbers are also decimal but they have non-zero numbers to the right of the decimal point. In other words, the plants in these three plots need decimal numbers; integers won't do. They are listed in no particular numeric order; instead they appear to be organized roughly by the dates they were removed from the field.

After that we are back to three more plots, labeled E, F, and H from 1990, again listed in numeric order, except that plant number 37.00 is missing. These plants again have decimal numbers but with zeros to the right of the decimal point. Once again, integers would have done just as well. Why use 35.00, 36.00 and 38.00 when 35, 36, and 38 carry the same information? Except for plot F, they are also organized according to date harvested. Plot A also suffers from this strict lack of order according to date harvested.

Why is the data mixed from one year to the next and back again? Why are decimals used for the 1990 data and not simply integers? Why do the three 1991 plots not have plot letters but the other six do?

But of course this is only Lewis hard at work with his magic scissors and paste. Lewis erases and manipulates the content to get the results he wants. But afterwards he has to cover his tracks. He has to make sure no one could ever reconstruct the field from the data given in Attachment 1.

So Lewis changed the plant identification numbers in the 1990 plots. These were originally decimals, with non-zeroes to the right of the decimal point, just like the so-called 1991 plots. He thought he could hide them by simply numbering them in the order listed. But he calls attention to their oddity at the same moment he is trying to make them look like the decimal numbers in the three 1991 plots. Lewis doesn't understand the principle of simplicity.

But he couldn't very well alter the 1991 numbers because they had already been used in the body of the paper that refers to the two anomalies. Perhaps it would have been simpler to have changed the two plant numbers 107.01 and 103.01 to 51.00 and 52.00. But Lewis was lazy.

To try to cover his tracks, he cuts and shuffles the data for the plots. He alters the plot titles. He changes identification numbers. He cuts one field of plants grown in one year into two fields grown in two separate years. This was his *modus operandi* in Attachment 2 as well, when he excised the Week column data from the 1986 plants and re-sorted the plants, again chopping one year into two.

Lewis cuts and shuffles, cuts and shuffles, like no dealer in Vegas is allowed to anymore. He sanitizes and obscures how, when and where the plants were grown before the once secret report is released into general circulation.

Perhaps Lewis didn't think anyone would bother to try to reconstruct the field. Perhaps he didn't think anyone could. So let's do it.

F.   The North End of the Field

We make a single assumption: The identification numbers for the plants in the 1991 plots refer to the plant's row and column. You wouldn't lay out these plots without having some method of referring to an individual plant; after all, you have to tell the harvester which plants to cut. Identifying the plant by its row and column would be sufficient.

Hence, the decimal identification numbers. The corollary to this assumption is that the digits to the left of the decimal point indicate the row and the digits to the right of the decimal point indicate the column in that row. You could do it the other way but then you would have 100 or more plants in a single row. Not exactly an efficient use of land. And the protocol says we have roughly 100 plants in a given plot which has outer rows.

In all this we follow Occam. Decimals contain more information than integers. But why use the former if the latter will do? The principle of simplicity supposes that no one will needlessly complicate his design if he doesn't need to. And remember the plots were originally designed not by Lewis but by Dr. Sly. Whether you like his morals or not, you have to admit he has the ability to prepare one of these studies.

Thus, by our scheme, identification number 99.16 refers to plant number 16 in row 99. Plant number 87.12 refers to the twelfth plant in row 87. This means we have to count from a first column. Without loss of generality, we can let the first column run alongside the Westside bleachers.

Now that we have rows and columns, we can recreate at least one end of the football field on which the plants were grown. Why a football field? Because the plants were spaced out in yards but harvested in meters.

In the first chapter we noted the mixed use of metric and English measures. In Attachment 1, the plant data is reported using the metric system. The amount of space allotted to each plant is given in the metric system. Thus, plot A is described as a "1.8 x 2.7 m Planting (page 1 of Attachment 1)."

But why report the growing space for each plant in fractions of meters? Eventually your results have to be reported using the metric system. That's the convention with scientific papers.

Suppose you have a large empty field in the piney woods of Yoknapatawpha County on which you are going to grow your plants. You can just as easily mark out your plots with a meter stick as you can using a yardstick.

But this wasn't done. Because 1.8 meters is two yards and 2.7 meters is three yards. So why lay out your plots in yards, forcing you later to convert them to parts of meters? Where is the advantage for this added layer of complexity?

Ontogeny doesn't really recapitulate phylogeny. You didn't really once resemble an adult tadpole, newt, frog, and tree rat in the womb. But the Pachamama does build with what she has. It's cheaper than reinventing the wheel.

The DEA could have laid out its plots in meters. They probably should have. The only reason they wouldn't is if they already had a field marked out in yards ready to be used. And what kind of field is already marked out with handy yardlines?

Go Rebels! A football field is already marked off in yards. What more could you ask for? The athletic department already has the equipment to easily chalk up some crosslines and even some lines in the end zones. A hypothetical football field could so easily accommodate a yield/density study.

Question: Did they plant on the lines or in the center of the squares formed by the lines? Either one will work. But I'll choose the center of the squares, again without loss of generality. If so, then a plant identification number beginning with 87 means they planted this plant between the 86th and the 87th yard lines. Any plant identification number beginning with 100 would have been planted

FIELD OF DREAMS

between the 99th and 100th yard lines. They could just have easily planted directly on the intersections of the chalk lines.

1. The 1x1s. First, let's look at the 1x1s. The range of the numbers for the rows that we have in Attachment 1 run from 87 to 100. The range of the numbers for the columns, the two digits to the right of the decimal point, run from 2 to 23. If you wanted a hundred plants in this plot, you could have planted five rows of twenty plants. But the existence of a plant with number 23 in its column suggests they used four rows of twenty-five plants instead.

If they followed the protocol, then they also planted two outside rows, one on each side of the four inner rows from which they wanted to choose their plants so as not to disturb the density. In other words, for the four rows of twenty-five plants they wanted for their sample space, they needed to plant six rows of twenty-five plants.

So in Figure 107 we have drawn a grid of twenty-five columns by sixteen rows and numbered the rows from 85 to 100 corresponding to those yardlines. After that, we can put a capital letter P in the center of every square that contained a plant that was reported in Attachment 1. What's interesting about this hypothetical construction of the 1x1s?

First, there are no plants chosen from column number one. Again, this makes sense. The plants in column one can be considered an edge column, which you would want to control the density. Second, the plants chosen come from two distinct groups. One group of plants was chosen from rows 95 to 100 and another from rows 85 to 90. Again, this makes sense, since there are six rows in each group. There were no plants chosen from rows 91, 92, 93, and 94. These rows are the space between the plots.

195

Figure 107.
The mature plants chosen from the plot of 1×1s.

So the 1x1s, although they have been gathered together into one plot in Attachment 1, were originally divided between two distinct plots. Only nine different plots appear in Attachment 1: one 1x1, three 1x2, one 2x2, three 2x3, and one ˜3x3, dimensions expressed in yards. Usually you use ten plots for these studies. The missing plot was simply another 1x1, combined together in Attachment 1 as a single plot. Four yards separated the two plots of the 1x1s. We'll call the two distinct plots G and H.

In plot H the two plants from row 95, numbers 95.11 and 95.23, as well as the two plants from row 100, numbers 100.15 and 100.17 came from edge rows. This breaks the protocol.

We could also use row 86 and row 91 as edge rows for Plot G. But then which would be the edge rows for plot H? If all six rows in Plot H had plants chosen from them in the original lay out, then Plot H would have had six rows of twenty-five plants each for a total of one hundred and fifty plants in its sample space. This would contradict the protocol which assures us that each plot had roughly only 100 plants.

Why were no plants chosen from row 86 in Plot G? Under this more or less completely unreasonable scheme, row 85 was an edge row, as was row 90 for Plot G. So row 86 could have used. I don't know why no plants were chosen from it. Of course, it could be they simply had enough from the other rows. No rule demands they choose plants from every row available. We can also notice that there were a total of nine plants chosen from Plot G as well as nine chosen from the interior rows 96 through 99 in Plot H.

In the next diagram, we can draw the same row and column grid but this time we can put the number of grow days the plant had accumulated by the time it was harvested. At this point it's even clearer that column one was meant to be an outer column from which no plants were to be selected so as to preserve the density of the two plots. All of the thirty day plants were chosen from the first nine columns.

	1	2	3	4	5	6	7	8	9	10	11	12	13	14	15	16	17	18	19	20	21	22	23	24	25
85	P																								
86	L																								
87	O	30																							
88	I																								
89										91															
90	G										65	91		91			120		120						
91											65	91													
92											65														
93																									
94											65		91	91											
95	P										65			91		121			120			120			
96	L													91		121							120		
97	O	30							30																
98	I								30		65					121									
99									30		65				122		122								
100	H																								

Figure 108.
The harvest dates of the plants of the 1×1s.

Notice also that all of the sixty-five day plants were chosen from column eleven. This would have followed the protocol if column ten became the new outer column after the first cutting. In other words, they could have cut the first nine columns on day thirty. The next cutting, on day 65, came one column in.

But already the protocol has been violated in three different ways. First, it's even more clear that rows 95 and 100 were originally edge rows; more than likely the same is true of rows 90 and 85. Second, instead of cutting all of column ten, they left one plant, number 89.10 in place for another twenty-six days though the plants around it, numbers 88.11, 89.11, and 90.11 were all harvested on day 65. This would have given plant 89.10 extra sun, water, nutrients and so forth for almost an additional month. Third, the other 91 day old plants were all cut from columns 12, 13 and 14. But column 12 would have been a new edge column on day 65 when all of column 11 was cut. So edge effects are clearly present.

Thirty days later, the last cutting took place over three days, day 120, day 121 and day 122. Nine plants were chosen from the remaining plants in columns 15 through 25. Again, column 15 became a new outer column when column 14 was cut so plant 100.15 was harvested both from an outer column and an outer row. Number 100.15 was the second largest plant by weight of the mature 1x1s, weighing 2123.1 grams fresh. Again, edge bias is evident.

In the next diagram of the same grid, a capital letter S has been placed where a plant was designated as sinsemilla and a capital letter N has been placed where a plant was designated non-sinsemilla. The 1x1s are the only plots to contain both sinsemilla and non-sinsemilla mature plants together. All of the mature sinsemilla plants were 120 days old.

	100	99	98	97	96	95	94	93	92	91	90	89	88	87	86	85
1	H		T	O	L	P					G		T	O	L	P
2				S												
3																
4																
5																
6																
7																
8																
9		S	S													
10											S	S				
11		S				S				S	S	S				
12														S	S	
13				S	S											
14				S	S									S		
15	N															
16		N		N												
17	N													S		
18																
19				S										N		
20																
21																
22					N											
23						S										
24																
25																

Figure 109.
Sinsemilla and non-sinsemilla in the 1x1s.

Though we have already dismissed such claims in Chapter 4, it is interesting to see how Lewis decided which plants would be sinsemilla and which seeded. He scrambled the order of the plants but we can relist them by ascending row and column numbers:

87.17   S
87.19   N
95.23   S
96.22   N
97.19   S

Since the males admittedly weren't pulled, somewhere in Plot H there must have been a male that pollinated the group of four plants in columns 15 to 17, rows 97 to 100, numbers 97.16, 99.16, 100.15, and 100.17. Yet pollen from this male did not touch plant 97.19 very nearby. Wind blew pollen from a male to plant 96.22 but 95.23, diagonally next to it, was left a pure sinsemilla. Plant 87.19 became seeded but 87.17, one yard distant, was left sinsemilla.

2.   The 2x2s.   The row numbers range from 101 to 105, and the column numbers from 1 to 17 for the 2x2s. We can draw a grid with five rows of twenty squares that would have contained all of them and fit the declared protocol of approximately 100 plants per plot. What about the edge rows?

We could place two more rows, for seven total, around the rows numbered 101 to 105. But we notice that the 1x1s extend to row 100. And row number 106 is included in the almost 3x3s. So were the 2x2s given edge rows? Probably not. Does this violate the stated protocol? Yes. Is this a serious violation? You could argue that edge row 100 could do double duty as an edge row for both the 1x1s and the 2x2s. Perhaps it was designed that way. Later, of course, two plants of the 1x1s were selected from this row. It is more difficult to argue that row 106 of the almost 3x3s was meant as an edge row on the other side. Call this a technical violation.

Let's label this cultivation area for the 2x2s, Plot I. Again, we assume row and column for the decimal plant numbers. We place the plant's final grow day number in the square corresponding to its identification number from Attachment 1.

Once again, we see that, with one notable exception, the DEA harvested by columns. All the plants cut on day 30 were taken from column two, leading once again to the supposition that column one was originally meant to be an outer column from which no plants were to be selected. Column three was another outer column and all the plants harvested on day 64 came from column four. Column five was another outer column and the next cutting, on days 91 and 92 came from columns six and seven.

This is the most generous interpretation, given the declared protocol. But nothing supposes that column three was not cut on day 30, or column five on day 64. Had this happened, the plants for the subsequent cutting would have effectively been on an outer row for an extra thirty days of sun, water and fertilizer.

The remaining plants, the mature ones, came from columns eight through twenty with one very important exception. The last plant to be cut from the 2x2s, on day 129, came from column one! This was 103.01, one of the two by now famous anomalies, the very largest plant of all the plants grown by the DEA that summer, with a whopping 2308.4 grams of Leafnbud®, referred to proudly not once but twice in the paper.

And now we see why. Column one was not cut down, well not completely. No doubt the other plants in column one were cut down on day 30. But plant 103.01 was allowed to gather as much sunlight as it could handle. It was harvested last. And surprise, surprise, when a plant is grown without any competition whatsoever from its neighbors, it expands to fill as much space as it can.

Row	101	102	103	104	105
1			129		
2		30	30	30	
3					
4		64	64		64
5					
6		91		92	
7					91
8		122			
9		128	121		
10	122				
11					
12	122		127		
13					
14					
15					
16					
17				127	
18					
19					
20					

Figure 110.
The harvest dates for the 2x2s.

203

One thing is a plant that grows large within a given density as if by chance and quite another is a plant that has deliberately been grown to be as large as possible by removing all constraints of that density upon it. Plant 103.01, besides residing in a "low area" which received "additional water and possibly additional fertilizer" also received significantly greater sunlight throughout the entire summer. To this procedure we can rightly give a large raspberry and call out to the ref, "Unfair!"

3.   The ˜3x3s.   But the same exact thing occurred with the almost 3x3s. Why not have measured out exactly three yards by three yards instead of eight feet by nine feet? If we assume that the 100 yard line was the end of the football field, and the row numbers for the 2x2s and the almost 3x3s simply continued after that into the North end zone, then the answer is obvious: the designer was running out of space.

A college football field regulation end zone is ten yards. This was taken up by rows 101 to 105, the 2x2s. But beyond the end zone there is still more space on the field before the North end zone bleachers. How much? We don't know.

If the almost three by threes followed the two by twos on the field, then the remaining space on the field contained rows 106 to 109, the four rows of the almost 3x3s. The column numbers run from 1 to 19. So we assume this plot contained four rows of twenty plants each for a total of 80 plants. Again, given the lack of space implied by the dimensions of 8 feet by 9 feet, we can guess this plot also did not have edge rows. We can call this plot, Plot J.

How was the longest side aligned? Three yards by four rows gives twelve yards. Was there an extra twelve yards between the end of the end zone and the North bleachers? (This will become an important question when we discuss where the plants were grown, that is on which football field, in a subsequent chapter.) This would have allowed the short side, the eight feet to have been aligned across the field. Eight feet by twenty give 160 feet, exactly the regulation dimensions of the width of a college football field.

With a little fudging, the opposite probably could have been done too. Eight feet by four rows is thirty-two feet, meaning only a little over ten yards left before running into the North bleachers. Nine feet by twenty columns is 180 feet, but given the extra five or so yards on either side of the field before the East and West bleachers, this plot could also have been laid out with its longest side along the width of the field. If there had not been enough space we could also have placed it in the South end zone, its long side running in either direction.

Once again, we can draw the grid for Plot J. All the plants harvested on day 30 came, as in the 2x2s from column two. All the plants cut down on day 64 came from column 4, again exactly as with the 2x2s. Once again we suppose that column one was meant to be an outer column as was column three. Again, like Plot I, the plants harvested on the next cutting came from columns six and seven. After that, the mature plants were taken from columns nine through twenty, except for that nagging exception.

The second anomaly, plant number 107.01 also came from column one. This shows that not all the plants from column one were harvested on day 30. Once again, plant 107.01 received an entire summer's worth of sun, water and fertilizer without the messy intrusion of neighbors called for in the original protocol which so firmly declared its intention of controlling the density within each plot. Another raspberry for this second data-skewing super-sized plant.

Naturally, this makes one wonder legitimately if these were the only two anomalies grown on the field. We note the presence of plant number 44.00, original digital identification number obscured by Lewis, weighing better than ten kilos freshly harvested, almost five times as much as any other mature 1x2 in the so-called Hybrid plot. It seems to have been mostly stalk and branch, though, as its quantity of dry Leafnbud® was only a little over three times as great as the other mature plant listed in that plot, and only two and a half as great as the largest of the 1x2s in the Colombian plot.

109	108	107	106	
		129		1
30	30	30		2
				3
	64	64	64	4
				5
	91		91	6
91				7
				8
123				9
				10
123				11
128				12
				13
				14
				15
				16
128				17
				18
	128	128		19
				20

Figure 111.
The harvest dates in the almost 3x3s.

4.   The Harvest by Columns.   By   comparing   the
harvest dates of the 1x1s, 2x2s and almost 3x3s, we can see how the
harvest was conducted.   In this we will give the most generous
interpretation possible. The number of edge and neighbor effects will
be minimized.   These three plots we assume to have been planted
more or less at the same time.

On day 30 the first nine columns of Plots G and H, the 1x1s,
were cut. On day 30 (perhaps the same day), the first two columns of
the 2x2s (Plot I) were cut, except for 103.01 in the first row. On day
30 the first two columns of Plot J (the almost 3x3s) were cut, except
for 107.01.

On day 64, columns 3 and 4, the next two columns of Plot J
were cut. On day 64, columns 3 and 4 of Plot I were cut. On day 65
two columns, number 10 and 11, were cut from the 1x1s except for
89.10.

On day 91 three more columns, number 5, 6 and 7, were cut
from Plot J, the almost 3x3s. On day 91 three more columns from
Plot I, the 2x2s, were cut, except for 104.06 which was cut the next day.
On day 91, three more columns from the 1x1s, Plot G and Plot H,
numbers 10, 11 and 12, were cut, as well as 89.10.

On day 120 the remaining columns of the 1x1s were cut,
columns 15 through 25, except for 97.16 and 99.16 which were cut the
following day, and 100.15 and 100.17 which were cut the day after that.
On day 121 the rest of the plants of Plot I, the 2x2s, were cut, columns
8 through 20. The beginning of column 8 of the 2x2s corresponded to
the beginning of column 15 of the 1x1s. The exceptions were six:
numbers 102.08, 101.10, and 102.12 cut on day 122, numbers 103.12
and 104.17 cut on day 127, 102.09 cut on day 128, and the anomaly
103.01 cut on day 129. On day 123 the rest of the plants of Plot J, the
almost 3x3s were cut, except for numbers 109.12, 109.17, 107.19 and
108.19 cut on day 128, and the anomaly 107.01 cut on day 129.

G.   The Lay Out of the Field

Can we lay out all the plants on a single football field?   A
college football field is 160 feet by 300 feet. It has two end zones, each
of thirty feet, at either end.   Plus, there is more space at each end
before the North and South bleachers. There is at least one possible
arrangement of a 950 plant sample space that fits on a regulation
college football field, including edge rows.

In this arrangement the identification numbers for the 1x1s
suggest they could have been located between the 85th and 100th
yardlines. The 2x2s fit nicely in one of the ten yard end zones. The
eight feet by nine feet almost 3x3s almost fit in the other end zone. Or,
if we can find twelve yards between the end of the North end zone and
the North end bleachers, we can fit them in just after the two by twos.
Eight feet by twenty columns is 160 feet, exactly right for the width of
the field, with 80 plants in the plot of almost 3x3s.

The 2x3s at the other end of the field we can orient the other
way. In these plots we lay out five rows of 18 columns for our sample
space. So we need seven rows of two yards apiece or 14 yards, to
include the edge rows. Let's put Plot A between the 0 and 14 yardlines.
That allows us five inner rows and two outer rows. Each of the five
inner rows has eighteen plants, which fits in 162 feet, not perfect but
close enough for government work. In the same way we can put Plot
B between the 18 and 32 yardlines. That leaves us four yards between
plots A and B. Plot C then belongs between the 36 and 50 yardlines,
again with four yards separating B from C. Then each of the plots, A,
B, and C have 90 plants for their sample space.

All we have left are the three plots of the 1x2s. This time let's
orient the short side toward the end zones and the long side toward
the sidelines. Plot D will be the Colombian (deliberately mislabeled by
Lewis as plot E). Plot E, the Hybrid (mislabeled as plot F) will be next.
Plot F, the Jamaican, (mislabeled as plot H) can be third. For each of
the 1x2s we need six yards, four inner rows and two outer ones.

LAYOUT OF THE FIELD

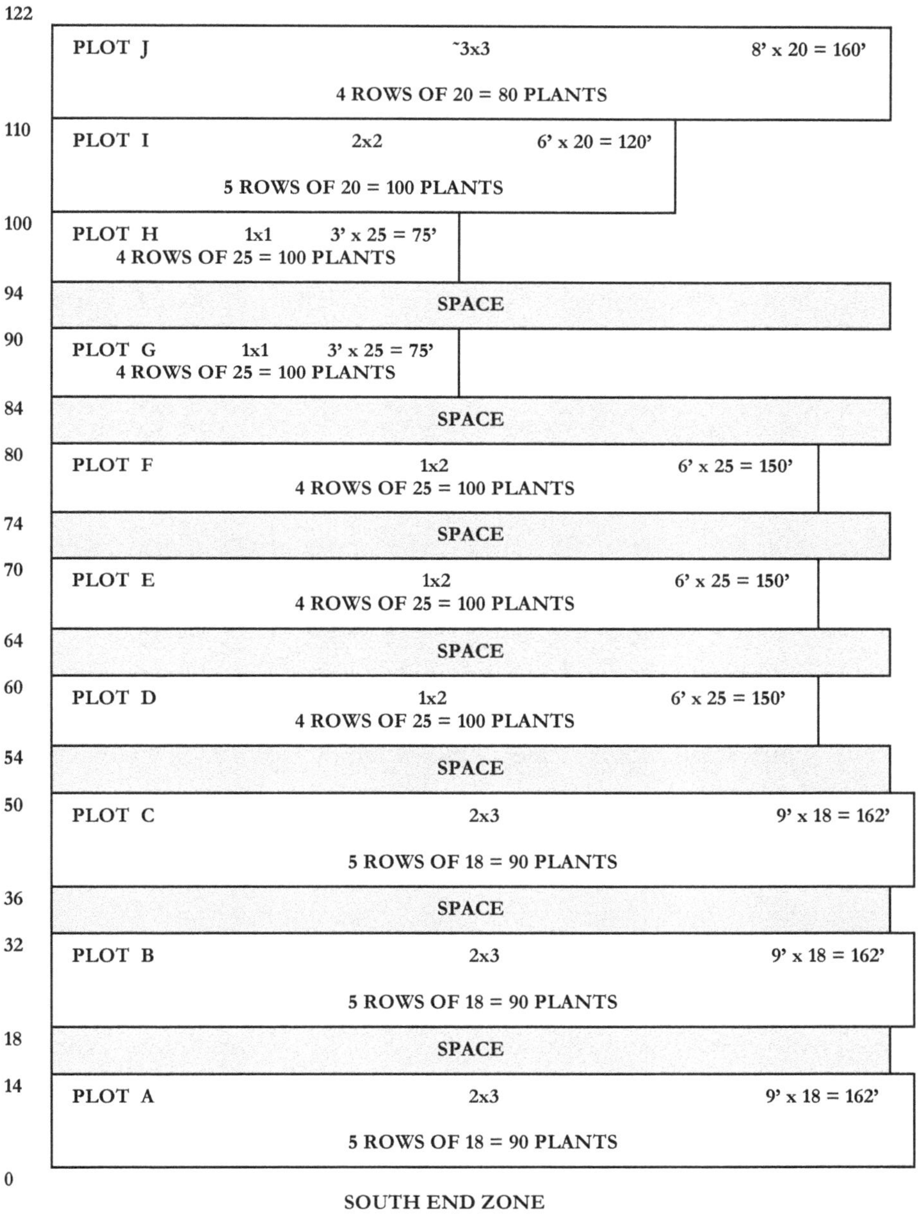

122			
	PLOT J	˜3x3	8' x 20 = 160'
		4 ROWS OF 20 = 80 PLANTS	
110	PLOT I	2x2	6' x 20 = 120'
		5 ROWS OF 20 = 100 PLANTS	
100	PLOT H	1x1	3' x 25 = 75'
		4 ROWS OF 25 = 100 PLANTS	
94		SPACE	
90	PLOT G	1x1	3' x 25 = 75'
		4 ROWS OF 25 = 100 PLANTS	
84		SPACE	
80	PLOT F	1x2	6' x 25 = 150'
		4 ROWS OF 25 = 100 PLANTS	
74		SPACE	
70	PLOT E	1x2	6' x 25 = 150'
		4 ROWS OF 25 = 100 PLANTS	
64		SPACE	
60	PLOT D	1x2	6' x 25 = 150'
		4 ROWS OF 25 = 100 PLANTS	
54		SPACE	
50	PLOT C	2x3	9' x 18 = 162'
		5 ROWS OF 18 = 90 PLANTS	
36		SPACE	
32	PLOT B	2x3	9' x 18 = 162'
		5 ROWS OF 18 = 90 PLANTS	
18		SPACE	
14	PLOT A	2x3	9' x 18 = 162'
		5 ROWS OF 18 = 90 PLANTS	
0			

SOUTH END ZONE

Figure 112. The Lay Out of the Field of Dreams.

We also add four yards between the plots for a total of ten yards per plot. Three times ten is thirty so the 1x2s fit between yardlines 54 and 84. This includes a four yard gap before the 1x1s begin on yardline 85. Plot G of the 1x1s goes between yardlines 85 and 90 and Plot H of the 1x1s fits between yardlines 95 and 100.

Why should we leave a four yard gap between plots? So we can drive in the leaf shredder? So we can pick up the freshly harvested plants in our truck and take them to the leaf shredder? So we can bring in the wood chipper to grind up the stalks and branches so they will fit on the trays that slide into the convection oven? So we can drive in the water cannon to irrigate the plants? I don't know. It does have the advantage of a certain consistency, though. And it repeats the four yard gap found between the two plots of the 1x1s.

By placing all the plants together on a single field, we can grow them in a single season. We already recognized that the so-called 1985 to 1986 plants were clearly one set of data, one set of plants that had been cut in two by Lewis. It must also be clear that the so-called 1990 to 1991 plants could also have been cut in two and scrambled, again by Lewis, trying to cover his tracks.

In Attachment 1, the plots are not organized by year or by density. First come the 2x3s from 1990, then the almost 3x3s, the 2x2s, and the 1x1s from 1991, followed by the 1x2s from 1990. Why would anyone do this? Either present them by year or present them by density.

Just for a moment, think like Lewis. What did he see originally in front of him? What he saw was the plots organized by density (this began as a yield/density study, after all). What he did in order to scramble them is the same thing he did when he scrambled the data from the 1x1s to make some of the five 120 day old plants sinsemilla. He assigned three of them randomly to be 1991 plants and the other two to be from 1990:

1x1s   1991
1x2s   1990
2x2s   1991
2x3s   1990
~3x3s   1991

But if he had left them in this order, what he had done would have been obvious. So he shuffled the result and this is the order in which they appear in Attachment 1:

2x3s   1990
~3x3s   1991
2x2s   1991
1x1s   1991
1x2s   1990

He left the letters for the 1990 plots in place, though he shuffled the letters for the 1x2s. He struck out the letters from the 1991 plots, though it is clear that he is only changing the titles and that originally the titles for these plots also took the form of variety, plot letter, and size. The dates he tacked on after the comma. After all, he used this same method for altering the titles of the data in Attachment 2.

What is certainly not in dispute is that the data as presented in Attachment 1 has been deliberately obscured. Not only are the plots mixed without regard to order of any kind, but much of the data internal to the plots had been deliberately cut and shuffled. No scientist, concerned with ordering his results in some logical fashion, would ever have done this.

H.   Discussion

The protocol wasn't followed. There were edge effects in the plots. In the 1x1s, plant numbers 90.11, 95.11, 95.23, 100.15 and 100.17 probably came from edge rows. In the 2x2s, plant numbers 101.10, 105.04 and 105.07 were most likely from edge rows. In the almost 3x3s, plant numbers 106.04, 106.06, 109.02, 109.07, 109.09, 109.11, 109.12 and 109.17 were probably grown on edge rows. In fact, the 2x2s and almost 3x3s do not appear to have had any edge rows at all. In the larger plots and for the younger plants, this may not have made much difference. For the older plants, there could very well have been some effect.

There were neighbor effects. In Plot G of the 1x1s, plant 89.10 was let stand after its neighbor 89.11 was harvested 26 days earlier. A similar thing occurred with plant 88.11 which was cut down on day 65 while its neighbor 88.12 was let stand until day 91. There were other minor neighbor effects in the 2x2s and the almost 3x3s but there the difference in harvest dates between the neighbors did not amount to more than a week.

There was selection bias. We know this because they admit it. The purpose of random selection is to eliminate investigator bias. In this case, it is clear that the investigators made a point of choosing the plants they liked, in particular the largest ones they could find. This dooms this study to be generalized to other plantations.

The anomalies, plant numbers 107.01 and 103.01, were deliberately manufactured; they did not occur by accident. Assuming row and column for the decimal plant numbers of the so-called 1991 plots, we can graph which plants were chosen, from which rows and columns, and when. We can see that these two anomalies were both grown on column one. In a sense, they are the mother of all examples of what happens with neighbor effects. They were allowed to remain alone without neighbors for the duration of the season in order to skew the calculations for that density, which would in turn bend the curves and allow for the production of the Poundaplant®.

All of the plants could have been grown on a single football field in a single season. The plants were planted in meters and harvested in yards. There is at least one arrangement of the ten plots that would allow all 950 plants in the sample space to be sited on a single football field of 300 by 160 feet, including their edge rows. Admittedly, this means the 2x2s and the almost 3x3s had to be grown at the end of the field, or at both ends. Neither of these two plots appears to have had edge rows.

Afterwards, Lewis did his best to obscure this information. He jumbled the plots, eliminated some letters and changed others. He cut the field in half, placing one half in one year and the other the following year. He jumbled up the plant numbers and zeroed out others, replacing them with empty decimals. He followed this same method of operations with the plants from the other study, those from 1985 and 1986.

But what exactly is Lewis trying to hide? He clearly doesn't want anyone to know at least three things. First, he doesn't want the reader to know the plants were grown in a single year. To do this he splits the year into two consecutive years. He also removes the original plant numbers from the 2x3s and the 1x2s, instead numbering them sequentially, though he mindlessly keeps the now useless decimal form. He takes off the plot letters for the 1x1s, 2x2s, and ~3x3s, but keeps the plot letters for the other six. The 1x1s that were originally two plots, Plot G and Plot H, he combines together in a single plot. But why is he so concerned about us finding out that the plants were grown in a single year?

Because if we know that, we can put the plants back together on a single field. And that field looks suspiciously like a college football field. And which college football field in Yoknapatawpha County would that be?

The second thing Lewis doesn't want us to know is *where* the plants were grown, that is on which football field. And the third thing he doesn't want us to know is *when*. But speculation on these two questions are the subject of Chapter 11.

Figure 113. Weighing #4, Espontanea, 2001.

Figure 114. Weighing #7, Warlock 00, 2001.

9
Les Miz

Enjolras: It is time for us all to decide who we are.
Do we fight for the right to a night at the opera now?
Have you asked of yourself what's the price you might pay?
... The colors of the world are changing days by day!
-- Les Misérables (2012)[1]

---

[1] Hooper, Tom, dir. Produced by Tim Bevan, et al., distributed by Universal Pictures, imdb.com.

By examining the section titled Miscellaneous Data Analysis, it is once again possible to conclude that some of the data is missing. Much of this was written by Dr. Sly and left as is by Lewis the Liar. It is worth taking this section apart because it reveals hidden insights into the minds and characters of the authors.

A.   Air Dry Weight

This subsection begins with a curiously ideological statement that, while purporting to be scientific, betrays the true purpose of the study. "The use of oven dry weights, although scientifically acceptable because it can be reproduced, under-represents the amount of *usable* material in the *illicit* market (page 8, italics added)." There is that lovely word, usable again. The word appears to be very usable to obfuscate the fact that the plants were shredded into three parts: a woody stem and denuded branches, seeds, and our favorite melange of Leafnbud®. It assumes a market for Leafnbud®, though none but DEA agents seem to be able to find it.

Is there a market for leaf? Will anyone get up in court and testify under oath to the huge black market in cannabis leaf? I have seen leaf given away, to the needy, who hope to comb through it for the leftover bracts. I have seen it composted.

Is there a huge market for Leafnbud®? I don't know anyone who buys a raw collection of mixed leaf and flower. Do you?

"Most *illegal* material is air dried or at the time of sale, is in equilibrium with surrounding atmosphere which contains a certain amount of moisture (page 8, italics added). I will add a nitpicking note on language. We often speak of black and white markets, as a shorthand. But illegal and illicit refer to a legal status. Sadly, our solons don't seem to be able to go a day without making something illegal. Nevertheless, technically, people, things, material, and markets cannot be illegal or illicit, as much as many would like to believe.

Human conduct can be sanctioned, that's all, whether rightly or wrongly.

But once again it is clear that there is not a whit of scientific objectivity here. The purpose of the paper is to convict. So far, we have seen them lie in almost every way possible, from altering data to simply making it up.

"*It is estimated* based upon *the* DEA studies that the leaf and bud material of cannabis would weigh an additional 10% to 20% if allowed to air dry naturally and equalize with the surrounding atmosphere (page 8, italics added)." Beware third person passive anonymity. Who estimated this? Certainly not the author.

What is this based on? *The* DEA studies? Which studies would those be? No doubt these unnamed studies, whose authors remain anonymous, were peer-reviewed by in-house DEA journals whose reviewers are also anonymous and whose reviews are still classified. Certainly nothing in *Cannabis Fields* permits one to draw a conclusion with regards to air dry versus kiln dry weights.

Is this self-declared fudge factor reasonable? Personally, I think it quite high as an estimate, but I admit freely that I have nothing to base that on. Then again, neither does the author. The range of this fudge factor is on the order of a hundred percent which is another reason I distrust it. If this is true, then bring these so-called studies into the light of day and allow a defendant the right to refute them. Until then, this is more faith-based policing.

Growers could add a fudge factor of their own, to the effect that any estimate based on the weight of the wet plant does not take into account the real world problems of handling and processing raw agricultural material. Based on secret unnamed studies that cannot be revealed to mere mortals, I can categorically state that handling losses *will be* 10 to 20 percent. Further, these same studies show without any doubt whatsoever that losses due to molds and pests, both two and multi-legged, *will be* another 10 to 20 percent. I lied. [See Appendix Three.]

B.   Water Content

"In addition to the yield [Leafnbud®] measurements, the amount of water contained in each plant was *measured* (page 8, italics added)." Well, not exactly. The plant wet weight was calculated from summing the weights of its three parts wet, the plant dry weight was calculated from summing the weights of its three parts dry, and the water content was calculated, not measured, by comparing the plant wet weight and the plant dry weight.

The second sentence in the paragraph reads, italics added: "A *mature* cannabis plant has, on a fresh weight basis, 66% water and 34% dry plant matter (leaves, buds, seeds, stems/branches)." Is it cheeky to ask at this point just what a mature cannabis plant is, for the purposes of this section of the paper? When we started it was 120 grow days. Then it morphed, strangely, to 119 days. After that, it became 90 days, but only for the non-existent sinsemilla of Figure 2.

Therefore, a mature cannabis plant *will be* considered one of the 38 plants listed in Attachment 1 that had obtained at least 120 grow days as per the original definition on page 2: "Table 1 depicts the average yield [Leafnbud®] for all mature (120 days or older) cannabis plants ...." Noted are rounding errors on plants 107.17 and 107.01 which should have been listed as 63 and 69 percent water, not 62 and 68. As well, plant 102.08 should have been 57 not 56 percent water. The percentage of water for each plant was calculated to seven decimals which was then rounded to integers, since that is how these numbers are presented in the paper. I summed these integer percents to get 2401 altogether, which, divided by 38, is 63.1821, or 63 percent, not 66. This tells us nothing but that a different set of data was used to make this calculation. Plant dry matter (stalk/branches, seeds and Leafnbud® amounted to 37% on average of the DEA's mature cannabis plants in Attachment 1.

The third sentence in this paragraph reads, truthfully: "Plant water content can vary with plant age." It then lies: "Young plants less than 55 days old have a water content ranging from 75% to 82%." There are 13 plants in Attachment 1 with harvest days less than 55 days old: nine 30 day old plants from 1991 and four 36 day old plants from plot B. They range in water content from 67% for plant 107.02 to 78% for plant 103.02. If the author meant to include the four 55 day old plants in plot A, then his statement should have read: "Young plants less than *or equal to* 55 days old ...." If we add these four to the original 13, we have 17 so-called young plants with less than or equal to 55 grow days. These have a water content from 67% for plant 107.02 to 82% for plant 1.00.

The last sentence of this paragraph states: "Older plants have water content ranging from 60% to 70%." In fact, 55 day or older plants have a range of water content from 56% for plants 97.16 and 100.17 to 82% for plant 1.00. Plants older than 55 days ranged in water content from 56% for plants 97.16 and 100.17 to 79% for plants 27.00 and 28.00.

I don't know why young plants are those defined to be ones with less than 55 grow days. At any rate, the comparison he makes is between young plants with a range of 67 to 78 percent water content to the so-called older plants with a range of 56 to 82 percent. If you pretend he meant to include 55 day old plants as young, then the comparison is between 67 to 82 percent for young and 56 to 79 percent water content for older plants. I fail to see the point.

The distinction between mature and non-mature was not made. I corrected the rounding errors for the non-mature plants, as well. Plant 109.07 should have 69% water content listed, not 68. Plant 88.12 should have 71% not 72. Mature plants (with at least 120 grow days) had a water content ranging from 56% for plants 97.16 and 100.17 to 75% for plant 44.00. Non-mature plants had a range of water content from 63% for plant 105.07 to 82% for plant 1.00. The range within each category is 19%. The end points of the range shift by 7% when changing to the other category.

C.   Plant Height

The section begins: "The average height of a mature cannabis plant was between 270 cm and 350 cm (8.6 – 11.5 feet)." Here, mature must be taken to mean plants with at least 120 grow days. Actually, the data in Attachment 1 tells us that the range is from 152 cm for plant 43.00 to 338 cm for plant 104.17. Again, this is only more evidence that this observation was made on a different set of plants.

We know there were plants that were measured but not included in Attachment 1 because of the next two statements: "A few cannabis plants were measured in excess of 400 cm (13.1 feet). The tallest plant recorded was 430 cm (14.1 feet)." But Attachment 1 has no plants that have heights above 341 centimeters, specifically number 11.00, in plot A. So, no plants in Attachment 1 have heights greater than 400 cm and the tallest plant in Attachment 1 was nearly 90 cm less than that recorded in this section. Why were these taller plants not included?

Generally but not always, the taller plants will also be the plants that grow in reduced space. They grow taller not because they can but because they have to, to compete with the other plants in the vicinity. Given enough space, they will tend to spread out. This makes one suspect that the omitted taller plants came from the higher density plots, probably giving smaller quantities of Leafnbud® and making them less usable for achieving a Poundaplant®.

D.   Crop Cycle

This section is boilerplate. It seems the author was in a bit of a reverie as he copied it. In the Linda Smith version, we have: "The first stage is the vegetative *state* [sic] .... and the vegetative *state* [sic] extends until late July and early August (page 8, italics added)." The second error has been corrected in the Konrad version, but the first remains.

It would be nice if it were true, that the vegetative and fruiting stages are so distinct and clearly delineated. What I found from taking measurements at the ARSECA Research Centre is that the plants are often growing as they are flowering, though it is certainly true that the growing eventually tapers off toward the end of the season. I also found a great deal of diversity as to when this happens, depending upon the variety of the plant. Some began flowering quite early and others seemed to hang on until nearly Christmas.

"The transition ... results from the reduction in day length associated with the photoperiod peaking on the summer solstice of June 21 (pages 8, 9)." Certainly, this is important. Researchers at ARSECA grew plants beginning in January and February which flowered in April and early May. These flowers were harvested and the plants allowed to remain in the ground. Some of these plants went back into growth mode until they flowered again in September and October. So yes to photoperiod but some of the plants also have an internal clock that is at least as important in flowering.

"Beginning in August ... huge amounts of pollen are released (page 9)." The plants grown in southern Spain often received pollen from Morocco, or so many were convinced. In Hawaii, a grower who had not properly pulled his males routinely endangered the other plantations downwind across the island.

Males develop at different rates, like the females. Some show up early, others quite late. But if there is any pollen in the vicinity, and pollen shadows can extend for miles or tens of miles, it is almost certain to pollinate any existing female plants. This experience caused me to laugh out loud when the DEA claimed in the paper to be able to produce sinsemilla plants without pulling the males.

"The male plants usually die by the middle of September or soon after they release their pollen (page 9)." I do not believe male cannabis plants are like salmon. But honestly I can only speak from experience, and I have never tried to keep a male plant alive in the field just to see what it would do. I have always pulled them at the first opportunity. I have seen male plants in the middle of September and they appeared to be quite robust. In South America I have observed male plants quite late in the season. I doubt very much this theory of spontaneous self-extinction promoted by the author of these words.

It would suit the DEA very much if every plant they seized would be female. I doubt the average agent can tell one from the other. It's not that it can't be done but it's a bit of a learned art. There are those who are good at it and those who are better. But no DEA agent acts as an impartial agent in these matters. If all plants are female, then every plant seized could have produced a quantity of flowers, whether male or female, and the magic number that will convict the home gardener just became that much larger.

E.   Yield Adjustment Factors

This is a strange subsection. The first paragraph continues the discussion of males versus females. The first line reads: "There is no need to adjust yield [Leafnbud®] estimations of outdoor mature cannabis crops if at the time of seizure there are no male plants (page 9)." Notice that in this case the so-called yield of male plants is nothing but male leaves. But if the DEA can tell male from female, why are they seizing male plants? If they did not seize them, then they would not have to "adjust yield estimations."

The second line is: "If male plants are present, then evidence of this fact should be apparent by early August (page 9)." Should be but often isn't. Hence, the importance of good plant doctors who can read a plant's sex early.

"The estimated yield [Leafnbud®] of a male plant in early August, the point at which it begins to senesce and loose [sic] leaf cover, *will be* approximately 50% of the weight of a female plant of similar age and growth stage (page 9, italics added)." Too bad no evidence is presented for this statement. By this time, whenever I read this author using the existential future tense I detect the whiff of a little man making categorical statements he does not intend to prove. Here he is using the future tense in place of the conditional or the subjunctive, as in, might be, could be, would be, should be, I sure hope it is, it would sure be convenient if it is, sounds good so let's put it in.

"By late September or October, the only harvestable plants remaining will be female plants." He hopes so, anyway. Even if generally true for many home growers who are trying to grow sinsemilla, making a categorical statement like this is silly. The author does not know.

The second paragraph in this section is more interesting. It begins: "If the female cannabis plants are unfertilized, then no seed will be produced." You would think a statement like this would be so obvious it would not need inclusion in a supposedly scientific paper. But in fact, it is not true. While this may be true for other plants, this is not true for cannabis.

Cannabis retains the ability to clone itself. Most plants lost this useful talent when they developed sex. But female cannabis plants, late in the season, when they are not becoming fertilized, will sometimes, even often, develop hermaphrodite characteristics and pollinate themselves. Though a grower may believe he has succeeded in growing a sinsemilla plant, next Spring there will be a half dozen or more seeds at the bottom of the box. Hermaphroditism is not discussed in *Cannabis Fields*, as noted by Konrad.

The second paragraph in this subsection continues: "The average usable yield (leaf and bud) of a mature female plant will be 57% of the plant's dry weight where as [sic] the yield [Leafnbud®] for a typical fertilized seed bearing cannabis plant will be 34% of the the [sic] plant dry weight (Figure 2)." (The Linda Smith version has "tile the.") This is a typical line ending mistake and a popular sight puzzle which only shows there is a third copy somewhere on a DEA floppy that is an earlier version of the Konrad.

For me this is more of the tremor of forgery. There are no sinsemilla plants. The first part of the sentence should have read:

"The average usable yield (leaf and bud) of a mature female *sinsemilla* plant ...." The author is attempting to make a distinction between seeded and seedless cannabis. But there were no sinsemilla, as the author of this sentence well knows. It looks to me like Lewis the Liar has grafted the first part of the sentence onto Dr. Sly's original note with regards to all female cannabis plants, all of which were non-sinsemilla.

But both numbers in this sentence are incorrect as we showed in Chapters 3 and 4. The data set has been altered, so the 34% of Leafnbud® referred to in the top pie chart of Figure 2 should really be 37%. Of course, there was no separation of bud. The bottom pie chart we showed in Chapter 4 to be completely cut from whole cloth. The data in Attachment 1 suggest the correct average weight of Leafnbud® for the so-called sinsemilla plants was 38%, not 57%. This is because there were no sinsemilla and Lewis the Liar simply added the missing seed data that he had zeroed to the stalk/stem data producing the absurd result that a mature sinsemilla plant had 62% of its dry weight in stalk, versus 41% for a non-sinsemilla.

F.   Discussion

Repeatedly, the numbers do not add up. The percentage of water content for mature female plants is incorrect. The ranges are incorrect for both young and older plants. The ranges are inaccurate for plant heights. The section on crop cycle ignores hermaphroditism and asserts the dying salmon theory of male plants. The section on yield adjustment asserts statements about the relative weight of male to female plants without even attempting to refer to some unnamed study. The statements referring to Figure 2, comparing dry weights to the weights of Leafnbud® have already been shown to be false in Chapters 3 and 4, both because the data set has been altered and because the data that does exist has been altered.

Figure 115. Secadero, 2008; 2007.

Figure 116. Secadero, 2004.

10
The Domestic Overestimate

Bedevere: There are ways of telling whether she is a witch. ...
What do you burn apart from witches? ... First Peasant: Wood.
Bedevere: Does wood sink in water? ... Second Peasant: No. It floats.
Bedevere: What else floats in water? ... Knight in crowd: A duck.
Bedevere: Exactly. So, logically, if she weighs the same
as a duck, she's made of wood. ... Use my larger scales.
(The peasants place the suspected witch
and a duck on either side of the huge balance.)
Bedevere: Right. Remove the supports!
(The scales rise, fall and then even out. The peasants
merrily go off to burn the witch. Bedevere (to the Knight):
Who are you who are so wise in the ways of science?
-- Monty Python and the Holy Grail (1975)[1]

A.   **Methodology to His Madness**
    1.   **Non-sinsemilla**
    2.   **Sinsemilla**
B.   **Averaging the Average**
C.   **Ideology Betrayed**
D.   **Discussion**

---

[1] Gilliam, Terry and Terry Jones, dirs. Produced by Mark Forstater and Michael White, distributed by EMI Films/Rainbow Releasing/Cinema 5 Distributing, imdb.com.

And then a miracle occurs. The Domestic Estimate has clearly been tacked on, like the tale of Job's fourth false friend. It is a poorly explained jumble of unconnected and preposterous statements. No rational person would have tried to string one unrelated bit of nonsense after another and expected it to convince. Nevertheless, this section eventually becomes the whole point of the study. Agent Lost may be the reason the War on Drugs is lost.

A.   Methodology to His Madness

It begins hopefully: "The identification of accurate plant yield [Leafnbud®] estimation methodologies makes possible the opportunity to estimate the average domestic yield [Leafnbud®] using eradication statistics and plant canopy diameter information (page 9)." As we have already seen, the use of diameters to predict anything is problematic. Only the longest diameter was measured, the measuring process is imperfect, and the diameters do not predict well the dry weight of the plant. More importantly, the presence of the two manufactured anomalies has warped the curve in Figure 4 between diameter and plant dry weight.

Another unpublished, classified, non-peer reviewed study is introduced: "A survey of *15 leading producer states* was conducted by the DEA to determine the average diameter of *mature* plants eradicated in September 1991 (page 9, italics added)." If after a century of drug war, there are 15 leading producer states for cannabis, my best advice would be to try something else. But I particularly like how the language approaches a business or economics report; we could be talking of soybean or wheat production. The definition of mature is unexplained so we have no choice but to revert to the original, that of a plant with 120 or more grow days.

The survey seems to be some bureaucrat's brainstorm. There is no mention of previous surveys. Here is some more paperwork for some office drone to fill out. Someone must get blamed.

"Table 4 lists the average plant diameter of mature plants observed in that state as reported by the DEA state eradication coordinator (page 9)." What a thankless job. So some clown has circulated 50 copies of a questionnaire to the poor fools designated this week as the eradication coordinators, who immediately turn them over to their secretaries.

Looking at Table 4, you can almost read the options on the form they have received: What would you estimate to be the average diameter of the plants eradicated in your state this year? A) Three feet three inches? B) Three feet six inches? C) Three feet nine inches? D) Four feet? Or, E) Four feet three inches?

How am I supposed to know this, sir? Oh Mabel, just put down something. Here is a survey asking questions for which no one had ever bothered to collect data. Which state eradication coordinator was out in the field with a tape measure that fall? The truth is, no one really knows the answer, the questionnaire has to be completed, and there are five choices. Pick one.

Coupled with the inaccurate diameter to plant dry weight formula, this newly made up survey information is duly processed as if it had some meaning. The most popular choice was four feet. They might as well be recording the weights of the witches they threw into the pond to see if they would float.

The most interesting thing about Table 4 is that it is made up of two unrelated bits of information crammed together into a single table. On the left are the names of 15 states and to the right of them the totals, to the plant, of all the cannabis macheted that year by all the different police agencies, city, county, state and federal in that state. Let us assume, for purposes of argument that the total for Texas was, in fact, exactly 22,997 and not 22,996 or simply somewhere north of

20K. How many angels can dance on the head of a pin. And the purpose of this information is?

We are not going to use any of this except the average. The names and numbers in the two left columns of Table 4 will not be used in any calculation the author is going to make to arrive at his domestic overestimate. The only purpose of listing this information is to prove that someone is busy diligently making up numbers to report to someone else further up the chain of obedience and command, much like the inflated body counts in Vietnam. The numbers are not aligned to the right in the Konrad version; they are in the earlier Linda Smith, with the exception of Texas. It wasn't intended that they be summed. They add to 3,294,917. That leaves 1,962,569 plants to be eradicated in the thirty-five other producer states. Why didn't they use the average for all 50 states?

But the right half of Table 4 has no connection with the left. The center column lists the numbers chosen by the secretaries of the state eradication coordinators filling out the survey form and making guesses as to what an average plant would look like if you took it in for a line-up. But the right two columns are not data provided from the states or connected in any way with the plant totals. The right two columns are what a given diameter would correspond to in grams of Leafnbud®, depending on whether it was sinsemilla or non-sinsemilla.

The rightmost three columns could have been presented alone, along with the formula from Figure 4 that generated them. There is no connection to the plant totals. The Arkansas state eradication coordinator reported 106,405 plants eradicated in 1991. The Alabama state eradication coordinator reported 163,294. Both of the secretaries to their respective state eradication coordinators chose option D, four feet, to be their best guess as to what the diameter of an average plant would be. Both have the same data reported in columns four and five, 369 and 630 grams respectively, which add suspiciously to 999 grams. A four foot diameter plant produced the same amount of Leafnbud® in each state. But what does this have to do with the plant totals?

The second thing you notice about Table 4 is that the numbers of sinsemilla and of non-sinsemilla are not reported. Instead, only the grams of Leafnbud® are listed, corresponding to the plant diameter. This suggests that the data as to whether a plant was sinsemilla or not was never collected either in the Fall of 1991, along with the non-existent data with regards to plant diameters. What we are given instead is a hypothetical: this plant diameter corresponds to that amount of grams of Leafnbud® if that plant had been sinsemilla and to this amount of grams of Leafnbud® if that plant had been non-sinsemilla.

"The estimated usable yield [Leafnbud®] for each state's eradicated plant total was calculated using the predictive methodology described in Figure 4 (pages 9, 10)." No, the diameters selected by the secretaries of the state eradication coordinators were plugged into the formula in Figure 4 to generate the grams of Leafnbud® the plant might have produced depending on whether or not the plant was sinsemilla or non-sinsemilla, which is obviously not known. These numbers in columns four and five of Table 4 depend on the formula in Figure 4, which we have already shown in Chapter 6 to be based on some other set of plants than the one given in Attachment 1, as well as the percentages of Leafnbud® in Figure 2, which were also demonstrated to be faked in Chapters 3 and 4.

So far we have a faked, after the fact seat-of-the-secretary's-pants-suit guesstimate of an average plant's diameter married to a formula that isn't based on anything other than a deliberately skewed data set and percentages of Leafnbud® also taken from some other set of plants. This can only give us a wildly inaccurate plant dry weight. But the madness of this methodology has only begun.

1.   Non-sinsemilla.   "This methodology uses average plant canopy diameter information as the predictor variable to estimate plant dry weight. The plant dry weight is adjusted to estimate usable air dry weight by first taking 34% of the dry weight to calculate usable yield [Leafnbud®], and adding 10% to the oven dry weight to obtain the air dry yield [Leafnbud®]. This estimate is valid for female cannabis plants at maturity which contain seeds." Did you get that?

First, plug in the plant diameter in the formula given in Figure 4, which is -3.768 + 0.0666 (X)^2 and is incorrect based on the data given in Attachment 1. X is measured in centimeters, not feet, so we have to convert. For example, 3.25 feet is 3 feet three inches, or 39 inches, which is 99.06 centimeters. Squaring this gives 9812.8836, times 0.0666 gives 653.53804 and minus 3.768 is 649.77004 grams for the plant dry weight. Multiply this by 0.34 gives 220.92181. Add ten percent and we have 243.01399 grams of air dried Leafnbud® for this seeded plant. Table 4 gives 243 grams.

Or we would have 243.01399 grams of air dried Leafnbud® if Figure 2 were correct. But it isn't. The Figure 2 drawn from the data in Attachment 1 should have 36.74% Leafnbud®, as we demonstrated in Chapter 3. If we multiply 649.77004 by .3674 we get 238.72551. Add ten percent and we have 262.60306 grams of air dried Leafnbud®.

Are there any mature seeded plants in Attachment 1 with a diameter of 99.06 centimeters? No. Plants with diameters close to this are only reported in the 1x1 and 1x2 plots. What if we look at all the mature plants between 80 and 120 centimeters? There are only three non-sinsemilla plants that fit this range: plant number 87.19 with a diameter of 112 centimeters and a yield [Leafnbud®] of 244.7 grams, number 96.22 with 113 cms and 214.2 grams of Leafnbud® and number 99.16 with 83 cms and 162.8 grams. The yield [Leafnbud®] sums to 621.7, which divided by three is 207.23333. Add ten percent to get 227.95666. So our unofficial spot check is overestimated by the formula in Figure 4 and the false numbers in Figure 2 by about 15%.

2.   Sinsemilla.   But this is only for seeded plants. What about the seedless (of which there were none) in Attachment 1, as noted in Chapter 4? The Domestic Estimate section has a methodology for these also on page 10:   "An estimate for seedless cannabis (sinsemilla) is derived by first taking 58% of the plant dry weight, and then adjusting upward by 10% to convert from oven dry weight to an air dry yield [Leafnbud®]." The Linda Smith has a line missing. It reads: "An estimate for seedless cannabis weight, and then adjusting upward by 10% to convert from oven dry weight to an air dry yield [Leafnbud®]." Missing is: "(sinsemilla) is derived by first taking 58% of the plant dry." This tells us that Dr. Sly calculated the seeded formula and Lewis added on the seedless formula.

This 58% contrasts with the 57% reported in the previous subsection, Yield Adjustment Factors, on page 9: "The average usable yield (leaf and bud) of a mature female cannabis plant will be 57% of the plant's dry weight ...." So, which is it, 57% or 58%? The answer, like the definition of mature, depends on which section of the report you are reading at the time.

The bottom pie chart of Figure 2 does indeed show its bud and leaf percentages add to 58%. But we saw in Chapter 4 this is an absurdity. The sinsemilla in Attachment 1 were manufactured after the fact. Lewis simply zeroed the seed data. The excised seed data was then added to the stalk data. In fact, one of their mature sinsemilla plants has 38% Leafnbud® on average, almost exactly that of a mature (>/= 120 grow days) seeded plant (36.74%), the only kind that ever existed before Lewis the Liar altered Attachment 1.

Are there any mature seedless plants in Attachment 1 with a diameter of 99.06 centimeters? No, so once again let's look at those between 80 and 120 centimeters. There are four: plant number 97.19 with a diameter of 83 centimeters and a yield [Leafnbud®] of 126.8 grams, number 95.23 with a 99 centimeter diameter and 198.1 grams of Leafnbud®, 87.17 whose diameter of 95 cms corresponded to 157.8 grams, and number 40.00 with 100 cm diameter and 153.5 grams of Leafnbud®. Sum them to get 636.2 and divide by 4 to get 159.05. Add ten percent and we have 174.955 average grams of Leafnbud®, air dried, for a sinsemilla in Attachment 1.

What does the methodology in the domestic estimate suppose it to be? Once again, the formula in Figure 4 estimates the plant dry weight as 649.77004. But according to the bottom pie chart of Figure 2, we must now take 58% of this number to find the oven dry yield of Leafnbud®, or 376.86662. Adding ten percent gives in grams of air dried Leafnbud® 414.55328. Compare this to our unofficial 174.955 average from the four plants closest in diameter to 99.06 centimeters in Attachment 1, a whopping 137% difference.

This occurs because Lewis added the seed data to the stalk data in Attachment 1 but added the percentage of seed to the Leafnbud® in Figure 2 to create his pie chart of a mythical sinsemilla. He appears to believe that a sinsemilla plant would have as much extra Leafnbud® as a nonsinsemilla plant has seed. This may well be true. But plants in their flowering stage are unlikely to grow new leaves and stalk. So all of this increase has to come from new flowers. This contradicts not only his division of leaf from bud in Figure 2 but the data in Attachment 1 where a sinsemilla plant has almost the same weight in Leafnbud® (38%) as a seeded plant (36.74%). Do sinsemilla plants generate more weight in flowers than seeded plants? I have no data to support this and neither does he.

B.   Averaging the Average

After all this, we could use a miracle. We are ready to find the average quantity of Leafnbud® for any given female cannabis plant in North America. We are ready for Poundaplant®!

"The average yield [of Leafnbud®] for the entire outdoor domestic cultivated cannabis crop can be calculated by averaging the non-sinsemilla and sinsemilla yields [of Leafnbud®] in the same proportion as reported in the 1991 end of year eradication program results (page 10)." But none of that is in Table 4, which does not show the proportion of sinsemilla to non-sinsemilla plants for any given state, because no one had ever bothered to ask and no one could be bothered to check.

That, however, will not stop Lewis: "The total number of cultivated outdoor cannabis plants eradicated in 1991 was 5,257,486. The number of sinsemilla plants was 2,251,735 or 42.8% of the total, and the number of non-sinsemilla plants was 3,005,751 or 57.2% of the total (page 10)." No data is presented to substantiate these two sentences. The totals are not broken down by seeded or seedless, and only a hypothetical is presented, evidence no data was ever collected.

Moreover, these numbers are only suspiciously close to those the Deaity® decided upon in Attachment 1. There, 17 of the mature plants were sinsemilla or 44.73684% of the total while 21 of the mature plants were non-sinsemilla or 55.26315% of the total. Compare 42.8% and 57.2% percent. But in fact Lewis manufactured the sinsemilla by zeroing the seed data. So he can make up any percentage he wants. He argues that it is a general principle of nature that in any group of mature female cannabis plants anywhere in North America some 55 to 57% will become seeded and some 42 to 44% will be sinsemilla.

Finally: "A weighted average using the yields reported in Table 4 results in an average domestic plant yield of 448 grams or approximately 1 pound per plant [of Leafnbud®]." But all of the supposed numbers in the left two columns of Table 4 are roughly 63% to 37% of air dried Leafnbud®. Thus, 589/934 is .6306209 and 345/934 is .369379. So, working backwards, 42.8% of 63% of X plus 57.2% of 37% of X must equal 448, where X is air dried Leafnbud®. In other words 48% of X is 448. Now we just choose some number to be the average (3.85 feet, roughly 117 centimeters) that will give us X. Once we have warped the curve in Figure 4, there must be some such number, in this case 934. Magic.

C. Ideology Betrayed

In the last paragraph, the gloves come off: "The application of detailed field measurements and mathematical analysis techniques has shown that cannabis plant yields can be accurately estimated (page 11)." Well, no. Perhaps cannabis plant yields can be accurately estimated. But *Cannabis Fields* has only demonstrated that they weren't. Their "detailed field measurments" were made on plants they chose for their own biased reasons, plants manufactured to be the largest they could grow, the others being obscured, erased, obfuscated and hidden. Their "mathematical analysis techniques" were bogus, chosen only to support the conclusions they wanted to get.

It ends hopefully as well: "Continued field observations at illicit cultivation locations, both domestically and overseas, will provide the opportunity to further validate the relationships reported." We're not narcs busting growers, we're scientists. "Development of cannabis yield methodologies is essential for understanding of the size of illicit cultivation problem and the drug abuse threat." What you eat, drink or smoke is our business. Even if it isn't, it is certainly our rice bowl.

D. Discussion

Another unpublished, non-peer reviewed study is introduced, a survey of 15 leading producer states that will never be used again. The survey was ad-hoc and no data was actually taken from plants. These phony diameter estimations of some poor office drone are then plugged into the formula from Figure 4. Neither the diameters nor the ratio of sinsemilla to non-sinsemilla were ever recorded in the field. These are then multiplied by the demonstrably faked percentages derived from the non-sinsemilla and non-existent sinsemilla pie charts of Figure 2. The over-estimation of sinsemilla yields [of Leafnbud®] is particularly absurd. An average is chosen that gives the answer they want. But this is what happens when science is used to weigh witches.

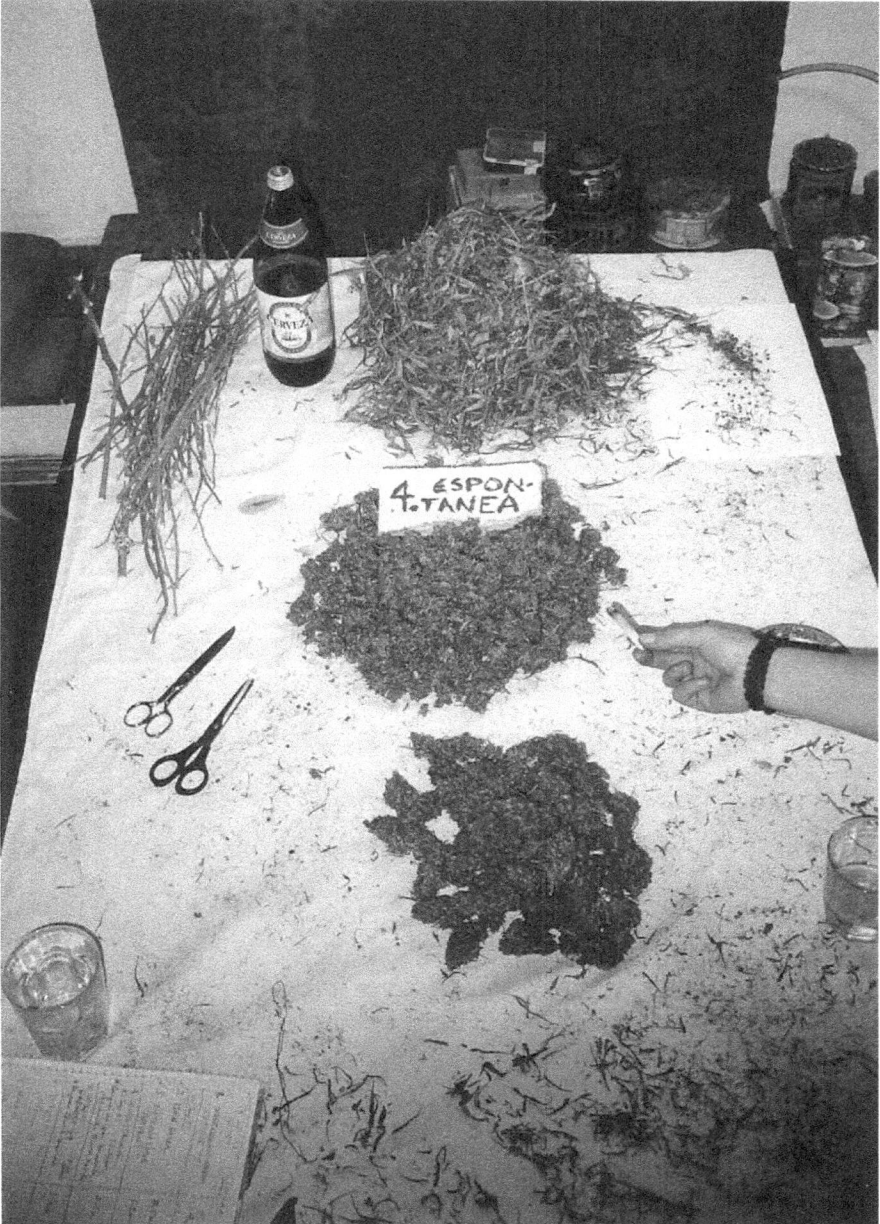

Figure 117. What the DEA did not do.
Separating #4, Espontanea, 2001.

Figure 118. Separating #6, Warlock, 2001.

11
Mouth-to-Mouth Tales

We have a few old mouth-to-mouth tales;
we exhume from old trunks and boxes
and drawers letters without salutation
or signature, in which men and women
who once lived and breathed are now
merely initials or nicknames ....
-- William Faulkner (1897 – 1962)[1]

A.   **Where**
    1.   **The Final Frontier**
    2.   **An Existential Problem**
    3.   **They Built That**
    4.   **A Mythical Stadium**
B.   **When**
C.   **Discussion**

---

[1] Absalom, Absalom! New York: Random House, a photographic reproduction of the first printing of 26 October 1936, pp. 100-101; see also www.seno.edu.

$\mathbf{A}$ll the plants in Attachment 1 could have been grown on a single football field. The deliberate altering and obscuring of the data in Attachment 1 and Attachment 2 suggests that at least one of the authors of *Cannabis Fields* is attempting to hide both where and when the plants were grown. But which field and when?

A.   Where

Okay, so the plants fit on a football field.   We have seen that the plot labels and plant numbers have been altered in Attachment 1, which leads us to suspect that the plants said to have been grown in 1990 and 1991 were likely grown together in the same year. The same reasoning leads us to suspect the same about the plants said to have been grown in 1985 and 1986. A single year supposes a single space.

1.   The Final Frontier.   So why couldn't this space have been a football sized space cut into the many thousands of acres of piney woods in Yoknapatawpha County? This makes sense and appears to be exactly what they eventually did. Under this scheme, the field was laid out, the sections were labeled, and the plants were grown and harvested miles from any civilized community.

So why are the almost 3x3s not 3x3s? If they can cut a football field and both end zones, why not cut enough space to make the final plot as a full three yards by three yards instead of eight feet by nine feet? After all, they can cut the field any size they want and they have plenty of piney woods.

The answer that keeps demanding to be considered is simply, they were running out of space. Which is to say, the designer, Dr. S, had only a limited amount of space in which to grow all ten plots. He did the best he could with what he had.   But there were certain physical limitations he had to work within.

2.   An Existential Problem.   Which forces a return to the idea of an existing facility, that is, a football field that existed prior to the idea of growing a cannabis plantation there. Let's make it a regulation college football field of 300 by 160 feet, two ten yard end zones and probably some extra space between the end zones and some obstruction that we can suppose to be a set of bleachers.

An existing football field solves a number of problems. It explains the almost three by threes. It explains the lack of edge rows for the last two plots, the 2x2s and the almost 3x3s. It also explains why the plots were laid out in yards but were harvested in meters.

The designer uses an existing football field's already existing grid of yard lines and hash marks to save the time, expense and trouble of cutting a new one. He lays out his plots not in meters but using the existing yard lines. The conversion from the English to the metric system is comparably less onerous, if somewhat inconvenient, than the alternative.

3.   They Built That.   Where are regulation college football fields usually built? Junior high, high school, college, and university campuses, and professional fields, bowls and stadiums come to mind. But the technology of creating a modern football field is no easy task. It requires considerable infrastructure.

Just for this study, they would only have needed to repurpose such a field. But to grow and process this much cannabis would have required no small amount of work. This field contained roughly 1000 plants. This is not your three potted plants on a sunny balcony.

First, you'll need some order. Yard lines are already marked. You would want some more. Ideally, you might want to cross hatch the entire field, at least those portions where the plots are going to be. Thus, the 1x1 plots might have had north to south one yard lines marked to go with the east to west yard lines already there on the field. This would have given the planting team clearly marked spaces in which to transplant the seedlings for the 1x1s, for example.

Marking a field is done with a line marker. An athletic department would have one and the personnel who have the experience to know how to use it, and the extra bags of chalk. Of course, you could just buy one on the open market.

You'll need some greenhouses to house the seedlings. The footnote to Table 2 on page 3 begins: "Seedlings for the 1990 measurement program ...." You wouldn't really try growing this many plants by simply putting seeds in the ground, would you? Not all cannabis seeds will germinate. You might lose 20 to 30 percent of your crop from day one by simply planting seeds and hoping for the best. Even home growers prefer to transplant only healthy, vital plants into the limited space of their home gardens. Non-viable seeds would create holes in the plots that would skew the density and controlling the density originally was the whole point of the project.

A thousand seedlings needs some larger number of seeds, say twelve to thirteen hundred pots, let's make them a quart of dirt each, say five by five foot tables of a hundred plants each, or a greenhouse roughly ten feet by twenty-five or thirty feet, or maybe two greenhouses, fifteen feet by ten. At this stage you could water them by hand, for say the first six to eight weeks. A few lights would be nice and a sprinkler system, but let's try to keep this as low-tech as possible. A university agricultural department could do this, but you could create your own greenhouse, just for this project.

You'll need a crew of planters. The footnotes to Tables 1 and 2 suggests a single plot was planted on a single day, three separate days a week apart, for the 1x2s and 2x3s, staggered to check whether planting date affects yield [Leafnbud®]. It's possible this same crew planted the 1x1s, 2x2s and almost 3x3s on the same day but even the footnote to Table 2 suggests they needed least a week. They could have transported the seedlings in small utility trucks from the greenhouses to the plots using the four yard gaps between each plot on the field. A mechanical seedling planter would have been nice.

You'll need to prepare the soil of the field. They must have plowed it, at least once, to turn in the existing grass. Alternatively, they could have rolled up the existing grass, to be put back down later. This football field would have been using some system of natural grass for its field, not an artificial turf. The athletic department would know how to apply the liquid fertilizer.

A football field is naturally crowned, its high point along the center line of its longest diameter. This helps drain off the water. Irrigation could have been done with a water cannon. Some fields have irrigation systems built in. The piping runs under the field and the grass can be irrigated from below.

At harvest time, the plants have to be moved off the field in some way. They could have brought in the leaf shredder and used it there on the field. The resulting seed and Leafnbud® would be ready to be placed on trays. The stalk and attached branches would have to be ground up first, perhaps in a wood chipper. The trays need to be transported to the oven in one of the utility trucks.

The scale could be separate or it could be built into the oven. It needs to be able to weigh many kilos to a tenth of a gram. These kinds of scales are commercial grade. A university would have one of these. The oven is a convection oven capable of drying to 70 degrees centigrade. This is a professional and reasonably expensive model. This oven would have to be able to handle a large amount of material in a single day. After we're done cooking and weighing the material, we need to destroy it. A large boiler room would do just right. A university might have one, used to provide heat to the dorms. If it were located reasonably close to the football field, that would be a plus.

After the last plant is harvested, we need to lay back down the grass. The professionals in the grounds department will be able to do this relatively quickly, within a week in some cases. But certainly within two or three weeks, the grass will be ready for the first football game of the season.

4.   A Mythical Stadium.   Let me introduce you to Yoknapatawpha County.   It has a university and a very fine professional stadium, the Naughty Hemmingway, not far from the main campus, though far enough away to have its own complex, with athletic department, grounds department, boiler room, and storage for all the various vehicles and equipment needed to keep a modern football field in good shape. The bleacher seating on the West side is marked off in nine sections labeled A through J:

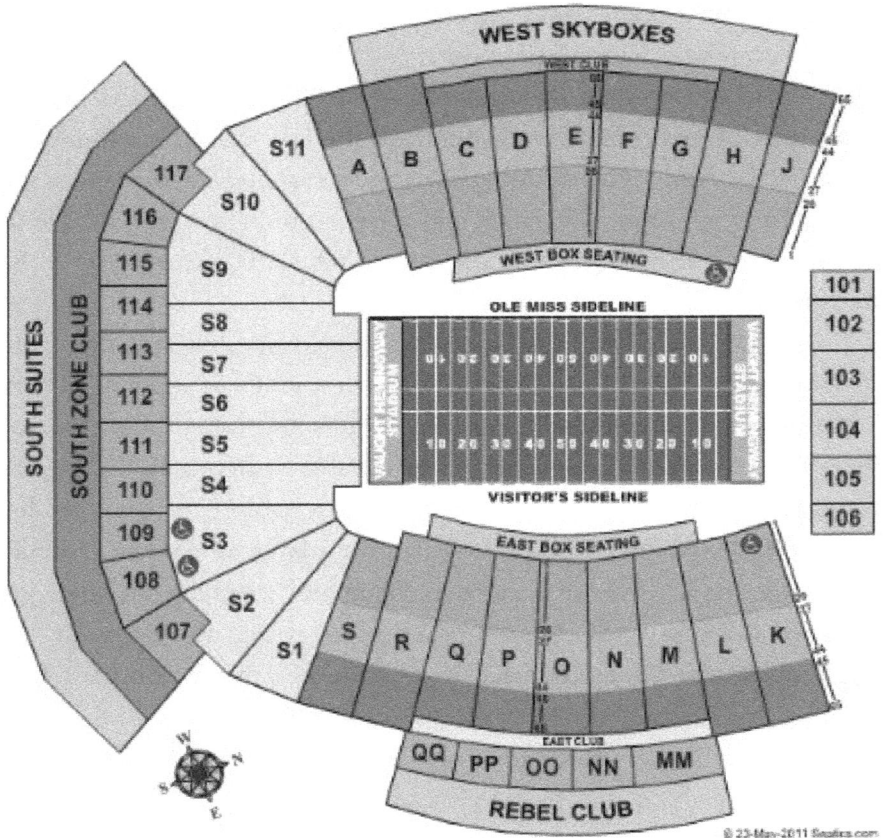

Figure 119. The Mythical Naughty Hemmingway Stadium.

Section I is missing. Hey, there is no I in Team. The stadium was using natural grass from 1985 to 2002 which was irrigated from below.[2] Before and after this period, they used artificial turf, though significantly not in the end zones.

Security would be important. There would have to be a way to close down the stadium for the spring, summer and some of the fall. The reason for this could be some kind of construction project, say a "new press box, new aluminum sideline seating, restrooms and concession stands, plus a club level section for 700 people."[3] This might also be the reason that this small town with limited resources in a relatively poor state might permit the stadium to be taken over for this admittedly out of the ordinary project.

B. When

The only year in which the Naughty Hemmingway could have been turned into a giant cannabis plantation would have been 1988. *Cannabis Fields* is dated on its face, June 1992. The release date on the Konrad version is February 1993. From 1970 to 1985, the field was topped with Astroturf.[4] So the seven years between 1985 and 1992 are the only ones available.

Why 1988? To take over the stadium for this project would have required shifting the college football season until the harvest was completed. The football schedules for the seasons from 1984-1985 to 1991-1992 all show games played at Yoknapatawpha within the first three weeks of September. The 1988-1989 season had its first five games played away. The first game in that year in the stadium was played on Saturday, the 15th of October.

---

[2] "Facilities," www.olemizzsports.com/ole-facilities-naughtyhemmingway.html.

[3] "Facilities," www.olemizzsports.com.

[4] "Facilities," www.olemizzsports.com.

It takes anywhere from a week to three weeks to lay in prescription athletic turf and get it rooted well enough to play a football game on. The longest a plant was in the ground was 153 days, plant number 13.00 of Plot A. The footnote for Table 2 says Plot A was planted on Sunday, April 17. If this were true, then this plant would have been harvested on Thursday, 16 September. This would have left four weeks to lay in the turf. The same footnote says the 1x1, 2x2 and almost 3x3 plots were planted the first week of June. The longest one of these plants was in the ground was 129 days, numbers 107.01 and 103.01, the two anomalies. Had they been planted Wednesday, 1 June, then they would have been harvested 8 October. This still leaves a week to get the field ready. Both these plants were in the end zone and between the end zone and the bleachers. The re-turfing of the field could have taken place as the plants were removed so most of the plants may have been gone by this time. It would have been close but it could have been done.

C.   Discussion

Now let's be serious. There is no way the DEA could have taken over a major college football stadium like the Naughty Hemmingway. First off, no one in their right mind would ever have given permission for this. It would have meant rescheduling most of the fall football season.

Also, someone would have noticed. All the contractors would have noticed. The odor from all those plants would have wafted across campus and the nearby town. Though it makes for a wonderful fantasy, this could never have happened. But it is fun to imagine what might have been. Until someone comes forward with some eyewitness testimony and some photos, this will have to remain speculation, an old mouth-to-mouth tale, passed down as just another legend of Yoknapatawpha.

Figure 120. 13Durbos5; 8Durbos6.

Figure 121. One happy gardener.

12
Summary Judgment

---

*"Now, I hate credentialism:
there are plenty of fools with Ph. Ds,
some fools with fancy prizes, and a fair
number of first-rate economic thinkers
without formal qualifications."*
-- Paul Krugman (1953 -   )[1]

A.   **Table 1 and Table 2**
B.   **Figure 1**
C.   **Figure 2, Top Pie Chart**
D.   **Figure 2, Bottom Pie Chart**
E.   **Figures 3, 4 and the CM**
F.   **Field of Dreams**
G.   **Les Miz**
H.   **The Domestic Overestimate**
I.   **Where and When**
J.   **History**
K.   **Conclusion**

---

[1] Krugman, Paul. "Who Should We Listen To?" in his blog, *The Conscience of a Liberal*, retr. 3 Mar 13, at //krugman.blogs.nytimes.com.

What can be said of the very dishonest study titled *Cannabis Fields*? How much, if anything, can we use from it? Let's recap what we have been able to discover after a reasonably thorough investigation.

A.   Table 1 and Table 2

In Chapter 1 it became apparent that at least two people had gotten their hands dirty with *Cannabis Fields*. One was familiar with the metric system while the other did not like it on principle. The first we've called Dr. Sly, who completely understood the intentions of his DEA masters. The second did so much lying and obfuscation that he deserves the nickname, Lewis the Liar.

Cannabis Fields began as a yield/density study. But it quickly morphed into another bogus piece of evidence that could be used in a courtroom to convict hapless growers. The weighmaster had his fat foot on the scale and had been paid off to overestimate the weight of the witch's plants.

Tables 1 and 2 were split off from an original table, Table I. Cannabis does not come in high and low density. The one is no better, no more normal, no more natural than the other. Many plants are sensitive to the amount of space in which they have to expand.

Combining results from some other study, the data given in Attachment 2, to fill out these new tables, only corrupts the original study. Nothing supposes the data from Attachment 2 was taken from plants grown under conditions in which their density was controlled. The data, read literally, describes male plants, with their lack of seed and flower. The leaves from Attachment 2 cannot be made to read the Leafnbud® of Attachment 1. Just as tables 1 and 2 have been split off from some previous Table I, so the two tables in Attachment 2 have been created from a single source. Further, many of the entries in Table 1 and Table 2 (on page 3) are simply incorrect.

B.   Figure 1

Figure 1 should have been a graphic illustration of Table I. It should have shown the change in yield versus density for all the mature plants. This missing figure we've called Figure I.

We graphed it as a column graph for yield versus square feet, yield versus density, yield versus square feet w/o the two anomalies, and yield versus density w/o the anomalies. For each of these categories, we also fitted it five different ways, as an exponential, linear, logarithmic, polynomial and power series curve, to see which one fits the data best. With the anomalies removed, the Leafnbud® can be predicted from the density using a polynomial expression, $Y = 718 X^2 - 1567 X + 1056$, with an R-squared of .999.

Instead, Lewis's Figure 1 is a representation of height/diameter ratios versus square feet. Lewis makes the same mistake he did with his Table 2: $6 \times 9 = 54$, not 81. Again, he splits one density into three, and leaves another out entirely, to emphasize the larger plants.

We corrected it. We also graphed the height/diameter ratio versus square feet of growing area and against the density for all the plants and all the densities. And we graphed the height/diameter ratios versus density without the anomalies.

Height/diameter ratios are interesting and density certainly will affect canopy shape to a degree, more for the plants grown closer together, less for the larger plants with more space in which to expand. But they chose only the longest diameter to use as an estimate. Canopy predicts the quantity of Leafnbud® much less accurately than either fresh weight or density. The purpose of *Cannabis Fields* however is not to find an accurate predictor variable but to arrive at a pre-ordained conclusion, the magical Poundaplant®.

C.   Figure 2, Top Pie Chart

Both pie charts in Figure 2 suppose that the leaf was separated from the flowers after the plants were harvested. Each pie chart has a line that divides bud from leaf. The methodology section assures us that the plant was separated into four parts, not three.

But the data in Attachment 1 does not show this. There we have separate weights for the stalk/branch and separate weights for the seed. But for the leaf or the flower we have only a catch-all designation, called the yield, which is nothing but Leafnbud®. To disguise this lack of data, they have added the word usable to yield, which means leaf and bud, or just leaf, depending.

There are two reasons for this. The first is ideological. The DEA has maintained for its entire existence that cannabis addicts will smoke anything, including leaf. No one else seems to be able to discover this enormous black market for leaf. In fact, this is just one more way to add weight to the magic number that might convict the modern witch, much as they used to have no problem weighing the plants with the roots and dirt attached.

The second reason is methodological. The plants were not separated during some DEA sponsored trimming party. Instead, they were fed through a leaf shredder with a screen at the bottom to catch the seeds. There was no separation of flower from leaf.

The ratio of flower to leaf and flower to plant will become important in the last section. This is the whole point of the paper, the Domestic Estimate. There, these ratios that are based on nothing will be used in an attempt to produce the mythical Poundaplant®. There is no data in Attachment 1 that supports the idea of the separation of flower from leaf.

D.   Figure 2, Bottom Pie Chart

There is also no data to support the notion that there were any sinsemilla plants. In fact, there is evidence against this. First, "no attempt was made cultivate unfertilized female plants, commonly known as 'sinsemilla' (page 1)." In other words, no one pulled the males. But half the plants were male which release "*huge* amounts of pollen are released (page 9, italics added)." Zero plants were sinsemilla.

Second, by assuming row and column for the decimal plant numbers, one plant became pollinated while its neighbors were seedless. The DEA pollen was incredibly selective. All the plants from 1990 were sinsemilla while in 1991 all but three were sinsemilla.

Third, the definition of mature changed one more time, from 120 grow days or more for the non-sinsemilla to 90 days or more for the sinsemilla. This added new sinsemilla plants, only for the bottom pie chart of Figure 2 and not for Figure 1 or Tables 1 or 2. The only reason to do this was to hide the real numbers in a larger mass of data.

Fourth, once the real numbers were calculated, it was clear what had happened. Lewis the Liar had simply zeroed the seed data to create his sinsemilla. Unfortunately, now he had to hide the data somewhere. His only choice was to add the missing seed data to the data for the stalk and branch. The stalk and branch of the mature sinsemilla, those with 120 or more grow days, comprised 62 percent of the plant's dry weight, versus 41 percent for the non-sinsemilla. The sinsemilla show a sudden increase in stalk and branch between 90 and 120 days compared to the non-sinsemilla. Sinsemilla with more than 120 grow days show an even larger increase in the weight of stalk and branch. Biologically, this is impossible but further the sinsemilla plants would have to be psychic to know they would never become pollinated.

E.   Figures 3, 4 and the CM

Figure 3 is also incorrect. Dr. S calculated this formula for the fresh weight to dry flower ratio for a different set of data than what is in Attachment 1. We graphed this relationship for five different curves of best fit, for all the plants, for all the plants without the anomalies, for the mature plants and for the mature plants without the anomalies.

Figure 4 is inaccurate for the same reason. The formula will become important in the calculation of the Domestic Estimate. It too was created from a different data set. The anomalies warp the curve toward the upper right hand corner. We graphed this figure from the data for five different curves of best fit, for all the plants, for all the plants without the anomalies, for the mature plants and for the mature plants without the anomalies. None of the formulas for the canopy predicted from the diameter are as accurate as those drawn from the density or fresh weight.

The correlation matrix is also wrong because the data set has been replaced. The real relationships can be calculated from the data in Attachment 1. This was done for all 102 plants, for all 100 plants of any age without the anomalies, for the 38 mature plants, and for the 36 mature plants without the anomalies.

F.   Field of Dreams

We assume row and column for the decimal plant numbers. When we place the plants in the field defined by these rows and columns, it is clear there were edge effects, neighbor effects and selection bias. Plants were chosen from outer rows. Plants were chosen and then their neighbors were chosen a month later. The selection was non-random which dooms the study to be used as a comparison to other plantations.

In particular, the two largest plants were left alone in the field for five months, to expand as large as they could, very much like the lone oak tree in the cow pasture. These two anomalies were manufactured for the purpose of skewing the data. The reason they grew so large was then hidden.

The north end of the field can be recreated by assuming row and column for the 1x1s, 2x2s and almost 3x3s. Here it is even more apparent the edge and neighbor effects and the selective pollen brush of the Deaity®. The two anomalies stand out when the harvest day numbers are graphed.

The entire field can also be recreated. Assuming four yard spaces between plots, all of the plants in Attachment 1 can be put on a single football field. This would allow for 950 plants in a sample space from which 38 mature plants can be selected, or four percent for a statistically useful survey.

G.   Les Miz

The Air Dry Weight is calculated from unnamed DEA studies for which no data is provided. This fudge factor will become useful when they calculate the Domestic Estimate. One might also subtract 10 to 20 percent for losses due to handling of organic material by home growers.

The subsection on water content betrays a separate set of data that was used to calculate it. The percentage water of a mature cannabis plant based on the data in Attachment 1 gives 63% not 66%. The water content of young plants was also reported incorrectly.

The paragraph on plant height again shows it came from a different set of data. The range for the height of the plants is incorrect. The tallest plant recorded does not exist in Attachment 1.

The crop cycle is divided into two sharp periods while in reality there is simply a steady drop in the growth rate over the summer and early fall. Males are said to spontaneously self-destruct but I have never seen this. If this were true, then the gardens of inexperienced home growers would be nearly twice as large as those who know how to grow sinsemilla.

The amount of Leafnbud® per male plant is estimated without any accompanying data in the final subsection, Yield Adjustment Factors. Hermaphroditism is not discussed. Lewis the Liar appears to have tacked on his line about how to calculate the weight of a sinsemilla plant to the original from Dr. Sly about a non-sinsemilla plant, which were the only kind grown on the DEA plantations.

H.   The Domestic Overestimate

This section was added onto the original report. It uses the anomaly-distorted formula from Figure 4, a fudge factor, the non-existent separation of leaf from flower in Figure 2, and a wildly unsubstantiated statement as to the ratio of sinsemilla to non-sinsemilla to calculate the Poundaplant®. What it doesn't use is the left two columns of Table 4. The right three columns come from the skewed and inaccurate formula of Figure 4. It is very unlikely any survey was conducted and completely probable that no canopy was measured in the field. That it was calculated for both sinsemilla and non-sinsemilla suggests those who answered the survey did not know the difference. The method for estimating sinsemilla shows no correlation with the plant data from Attachment 1.

I.   Where and When

It is fun to speculate as to where and when the plants were really grown. The mixing of the data in Attachment 1, the excising of the plant numbers for the sinsemilla of 1990, the fact that all the plants could fit on a single football field, the evidence that the cannabis was planted in yards and harvested in meters, and the lack of sufficient space in which to grow the almost 3x3s taken together point to a football field as the site of where the plants were grown. But which?

The necessity of a certain amount of infrastructure for marking the field, irrigation, transport, measuring and drying and the subsequent disposal all suggest a university athletic department. There is a stadium in Yoknapatawpha County sited near to a university that would have done perfectly, the Naughty Hemmingway. This would have required some considerable security.

There is at least one year in which the plants could have been grown in this same stadium: 1988. In that year, the first home game was advanced to the middle of October because of construction. This would have been enough time to grow the plants, harvest them and reseed the field for the first game.

Naturally, this could not have taken place.

J.   History

Why would anyone allow *Cannabis Fields* into court in the first place? There are at least two different circulating copies, no author signed his name to it, and it has never been peer reviewed. The only reason it has been allowed in, is the willingness of a DEA agent to testify to its existence. This should make us all suspicious.

Only recently, after twenty-five years, have two different people chosen to sign their names as lead authors (with the same group of others) and dared to claim it. But first they changed the title, twice. And neither of the new lead authors know anything about it. Instead they refer one to Dr. Sly or they clam up at any questions with the modern wonderword, classified.

It appeared first as a poster abstract under the new title, "Estimation of Usable Biomass in a Field of Outdoor Cultivated *Cannabis Sativa* L. plants."[2] This occurred at the IACM, the 6th

---

[2] *LACM 6th Conference on Cannabinoids in Medicine and 5th European Workshop on Cannabinoid Research*, held September 8-10, 2011 at the University of Bonn, Germany, http://www.bonn2011.org, pp. 134/150.

Conference on Cannabinoids in Medicine and 5th European Workshop on Cannabis Research, held from 8 – 10 September, 2011, in Bonn, Germany. The lead author on this was Bupkis Mnemonic. The others, including Ticklish Cant, Hernan De Soto, Dr. Sly, and Supra Chapstick, are all part of the Yoknapatawpha National Center for Natural Products Research. The poster abstract does not appear to be much more than a notice that such an abstract claims to exist. It was presented as one of some forty others on Friday, September 9, during poster session number one held between 15:00 to 17:00.

The second time the abstract had a different name: "Biomass Field Studies of Field Cultivated Cannabis sativa L. Plants." It appeared in *Planta Medica* 2012; 78 – P_5, DOI: 10.1055/s-0032-1307513. The lead author was Supra Chapstick with the same names as above listed as secondary authors. Both Cant and Sly are part of the same group at Yoknapatawpha. Again, what was published is only an abstract, not a paper, and was not peer-reviewed.

It is very clear that this abstract is meant to refer to *Cannabis Fields*. It quotes from the paper liberally: "planting density is a significant factor affecting the shape of plant canopy, which in turn affects the total plant yield" [the word 'total' is the only addition to the same statement on page 3]; "larger branching structures coupled with increased available sunlight, soil nutrients and water which in significantly greater biomass yield" [an 's' has been added to 'structure' and 'biomass' has replaced 'plant' but the phrase is identical to that found on page 3]; and "The fresh weight at the time of harvest multiplied by the number 0.1437 would result in an estimate of dry weight of useable plant material" [Here, "at the time of harvest" has been added and the latter six words have replaced "usable dry weight material" but the same can be found on page 6 of *Cannabis Fields*].

The densities in the abstract are inexplicably different from the original; at one point there are five, then six. The word biomass has now replaced yield. But the formulas given for the fresh weight to dry leaf and bud ratio, as well as the formula for the plant dry weight to canopy diameter are exactly the same.

I defy you to arrive at the same formula without using the exact same data set. If you substitute different plants you get different formulas. Whatever study this newly titled abstract is supposed to be an abstract of, it must have used exactly the same data from exactly the same plants as those used in *Cannabis Fields*. Even more amusing is that the data given in Attachment 1 of *CF* do not yield the formulas repeated here. This is because larger plants were substituted for smaller ones. So both the formulas in these supposedly new abstracts and the formulas in *Cannabis Fields* are incorrect. But academics are notorious for propagating errors without bothering to check.

I telephoned the gang at Yoknapatawpha in late February 2013. I spoke to the project coordinator. Later that day, I called and spoke to Supra Chapstick, lead author on the abstract from 2012. I asked him several questions about the abstract of the paper he had submitted.

At first, he did not seem to know what I was talking about. I asked him about this new paper he was the lead author of. I asked him how many plots there had been. He said, "Ten." I asked him, did he separate leaf from bud? He assured me he had. I asked him where it was because it wasn't in the data. He assured me it was. I asked him to show me.

Then his story began to change. He told me that there hadn't been a paper, only the abstract. He said they hadn't published a paper or the data. "Was there a study?" I asked. He said there was a study ongoing, both this year and last year.

This did not make any sense, since the abstract appeared in late 2011. Normally, an abstract is an abstract of a paper, published or not. That's why it's called an abstract, as in, taken from. The abstract references a study in its first words: "This study ...." I am expected to believe that only an abstract exists of an incomplete study but that conclusions have been drawn and formulas compiled but that no research paper exists?

I noted to him on the phone that the results were exactly the same as in *Cannabis Fields*. He didn't seem to know what I was referring to. I directed him to a website with a copy. He brought up the website. I pointed out the similarities between the conclusions in this new abstract and those of *Cannabis Fields*. Only when he saw the paper on the website did he declare that, yes, yes, he knew all about it.

Then the story changed again. Supra Chapstick told me that "they had noticed that *Cannabis Fields* had never been submitted to a peer-reviewed journal and had never been published." So that is why they decided to submit the study in the form of an abstract to *Planta Medica*. There was no new study, no new paper. At least we finally agreed that it was just a recycled abstract of *Cannabis Fields*.

So it was your group in Yoknapatawpha County that did the original work on *Cannabis Fields*? "Yes," he said. "It was definitely our group." But you personally did no work on the study? "No, that was Dr. Sly. He has been here 35 years. That was before my time."

"So what did you do?" I asked. "I compiled the study," he said. "What exactly did you compile?" I asked, since I had heard this typical academic response before. "I reviewed the literature," he answered. Obviously this was not true as he had never seen or heard of the paper before I mentioned it to him.

"So you didn't do any of the work on the study?" I asked again. "No," he admitted, "that was done by Dr. Sly some twenty years ago." I mentioned that the original paper had no author and he said he was sure that Dr. Sly had put his name on it. I assured him that he had not. "So why did Dr. Sly have you put your name on this new abstract since you never saw the plants?" I asked. "Well, maybe you should ask him that," he said.

I came away from our conversation feeling that Dr. Chapstick had never seen the plants, had never done any review, and had never done any work whatsoever on *Cannabis Fields*. It seemed to be just another example of the eternal search by oxymoronic respected academics for naming rights to supposed articles that didn't exist and that they never had anything to do with. In this case, there had not been an article, not a paper, not even a new study, just an abstract and not a particularly accurate one of *Cannabis Fields* and nothing more. It had appeared in *Planta Medica* which recently seems to have gone to an all-electronic format and undergone a change of management. Had no one at the journal bothered to ask for the paper from which the abstract had been taken?

Could this also be the DEA's attempt to pretend that the study had been published in a peer-reviewed journal? This would lend it some weight and credibility among the less sceptical. But then why change the name, not just once, but twice? And why change the densities? And why change yield to biomass?

I called Ticklish Cant. "How many plants were in the study?" I asked. He did not seem to know and seemed aggrieved that I was asking him a question about an abstract that had appeared less than a year ago, a conference title that had appeared less than two years ago. He wasn't eager to speak to me.

I felt that I was getting the runaround so I called back the next day. Suddenly, no one was available. A new person answered the phone, not the project coordinator. This woman said they were all in a conference going over their posters. I asked one by one to speak with the names on the study but they were all in the same conference. I asked to speak with the project coordinator. She came on but could not and would not converse further with me. She sounded scared and stressed.

I called back the next day, Wednesday. The project coordinator answered and told me, as if reading from a script: "I have been instructed to tell you that these were only abstracts. No paper was published."

"Instructed by who?" I asked.

"By higher ups," she said.

"Where is the paper the abstract is taken from? Where is the data?" I asked.

"I have been told to tell you that you must speak to Dr. Chapstick."

"Is Dr. Sly there?"

"He is very busy."

"Is Dr. De Soto there?"

"No."

"When will Dr. Sly be in?"

"I am only the middleman here and I can only tell you to speak to Dr. Chapstick," she answered.

"Seems like everyone is suddenly busy," I noticed.

"Look," she said. "We got inspected yesterday. By the DEA. You said you were a grower?"

"No," I said. "I'm an investigator."

She refused to disclose anything else. Dr. Chapstick's phone no longer rang except to the answering machine. Dr. Sly's phone did not answer at all. My emails went unanswered.

I called Dr. Mnemonic.

"Do you remember the paper?" I asked.

"Are you saying that I do not remember my own work?" he shot back, very unhappy with the question.

"Did you see the plants?" I asked, thinking it might be better to get down to specifics than deal with this fake professorial outrage.

"I do not understand what you are asking me," he said, quite diffident.

"Did you see the plants?" I asked again. It was a simple question.

"I am not authorized to give you that information. You must go through NIDA. I cannot give you any information," he replied.

Clearly, the walls had come down. And rather quickly. Big Brother was either monitoring my Skype account or the phone lines at Yoknapatawpha or both. They had quickly nixed any further inquiries on my part. Next, I discovered that all of my emails through Google that I use for academic research had been blocked. I also discovered that any emails sent from Yoknapatawpha to any of my emails had been bounced back as undeliverable, unbeknownst to me.

Personally, I like conspiracy over incompetence. Whenever there is a choice, I just naturally gravitate toward the former. If you're not already paranoid, you're really not paying attention. As an explanation of human conduct, I prefer the idea that rational actors knowingly do wrong. There are two kinds of people in the world: those who have seen the black helicopters and those who haven't seen them yet. Get out your tin foil hats.

But let's face it. Incompetence really does rule. My feeling after all this is that the gang in Yoknapatawpha did not really think this through. Someone found an old study, retitled it, figured it would be good enough for an abstract and got everyone to sign off on it. A petty academic fraud? Sure. But hey, publish or perish, right?

Could it be more than that? Does the department receive federal money based in part on the number of papers they supposedly publish? In that case, we have a financial fraud as well.

And why did the DEA feel the need for a snap inspection? What are they trying to cover up? Did they knowingly introduce *Cannabis Fields* as false evidence into court in order to convict growers? This would be a very legal, right in the judge's face, fraud as well.

At this point, I am guessing that this was just a bunch of academics trying to get away with a little extra resume padding. But would this be enough to have stirred up such a hornet's nest? Someone is definitely unhappy they actually signed their names to this.

This means there is now someone to blame. Not a committee, not a group, but real human beings who can be called into a court of law and from whom testimony can be taken, work product demanded, and so forth. By adding their names to *Cannabis Fields* after twenty-five years, they have opened up a whole new line of investigation. We may finally get to the bottom of who did or did not write the study, who did or did not see the plants, and who did or did not alter and rewrite the study, then sanitize it for release to the judge.

Until then *Cannabis Fields* remains the unwanted guest at the party, the black sheep in the family no one wants to know. Just last year they were so happy to include it on their professional resumes. Yet, as soon as someone starts asking questions about the work they were so proud to share, they clam up, tell stories, change those stories and suddenly have nothing more to say. An outside observer has every right to distrust not only the report but its pedigree.

As for Dr. Sly, up until recently he was too modest to put his own name (or anyone else's) on the disaster that the study became. When he finally did, he conned some fellow colleagues of equally dubious morals into pretending to be the lead authors of a paper they hadn't read describing a study they hadn't done of plants they hadn't seen. In academia, this unquenchable thirst for naming rights for things you have little or nothing to do with is known fondly as *credentialism*. The Spanish have an expression for people like this: *sin verguenza*, without shame.

K.   Conclusion

The study could have been a contender. Had the DEA actually tried to form an accurate estimate of what an outdoor plant might yield in dried flowers, this information could have been useful. Sadly, like their medieval counterparts, they were only interested in their own personal and institutional gain. With *Cannabis Fields*, the DEA became merely the latest modern example of the corrupt medieval weighmaster.

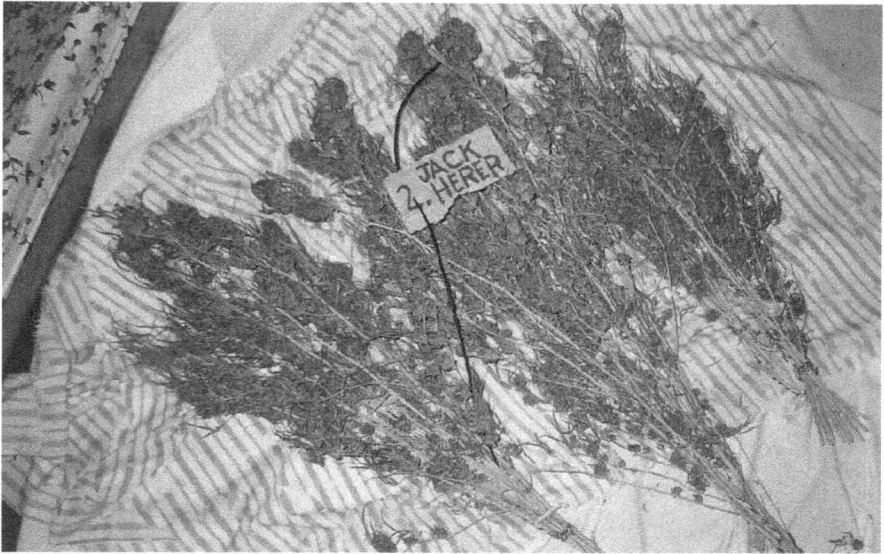

Figure 122. Previous page: Jack Herer; Above, Fernanda de la Figuera.

Appendix A
The Konrad Version

There are at least two versions of the report, *Cannabis Fields*. The first I received from Kris Konrad. It can be found at a number of websites. Unfortunately, many of them only contain the body of the paper.

They leave out the data from Attachment 1 and Attachment 2. These kinds of papers are data driven. That is, the results or conclusions in the body of the paper have to be drawn from the data. Without the data, the paper amounts to a series of unsubstantiated claims.

The Konrad version appears to be a later version of the study. Too bad I couldn't reproduce it here. Instead, I have included a copy of a not completely unrelated study.

CANNABIS YIELDS

RECEIVED
FEB ¨° 1993
DISTRICT ATTORNEY

JUNE 1992
DRUG ENFORCEMENT ADMINISTRATION

APPENDIX A – THE KONRAD VERSION

SUMMARY

Outdoor Cannabis sativa L. (cannabis) yield studies conducted during the summers of 1990 and 1991 have determined that the usable dry weight yield (leaf and bud) for female cannabis plants can be up to 2.3 kilograms (5.1 pounds). Based upon a survey of 15 leading producer states, the average plant yield for mature, domestically grown female cannabis plants in 1991 was 448 grams (1 pound). An accurate yield estimate can be made by weighing the fresh weight of a plant or measuring the plant's diameter at the broadest point in the canopy. A very significant factor affecting yield was planting density.

BACKGROUND

The Drug Enforcement Administration (DEA) during the summers of 1990 and 1991, conducted a detailed cannabis yield measurement program at the University of Mississippi in Oxford. The purpose of the project was to determine the average yield of outdoor cultivated cannabis plants and identify factors to predict usable yield. Prior to the project's initiation, the only quantitative studies undertaken were two studies self-initiated by the University of Mississippi in 1985 and 1986. These two studies made a limited number of observations and did not identify factors influencing plant yield.

METHODOLOGY

The overall intent of the studies was to introduce variation into the research design in order to gain a basic understanding of some of the factors influencing plant yield. The DEA sponsored research used different seed stocks from Mexico, Colombia, Jamaica, and a hybrid of South African-Afghanistan origin.

The 1990 effort consisted of a progressive planting of 3 separate areas at 2 week intervals. Each area was planted with the same seed stock at an identical planting density. The varying of the planting date permitted analysis of the sensitivity of cannabis yield and plant development to planting date. The 1991 effort focused on the relationship between planting density and yield. Three different planting densities of Mexican seed stock were studied. Tables 1 and 2 describe the average plant yields which are associated with specific densities.

Yield measurements were made on 90 days or older female plants, which duplicated the preference of a majority of domestic growers to cultivate the larger yielding females. However, no attempt was made to cultivate unfertilized female plants, commonly known as "sinsemilla". The vast majority of observations were made on the very common, tall, narrow leaflet cannabis variety known as

271

"sativa". A very limited number of observations were made on the other major variety, "indica". The indica variety is a shorter, more compact, faster maturing plant with larger leaves.

Yield measurements were made on 102 plants during the course of the two year study. Physical measurements were made of the plant's height from ground level and the diameter at the broadest point in the plant's canopy. Upon completion of the physical measurements, the plant was cut at ground level and separated into four component parts - stem/branches, leaves, female flowering tops, commonly known as buds or colas, and seed. The individual components were each weighed to determine a "wet" or "fresh" weight. The material was dried in a convection oven at 70 degrees Celsius. The dried material was reweighed when it had reached a constant weight, typically after 24 to 48 hours. This second measurement is termed the "dry" weight. During both yield surveys, cannabis plants were harvested and measured on a monthly basis to quantify yield throughout the growth cycle. The selection of plants was based upon a determination of their representative physical size, shape, and overall vigor characteristics. The selection process captured the diversity or plant size by including cannabis plants ranging from the larger to the smaller plant specimens. The planting of approximately 100 plants per cultivation area insured that there was a large and representative population from which plants were sampled. If a particular plant was harvested for the measurement program, the neighboring plants were ineligible for future selection which avoided changing the planting density during the study. Similarly, no plants on the outer rows were selected to avoid edge affects which could skew results because of an asymmetrical planting density.

YIELD RESULTS

All measurements recorded in 1990 or 1991 are contained in Attachment 1. Table 1 depicts the average yield for all mature (120 days or older) cannabis plants grown using a dense planting pattern of either 9 square feet per plant or 18 square feet per plant. At this relatively high planting density, the lateral branches of adjacent cannabis plants were touching by the middle of July. Thereafter, the horizontal growth rate decreased in relation to the vertical rate of growth. The results were tall, narrow plant canopies.

272

APPENDIX A – THE KONRAD VERSION

Table 1
Average Cannabis Yields at
Maturity for High Planting Densities

SPONSOR	YEAR	DENSITY	YIELD*	SEED STOCK
Univ. of MS	1985	9 ft. sq.	222 grams	Mexico
Univ. of MS	1986	9 ft. sq.	274 grams	Mexico
DEA	1990	18 ft. sq.	233 grams	Colombia
DEA	1991	9 ft. sq.	215 grams	Mexico

*Yield = oven dry weight of usable leaf and bud from mature 120 day or older plants.

The similarity of plant yields contained in Table 1 is remarkable considering the variation in seed stock, year of cultivation, and other factors. However, if the planting density is decreased, the plants have more room to laterally branch out. The additional space allows the plant to assume a natural canopy shape, somewhat similar to a Christmas tree. The larger branching structure coupled with increased available sunlight, soil nutrients, and water resulted in significantly greater plant yields. Table 2 displays the yields for cannabis at maturity for identical seed stocks at three low planting densities and for different planting dates and years.

Table 2
Average Cannabis Yields at
Maturity for Low Planting Densities

SPONSOR	YEAR*	DENSITY	YIELD	SEED STOCK
DEA-A	1990	81 ft. sq.	777 grams	Mexico
DEA-B	1990	81 ft. sq.	936 grams	Mexico
DEA-C	1990	81 ft. sq.	640 grams	Mexico
DEA	1991	72 ft. sq.	1015 grams	Mexico
DEA	1991	36 ft. sq.	860 grams	Mexico

*Seedlings for the 1990 measurement program were planted at two week intervals: DEA-A was planted on 4/17, DEA-B was planted on 5/8, and DEA-C was planted on 5/17. The 1991 plantings were made during the first week of June.

Figure 1 reports select plant height-diameter ratios for the planting densities used in 1990 and 1991. The noticeably high ratio for the 9 foot square planting density confirms that this plant canopy shape is different than all of the other observations which had relatively large amounts of space in which to grow. The height-diameter graph of Figure 1 shows that planting density is a significant factor affecting plant canopy shape, which in turn affects plant yield. The significance of the relationship between planting density and plant yield will be

DEA Cannabis Yields (1992) Page 3

discussed later in this paper.

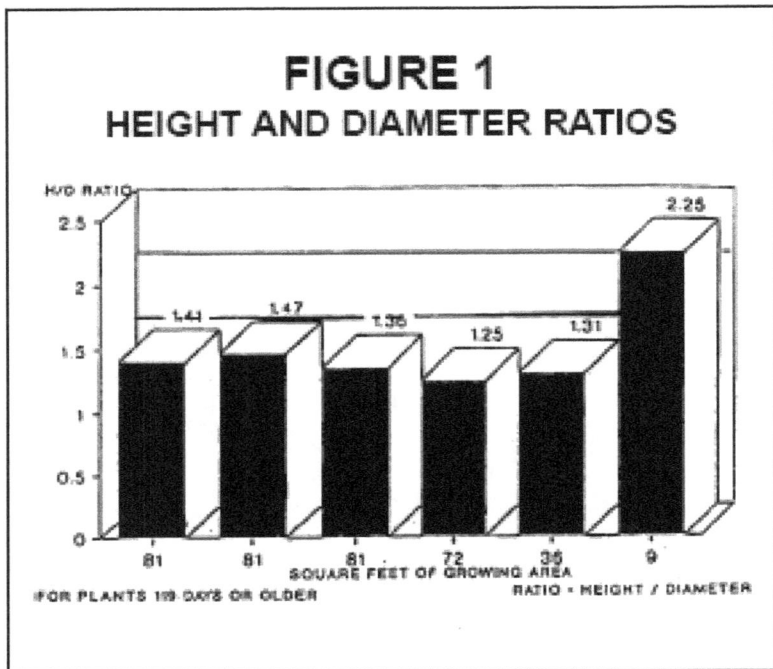

FIGURE 1
HEIGHT AND DIAMETER RATIOS

During both growing seasons, only standard irrigation, fertilization, and weeding activity were rendered as required. However,
two plants, identification numbers 107.01 and 103.01 in the 1991
low planting density plots, had extremely high yields in comparison to neighboring plants. The dry weight yield for plant 107.01
was 2,086.9 grams (4.6 pounds) and plant 103.01 yielded 2,308.4
grams (5.1 pounds). These two plants were located in a low area.
It is believed that the natural slope of the land caused these
plants to receive additional water and possibly additional fertilizer through run on water. The significance of these yields
is that they demonstrate that certain agronomic practices can
produce higher average yields than those reported in Table 2.

Analysis of the combined 1990 and 1991 DEA yield data shows that
usable oven dry weight material (leaf and bud) in a mature
cannabis plant is 14.4% of the plant's total (roots excluded)
fresh weight. A break down of the four types of material found
in a mature female cannabis plant is presented in Figure 2.

DEA Cannabis Yields (1992) Page 4

FIGURE 2
NON-SINSEMILLA CANNABIS COMPONENTS

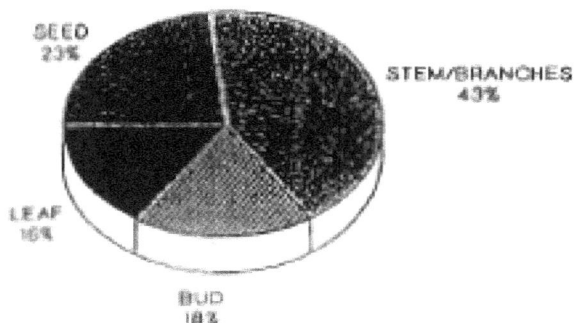

SEED
23%

STEM/BRANCHES
43%

LEAF
16%

BUD
18%

PERCENT OVEN DRY WEIGHT 120 DAYS OR OLDER PLANTS

SINSEMILLA CANNABIS COMPONENTS

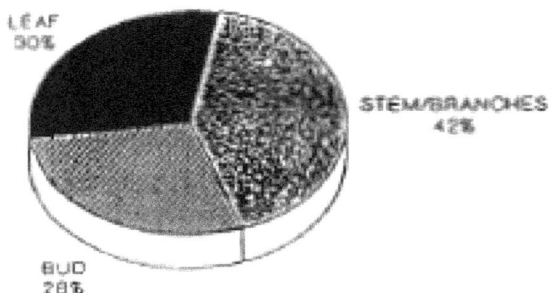

LEAF
30%

STEM/BRANCHES
42%

BUD
28%

PERCENT OVEN DRY WEIGHT 90 DAY OR OLDER PLANTS
WHICH DID NOT HAVE ANY SEED DEVELOPMENT

DEA *Cannabis Yields* (1992) Page 5

YIELD PREDICTION

The plant growth and yield data collected throughout the 1990 and 1991 growing seasons shows that plant yield can be accurately predicted from simple field measurements. Several field measurement techniques were assessed including plant height, diameter, fresh weight, and the number of grow days. The predictive models developed are valid for any sativa variety plants regardless of plant age or planting density.

The best predictor of plant yield was measurement of the plant's fresh weight. Figure 3 depicts the linear relationship between plant fresh weight and yield dry weight. The only required measurement is the weighing of the plant at the time of seizure in a timely fashion to avoid excessive loss of plant water. That fresh weight would not include the plant roots or any soil adhering to the plant. The fresh weight multiplied by the number 0.1437 would result in an estimate of usable dry weight material. This estimating technique is extremely accurate.

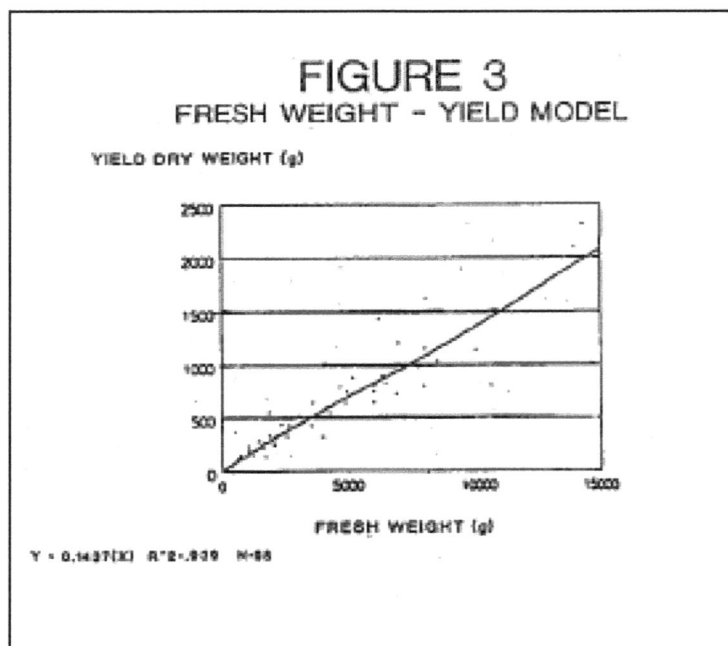

FIGURE 3
FRESH WEIGHT - YIELD MODEL

YIELD DRY WEIGHT (g)

FRESH WEIGHT (g)

$Y = 0.1437(X)$ $R^2 = .939$ N=86

DEA Cannabis Yields (1992) Page 6

APPENDIX A – THE KONRAD VERSION

Another accurate method for predicting plant yield is based upon measurement of the diameter of the plant at the broadest point in the canopy. Figure 4 depicts the curvilinear relationship between plant canopy diameter and the plant dry weight. The measurement of a plant canopy diameter is simpler than the measurement of the plant's fresh weight. However, the calculation of a yield estimate requires a two step process. First, the measured diameter is entered into the equation: Dry Weight = -3.76786 + (0.06666 * (Diameter ^2)). This first equation estimates the plant's total dry weight. Usable yield is then calculated using the percentages of bud and leaf described in Figure 2.

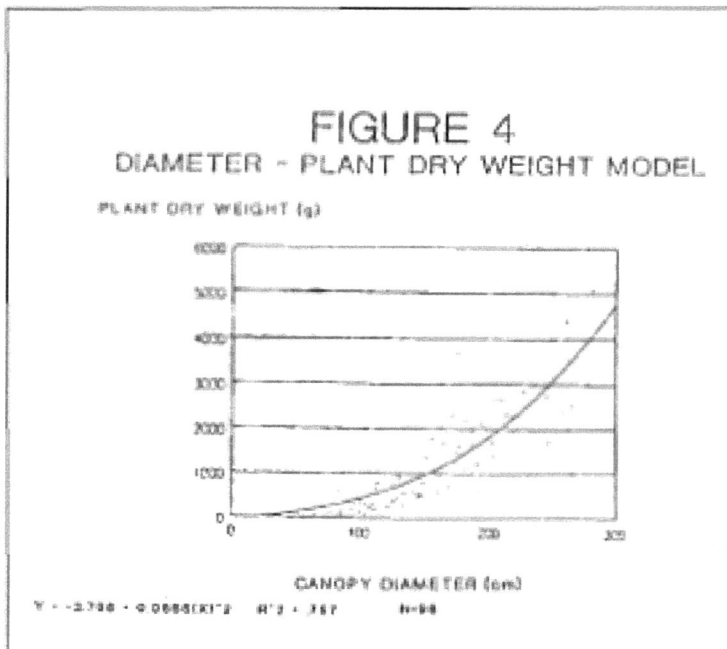

FIGURE 4
DIAMETER - PLANT DRY WEIGHT MODEL

DEA Cannabis Yields (1992) Page 7

WEEDING *CANNABIS FIELDS*

Neither plant height data or the number of grow days were as accurate a predictor of plant yield as were fresh weight or diameter measurements. However, weight was a good indicator of plant age and this relationship may be useful in estimating planting date. The correlation matrix included in Attachment 1 reports on the degree of association among 13 different plant measurements.

MISCELLANEOUS DATA ANALYSIS

Air Dry Weight

The use of oven dry weights, although scientifically acceptable because it can be reproduced, under-represents the amount of usable material in the illicit market. Most illegal material is air dried or at the time of sale, is in equilibrium with surrounding atmosphere which contains a certain amount of moisture. It is estimated based upon the DEA studies that the leaf and bud material of cannabis would weigh an additional 10% to 20% if allowed to air dry naturally and equalize with the surrounding atmosphere.

Water Content

In addition to the yield measurements, the amount of water contained in each plant was measured. A mature cannabis plant has, on a fresh weight basis, 66% water and 34% dry plant matter (leaves, buds, seeds, stems/branches). Plant water content can vary with plant age. Young plants less than 55 days old have a water content ranging from 75% to 82%. Older plants have water content ranging from 60% to 70%.

Plant Height

The average height of a mature cannabis plant was between 270 cm and 350 cm (8.6 - 11.5 feet). A few cannabis plants were measured in excess of 400 cm (13.1 feet). The tallest plant recorded was 430 cm (14.1 feet). Height was determined not to be very sensitive to planting density factors.

Crop Cycle

The crop cycle for the cannabis plants grown at the University of Mississippi was typical of cannabis crops grown in the contiguous states. The crop cycle consists of two stages. The first stage is the vegetative state which is characterized by a 30 to 90 day period of vigorous growth of sexually undifferentiated plants. Typical plantings occur in April or May and the vegetative stage extends until late July or early August. The transition from the vegetative stage to the second stage, known as the flowering or fruiting period, results from the reduction in day length as-

APPENDIX A – THE KONRAD VERSION

sociated with the photoperiod peaking on the summer solstice of June 21.

The flowering or fruiting stage lasts for the remainder of the plant's life cycle. Beginning in August, male plants form the stamens from which huge amounts of pollen are released. The male plants usually die by the middle of September or soon after they release their pollen. Female plants live a longer time in order to produce seed for the next generation. This reproductive stage is essential for naturally growing cannabis because it is an annual plant and can not survive the winter months. Female plants will produce a protective leafy bud to surround the pistulate reproductive organs and develop seed, if fertilized. The bud structure is highly desired by illicit growers because it contains the highest number of THC producing glands.

Yield Adjustment Factors

There is no need to adjust yield estimations of outdoor mature cannabis crops if at the time of seizure there are no male plants. If male plants are present, then evidence of this fact should be apparent by early August. The estimated yield of a male plant in early August, the point at which it begins to senesce and loose leaf cover, will be approximately 50% of the weight of a female plant of similar age and growth stage. By late September or October, the only harvestable cannabis plants remaining will be female plants.

If the female cannabis plants are unfertilized, then no seed will be produced. The average usable yield (leaf and bud) of a mature female plant will be 57% of the plant's dry weight where as the yield for a typical fertilized, seed bearing cannabis plant will be 34% of the the plant dry weight (Figure 2).

DOMESTIC ESTIMATE

The identification of accurate plant yield estimation methodologies makes possible the opportunity to estimate the average domestic yield using eradication statistics and plant canopy diameter information. A survey of 15 leading producer states was conducted by DEA to determine the average diameter of mature plants eradicated in September 1991. Table 4 lists the average diameter of mature plants observed in that state as reported by the DEA state eradication coordinator. The estimated usable yield for each state's eradicated plant total was cal-

DEA Cannabis Yields (1992) Page 9

culated using the predictive methodology described in Figure 4. This methodology uses average plant canopy diameter information as the predictor variable to estimate plant dry weight. The plant dry weight is adjusted to estimate usable air dry weight yield by first taking 34% of the dry weight to calculate usable yield, and adding 10% to the oven dry weight to obtain the air dry yield. This estimate is valid for female cannabis plants at maturity which contain seeds. An estimate for seedless cannabis (sinsemilla) is derived by first taking 58% of the plant dry weight, and then adjusting upward by 10% to convert from oven dry weight to an air dry yield.

Table 4
Estimated Cannabis Plant Yields

State	1991 Eradicated Plant Total	Average Diameter*	Estimated Non-Sinsemilla Yield (g)	Estimated Sinsemilla Yield (g)
Alabama	163,294	4 ft.	369	630
Arkansas	106,405	4 ft.	369	630
California	151,529	3.5 ft.	284	484
Florida	92,190	4.25 ft.	420	716
Georgia	300,583	4 ft.	369	630
Illinois	337,730	3.25 ft.	243	414
Indiana	206,494	4 ft.	369	630
Kansas	21,751	4 ft.	369	630
Kentucky	809,366	3.25 ft.	243	414
Louisiana	79,009	3.5 ft.	284	484
Minnesota	191,790	4 ft.	369	630
Missouri	104,493	3.5 ft.	284	484
N. Carolina	198,470	4 ft.	369	630
Tennessee	508,816	4 ft.	369	630
Texas	22,997	4.5 ft.	466	795
AVERAGE:		3.85 ft.	345 grams	589 grams

*Source: DEA Cannabis Investigations Section survey May, 1992.

The average yield for the entire outdoor domestic cultivated cannabis crop can be calculated by averaging the non-sinsemilla and sinsemilla yields in the same proportion as reported in the 1991 end of year eradication program results. The total number of cultivated outdoor cannabis plants eradicated in 1991 was 5,257,486. The number of sinsemilla plants was 2,251,735 or 42.8% of the total, and the number of non-sinsemilla plants was 3,005,751 or 57.2% of the total. A weighted average using the yields reported in Table 4 results in an average domestic plant yield of 448 grams or approximately 1 pound per plant.

DEA Cannabis Yields (1992) Page 10

APPENDIX A – THE KONRAD VERSION

CONCLUSIONS

The application of detailed field measurements and mathematical analysis techniques has shown that cannabis plant yields can be accurately estimated. Continued field observations at illicit cultivation locations, both domestically and overseas, will provide the opportunity to further validate the relationships reported. Development of cannabis yield methodologies is essential for understanding of the size of illicit cultivation problem and the drug abuse threat.

-- End --

DEA _Cannabis Yields_ (1992) Page 11

Attachment 1

1990-91 DEA CANNABIS YIELD DATA

Productivity Data for Mississippi Field Plots, 1990-1991

Index Number	Grow Days	Density #/m²	Plant Ht. cm	Plant Diam. cm	Plant Fresh g	Plant Dry g	Plant Water %	Stem Fresh g	Stem Dry g	Yield Fresh g	Yield Dry g	Seed Fresh g	Seed Dry g
Mexican Variety - Plot A, 1.8x1.7 m Planting, 1990													
1.00	55	0.20	29	20	11.9	2.1	82	4.7	0.7	7.2	1.4	0.0	0.0
2.00	55	0.20	47	36	57.4	17.3	70	24.0	5.2	33.4	12.1	0.0	0.0
3.00	55	0.20	45	42	72.9	19.6	73	6.3	0.8	41.2	13.5	0.0	0.0
4.00	55	0.20	27	24	12.9	2.7	78	4.7	0.6	7.6	2.1	0.0	0.0
5.00	93	0.20	145	116	590.2	148.2	72	311.3	79.0	278.9	138.9	0.0	0.0
6.00	93	0.20	156	107	967.6	251.4	74	511.9	112.9	455.7	138.5	0.0	0.0
7.00	93	0.20	228	147	1793.0	500.2	72	1004.3	266.0	788.7	234.2	0.0	0.0
8.00	94	0.20	142	111	860.2	177.7	73	307.2	70.7	383.0	107.0	0.0	0.0
9.00	111	0.20	172	124	1110.9	369.4	67	582.8	190.2	528.1	179.4	0.0	0.0
10.00	112	0.20	238	202	5906.0	1699.3	71	3280.2	951.6	2625.3	747.7	0.0	0.0
11.00	111	0.20	341	263	7581.4	2523.0	67	4362.4	1532.5	3219.0	990.5	0.0	0.0
12.00	152	0.20	245	203	3586.8	1314.1	61	2428.4	957.6	1158.4	427.0	0.0	0.0
13.00	153	0.20	303	245	8010.0	2737.9	66	4545.7	1639.7	3464.3	1098.2	0.0	0.0
14.00	146	0.20	324	170	7181.2	2287.0	71	4198.9	1481.6	2982.3	805.4	0.0	0.0
Mexican Variety - Plot B, 1.8x1.7 m Planting, 1990													
15.00	36	0.20	16	16	4.1	1.1	73	1.3	0.2	2.8	0.9	0.0	0.0
16.00	36	0.20	29	25	14.5	4.2	71	5.2	1.0	9.3	3.2	0.0	0.0
17.00	36	0.20	29	20	13.0	3.9	70	4.0	0.8	9.0	3.1	0.0	0.0
18.00	44	0.20	34	34	27.3	7.6	73	11.1	1.9	16.6	5.7	0.0	0.0
19.00	44	0.20	117	112	889.0	199.8	72	323.6	83.4	365.4	116.4	0.0	0.0
20.00	65	0.20	137	121	923.1	237.5	74	484.7	111.3	438.4	126.2	0.0	0.0
21.00	65	0.20	132	137	1040.7	273.3	74	513.7	116.8	526.9	156.5	0.0	0.0
22.00	91	0.20	255	190	4196.4	1199.9	71	2270.7	597.2	1925.9	602.7	0.0	0.0
23.00	91	0.20	205	160	3243.2	940.6	70	1684.6	438.7	1558.6	501.9	0.0	0.0
24.00	127	0.20	255	215	9356.9	2985.6	70	5771.6	1844.3	4085.3	1141.3	0.0	0.0
25.00	134	0.20	328	180	6770.1	2177.7	68	4339.0	1445.1	2431.1	729.6	0.0	0.0
Mexican Variety - Plot C, 1.8x1.7 m Planting, 1990													
26.00	56	0.20	63	56	103.4	23.5	77	45.8	8.2	57.6	15.3	0.0	0.0
27.00	58	0.20	88	64	153.7	32.4	79	75.3	11.3	78.4	21.1	0.0	0.0
28.00	56	0.20	90	85	239.9	49.5	79	132.4	19.5	107.5	29.6	0.0	0.0
29.00	83	0.20	175	145	1802.9	523.9	71	939.1	260.4	863.8	263.5	0.0	0.0

APPENDIX A – THE KONRAD VERSION

Cannabis Yield: Attachment 1: Productivity Data for Mississippi Field Plots, 1990-1991 (Continued)

Index Number	Grow Days	Density #/m²	Plant Ht. cm	Plant Diam. cm	Plant Fresh g	Plant Dry g	Plant Water %	Stem Fresh g	Stem Dry g	Yield Fresh g	Yield Dry g	Seed Fresh g	Seed Dry g
30.00	82	0.20	140	110	1186.9	308.8	74	565.0	127.5	621.9	181.3	0.0	0.0
31.00	124	0.20	301	185	4942.9	1652.0	67	2624.9	906.6	2318.0	745.4	0.0	0.0
32.00	124	0.20	230	150	4293.2	1340.4	69	2489.8	803.4	1803.4	548.6	0.0	0.0
33.00	124	0.20	220	180	3304.2	1086.1	67	1797.3	621.4	1507.5	464.7	0.0	0.0
34.00	124	0.20	210	190	5944.6	2008.3	66	3557.4	1205.7	2387.2	802.6	0.0	0.0
Mexican Variety - 2.4x2.7 m Planting 199													
107.02	30	0.15	30	16	6.6	2.2	67	2.0	0.6	4.6	1.6	0.0	0.0
108.02	30	0.15	40	25	22.2	6.7	70	7.1	1.6	15.1	5.1	0.0	0.0
109.02	30	0.15	100	64	166.9	44.9	73	70.4	16.6	96.5	28.3	0.0	0.0
108.04	64	0.15	150	167	2693.5	706.0	74	1163.2	276.0	1528.6	430.0	0.0	0.0
107.04	64	0.15	170	100	459.5	128.9	72	184.6	41.1	274.9	87.8	0.0	0.0
106.04	64	0.15	170	143	1608.6	440.0	73	816.4	201.2	792.2	239.6	0.0	0.0
106.06	91	0.15	200	229	6829.4	2026.6	70	2517.2	816.2	4311.2	1210.4	0.0	0.0
108.06	91	0.15	229	186	6221.8	1944.4	69	1657.2	513.5	4466.6	1431.0	0.0	0.0
108.06	91	0.15	186	175	5154.2	1612.9	68	2115.7	732.7	4311.4	880.2	0.0	0.0
109.07	91	0.15	297	246	1719.4	719.4	57	2627.3	732.7	3038.5	320.3	0.0	0.0
109.09	123	0.15	285	205	7014.9	2654.4	62	2822.4	1126.8	2717.3	615.4	0.0	0.0
107.19	128	0.15	292	215	5901.0	2150.0	64	2412.5	739.8	1442.4	1484.9	0.0	0.0
107.19	128	0.15	249	204	8315.0	2980.8	64	3937.2	1442.0	2764.5	766.1	0.0	0.0
108.19	128	0.15	309	227	7831.1	2812.0	64	2711.0	995.3	3030.6	1827.5	0.0	0.0
109.12	128	0.15	262	213	6255.5	2345.5	62	1621.1	1155.1	1155.1	1613.3	0.0	0.0
109.17	128	0.15	266	261	13957.6	4392.2	62	1621.3	902.0	2182.6	2182.6	0.0	0.0
107.01	129	0.15	270	261	13957.6	4392.2	68	4337.7	1509.9	7286.8	2333.1	0.0	0.0
Mexican Variety - 1.8x1.8 m Planting 199													
102.02	30	0.30	50	38	63.6	15.2	76	27.6	5.0	36.0	10.2	0.0	0.0
103.02	30	0.30	64	42	77.2	17.1	78	22.0	4.0	55.2	13.1	0.0	0.0
104.02	30	0.30	67	52	71.2	19.0	73	22.5	4.0	49.0	14.1	0.0	0.0
102.04	64	0.30	158	141	1947.1	546.7	72	823.4	212.5	1123.7	334.2	0.0	0.0
103.04	64	0.30	172	144	1754.3	486.0	72	816.5	208.5	937.8	277.5	0.0	0.0
105.04	64	0.30	140	158	2232.0	964.3	75	959.9	222.6	1272.1	341.7	0.0	0.0
103.06	91	0.30	247	184	3088.5	964.3	69	1290.6	438.4	1797.9	513.5	0.0	0.0
105.07	91	0.30	140	185	4109.0	1536.1	63	1348.7	523.6	2760.3	1012.5	0.0	0.0
104.06	92	0.30	314	173	3364.0	1269.0	65	1641.2	626.3	1998.9	642.7	0.0	0.0
105.07	91	0.30	173	193	5123.8	2107.6	59	1936.4	876.8	733.3	1259.3	0.0	0.0
104.06	92	0.30	267	154	4370.4	1779.8	59	1839.6	820.9	1646.6	884.2	0.0	0.0
103.09	121	0.30	218	195	4688.2	2037.5	56	1818.4	576.6	1963.0	906.6	0.0	0.0
101.10	122	0.30	240	173	3429.0	1461.7	57	1256.4	576.4	1212.6	960.1	0.0	0.0
102.08	122	0.30	245	191	4868.8	1986.1	59	2021.5	886.6	1688.9	635.3	0.0	0.0
103.12	127	0.30	220	191	4868.8	1986.1	59	2021.5	886.6	1688.9	635.3	0.0	0.0

Cannabis Yield: Attachment 1: Productivity Data for Municipal Field Plots, 1990-1991 (Continued)

Index Number	Grow Days	Density #/m²	Plant Ht. cm	Plant Diam. cm	Plant Fresh g	Plant Dry g	Plant Water %	Stem Fresh g	Stem Dry g	Yield Fresh g	Yield Dry g	Seed Fresh g	Seed Dry g
104.17	127	0.30	338	218	5814.1	2285.5	61	2483.1	1089.1	2264.1	814.3	1066.9	382.1
102.09	128	0.30	303	163	4143.5	1690.7	59	1849.5	811.2	1327.6	502.1	966.4	377.4
103.01	129	0.30	224	281	14290.0	5051.4	65	4812.4	1856.4	6784.6	2308.4	2693.0	886.6

Mexican Variety - 0.9x0.9 m Planting, 1991

Index Number	Grow Days	Density #/m²	Plant Ht. cm	Plant Diam. cm	Plant Fresh g	Plant Dry g	Plant Water %	Stem Fresh g	Stem Dry g	Yield Fresh g	Yield Dry g	Seed Fresh g	Seed Dry g
97.02	30	1.20	67	39	65.9	17.5	73	23.1	4.9	42.8	12.6	0.0	0.0
98.09	30	1.20	47	35	45.9	11.3	75	15.9	3.1	30.0	8.2	0.0	0.0
99.09	30	1.20	37	24	6.7	4.7	72	5.1	1.1	3.4	3.4	0.0	0.0
90.11	30	1.20	145	106	656.2	180.8	72	308.3	83.5	347.6	97.3	0.0	0.0
95.11	65	1.20	140	100	1131.6	324.0	71	576.5	161.2	555.1	162.8	0.0	0.0
89.11	65	1.20	123	76	4330.0	122.2	72	492.5	53.5	237.5	68.7	0.0	0.0
99.11	65	1.20	232	126	1078.3	346.2	68	533.2	173.5	545.1	172.7	0.0	0.0
88.11	65	1.20	160	86	4480.1	142.2	70	246.1	71.0	234.0	71.2	0.0	0.0
87.12	65	1.20	180	86	565.6	194.2	66	284.1	102.9	281.5	91.3	0.0	0.0
88.12	65	1.20	125	51	30.4	37.2	72	58.2	16.2	72.2	21.0	0.0	0.0
96.14	91	1.20	207	104	839.9	296.9	65	410.3	161.7	429.6	135.2	0.0	0.0
87.14	91	1.20	186	79	732.8	244.4	67	278.2	98.2	454.6	146.2	0.0	0.0
89.14	91	1.20	170	99	1078.2	321.5	70	290.4	89.8	787.8	233.7	0.0	0.0
96.13	91	1.20	224	133	1498.4	541.2	64	635.8	254.4	862.6	286.8	0.0	0.0
97.14	91	1.20	230	147	2427.6	763.3	69	955.6	326.0	1472.0	437.3	0.0	0.0
97.19	91	1.20	224	83	2653.8	261.2	60	334.8	132.4	319.0	128.8	0.0	0.0
95.23	91	1.20	256	99	1079.1	424.5	61	543.0	226.4	536.1	198.1	0.0	0.0
87.19	120	1.20	271	112	1181.0	650.2	61	690.4	267.1	637.8	244.2	352.8	138.4
96.22	120	1.20	221	113	1938.2	767.0	60	868.7	344.0	551.6	214.2	517.6	208.8
87.17	120	1.20	251	95	750.7	287.5	62	305.2	129.7	445.5	157.8	0.0	0.0
97.16	121	1.20	288	129	2326.0	937.1	56	1026.2	468.6	594.9	242.1	226.0	226.0
99.16	121	1.20	288	83	1305.6	555.0	57	560.7	238.9	391.7	162.8	353.9	153.9
99.15	121	1.20	234	130	555.6	560.7	59	759.3	342.3	835.9	326.0	527.9	203.8
100.15	122	1.20	234	130	2123.1	872.3	59	742.3	326.2	326.2	153.9	527.9	203.8
100.17	122	1.20	175	125	1721.8	752.4	56	495.4	193.5	591.7	258.4	634.8	300.5

Colombian Variety - Plot B, 0.9x1.8 m Planting, 1990

Index Number	Grow Days	Density #/m²	Plant Ht. cm	Plant Diam. cm	Plant Fresh g	Plant Dry g	Plant Water %	Stem Fresh g	Stem Dry g	Yield Fresh g	Yield Dry g	Seed Fresh g	Seed Dry g
35.00	91	0.60	77	72	159.9	37.8	76	75.4	13.7	84.5	24.1	0.0	0.0
36.00	91	0.60	111	104	341.3	85.0	75	169.3	32.9	172.0	52.1	0.0	0.0
38.00	93	0.60	137	108	752.0	214.1	72	387.9	100.2	364.1	113.9	0.0	0.0
39.00	110	0.60	182	128	1385.5	419.7	70	751.5	227.3	634.0	192.4	0.0	0.0
40.00	147	0.60	200	100	1131.8	389.6	66	533.4	236.1	598.4	153.5	0.0	0.0
41.00	147	0.60	220	140	1697.1	576.5	66	950.0	357.9	747.1	218.5	0.0	0.0
42.00	147	0.60	250	143	2627.9	883.5	66	1496.7	555.7	1131.2	327.5	0.0	0.0

APPENDIX A – THE KONRAD VERSION

Cannabis Yield: Attachment 1: Productivity Data for Mississippi Field Plots, 1990-1991 (Continued)

Index Number	Grow Days	Density #/m²	Plant Ht. cm	Plant Diam. cm	Plant Fresh g	Plant Dry g	Plant Water %	Stem Fresh g	Stem Dry g	Yield Fresh g	Yield Dry g	Seed Fresh g	Seed Dry g
Hybrid Variety – Plot F, 0.9x1.8 m Planting, 1990													
43.00	145	0.60	152	191	2201.2	593.6	72	1137.6	333.5	963.6	260.1	0.0	0.0
44.00	145	0.60	230	210	10477.2	2654.2	75	6716.7	1843.0	3760.5	811.2	0.0	0.0
45.00	91	0.60	67	84	369.7	92.9	75	153.6	33.6	216.1	59.3	0.0	0.0
Jamaican Variety – Plot H, 0.9x1.8 m Planting, 1990													
46.00	91	0.13	102	94	810.7	184.6	77	421.8	78.2	388.9	106.4	0.0	0.0

Correlation Matrix for Marijuana Plant Parameter Relationships, 1990-91

	Growth Days	Density	Plant Height	Plant Diameter	Plant Fresh Weight	Plant Dry Weight	Plant Water	Stem Fresh Weight	Stem Dry Weight	Yield Fresh Weight	Yield Dry Weight	Seed Fresh Weight	Seed Dry Weight
Growth Days	1.000												
Plant Density	0.015	1.000											
Plant Height	0.846	0.009	1.000										
Plant Diameter	0.729	-0.315	0.830	1.000									
Plant Fresh Weight	0.628	-0.350	0.687	0.867	1.000								
Plant Dry Weight	0.660	-0.328	0.704	0.870	0.989	1.000							
Plant Water	-0.689	-0.245	-0.664	-0.476	-0.378	-0.470	1.000						
Stem Fresh Weight	-0.365	-0.365	0.722	0.844	0.939	0.917	-0.417	1.000					
Stem Dry Weight	-0.336	-0.336	0.746	0.853	0.943	0.945	-0.442	0.985	1.000				
Yield Fresh Weight	0.696	0.609	0.824	0.962	0.932	-0.280	0.857	0.849	1.000				
Yield Dry Weight	0.658	0.630	0.843	0.969	0.958	-0.358	0.853	0.862	0.990	1.000			
Seed Fresh Weight	0.529	0.528	0.630	0.660	0.728	-0.490	0.452	0.530	0.565	0.637	1.000		
Seed Dry Weight	0.562	0.446	0.523	0.632	0.706	-0.527	0.430	0.511	0.528	0.604	0.994	1.000	

N=98

CRITICAL VALUE (2-TAIL, P<0.05) = +/- .198 ;

CANNABIS YIELDS: ATTACHMENT 2

1985-86 YIELD DATA, UNIVERSITY OF MISSISSIPPI

UNIVERSITY OF MISSISSIPPI 1985 YIELD STUDY DATA

Table 1. Statistics for the Production of Marijuana from Plants of Different Age

Week	Plant #	WET WEIGHT(s) Whole Plant	Stalk/ Stems	Stalk/ leaves	DRY WEIGHT(s) Stalk/ Stems	Stalk/ leaves	% of dry leaves to dry wt²	% of dry leaves to wet wt²	% of dry stalk/stem to wet wt²	% of dry plant to wet wt²	% of wet leaves to wet wt²	% of wet stalk/stem to wet wt²	% of dry leaves to wet leaves	Height (cm)
12	1	328	182	146	82	53.5	39	16	25	41	45	56	37	180
13	2	1309.7	702	607.7	380	130.5	26	10	29	39	46	54	21	231
14	3	1055	657	398	282	158.1	36	15	28	42	38	62	40	269
15	4	1588	966	622	372.5	241.0	37	17	29	46	45	55	39	286
16	5	2163	1197	704	726	268.2	25	11	33	43	68	68	34	281
17	6	2268	1533	735	823	221.5	25	12	36	48	68	67	36	300
18	7	1972	1331	641	655	171.4	20	10	39	44	74	74	35	326
19	8	1724	1278	446	668	171.4	20	11	35	46	73	74	38	259
20	9	3472	2535	937	1220	388.7	24	11	35	46	73	73	41	259
21	10	2164	1661	503	854	217.6	20	10	39	50	77	77	43	358
Average		1867.77	1259.4	608.37	630.9	222.37	27.7	12.3	32.6	44.8		65.4	36.3	275.1

wg² = Whole plant

UNIVERSITY OF MISSISSIPPI 1986 YIELD STUDY DATA

Table 2. Statistics for the Production of Marijuana from Mature Plants

Plant #	WET WEIGHT(s) Whole Plant	Stalk/ Stems	Stalk/ leaves	DRY WEIGHT(s) Stalk/ Stems	Stalk/ leaves	% of dry leaves to dry wt²	% of dry leaves to wet wt²	% of dry stalk/stem to wet wt²	% of dry plant to wet wt²	% of wet leaves to wet wt²	% of wet stalk/stem to wet wt²	% of dry leaves to wet leaves	Height (cm)
1	3869	2635	1261	1456	709	33	11	37	56	32	68	36	249
2	2680	1620	1060	688	361	34	16	26	40	40	61	34	231
3	1712	1200	512	620	181	23	23	36	47	30	70	35	213
4	2133	1292	861	680	289	30	14	32	45	39	61	34	216
5	1730	1218	512	570	171	23	10	33	43	30	70	33	221
6	2344	1314	1030	621	319	34	14	36	44	56	31	221
7	2283	1541	742	742	140	15	6	33	33	68	19	257
8	2231	1418	813	734	140	28	13	33	36	64	34	224
9	1168	808	360	400	280	25	11	31	36	69	36	224
10	1376	965	411	540	157	23	11	30	30	70	38	220
Avg.	2155.3	1401.1	754.2	731.9	273.7	26.8	12.2	33.3	45.5		65.7	34.5	220

Appendix B
The Lindy Smith Version

An earlier version also exists. I obtained this copy from the Lindy Smith Foundation. It betrays a number of errors some of which will be corrected in the Konrad. But it also supposes an even earlier version of the report.

Again, I cannot reproduce it here so I include another copy of that not completely unrelated study, the same one as in Appendix A. This one has a first page bearing the stamp of a DEA Special Agent. It also has two first pages, the summary page. In the first, the first paragraph states the plants were grown in 1990 and 1991. In the second summary page, the first paragraph states the plants were grown in 1990 and 1993. As well, there are two Figure 1s, identical except that one is vertical and the other horizontal, so I have only reproduced one of them. There is also a line missing on page 10 as well as a few other minor errors.

CHARLES A. STOWELL
SPECIAL AGENT

CANNABIS YIELDS

RECEIVED

FEB 1993

DISTRICT ATTORNEY

JUNE 1992
DRUG ENFORCEMENT ADMINISTRATION

SUMMARY

Outdoor *Cannabis sativa L.* (cannabis) yield studies conducted during the summers of 1990 and 1991 have determined that the usable dry weight yield (leaf and bud) for female cannabis plants can be up to 2.3 kilograms (5.1 pounds). Based upon a survey of 15 leading producer states, the average plant yield for mature, domestically grown female cannabis plants in 1991 was 448 grams (1 pound). An accurate yield estimate can be made by weighing the fresh weight of a plant or measuring the plant's diameter at the broadest point in the canopy. A very significant factor affecting yield was planting density.

BACKGROUND

The Drug Enforcement Administration (DEA) during the summers of 1990 and 1991, conducted a detailed cannabis yield measurement program at the University of Mississippi in Oxford. The purpose of the project was to determine the average yield of outdoor cultivated cannabis plants and identify factors to predict usable yield. Prior to the project's initiation, the only quantitative studies undertaken were two studies self-initiated by the University of Mississippi in 1985 and 1986. These two studies made a limited number of observations and did not identify factors influencing plant yield.

METHODOLOGY

The overall intent of the studies was to introduce variation into the research design in order to gain a basic understanding of some of the factors influencing plant yield. The DEA sponsored research used different seed stocks from Mexico, Colombia, Jamaica, and a hybrid of South Africa-Afghanistan origin.

The 1990 effort consisted of a progressive planting of 3 separate areas at 2 week intervals. Each area was planted with the same seed stock at an identical planting density. The varying of the planting date permitted analysis of the sensitivity of cannabis yield and plant development to planting date. The 1991 effort focused on the relationship between planting density and yield. Three different planting densities of Mexican seed stock were studied. Tables 1 and 2 describe the average plant yields which are associated with specific densities.

Yield measurements were made on 90 days or older female plants which duplicated the preference of a majority of domestic growers to cultivate the larger yielding females. However, no attempt was made to cultivate unfertilized female plants, commonly known as "sinsemilla". The vast majority of observations were made of the very common, tall, narrow leaflet cannabis variety known as

1

2/

103·01

SUMMARY

Outdoor Cannabis sativa L. (cannabis) yield studies conducted during the summers of 1990 and 1993 have determined that the usable dry weight yield (leaf and bud) for female cannabis plants can be up to 2.3 kilograms (5.1 pounds). Based upon a survey of 15 leading producer states, the average plant yield for mature, domestically grown female cannabis plants in 1991 was 448 grams (1 pound). An accurate yield estimate can be made by weighing the fresh weight of a plant or measuring the plant's diameter at the broadest point in the canopy. A very significant factor affecting yield was planting density.

BACKGROUND

The Drug Enforcement Administration (DEA) during the summers of 1990 and 1991 conducted a detailed cannabis yield measurement program at the University of Mississippi in Oxford. The purpose of the project was to determine the average yield of outdoor cultivated cannabis plants and identify factors to predict usable yield. Prior to the project's initiation, the only quantitative studies undertaken were two studies self-initiated by the University of Mississippi in 1985 and 1986. These two studies made a limited number of observations and did not identify factors influencing plant yield.

METHODOLOGY

The overall intent of the studies was to introduce variation into the research design in order to gain a basic understanding of some of the factors influencing plant yield. The DEA sponsored research used different seed stocks from Mexico, Colombia, Jamaica, and a hybrid of South African-Afghanistan origin.

The 1990 effort consisted of a progressive planting of 3 separate areas at 2 week intervals. Each area was planted with the same seed stock at an identical planting density. The varying of the planting date permitted analysis of the sensitivity of cannabis yield and plant development to planting date. The 1991 effort focused on the relationship between planting density and yield. Three different planting densities of Mexican seed stock were studied. Tables 1 and 2 describe the average plant yields which are associated with specific densities.

Yield measurements were made on 90 days or older female plants, which duplicated the preference of a majority of domestic growers, to cultivate the larger yielding females. However, no attempt was made to cultivate unfertilized female plants, commonly known as "sinsemilla". The vast majority of observations were made on the very common, tall, narrow leaflet cannabis variety known as "sativa". A very limited number of observations were made on the other major variety, "indica". The indica variety is a shorter, more compact, faster maturing plant with larger leaves.

(p. 2)

Yield measurements were made on [102] plants during the course of
the [two year] study. Physical measurements were made of the
plant's height from ground level and the diameter at the broadest
point in the plant's canopy. Upon completion of the physical
measurements, the plant was cut at ground level and separated
into [four] component parts - stem/branches, leaves, [female
flowering tops, commonly known as buds or colas, and seed.] The
individual components were each weighed to determine a ["wet" or
"fresh" weight.] The material was dried in a convection oven at [70]
degrees Celsius. The dried material was reweighed when it had
reached a constant weight, typically after (24) to (48) hours. This
second measurement is termed the ["dry"] weight. During both yield
surveys, (cannabis) plants were harvested and measured on a monthly
basis to quantify yield throughout the growth cycle. [The
selection of [plants] was based upon a determination of their
representative physical size, shape, and overall vigor
characteristics.] The selection process captured the diversity (or
plant size by including cannabis plants ranging from the larger
to the smaller plant specimens.] The planting of approximately 100
plants per cultivation area insured that there was a large and
representative population from which plants were sampled. If a
particular plant was harvested for the measurement program, the
neighboring plants were ineligible for future selection which
avoided changing the planting density during the study.
Similarly, no plants on the outer rows were selected to avoid
edge affects which could skew results because of an asymmetrical
planting density.

YIELD RESULTS

All measurements recorded in 1990 (or) 1991 are contained in
Attachment 1. Table (I) depicts the average yield for all mature
(120 days or older) cannabis plants grown using a [dense] planting
pattern of either 9 square feet per plant or 18 square feet per
plant. At this relatively high planting density, the lateral
branches of adjacent cannabis plants were touching by the middle
of July. Thereafter, the horizontal growth rate decreased in
relation to the vertical rate of growth. The results were tall,
narrow plant canopies.

(p. 3)

Table 1
Average Cannabis Yields at
Maturity for High Planting Densities

Sponsor	Year	Density	Yield	Seed	Stock
Univ. of MS	1985	9 ft.sq.	222 grams	Mexico	incorrect
Univ. of MS	1986	9 ft.sq.	274 grams	Mexico	
DEA	1990	18 ft.sq.	233 grams	Colombia	
DEA	1991	9 ft.sq.	215 grams	Mexico	

Yield = [oven dry weight of usable leaf and bud from mature 120
day or older plants.)

The similarity of plant yields contained in Table (I) is remarkable
considering the variation in seed stock, year of cultivation, and

other factors. However, if the planting density is decreased, the plants have more room to laterally branch out. The additional space allows the plant to assume a natural canopy shape, somewhat similar to a Christmas tree. The larger branching structure coupled with increased available sunlight, soil nutrients, and water resulted in significantly greater plant yields. Table 2 displays the yields for cannabis at maturity for identical seed stocks at three low planting densities and for different planting dates and years.

Table 2
Average Cannabis Yields at
Maturity for Low Planting Densities

Sponsor	Year	Density	Yield	Seed Stock
DEA-A	1990	81 ft.sq.	777 grams	Mexico
DEA-B	1990	81 ft.sq.	936 grams	Mexico
DEA-C	1990	81 ft.sq.	640 grams	Mexico
DEA	1991	72 ft.sq.	1,015 grams	Mexico
DEA	1991	36 ft.sq.	860 grams	Mexico

Seedlings for the 1990 measurement program were planted at two week intervals: DEA-A was planted on 4/17, DEA-B was planted on 5/8, and DEA-C was planted on 5/17. The 1991 plantings were made during the first week of June.

Figure 1 reports select plant height-diameter ratios for the planting densities used in 1990 and 1991. The noticeably high ratio for the 9 foot square planting density confirms that this plant canopy shape is different than all of the other observations which had relatively large amounts of space in which to grow. The height-diameter graph of Figure 1 shows that plant density is a significant factor affecting plant canopy shape, which in turn affects plant yield. (The significance of the relationship between planting density and plant yield will be discussed later in this paper.)

(p. 4)

(Figure 1)

During both growing seasons, only standard irrigation, fertilization, and weeding activity were rendered as required. However, two plants, identification numbers 107.01 and 103.01 in the 1991 low planting density plots, had extremely high yields in comparison to neighboring plants. The dry weight yield for plant 107.01 was 2,086.9 grams (4.6 pounds) and plant 103.01 yielded 2,308.4 grams (5.1 pounds). These two plants were located in a low area. It is believed that the natural slope of the land caused these plants to receive additional water and possibly additional fertilizer through run on water. The significance of these yields is that they demonstrate that certain agronomic practices can produce higher average yields than those reported in Table 2.

292

Analysis of the combined 1990 and 1991 DEA yield data shows that usable oven dry weight material (leaf and bud) in a mature cannabis plant is 14.4% of the plant's total (roots excluded) fresh weight. A break down of the four types of material found in a mature female cannabis plant is presented in Figure 2.

needs something to introduce figure 2

not two separate figures

(p. 5)

(Figure 2)

(p. 6)

YIELD PREDICTION

The plant growth and yield data collected throughout the 1990 and 1991 growing seasons shows that plant yield can be accurately predicted from simple field measurements. Several field measurement techniques were assessed including plant height, diameter, fresh weight, and the number of grow days. The predictive models developed are valid for any sativa variety plants regardless of plant age or planting density.

The best predictor of plant yield was measurement of the plant's fresh weight. Figure 3 depicts the linear relationship between plant fresh weight and yield dry weight. The only required measurement is the weighing of the plant at the time of seizure in a timely fashion to avoid excessive loss of plant water. That fresh weight would not include the plant roots or any soil adhering to the plant. The fresh weight multiplied by the number 0.1437 would result in an estimate of usable dry weight material. This estimating technique is extremely accurate. *b. s. !!!!*

(Figure 3)

(p. 7)

II. Another accurate method for predicting plant yield is based upon measurement of the diameter of the plant at the broadest point in the canopy. Figure 4 depicts the curvilinear relationship between plant canopy diameter and the plant dry weight. The measurement of a plant canopy diameter is simpler than the measurement of the plant's fresh weight. However, the calculation of a yield estimate requires a two step process. First, the measured diameter is entered into the equation: Dry Weight = -3.76786 + (0.06666 * (Diameter ^2)). This first equation estimates the plant's total dry weight. Usable yield is then calculated using the percentages of bud and leaf described in Figure 2.

(p. 8)

Neither plant height data or the number of grow days were as accurate a predictor of plant yield as were fresh weight or diameter measurements. However, weight was a good indicator of plant age and this relationship may be useful in estimating planting date. The correlation matrix included in Attachment 1

Analysis of the combined 1990 and 1991 DEA yield data shows that usable oven dry weight material (leaf and bud) in a mature cannabis plant is 14.4% of the plant's total (roots excluded) fresh weight. A break down of the four types of material found in a mature female cannabis plant is presented in Figure 2.

(p. 5)

(Figure 2)

(p. 6)

YIELD PREDICTION

The plant growth and yield data collected throughout the 1990 and 1991 growing seasons shows that plant yield can be accurately predicted from simple field measurements. Several field measurement techniques were assessed including plant height, diameter, fresh weight, and the number of grow days. The predictive models developed are valid for any sativa variety plants regardless of plant age or planting density.

The best predictor of plant yield was measurement of the plant's fresh weight. Figure 3 depicts the linear relationship between plant fresh weight and yield dry weight. The only required measurement is the weighing of the plant at the time of seizure in a timely fashion to avoid excessive loss of plant water. That fresh weight would not include the plant roots or any soil adhering to the plant. The fresh weight multiplied by the number 0.1437 would result in an estimate of usable dry weight material. This estimating technique is extremely accurate.

(Figure 3)

(p. 7)

Another accurate method for predicting plant yield is based upon measurement of the diameter of the plant at the broadest point in the canopy. Figure 4 depicts the curvilinear relationship between plant canopy diameter and the plant dry weight. The measurement of a plant canopy diameter is simpler than the measurement of the plant's fresh weight. However, the calculation of a yield estimate requires a two step process. First, the measured diameter is entered into the equation: Dry Weight = -3.76786 + (0.06666 * (Diameter ^2)). This first equation estimates the plant's total dry weight. Usable yield is then calculated using the percentages of bud and leaf described in Figure 2.

(p. 8)

Neither plant height data or the number of grow days were as accurate a predictor of plant yield as were fresh weight or diameter measurements. However, weight was a good indicator of plant age and this relationship may be useful in estimating planting date. The correlation matrix included in Attachment 1

There is no Table 3. 7/

structure is highly desired by illicit growers because it
contains the highest number of THC producing glands.

Yield Adjustment Factors
There is no need to adjust yield estimations of outdoor mature
cannabis crops if at the time of seizure there are no male
plants. If male plants are present, then evidence of this fact
should be apparent by early August. The estimated yield of a male
plant in early August, the point at which it begins to senesce
and loose leaf cover, will be approximately 50% of the weight of
a female plant of similar age and growth stage. By late September
or October, the only harvestable cannabis plants remaining will
be female plants.

Based ? No data

If the female cannabis plants are unfertilized, then no seed will
be produced. The average usable yield (leaf and bud) of a mature
female plant will be 57% of the plant's dry weight where as the
yield for a typical fertilized, seed bearing cannabis plant will
be 34% of tile the plant dry weight (Figure 2).

will be *p. 9* *I say so* *the the in C*

DOMESTIC ESTIMATE
The identification of accurate plant yield estimation
methodologies makes possible the opportunity to estimate the
average domestic yield using eradication statistics and plant
canopy diameter information. A survey of 15 leading producer
states was conducted by DEA to determine the average diameter of
mature plants eradicated in September 1991. Table 4 lists the
average diameter of mature plants (observed) in that state as
reported by the DEA state eradication coordinator. The estimated
(usable) yield for each state's eradicated plant total was calculated using the predictive methodology described in Figure 4.

Several May 92 *from canopy method* *dry*

(p. 10)

This methodology uses average plant canopy diameter information
as the predictor variable to estimate plant dry weight. The plant
dry weight is adjusted to estimate usable air dry weight yield by
first taking 34% of the dry weight to calculate usable yield, and
adding 10% to the oven dry weight to obtain the air dry yield.
This estimate is valid for female cannabis plants at maturity
which contain seeds. An estimate for seedless cannabis weight,
and then adjusting upward by 10% to convert from oven dry weight
to an air dry yield.

INSERT *"sensimilla" [Sensemilla] is derived by first taking 58% of the plant dry"*

usable yield Dry wt : air dry

Table 4
Estimated Cannabis Plant Yields

State	1991 Eradicated Plant Total	Average Diameter	Estimated Non-Sinse. Yield(g)	Estimated Sinsemilla Yield(g)
Alabama	163,294	4 ft.	369	630
Arkansas	106,405	4 ft.	369	630
California	151,529	3.5 ft.	284	484
Florida	92,190	4.25 ft.	420	716
Georgia	300,583	4 ft.	369	630
Illinois	337,730	3.25 ft.	243	414
Indiana	206,494	4 ft.	369	630
Kansas	21,751	4 ft.	369	630

Line missing in p. 10

Missing line

295

8/

		δ grams & Dw's		
Kentucky	809,366	3.25 ft.	243	414
Louisiana	79,009	3.5 ft.	264	484
Minnesota	191,790	4 ft.	369	630
Missouri	104,493	3.5 ft.	284	484
N. Carolina	198,470	4 ft.	369	630
Tennessee	508,816	4 ft.	369	630
Texas	22,997	4.5 ft.	466	795
Average:		3.85 ft.	345 grams	589 grams

Source: DEA Cannabis Investigations Section survey May, 1992.

The average yield for the entire outdoor domestic cultivated
cannabis crop can be calculated by averaging the non-sinsemilla
and sinsemilla yields in the same proportion as reported in the
1991 end of year eradication program results. The total
number of cultivated outdoor cannabis plants eradicated in 1991
was 5,257,486. The number of sinsemilla plants was 2,251,735 or
42.8% of the total, and the number of non-sinsemilla plants was
3,005,751 or 57.2% of the total. A weighted average using the
yields reported in Table 4 results in an average domestic plant
yield of 448 grams or approximately 1 pound per plant.

(p. 11)

CONCLUSIONS

The application of detailed field measurements and mathematical
analysis techniques has shown that cannabis plant yields can be
accurately estimated. Continued field observations at illicit
cultivation locations, both domestically and overseas, will
provide the opportunity to further validate the relationships
reported. Development of cannabis yield methodologies is
essential for understanding of the size of illicit cultivation
problem and the drug abuse threat.

296

10/

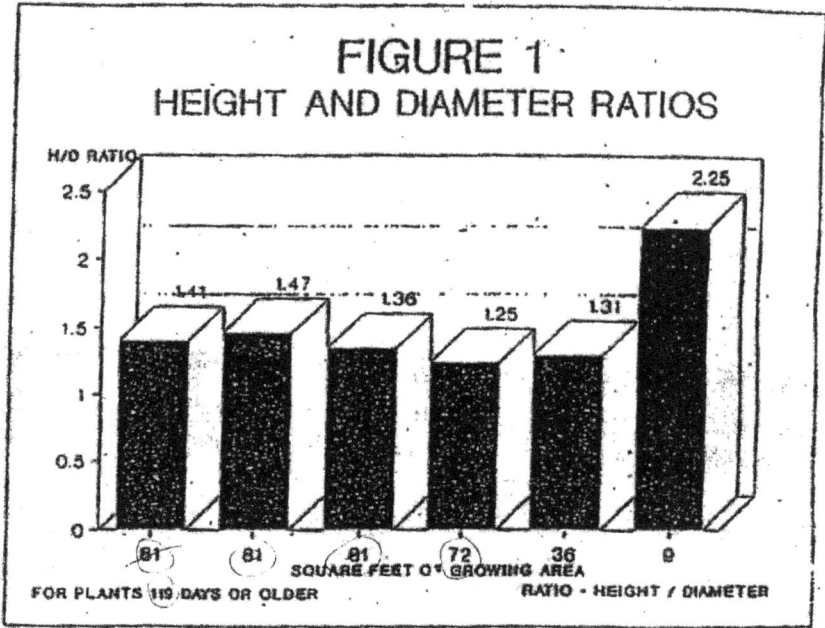

FIGURE 1
HEIGHT AND DIAMETER RATIOS

FOR PLANTS 119 DAYS OR OLDER

RATIO - HEIGHT / DIAMETER

Cannabis Yields 1992   US DOJ, DEA   p. 5

FIGURE 2
NON-SINSEMILLA CANNABIS COMPONENTS

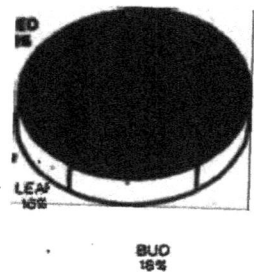

STEM/BRANCHES
43%

LEAF
16%

BUD
16%

PERCENT OVEN DRY WEIGHT FOR 120 DAY OR OLDER PLANTS

SINSEMILLA CANNABIS COMPONENTS

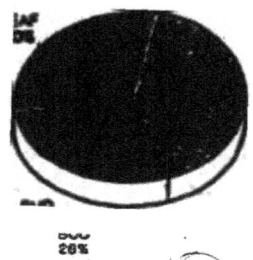

STEM/BRANCHES
42%

LEAF

BUD
26%

PERCENT OVEN DRY WEIGHT FOR 90 DAY OR OLDER PLANTS
WHICH DID NOT HAVE ANY SEED DEVELOPMENT

12/

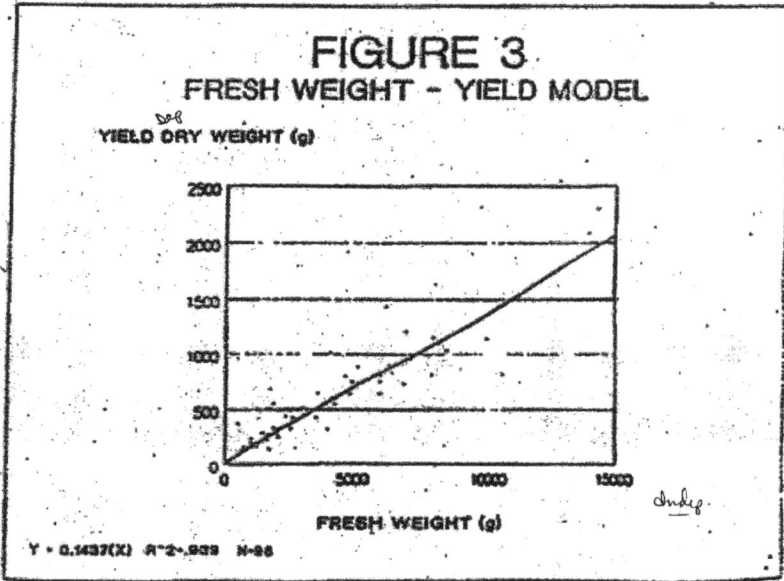

FIGURE 3
FRESH WEIGHT – YIELD MODEL

YIELD DRY WEIGHT (g)

FRESH WEIGHT (g)

Y - 0.1437(X) R^2-.933 N-88

13/

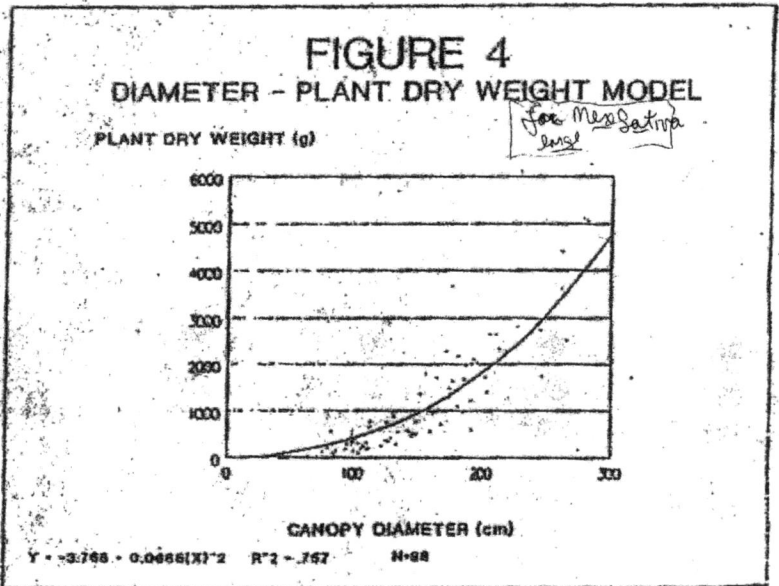

FIGURE 4
DIAMETER – PLANT DRY WEIGHT MODEL

14/

ATTACHMENT 1

cannabis

1990-91 DEA YIELD DATA

Productivity Data for Mississippi Field Plots, 1990-1991

Index Number	Grow Days	Density t/m²	Plant Ht. cm	Plant Diam. cm	Plant Fresh g	Plant Dry g	Plant Water %	Stem Fresh g	Stem Dry g	Yield Fresh g	Yield Dry g	Seed Fresh g	Seed Dry g
Mexican Variety – Plot A, 1.8x2.7 m Planting, 1990													
1.00	55	0.20	25	20	11.9	2.1	82	4.7	0.7	7.2	1.4	0.0	0.0
2.00	55	0.20	47	36	57.4	17.3	70	24.0	5.2	33.4	12.1	0.0	0.0
3.00	55	0.20	45	42	72.9	19.8	73	31.7	6.3	41.2	13.5	0.0	0.0
4.00	55	0.20	27	24	12.3	2.7	78	4.7	0.6	7.6	2.1	0.0	0.0
5.00	93	0.20	145	110	590.2	165.2	72	311.3	79.0	278.9	86.5	0.0	0.0
6.00	93	0.20	156	107	967.6	251.4	74	511.9	112.9	455.7	138.5	0.0	0.0
7.00	93	0.20	228	147	1793.0	500.2	72	1004.3	266.0	788.7	234.2	0.0	0.0
8.00	94	0.20	142	111	660.2	177.7	73	307.2	70.7	353.0	107.0	0.0	0.0
9.00	111	0.20	172	124	1110.9	369.6	67	582.8	190.2	528.1	179.4	0.0	0.0
10.00	112	0.20	238	202	5906.0	1699.3	71	3280.7	951.6	2625.3	747.7	0.0	0.0
11.00	111	0.20	341	265	7581.4	2523.0	67	4362.4	1532.6	3219.0	990.5	0.0	0.0
12.00	152	0.20	245	203	3586.8	1384.6	61	2428.4	957.6	1158.4	427.0	0.0	0.0
13.00	153	0.20	303	245	8010.0	2737.9	66	4545.7	1639.7	3464.3	1098.2	0.0	0.0
14.00	146	0.20	324	170	7781.2	2287.0	71	4798.9	1481.6	2982.3	805.4	0.0	0.0
Mexican Variety – Plot B, 1.8x2.7 m Planting, 1990													
15.00	36	0.20	16	16	4.1	1.1	73	1.3	0.2	2.8	0.9	0.0	0.0
16.00	36	0.20	25	25	14.5	4.2	71	5.2	1.0	9.3	3.2	0.0	0.0
17.00	36	0.20	20	20	13.0	3.9	20	4.0	0.8	9.0	3.1	0.0	0.0
18.00	39	0.20	34	34	27.9	7.6	73	11.1	1.9	16.8	5.7	0.0	0.0
19.00	64	0.20	117	112	689.0	199.8	71	323.6	83.4	365.4	116.4	0.0	0.0
20.00	65	0.20	137	121	923.1	237.5	74	484.7	111.3	438.4	126.2	0.0	0.0
21.00	65	0.20	137	132	1040.7	273.3	74	513.7	116.8	527.0	156.5	0.0	0.0
22.00	91	0.20	255	190	4196.6	1199.9	71	2270.7	597.2	1925.9	602.7	0.0	0.0
23.00	93	0.20	205	160	3243.2	940.6	71	1684.6	438.7	1558.6	501.9	0.0	0.0
24.00	127	0.20	255	215	9858.9	2985.6	70	5771.6	1644.3	4085.3	1141.3	0.0	0.0
25.00	134	0.20	328	180	6770.1	2177.7	68	4339.0	1448.1	2431.1	729.6	0.0	0.0
Mexican Variety – Plot C, 1.8x2.7 m Planting, 1990													
26.00	56	0.20	61	56	103.4	23.5	77	45.8	8.2	57.6	15.3	0.0	0.0
27.00	56	0.20	68	65	153.7	32.4	79	75.3	11.3	78.4	21.1	0.0	0.0
28.00	56	0.20	90	85	239.9	49.5	79	132.4	19.9	107.5	29.6	0.0	0.0
29.00	83	0.20	175	145	1602.9	523.9	71	939.1	260.4	663.8	263.5	0.0	0.0
30.00	82	0.20	148	110	1186.0	308.8	74	563.0	127.5	621.9	181.3	0.0	0.0
31.00	124	0.20	301	185	4942.9	1652.0	67	2624.9	906.6	2318.0	745.4	0.0	0.0
32.00	124	0.20	230	150	4291.2	1340.4	69	2489.8	791.8	1803.4	548.6	0.0	0.0
33.00	124	0.20	220	180	3304.8	1086.1	67	1797.3	621.4	1507.5	464.7	0.0	0.0
34.00	124	0.20	210	190	5944.6	2008.3	66	3557.4	1205.7	2387.2	802.6	0.0	0.0

APPENDIX B – THE LINDY SMITH VERSION

Productivity Data for Mississippi Field Plots, 1990-1991

Index Number	Grow Days	Density #/m²	Plant Ht. cm	Plant Diam. cm	Plant Fresh g	Plant Dry g	Plant Water %	Stem Fresh g	Stem Dry g	Yield Fresh g	Yield Dry g	Seed Fresh g	Seed Dry g
Mexican Variety - 2.4x2.7 m Planting, 1991													
107.02	30	0.15	30	16	6.6	2.2	67	2.0	0.6	4.8	1.6	0.0	0.0
108.02	30	0.15	40	25	22.2	6.7	70	7.1	1.6	15.1	5.1	0.0	0.0
109.02	30	0.15	100	64	166.9	44.9	73	70.4	16.6	96.5	28.3	0.0	0.0
108.04	64	0.15	150	167	2691.8	706.0	74	1163.2	276.0	1528.6	430.0	0.0	0.0
107.04	64	0.15	170	100	459.5	128.9	72	184.6	41.1	274.9	87.8	0.0	0.0
106.04	64	0.15	170	143	1608.6	440.8	73	816.4	201.2	792.2	239.6	0.0	0.0
106.06	91	0.15	200	229	6829.0	2026.6	70	2517.8	816.2	4311.2	1210.4	0.0	0.0
108.06	91	0.15	223	186	6121.8	1944.9	68	1857.2	513.5	4464.6	1431.4	0.0	0.0
109.07	91	0.15	297	175	5154.2	1612.9	68	2115.7	732.7	3038.5	880.2	0.0	0.0
109.09	123	0.15	285	246	4013.0	1719.4	57	2627.3	1126.8	770.3	320.3	615.4	272.3
109.11	123	0.15	292	205	7014.9	2654.4	62	2822.2	1142.9	2717.8	956.9	1484.9	654.6
107.19	128	0.15	248	219	5910.8	2150.0	64	2412.5	739.8	1670.8	644.1	1827.5	766.1
108.19	128	0.15	309	204	8315.0	2980.8	64	3937.2	1442.2	2784.5	1030.6	1613.3	508.0
109.12	128	0.15	262	227	7831.1	2812.7	64	2717.1	995.3	3294.7	1155.1	1819.3	662.3
109.17	128	0.15	266	213	6255.5	2345.2	62	1621.3	593.9	2451.6	902.0	2182.6	849.3
107.01	129	0.15	270	261	13957.6	4392.2	68	4337.7	1509.9	7286.8	2086.9	2333.1	795.4
Mexican Variety - 1.6x1.8 m Planting 1991													
102.02	30	0.30	50	38	43.6	15.2	76	27.6	5.0	36.0	10.2	0.0	0.0
103.02	30	0.30	64	42	77.2	17.1	78	22.0	4.0	55.2	13.1	0.0	0.0
104.02	30	0.30	67	52	71.2	19.0	73	22.2	4.9	49.0	14.1	0.0	0.0
102.04	64	0.30	158	141	1947.1	546.7	72	823.4	212.5	1123.7	334.2	0.0	0.0
103.04	64	0.30	172	144	1754.3	486.0	72	816.5	208.5	937.8	277.5	0.0	0.0
105.04	64	0.30	140	158	2232.0	564.3	75	959.9	222.8	1272.1	341.7	0.0	0.0
103.06	91	0.30	247	184	3088.5	951.5	69	1290.6	438.4	1797.9	513.5	0.0	0.0
105.07	91	0.30	140	185	4109.0	1536.1	63	1348.7	523.6	2760.3	1012.5	0.0	0.0
104.06	92	0.30	314	173	3640.1	1269.0	65	1641.2	626.3	1998.9	642.7	0.0	0.0
103.09	121	0.30	267	193	5123.8	2107.6	59	1936.4	876.8	1928.1	733.3	1259.3	497.5
101.10	122	0.30	218	154	4370.4	1779.8	56	1839.6	820.9	1646.6	810.4	884.2	348.5
102.08	122	0.30	240	195	4688.7	2037.5	56	1818.6	856.7	1963.0	791.1	906.6	389.7
102.12	122	0.30	245	173	3429.8	1461.7	57	1256.4	576.4	1217.6	485.6	960.1	399.7
103.12	127	0.30	220	191	4868.8	1986.1	59	2021.5	866.6	1684.9	635.3	1162.1	464.2
104.17	127	0.30	338	218	5814.1	2285.5	61	2483.1	1089.1	2284.1	814.3	1056.9	382.1
102.09	128	0.30	303	163	4143.5	1890.7	59	1849.5	811.2	1327.6	502.1	966.4	327.4
103.01	129	0.30	224	281	14290.0	5051.4	65	4812.4	1656.4	6784.6	2308.4	2693.0	886.6

17

Productivity Data for Mississippi Field Plots. 1990-1991

93

Index Number	Grow Days	Density g/m²	Plant Ht. cm	Plant Diam. cm	Plant Fresh g	Plant Dry g	Plant Water %	Stem Fresh g	Stem Dry g	Yield Fresh g	Yield Dry g	Seed Fresh g	Seed Dry g
Mexican Variety - 0.9x0.9 m Planting 1991													
97.02	30	1.20	87	39	65.9	17.5	73	23.1	4.9	42.8	12.6	0.0	0.0
98.09	30	1.20	47	35	45.9	11.3	75	15.9	3.1	30.0	8.2	0.0	0.0
99.09	30	1.20	37	24	16.7	4.7	72	5.1	1.3	11.6	3.4	0.0	0.0
90.11	65	1.20	145	106	656.2	180.8	72	308.3	83.5	347.9	97.3	0.0	0.0
95.11	65	1.20	140	100	1131.6	324.0	71	576.5	161.2	555.1	162.8	0.0	0.0
89.11	65	1.20	123	76	430.0	122.2	72	192.5	53.5	237.5	68.7	0.0	0.0
99.11	65	1.20	232	126	1078.3	346.2	68	533.2	173.5	545.1	172.7	0.0	0.0
88.11	65	1.20	160	86	480.1	142.2	70	246.1	71.0	234.0	71.2	0.0	0.0
87.12	91	1.20	180	80	565.6	194.2	66	204.1	102.9	281.5	81.3	0.0	0.0
88.12	91	1.20	125	51	130.4	37.2	72	58.2	16.2	72.2	21.0	0.0	0.0
96.14	91	1.20	207	104	839.9	296.9	65	410.3	161.7	429.6	135.2	0.0	0.0
87.14	91	1.20	186	79	732.8	244.4	67	278.2	98.2	454.6	146.2	0.0	0.0
89.10	91	1.20	170	99	1078.2	321.5	70	290.4	89.8	787.8	231.7	0.0	0.0
96.13	91	1.20	224	133	1498.4	541.2	64	635.8	254.4	862.6	286.8	0.0	0.0
97.14	91	1.20	230	147	2427.6	763.3	69	955.6	326.0	1472.0	437.3	0.0	0.0
97.19	120	1.20	221	83	653.8	261.2	60	334.8	132.4	319.0	126.3	0.0	0.0
95.23	120	1.20	256	99	1079.1	424.5	61	543.0	226.4	536.1	198.1	0.0	0.0
87.19	120	1.20	271	112	1681.0	650.2	61	890.4	267.1	637.8	244.7	352.8	138.4
87.17	120	1.20	221	113	1938.2	767.0	60	868.7	344.0	551.9	214.2	317.6	208.8
87.17	120	1.20	251	96	750.7	287.5	62	305.2	129.7	445.5	157.8	0.0	0.0
97.16	121	1.20	268	129	2144.0	937.1	56	1026.2	468.6	594.9	242.3	522.9	226.0
99.16	121	1.20	221	83	1305.6	555.6	57	560.7	238.9	391.7	162.8	353.2	153.9
100.15	122	1.20	234	130	2123.1	872.3	59	759.3	342.3	835.9	326.2	527.9	203.8
100.17	122	1.20	175	125	1721.8	752.4	56	495.4	193.5	591.7	258.4	634.8	300.5
Columbian Variety - Plot E, 0.9x1.8 m Planting, 1990													
35.00	91	0.60	77	72	159.9	37.8	76	75.4	13.7	84.5	24.1	0.0	0.0
36.00	91	0.60	111	104	341.3	85.0	75	169.3	32.9	172.0	52.1	0.0	0.0
38.00	93	0.60	137	108	752.0	214.1	72	387.9	100.2	364.1	113.5	0.0	0.0
39.00	110	0.60	182	128	1385.5	419.7	70	751.5	227.3	634.0	192.4	0.0	0.0
40.00	147	0.60	200	100	1131.8	309.6	66	533.4	236.1	598.4	153.8	0.0	0.0
41.00	147	0.60	220	140	1697.1	576.5	66	950.0	357.9	742.1	218.6	0.0	0.0
42.00	147	0.60	250	143	2627.9	883.5	66	1496.7	555.7	1137.2	327.5	0.0	0.0
Hybrid Variety - Plot F, 0.9x1.8 m Planting, 1990													
43.00	145	0.60	152	191	2101.2	593.6	72	1132.6	333.5	963.6	260.1	0.0	0.0
44.00	145	0.60	230	210	10427.2	2654.2	75	6716.7	1843.0	3760.5	811.2	0.0	0.0
45.00	91	0.60	87	84	369.7	92.9	75	153.6	33.6	216.1	59.3	0.0	0.0
Jamaican Variety - Plot H, 0.9x1.8 m Planting, 1990 ← confidence in title?													
46.00	91	0.13	102	94	810.7	184.6	77	421.8	78.2	388.9	106.1	0.0	0.0

(handwritten annotations: 1721.9 ; 883.2 ; 0.60 "could have been an error of 9 sq yd / 81 sq ft")

18

84

Correlation Matrix for Marijuana Plant Parameter Relationships, 1990-91.

	Growth Days	Density	Plant Height	Plant Diameter	Plant Fresh Weight	Plant Dry Weight	Plant Water	Stem Fresh Weight	Stem Dry Weight	Yield Fresh Weight	Yield Dry Weight	Seed Fresh Weight	Seed Dry Weigh
1 Growth Days	1.000												
2 Plant Density	0.015	1.000											
3 Plant Height	0.818	0.009	1.000										
4 Plant Diameter	0.729	-0.315	0.830	1.000									
5 Plant Fresh Weight	0.628	-0.350	0.687	0.867	1.000								
6 Plant Dry Weight	0.660	-0.328	0.704	0.870	0.989	1.000							
7 Plant Water	-0.689	-0.245	-0.664	-0.478	-0.378	-0.470	1.000						
8 Stem Fresh Weight	0.658	-0.365	0.722	0.844	0.939	0.917	-0.337	1.000					
9 Stem Dry Weight	0.696	-0.336	0.746	0.853	0.943	0.945	-0.442	0.985	1.000				
10 Yield Fresh Weight	0.529	-0.334	0.609	0.824	0.962	0.932	-0.280	0.857	0.849	1.000			
11 Yield Dry Weight	0.562	-0.328	0.630	0.843	0.969	0.958	-0.358	0.853	0.862	0.990	1.000		
12 Seed Fresh Weight	0.435	-0.155	0.396	0.528	0.660	0.728	-0.490	0.452	0.530	0.565	0.637	1.000	
13 Seed Dry Weight	0.446	-0.145	0.403	0.523	0.632	0.706	-0.527	0.130	0.511	0.528	0.604	0.994	1.000

CRITICAL VALUE (2-TAIL, P<0.05) = +/- .198; N=98

41

ATTACHMENT 2

1985-86 YIELD DATA
UNIVERSITY OF MSSISSIPPI

University of Mississippi 1985 Yield Study Data

UNIVERSITY OF MISSISSIPPI
1986 YIELD STUDY DATA

Appendix C
The Fifth Level

A.   Context
     1.   Unaskable Questions
     2.   Welcome to the Future, Citizen
     3.   Commercial vs Non-Commercial
     4.   Free Markets, Anyone?
     5.   Convicting the Non-Average
     6.   Consumption
B.   Materials and Methods
     1.   Site and Soil
     2.   Treatment and Design
     3.   Husbandry
     4.   Harvesting and Processing
     5.   Data Recording
C.   Statistical Analysis
     1.   Harvest Weight v Dried Flowers
     2.   HW v DF Scattergraphs
     3.   House Brand Seeds
     4.   Canopy v Dried Flowers
     5.   Male Plants
     6.   Separation
          a.   2001 Plant Separation
          b.   2004 Plant Separation
          c.   2006 Plant Separation
          d.   All Plant Separation
     7.   Losses
     8.   Discussion

The fifth level is the data. What some people say, what academics say, what those with special knowledge say, and what the original documents themselves say are all very interesting, in increasing importance, clarity, understanding and most of all confidence. But for what you would really like to know, the data should make you rethink everything.

The data provided by *Cannabis Fields* gives us something. All we need to do is run the numbers. But that data was deliberately altered and obscured after the study itself had been mauled. Hence the deconstruction.

A.   Context

The immediate question that still remains to be answered post-*Cannabis Fields*, is what a given weight of confiscated wet cannabis plants corresponds to in terms of their dried flowers. The average home gardener isn't particularly interested in this ratio. But repeatedly in courts of law around the world, it is this magic number that can determine the difference between freedom and captivity.

As it became clear that judges needed some clarity with regards to the quantity of dried flowers per plant, in the first decade of the twenty-first century ARSECA initiated a program of measuring and weighing the plants in their communal garden. The purpose was to be able to bring evidence into a courtroom to aid in the defense of hobby gardeners who were being charged with trafficking based solely on a single number, the weight of freshly seized plants.

But behind this lie a host of other questions beg to be asked and answered. The drug war notoriously forces a lack of rational discussion, preferring ever popular self righteous scapegoating in its place. For this reason it is useful to try to bring some much needed context to the issue.

APPENDIX C – THE FIFTH LEVEL

1.   Unaskable Questions.   What I eat, drink or smoke is nobody's business but my own, certainly not that of the state. But will any judge permit a challenge based upon the inherent right of the individual to eat, drink and smoke what she chooses? To do so would ultimately require the judiciary to formally declare an individual's body the property of the state, to do with as it so chooses.

The larger question of why we are weighing witches in the first place is also never addressed in any courtroom. This would require a judge to question why the corrupted, distracted, bought off solons feel the need to protect the global pharmaceutical cartel (which wrote the earliest international drug treaties) from the competition from the natural medicinal plants of the earth that have maintained the health of humans for uncounted millennia, and still do so today. No judge will ever permit this question to be asked either.

But once we enter the looking glass world of drug law, where the various constitutional protections afforded to murderers, rapists and thieves no longer apply, where the evidence *is* the crime, where draconian punishment *is* the norm, and where the witch's real crime *is* simply disobedience to the state, then we are forced to defend ourselves with the few tools left to us. Since the state defines dried flowers as dangerous, pure legal logic dictates the conclusion that more flowers are more dangerous. And again we are forced to confront the spectacle of otherwise rational men and women attempting to figure out how to separate the "good" home gardener who grows for personal or medicinal use from the "bad" trafficker, how to indemnify need while excoriating greed, using literally a balance. No one ever asks why greed, so accepted and even lauded in so many other endeavors, is so forbidden here.

2.   Welcome to the Future, Citizen.   Cannabis growers are routinely subjected to an indictment of future crime. The gardener is not charged for the amount of dried flowers that can be obtained from her seized plants. The gardener is charged with *what she might have been*

311

able to obtain from the same plants had she been allowed to carry her plants to harvest. The witch is not charged with what she did, but rather with *what she could have done*. By this reasoning, a seed is a seedling and a seedling an immature plant and an immature plant a mature one. Thus, the great hemp seed trials that took place in the US at the height of just-say-no.

The problem almost no one sees is that making such a calculation requires one to make a guesstimate of what the diabolical plant would have produced had it not died an untimely death at the hands of the machete-wielding axe murderers from the Holy Office of the Inquisition. Now, stop and think for a moment. The answer to the question of how many flowers the plant produced lies in the hands of those who seized the plants, does it not?

Why not ask them to determine themselves how many dried flowers are present? This would require our brave men in blue to sit around a table and conscientiously trim the beast in their laps, carefully and honestly separating the flowers from the leaves, stalk and seed. No doubt if you paid them overtime, they would only be too happy to hold a trimming party back at the police station. The uniformed thieves in possession of her stolen property have it within their ability to determine exactly what can be obtained from the plants.

Some judges in some countries are actually catching on to this rather obvious idea: that you don't charge a person for what they could have done but for what they did do, not for what their plants might have produced, but for what they did produce. This will vary depending on the relative maturity of the plants. Clearly the prosecutor has it within his power to discover this magic number he needs to convict the witch.

3.   Commercial vs Non-Commercial. On the other side of the looking glass, in the world of the so-called legal plants, this problem has long since been solved. There, the same distinction exists between the backyard gardener and the commercial cultivator. The former is a hobby gardener while the latter runs a business. Should you decide to grow a variety of sweet corn on your property, the state cannot find the time to be interested in your humble operation until it surpasses a certain size.

That limit is a simple one. It separates the non-taxable from the taxable. Ordinarily, this limit is expressed in terms of acres or hectares. It divides the commercially viable from the non-commercially viable, not only for the crop itself, but for the state's time, expense and ability to tax the crop. No one pays taxes on ten rows of sweet corn.

In Andalucia, for example, this limit is roughly 2500 square meters of land if irrigated and 25,000 square meters if not.[1] Those with less than this quantity of land under production pay no taxes in part because the government cannot bother paying their accountants and file clerks to keep track of such superficial results. After the repeal of the prohibition on alcohol, when the laws regarding the production and sale of alcohol were once more left to the various US states, some states simply exempted home production from taxes, setting limits as high as 500 gallons a year per person per household of any brewed or distilled beverage. Spain, which operated one of the first state monopolies on tobacco, still exempts twenty-five tobacco plants per person from state licensing and control.

4.   Free Markets, Anyone?   Economically, setting a high limit not a low one is not only more feasible but it has another very important advantage as well. Competition inevitable begets cartels, a fact of commerce noted by Adam Smith, among others. Businessmen routinely engage in restraint of trade as soon as they are able to control their market. They set quotas, raise prices and collude against the consumer. A high limit enforces much needed competition

---

[1] Figuera, Fernanda de la. *"El Número Mágico," Cañamo,* p. 40, the data obtained by phone from the office of the *Cámara Agraria de Malaga,* 15 February 2002, 11:30 am

in the marketplace, as higher prices will cause canny consumers to simply produce their own. A high limit also allows these home producers to swap, trade, and sell their minor excess, again forcing the larger cartel to suddenly compete with a thousand new producers as soon they raise the price of the commodity beyond a reasonable level.

5.   Convicting the Non-Average.   The needs of each person are different. From automobiles to *zapatos*, each person elects what she believes to be necessary but when we begin to talk of dried flowers we need the help of a judge. Some smoke only on the weekends. Others, the so-called chronics, we smoke much more, every day, now for pleasure, then for medicine. (Let's hope we are not going to examine the soul of the accused.) [Personally, I have smoked as much as 20 *porros* a day, especially when working with the plants.] How can we come to some reasoned and reasonable quantity that will cover us?[2] Or should we simply force each and every person to consume some average?

And should we be convicting someone not to the standard of beyond any reasonable doubt but for being non-average? Remember that this is the exact same standard in use in the Middle Ages when it came to weighing witches. Then, what was important was not what she weighed, but whether she weighed less than what she should have.

Suppose we discover that the ratio of dried flowers to wet plants is on average 12 percent. Should we establish a limit of 10 percent? Or should we use 6? Remember, we are trying to convict a human being and send her to prison based on this magic number.

---

[2] Figuera, Fernanda de la. *"El Número Mágico," Cañamo*, p. 39: *Las "necesidades" de cada persona son diferentes. Desde automóviles hasta zapatos, cada individuo elige según sus necesidades, pero si hablamos de flores secadas necesitamos de la ayuda de un juez. Algunos fuman solamente durante los fines de semana. Otros, crónicos, fuman – fumamos – más, muchas veces cada dia, ya por placer, ya por medicina. (No vamos a examinar el "alma" de encausado, espero.) Si no podemos llegar a un acuerdo sobre una cantidad suficiente para éstas últimas, por lo menos podiamos tener una directriz razonada y razonable.*

This is for a victimless crime. And whatever number we use, ultimately we will be convicting someone for being non-average.

For that matter we could use the maximum, not the average. By cherry-picking the data, we could readily arrive at a pound of dried cannabis flowers for each plant. Every amateur grower would then be guilty of not achieving this rare and normally unobtainable goal.

But if what we are trying to do is use this information to convict someone in a criminal trial where the standard is beyond any reasonable doubt, why shouldn't we be using the minimum? From the plants I was able to examine at the ARSECA garden, I could state that I found no plants with a ratio of dried flowers to wet plant below four percent. This does not say such plants do not exist, only that I have not found them, so far. But at what point is it not clear that we are weighing witches in the twenty-first century, albeit with an electronic balance?

6.   Consumption.

Finally, once a given figure is arrived at, just what does this mean? Suppose a defendant has effectively the number of plants able to produce say, three kilos of dried flowers. So what? Only the denominator of the equation consumption/production has been established. Is three kilos enough, too much or too little?

Various estimates exist as to how much people actually consume. In the now closed compassionate use program, the FDA of the US distributes to a few lucky patients a monthly ration of 300 cannabis cigarettes, each about 0.9 grams.[3] This is 270 grams a month

---

[3] A follow up report from the Medical Marijuana Working Group regarding the city's low law enforcement policy towards medical marijuana. Robert C. Bobb, 23 June 1998, www.rxcbc.org, www.saveacownow.org.

or 3.240 kilograms a year. This occurs in a nation historically almost talibanistic in its views on drugs.[4]

When in 1996 the State of California implemented a new law on the use of medical marijuana, the progressive City of Oakland adopted this same measure for its patients. We can also compare this standard with the quantity for a smoker of tobacco. It is common enough to smoke 10 cigarettes a day of tobacco, for example. If one cigarette contains 1 gram of tobacco, we would need 3.650 kilograms a year.[5] Jamaican rastas are reputed to smoke some 25 joints a day; Hindu sadhus smoke constantly. One judge in one trial of a grower in Chile simply could not believe that she smoked ten joints a day for her neuralgia. Yet such consumption is more the norm than many judges would like to believe based on that one puff they had at that frat party, Freshman year.

If we suppose an average grower might obtain on average 200 grams of dried flowers per plant, 25 plants would give some five kilos. But this is a year's supply. If the same grower smokes ten joints a day, she uses us 3.65 kilos even before her friends come over to help her smoke it. By August of the following year she is smoking the dregs of the last jar.

So should a judge set a limit of some 25 plants per person? But setting such limits are bound to limit the needs of at least some. A better course of action would simply be to consider that some 25

---

[4] Figuera, Fernanda de la. *"El Número Mágico," Cañamo,* p. 39: *Existen estimaciones varias. En un programa de uso compasivo actualmente ya clausurado, la FDA (administracion de Farmacia y Alimentacion de Estados Unidos) distribuía entre ocho pacientes una dosis mensual de 300 porros de 0,9 g de marijuana por porro. Esto es 270 g al mes o 3,240 kg al año. Y esto desde la óptica de un estado casi taliban en materia de drogas.*

[5] Figuera, Fernanda de la. *"El Número Mágico," Cañamo,* p. 39: *Cuando en 1996 el Estado de California implementó una nueva ley acerca del uso médico de la marihuana, la progresista ciudad de Oakland adoptó este mismo baremo para sus pacientes. También podríamos compararnos con un fumador de tabaco. Es bastante habitual fumar 10 cigarrillos de tabaco cada día, por ejemplo. Si un cigarrillo contiene 1 g de tabaco, necesitaremos 3,650 kg al año.*

outdoor plants per person is simply reasonable, uncontroversial and not worth prosecuting. In other words, 25 plants per individual would be better treated as a minimum.

How many plants does a grower need, either personally or medically? In Spain a judge has accepted 156 plants as personal use while in another case a person with only 10 was declared guilty.[6] In California the limits vary from county to county. Colorado and Washington are in the process of establishing their own limits for personal use. Each of the states in the US with medical use has attempted to come up with something that seems reasonable. But often this limit is based on nothing more than what feels good or is politically expedient at that moment.

B.   Materials and Methods

In order to try to get some real world numbers on what a plant can or cannot produce, and what a garden can or cannot produce, I was allowed me to take measurements from a number of plants grown in the ARSECA research garden over a number of years.

1.   Site and Soil.   The   site   was   the
ARSECA Research Station near Malaga in Andalucia, southern Spain. The latitude and longitude are 36° 43' 0" N, 4° 25' 12" S. Compare that of Yoknapatawpha: 34° 21' 35" N, 89° 31' 34" W. The elevation is 500' above sea level. The climate is Subtropical-Mediterranean. Rainfall averages 526 mm (20.71") annually. The most rain falls in November, about 95 mm (3.74"); the least occurs in July, roughly 2 mm (0.08"). The average relative humidity is 66%. It receives 2800 to 3000 sunshine hours a year, 5 to 6 hours a day in December and

---

[6] Figuera, Fernanda de la. *"El Número Mágico," Cáñamo*, p. 39: *En España un juez has aceptado 156 plantas como uso personal, mientras en otra causa se ha declarado culpable a una persona con sólo diez.*

roughly twice that in July. It is an area of mild winters and hot summers. The average annual temperature is 23° C (73° F) during the day and 13° C (55° F) at night. January is the coldest month, averaging 12 - 20° C (54 - 68° F) during the day and 4 - 13° C (39 - 55° F) at night. August is the warmest with temperatures ranging from 26 - 35° C (79 - 95° F) in the daytime and better than 20° C (68° F) at night.

The research station is located in an old olive and almond orchard. The soil is generally an alluvial, lime-bearing barl. It is enriched each year with potting soil, forest soil, earthworms and various kinds of manure and compost.

2.   Treatment and Design.   Thirty-six known kinds and more than thirty unknown varieties were planted in three separate years during the first decade of the twenty-first century. The ARSECA communal garden approximates 100 square meters. There was no attempt to control for density. Each plant began with a meter to a meter and a half of growing space. Males were pulled at the earliest opportunity. Occasionally the holes in the field were filled in with a second germination, but generally this was not done because the taller plants tended to shade the newer, smaller ones.

3.   Husbandry.   Growing cannabis is a year-round occupation. Typically, in January or February, the soil of the garden was turned in with a large number of sacks of one year old horse manure. The residual heat of the manure helps cure the soil, slowly sterilizing it. The rains of early Spring help to cool it so it will be ready for transplanting in May or June. Forest soil from the mountains was gathered and added along with a healthy helping of homemade compost.

The basic principles of organic gardening were applied. For example, stinging nettle, also known as bull nettle and called locally *ortiga (Urtica dioica* L.) blooms early in the Spring and can be gathered using gloves. This plant has a property that touching it will cause a skin rash. Mixed with raw tobacco and chopped up chunks of garlic it makes an excellent plant tonic and bug repellent. The worms that show up in the Fall particularly do not like crawling across it and the smell of the tobacco and garlic disorient them. For this reason the garden was also ringed and cross hatched with other aromatic plants like lavender, thyme, and mint.

In late March and early April seed selection takes place. This requires one to sit for hours before a strong light, examining each seed with a hand *loupe*, checking for flaws and patterns and to see how each one feels. At the right time of the moon, these seeds were planted in small, cleaned and sterilized seed trays of potting soil. Sometimes they were germinated between wet pieces of tissue paper before putting them in the trays. Each one was wished *un buen viaje*, a good journey.

These trays were set out in a homemade greenhouse where the rest of the seeds germinated over the next two weeks. The soil was kept moist with a spray bottle. Just because a seed germinates does not mean it is viable. Some seeds sprout well and then die off early. Some of these small seedlings came up twisted and distorted and did not make it past the first month.

Germination rates vary. In 2001, for the first thirty seeds chosen, some 96% germinated. However, inevitably there is regression to the mean and the averages take over. It is a good batch of seeds that will fully germinate and healthily grow some 80 out of a 100 seeds.

Around this time the soil in the garden was turned over a second time. The rains raised a good crop of thistles and poppies and *ortiga*. By turning in the soil again, the nitrogen in their roots becomes part of the new soil. Depending on the taste of the soil, a second helping of kitchen compost was added. Worms were also be added at this time.

Once the plants germinated well in the trays, they were transplanted into larger quart pots and returned to the greenhouse. If the weather had warmed enough, they were placed in the full sun on a foldout table placed directly in the garden. Again, the soil in these pots was kept moist. The plants were checked on a regular basis to see how well they were getting along. Those that did not thrive were removed.

May is the moment to transplant. This is done by consulting an almanac to determine the proper cycle of the moon. Some seeds from the previous year's crop had spontaneously came up by then. These were carefully transplanted into other pots. These spontaneous plants are the ones that have adapted to the garden, the soil, the geography, the climate, the pests, and the range of temperatures they have to withstand during the year. Later, some of these will be crossed with various house brand seeds. In this way, the genetics of the garden can only improve from year to year.

The garden was marked off into *jaulas*, roughly square sections. Each section had about nine to twelve seedlings. To transplant, each quart pot containing one small plant was let sit in a bucket of water until the water floated out the top. The holes in the garden were dug and were given a small dose of compost and manure and filled in with more potting soil. This was then soaked with a garden hose. In this way, the plants go from wet to wet. If done well and quickly, the plant should never notice it has been moved. The reason for letting the pots grow on a table in the garden beforehand is to orient them to the full sun. When they are transplanted, one takes care to keep them oriented to the same compass direction in their new places.

June, July and August bring little rain and hot sun. Water is critical. Irrigation was done in four different ways: at ground level by plastic irrigation hoses, flooding via a garden hose, and through an overhead spray system that mimics a rain shower. Each one has its uses, depending on the time of day or evening, the weather, the dryness of the soil and the dustiness of the plants. The soil was kept moist to a finger's distance beneath.

There is not much weeding necessary. Cannabis tends to outgrow the surrounding vegetation. But the excess was removed with a hoe or by hand and went into the compost bin to become next year's soil.

APPENDIX C – THE FIFTH LEVEL

When the weather becomes too hot, flat stones were placed around the base of the plant, a practice still used in country farming in this region. This keeps the soil around the plants cool and moist. If you watch them closely, the plants will tell you when they need water. In an afternoon breeze, the leaves will turn too much or too little, the branches will droop or spring upwards.

If a pest has gotten at the roots, the leaves will change color, the branches dry out. This can be a good moment for a root tonic to help chase away the unhealthy bugs. The ARSECA garden used only organic and natural pest dissuaders. Ladybugs are a good sign of a healthy garden and were introduced if not already apparent.

Sexing takes place throughout this period. There is no possibility of sacrificing plants early in order to weigh them. This is home gardening and each plant is too useful and the space too limited. Males were pulled as soon as they showed up. The garden must be checked daily. This means examining every node on every branch of every plant. When the plants are small this is readily done. But some plants make it into September without showing signs that it is either male or female.

A few plants became hermaphrodites. They showed themselves female but then later in the season suddenly produced some nodes or branches male. If caught early enough, these male pollen sacs can be pinched off. But if there were too many, then the entire plant was pulled.

4.   Harvesting and Processing.   The harvest occurred in September and October. But the long sativas sometimes stay in the ground until almost Christmas. Each grower has her own time to harvest. Fernanda generally lets them remain until the very end. She calculates the best time to harvest by using the color of the resin globules as you hold the branch so the evening sun can glance through the flowers. White is green and highest in THC. Silver means not quite, 10 percent gold is a sure sign, but covered in twinkling gold is best for her. She prefers her cannabis to be field ripened. To some degree this reduces the THC and tends to increase the amount of CBD, CBN and the other cannabinoids but the taste and quality is worth waiting for.

The exact day of the harvest can vary depending on the weather. An approaching storm that might threaten to stay for a week when a plant is nearly ready. This often means it will be pulled slightly early to avoid molds and mildews. It takes a day or two after a good storm to dry out the plants. Storms, like rippers, can break branches so sometimes it's best to bring them in early.

By November, almost all the plants were in the drying room. The plants were hung in a drying room with wooden walls and ceiling, kept dark with a circulating fan, the light off. Thirty days is usually sufficient for the initial drying of a good sized plant. Typically, after about four days the plant stiffens up and this was a good moment for trimming the shade leaves. Sometimes mechanical trimmers were used that can remove the leaves green. But often the plants were field trimmed before being harvested. Then the rest of the plant was returned to the drying room, hung upside down. There was no commercial oven available to bake each part of the plant in order to get a reproducible weight. Instead, the plants were air dried to the surrounding humidity. On the other hand, they were not sent through a leaf shredder either.

By November or December the first plants were ready to be trimmed and graded. This can be a long and tedious process. The plants were cut in sections and the branches were separated. This was usually done in concert, known as a trimming party. Volunteers were easily found for this otherwise tiresome job. Each person with a pair of scissors sat around a table and separated the dried plant into stalk and branch, bud leaves and flowers. Sometimes this was done over a set of screens to catch the best pollen. It was also a good moment to collect finger *charas*.

APPENDIX C – THE FIFTH LEVEL

The stalk and branches made excellent fire starters, still full of resin. The shade leaves were composted. The bud leaves often found themselves into the ice-o-lator. Some medium-grade hashish can be extracted depending on the plant.

The dried flowers were then packed in cans or glass jars. Some needed to be cured more than others so they were packed in butcher block paper and cardboard boxes and set aside for six months. The very best ended up in special wooden boxes. Good cannabis continues to mature in flavor and complexity for up to two years without noticeable decline. But almost all of it was usually smoked by the beginning of the next year's harvest.

5.   Data Recording.   The plants to be measured were selected at random. But there were biases. Most of the plants measured were harvested early in the season, meaning they matured first. During the harvest I measured height, canopy, grow days, wet plant weight, dry plant weight, and the weights of the component parts dry.

But this is a working garden and often the exigencies of time limited my ability to collect all of this data for all of the plants. During one summer I took heights and canopy measurements. During another I collected information on grow days. Heights and weights at harvest were collected in each of three years, 2001, 2004 and 2006.

Height and canopy measurements were taken with a simple meter stick. This was constructed by painting a four meter long 2" x 2" pole at ten centimeter intervals in different colors. The accuracy of this instrument is only good to a tenth of a meter.

I weighed the wet plants with a simple agricultural balance sensitive to a half kilo. Plants less than one half kilo were rejected as being too small to take data from. This skewed the sample toward larger plants. Accuracy of this balance was good only to a quarter kilogram.

The trimmers separated each plant. I weighed with a simple kitchen balance the stalk and branches, the shade and bud leaves, and the dried flowers. This balance had accuracy to only a gram.

As a result what data I obtained was data from a real medicinal garden, albeit one under the direct supervision of a master grower. It is only an N = 1 study, meaning this is what was grown during a number of seasons in one garden. It may have some utility in judging what it is possible to obtain, in other words, an upper bound, not an average nor a minimum.

C.   Statistical Analysis

The purpose of gathering the data in the first place was to try to get some good numbers on the ratio of dried flowers to wet plants. Along the way I was able to record some other data as well. But this magic number was the most important bit of information at trial.

1.   Harvest Weight v Dried Flowers.   For this I recorded the heights, fresh weights and weights of the dried, separated flowers from seventy-six plants over three different years:

#	NAME	HT (KG)	WT (KG)	DF (G)
1	Refugio	1.9	1.5	160
2	Jack Herer	2	2.1	260
3	Desc	1.8	1.4	220
4	ESP1	2.1	2.6	240
5	Harv 99	1.6	1.3	190
6	Warlock 99	1.7	1.3	140
7	Warlock 00	1.5	1.2	100
8	BF 99a	2.3	1.3	130
9	Esp x BF	1.9	5.2	620
10	H99a	1.9	0.9	90
11	H99b	2.1	0.9	145
12	Him Widow	1.9	0.8	67
13	Col. 98	2	2.4	230
14	BF99b	1.4	1	120
15	Ref 98a	1.9	1.4	200
16	Ref 98b	1.4	0.6	120
17	Ref 98c	1.7	0.8	160
18	Ref 98d	1.8	1.4	240
19	Caladan	2	2.2	275
20	N. Lights	1.6	2.6	110
21	Ref B	1.9	2.1	300
22	Notoz	1.8	1.7	150
23	BT1	1.1	0.6	63
24	Esp Grande	2.7	3.6	235
25	Esp Alta	2.5	1.6	200
#	NAME	HT (KG)	WT (KG)	DF (G)

Figure 123. The data for the harvest weights and dried flowers, first page.

#	NAME	HT (KG)	WT (KG)	DF (G)
26	Esp Altissim	3.2	3.6	390
27	Che	1.2	1.6	180
28	BO2	1.9	0.6	40
29	BT2	2	2.7	220
30	Bush	1.7	0.5	60
31	Ref x Skunk	2.3	0.9	97
32	Esp Excel	2.5	1.1	120
33	Esp Bueno	1.9	1.1	150
34	Esp 2	2.2	1.4	150
35	MM73	1.7	4.3	560
36	MM72	1.5	2.4	300
37	Manolito 6	2	3.3	430
38	Tusk 23	2	2.5	410
39	Tusk 22	1.6	3.6	480
40	Manolito 5	1.6	2.9	450
41	Lui 52	1.5	3.9	610
42	Tusk 24	1.6	1.6	300
43	Highland 13	1.9	2.7	480
44	Hashballs 2	1.9	2.9	320
45	Red Horz 19	1.7	1.7	220
46	Red Horz 17	1.6	2	320
47	Nuvola 26	1.5	3.4	560
48	Nuvola 27	1.2	0.5	80
49	BE 155	1.9	1.3	220
50	B2002109	1.3	0.8	110
#	NAME	HT (KG)	WT (KG)	DF (G)

Figure 124. The data for the harvest weights and dried flowers, second page.

#	NAME	HT (KG)	WT (KG)	DF (G)
51	Col. 47	2.6	2.2	260
52	Sp. AK	2	5	490
53	Blckhead 48	1.8	4	660
54	2G2	1.4	2.1	340
55	Lui 54	1.6	2	390
56	Swtooth 57	1.4	2.5	340
57	2G1	1.9	1.5	245
58	DB128	2	1.7	280
59	Afr 43	3.4	5	403
60	Col. 45	2.3	3.3	457
61	B2002111	1.6	1	159
62	B2002112	1.7	1.7	120
63	Red Horz 18	1.5	2.1	236
64	MM 64	2	3.5	420
65	Highland 15	1.5	2	290
66	Sheherzad	1.1	0.6	131
67	C3	1.1	0.7	131
68	PSK1	1.2	1.4	300
69	C2	1.2	1.5	275
70	Dblfun5	1.2	0.7	106
71	J2-1	2	1	133
72	D. Haze	1.2	1.7	286
73	J2-16b	2.3	1	92
74	Psk2	1.2	1.4	202
75	Honeymn 1	1.2	1.3	177
76	J2-26	2.3	1.4	214
#	NAME	HT (KG)	WT (KG)	DF (G)

Figure 125. The data for the harvest weights and dried flowers, third page.

2. **HW v DF Scattergraphs.** Here are the scattergraphs comparing harvest weight to dried flowers:

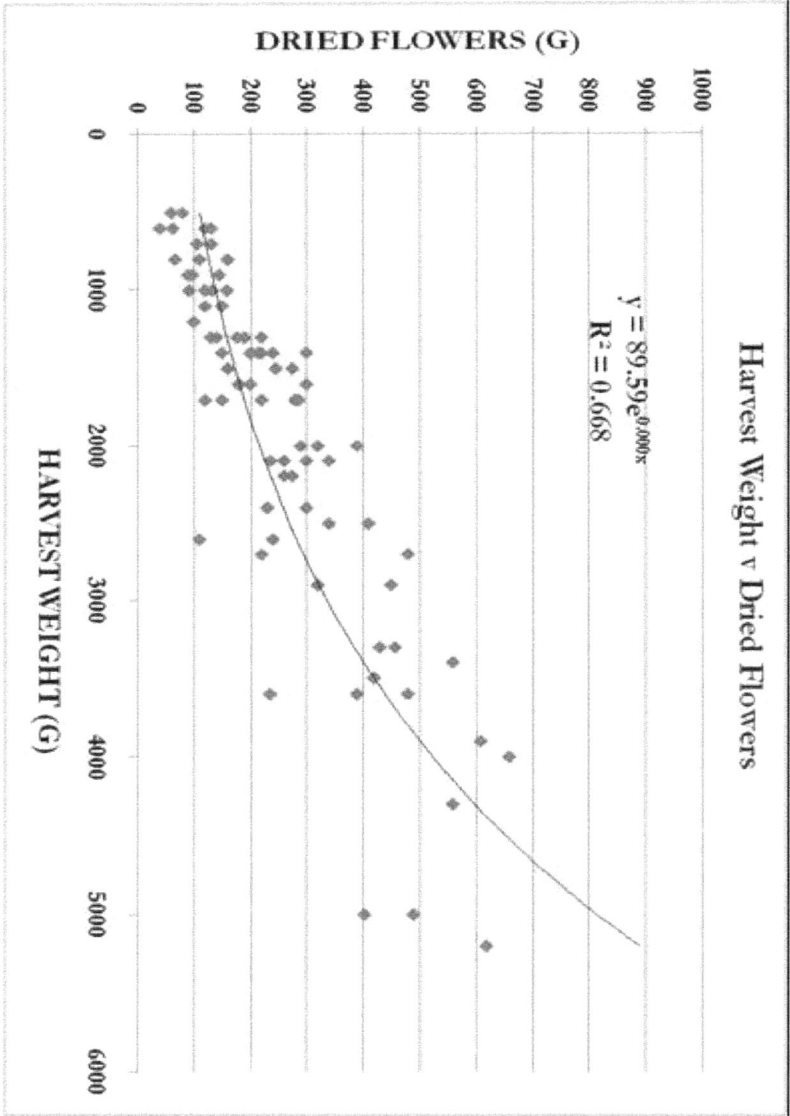

Figure 126. Harvest weights v dried flowers, exponential CBF.

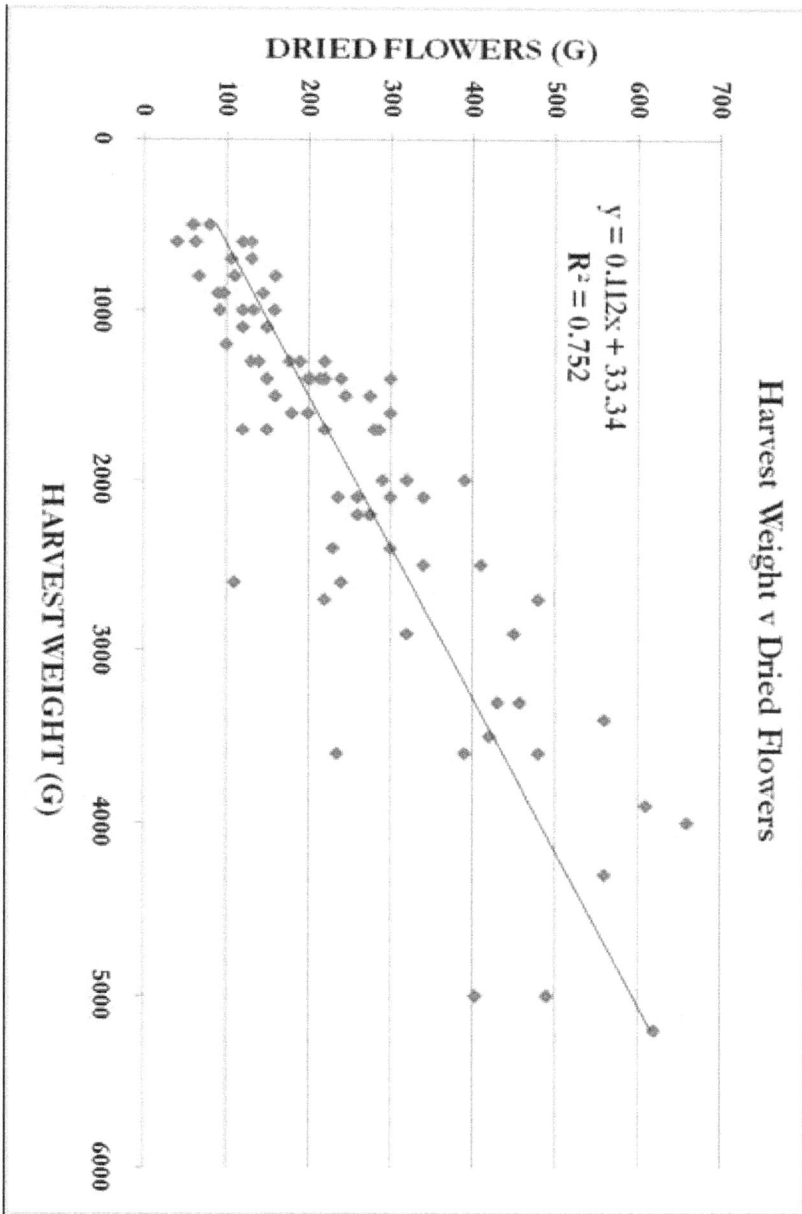

Figure 127. Harvest weights v dried flowers, linear CBF.

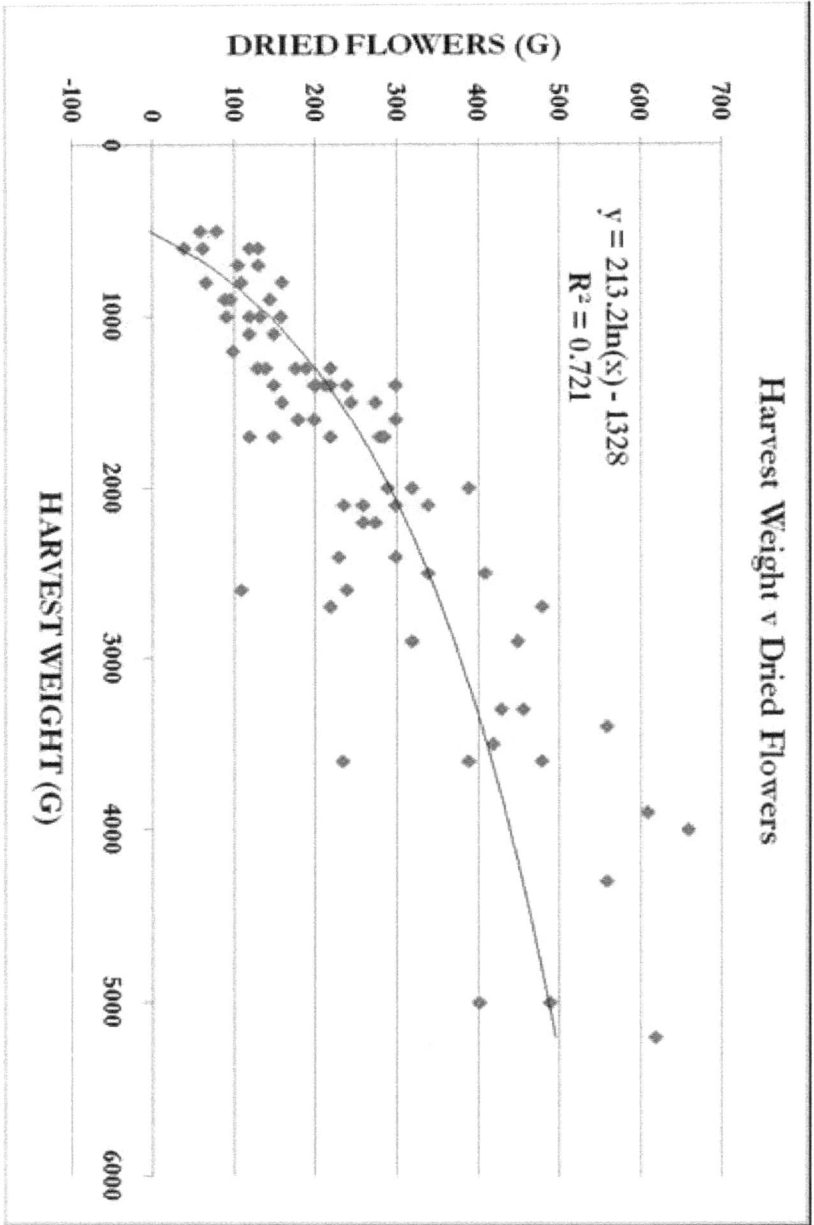

Figure 128. Harvest weights v dried flowers, logarithmic CBF.

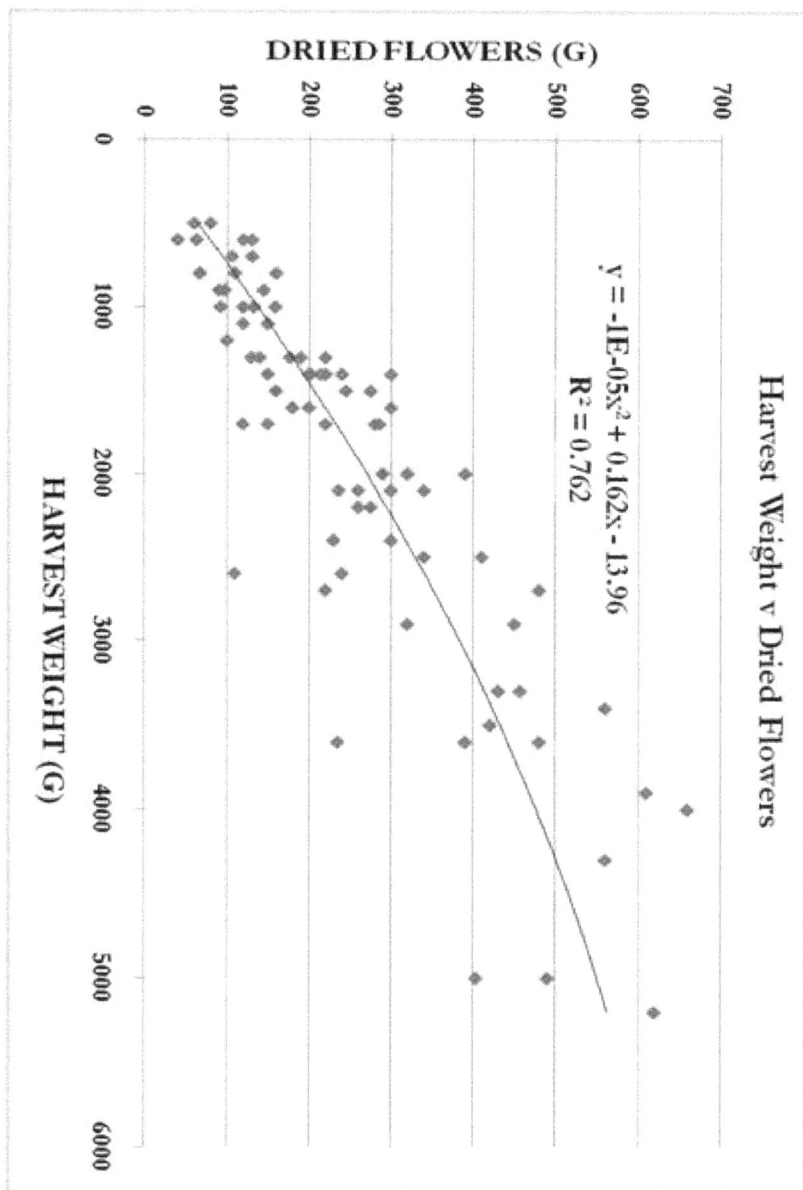

Figure 129. Harvest weights v dried flowers, polynomical CBF.

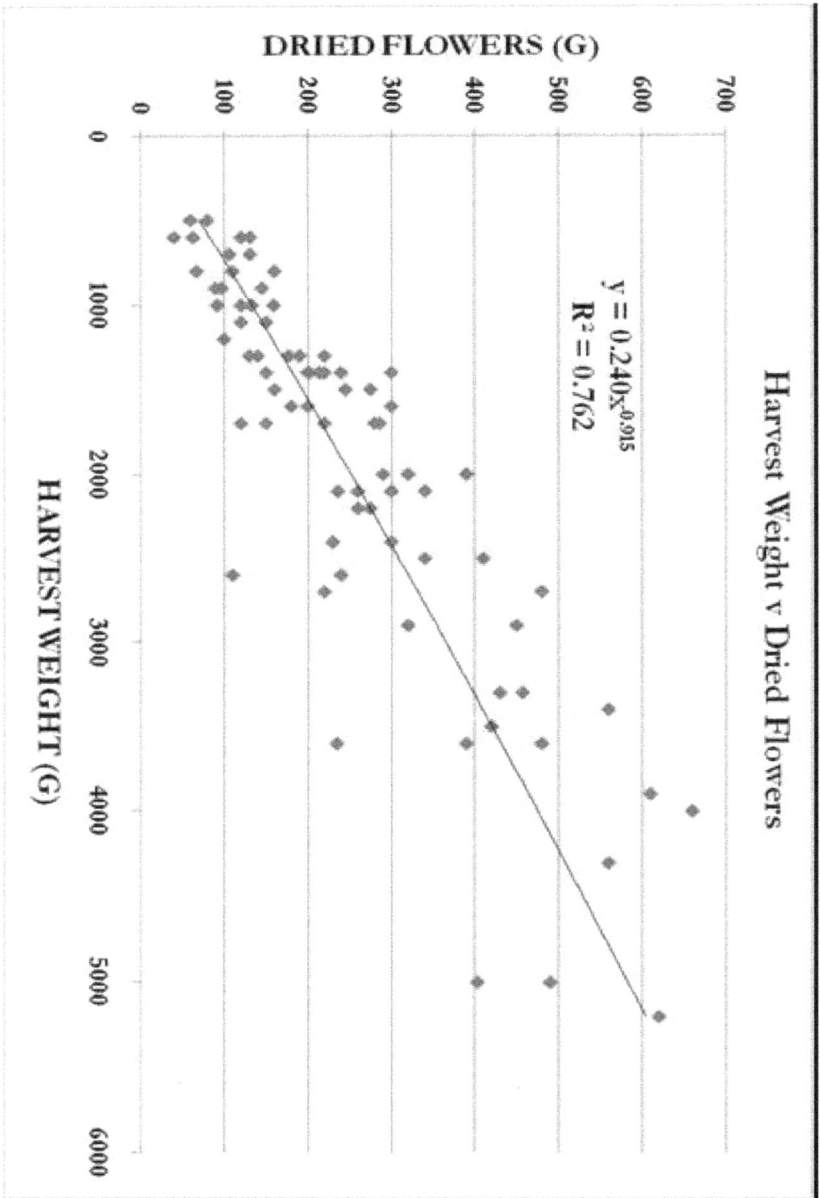

Figure 130. Harvest weights v dried flowers, power series CBF.

APPENDIX C – THE FIFTH LEVEL

The best R-squared are the polynomial and power series curves but the linear is not far behind. These curves of harvest weight versus dried flowers fit the data less well than those given by the data in *Cannabis Fields*. This might well be explained by the much larger variety of plants grown in the ARSECA garden compared to the few grown by the DEA (sixty-six versus four). It also suggests the limits of the applicability of this data, something that should be taken into account when comparing one garden to another.

The average height of these seventy-six plants was 1.8 kilograms; the average weight was 1.9 kilograms and the average quantity of dried flowers over the three seasons was 252 grams. The maximum height was 3.4 meters, maximum weight was 5.2 kilograms and the maximum weight of dried flowers was 660 grams. The minimum height was 1.1 meters, the minimum weight was 0.5 kilograms and the minimum quantity of dried flowers was 40 grams.

There was little correlation between height and dried flowers, a coefficient of 0.12569666. The same was true of the correlation between weight and height, 0.36843246. But harvest weight correlated well with dried flowers, 0.86720655. The number of plants was 76, the test was two-tailed, the degrees of freedom 74, P was less than or equal to .05 and the critical value .2257. This means the coefficient between height and dried flowers could have occurred by chance.

The ratio of dried flowers to harvest weight varied between a minimum of 4.2% to a maximum of 21.8% with an overall average of 13.3%. At first sight this compares well with the 14.4% reported on page 4 of *Cannabis Fields*, actually 14.25% when taken from the data in Attachment 1. The latter ratio falls to 13.14% when only the mature plants (those with greater than or equal to 120 grow days) are considered. It falls further to 12.71% when the two mature anomalies are subtracted from the data set.

But these numbers taken from the data in Attachment 1 of *Cannabis Fields* are not for the ratio of dried flowers to harvest weight but for Leafnbud® to harvest weight, that is, a mass of ground up leaf and flowers versus the fresh plant weight. If we accept [and we don't] the ratio of leaf to bud given in Figure 2, then the weight of the dried flowers grown by the DEA would be somewhere between six and seven percent. But the leaf was not separated from the flowers in the DEA plantation. Thus, their estimates differ from the ARSECA data by almost 100%.

How can we explain that the DEA brought in a smaller ratio than the crew at the ARSECA garden? This is understandable since the DEA chose the very largest plants from their sample space. Larger plants mean more wood, thicker stalks and longer branches. Had the DEA wanted a higher ratio of dried flowers to harvest weight, they should have grown smaller plants, mostly indica. But this would have defeated their purpose, the Poundaplant®.

We can also compare the formula for the linear curve of best fit for the ARSECA plants (page 329) with that for the DEA mature plants without anomalies (page 141). The first is $Y = .112X + 33.34$, the second $Y = .110X + 72.84$. They are remarkably similar. But the former expresses a relationship between the harvest weight in grams and the weight of the dried flowers in grams, while the latter that between the harvest weight in grams and the dried Leafnbud® in grams. Both describe mature female plants. For smaller plants, these formulas suggest the DEA plants were some 40 grams heavier. For larger plants, it also suggests that a rough estimate of the weight of the dried flowers from ARSECA is close to 11% of the harvest weight. If we accept that one half of the Leafnbud® from the DEA is flowers (and there is no data to support this) then a reasonable estimate for said Leafnbud® is some 5% to 6%.

3.   House Brand Seeds.   Can a grower obtain a pound of dried flowers from a cannabis plant? I took a limited amount of data on house brand seeds, those seeds deliberately bred by seed houses to produce the largest yields possible. I deliberately cherry-picked this data.

NAME	HT(M)	HW(G)	DF(G)
MM73	1.7	4300	560
MM72	1.5	2400	300
Manolito 6	2	3300	430
Tusk 23	2	2500	410
Tusk 22	1.6	3600	480
Manolito 5	1.6	2900	450
Lui 52	1.5	3900	610
Tusk 24	1.6	1600	300
Highlnd 13	1.9	2700	480
Hshballs 2	1.9	2900	320
Redhorz 19	1.7	1700	220
Redhorz 17	1.6	2000	320
Nuvola 26	1.5	3400	560
Sp. AK	2	5000	490
Blkhd 48	1.8	4000	660
Lui 54	1.6	2000	390
Swtooth 57	1.4	2500	340
MM 64	2	3500	420
NAME	HT(M)	HW(G)	DF(G)

Figure 131. The data for eighteen plants grown from house brand seeds.

	HT(M)	HW(G)	DF(G)
HT(M)	1		
HW(G)	0.30979	1	
DF(G)	0.0777299	0.7852272	1
	CV = +/- .4683		P </= 0.05

Figure 132. The correlation matrix for eighteen house brand plants.

The number of plants was eighteen, the degrees of freedom 16, and the test was two-tailed. Only the correlation between the dried flowers and the harvest weight has validity; the others could have occurred by chance.

	HT(M)	HW(G)	DF(G)
TOTALS	30.9	54200	7740
AVG	1.7166667	3011.1111	430
MIN	1.4	1600	220
MAX	2	5000	660

*Figure 133. Totals, averages, minimums and maximums for
the eighteen cherry-picked house brand plants.*

The ratios of dried flowers varied from a minimum of 9.8% for the Special AK to a maximum of 19.5% for the Lui 54 with an average of 14.6%. The smallest quantity of dried flowers from a single plant was 220 grams from the Red Horse 19 and the largest was 660 grams from the Blockhead 48. The average weight of the dried flowers from these eighteen cherry-picked house brand plants was 430 grams, roughly 96% of the 448 grams reported in *Cannabis Fields*. This was remarkable considering that the seed packets themselves suggested this was at the high end of the range of the possible. It helps to have a crew to help you grow. It also helps to have a master grower overseeing the garden.

So yes, Virginia, it is possible to obtain a pound of dried flowers from a set of plants. These were of course carefully selected from all the plants to be only plants grown from house seeds and then only those with the largest weights of dried flowers. But will the average grower manage this? Notice that the average of the seventy-six plants fell to just over half this, 252 grams, still an above average result. One other master grower told me he had managed 200 grams per plant and was happy to get it. But these are generally upper bounds, not averages or minimums.

4.   Canopy v Dried Flowers.   In 2004 and 2006 I took data on the canopy diameters of 38 plants. The diameter was measured with the same homemade pole used to measure the heights. Two diameters were taken for each plant, at right angles to one another, one of which was the longest diameter. The diameters were then averaged. The data was taken along with the heights just before the plant was harvested and weighed.

This data has biases. First, most were taken from the 2004 House Brand plants. Second, most were taken early in each harvest season, favoring not only larger plants but those that matured first. Plants that weighed less than half a kilo were excluded.

Figure 134. Following page. Canopy v Dried Flower Data.

NAME	HT(CM)	DIA(CM)	HW(G)	DF(G)
MANO 6	200	140	3300	430
TUSK 23	200	130	2500	410
MANO 5	160	140	2900	450
LUI 52	150	140	3900	610
TUSK 24	160	120	1600	300
HLND 13	190	130	2700	480
HBALLS 2	190	130	2900	320
LUI 54	160	100	2000	390
SWTH 57	140	100	2500	340
2G1	190	100	1500	245
DB128	200	60	1700	280
AFR 43	340	240	5000	403
COL 45	230	150	3300	457
B2002111	160	100	1000	159
B2002112	170	40	1700	120
RH18	150	110	2100	236
RH19	170	100	1700	220
RH17	160	100	2000	320
NUV 26	150	120	3400	560
NUV 27	120	50	500	80
BESP 155	190	100	1300	220
B2002109	130	50	800	110
COL 47	260	100	2200	260
SPAK	200	140	5000	490
BLKHD 48	180	150	4000	660
2G2	140	100	2100	340
2G1	190	100	1500	245
SHEZD	110	100	600	131
C3	110	90	700	131
PSK1	120	110	1400	300
C2	120	110	1500	275
DHAZE	120	130	1700	286
J216BA	230	110	1000	92
PSK2	120	110	1400	202
HNYMN1	120	110	1300	177
J226	230	120	1400	214
DBLFN5	120	110	700	106
J21	200	100	1000	133
NAME	HT(CM)	DIA(CM)	HW(G)	DF(G)

APPENDIX C – THE FIFTH LEVEL

	HT(CM)	DIA(CM)	HW(G)	DF(G)
TOTALS	6480	4240	77800	11182
AVG	170.52632	111.57895	2047.3684	294.26316
MIN	110	40	500	80
MAX	340	240	5000	660

Figure 135. Totals, averages, minimums and maximums, canopy data.

	HT(CM)	DIA(CM)	HW(G)	DF(G)
HT(CM)	1			
DIA(CM)	0.5276933	1		
HW(G)	0.5106483	0.7298053	1	
DF(G)	0.2464927	0.6111817	0.8638311	1
	CV = +/- .3202		P </=0.05	

Figure 136. The correlation matrix, canopy data.

The test is two-tailed, the degrees of freedom are 36, the height to dried flower correlation could have occurred by chance.

The x-y scattergraphs between canopy diameter and dried flowers do not show high R-squared, the best coming from the polynomial and power series curves of best fit. Here they are on the following pages:

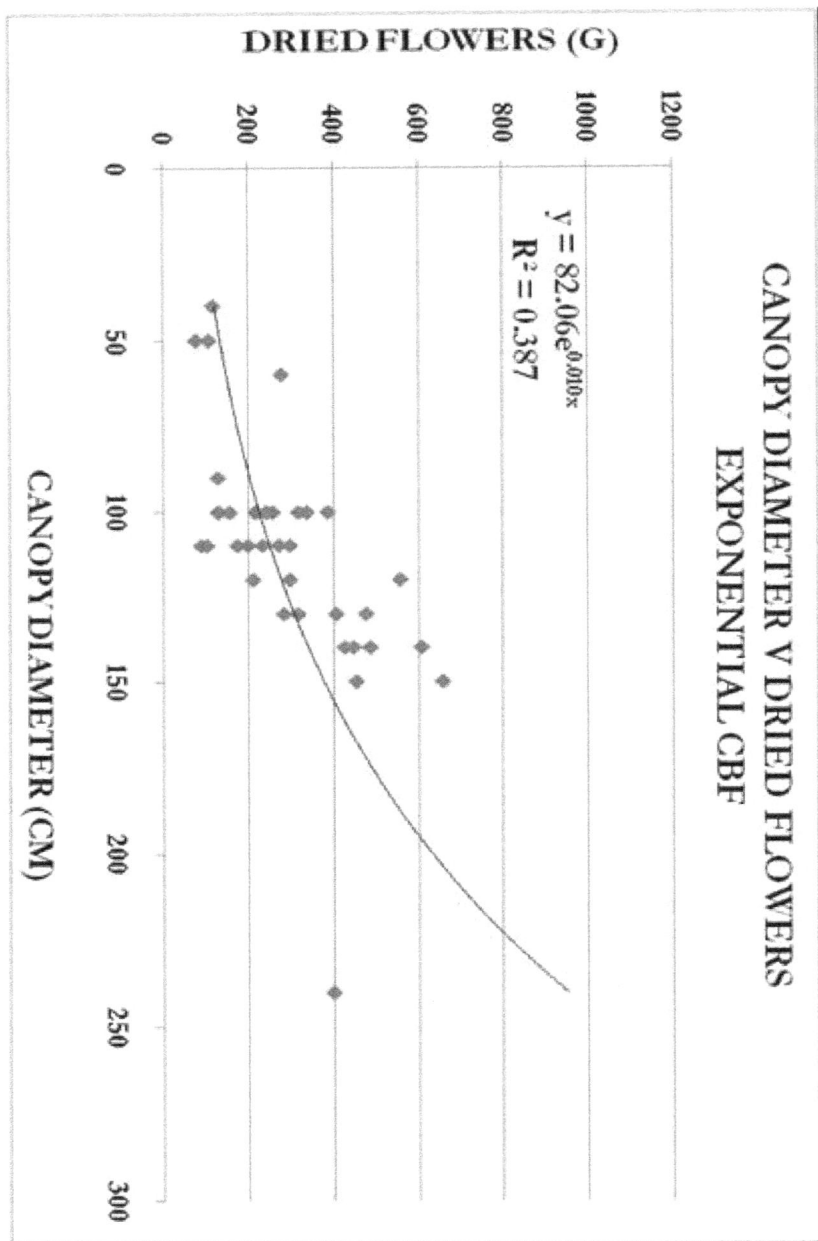

Figure 137. Canopy diameter v dried flowers, exponential CBF.

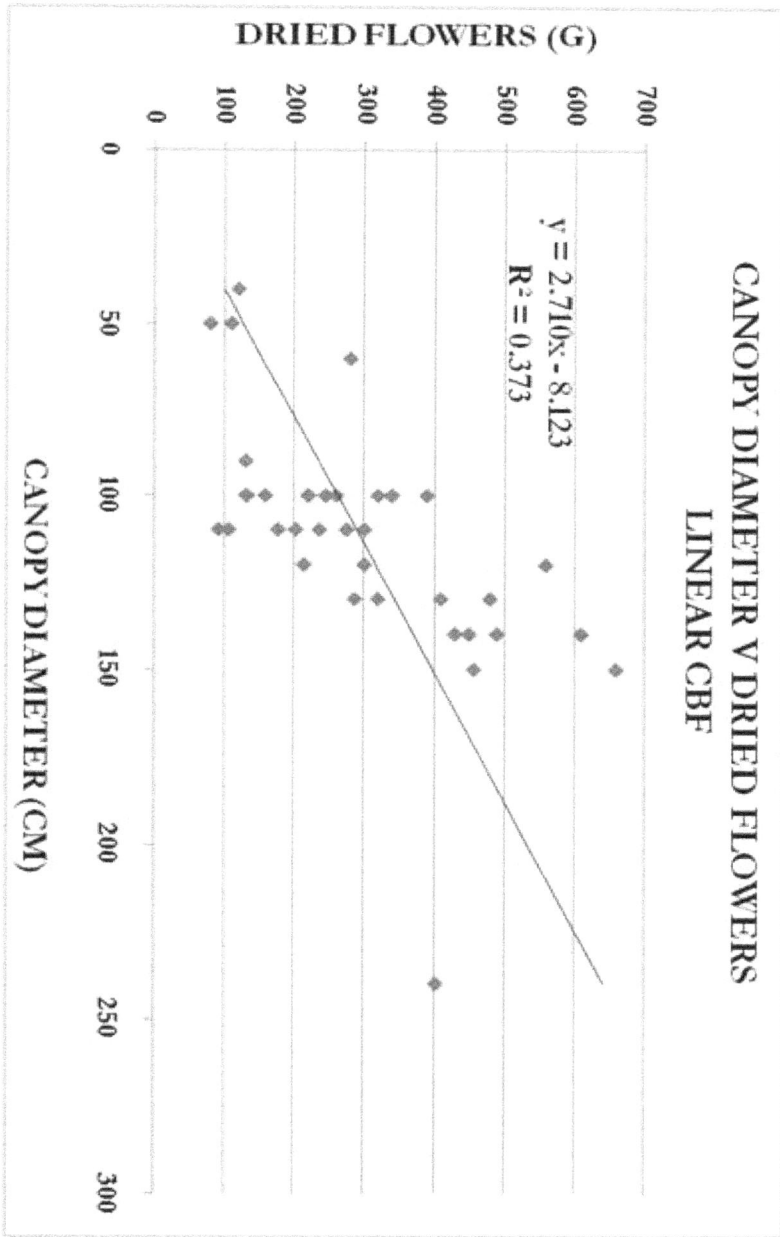

Figure 138. Canopy diameter v dried flowers, linear CBF.

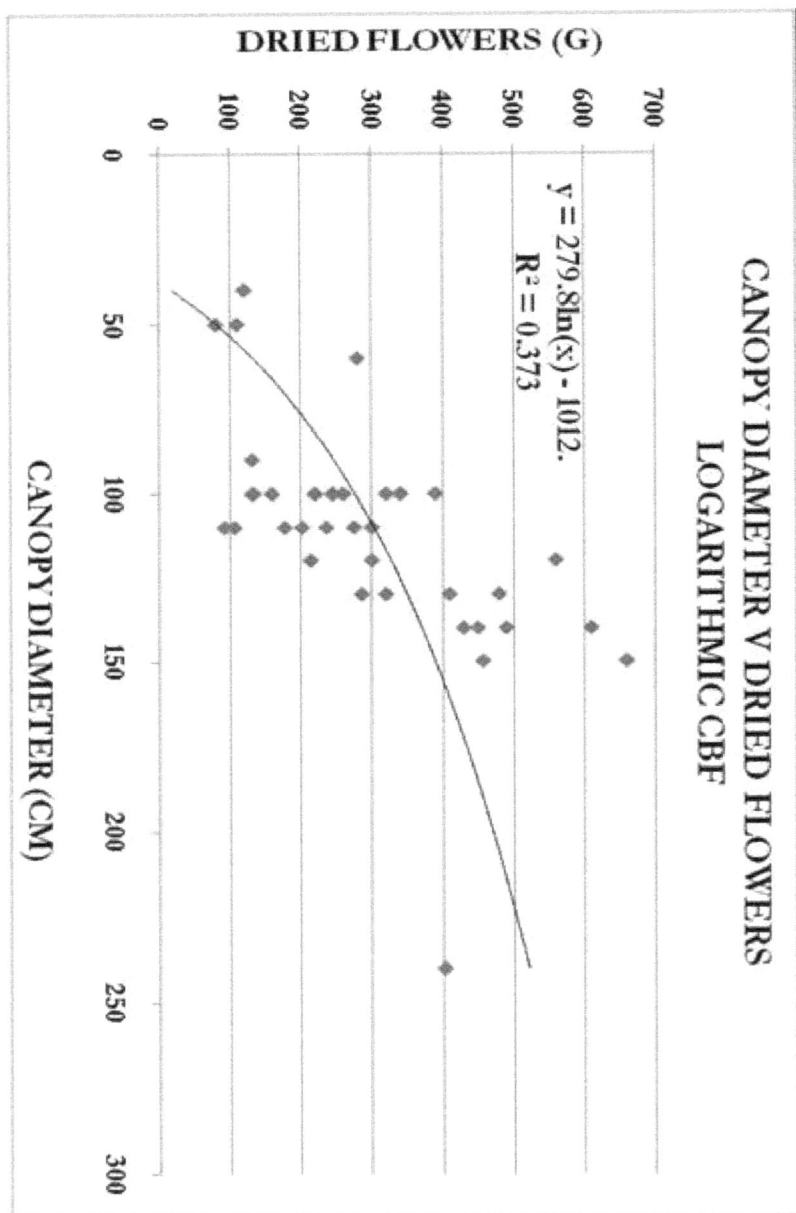

Figure 139. Canopy diameter v dried flowers, logarithmic CBF.

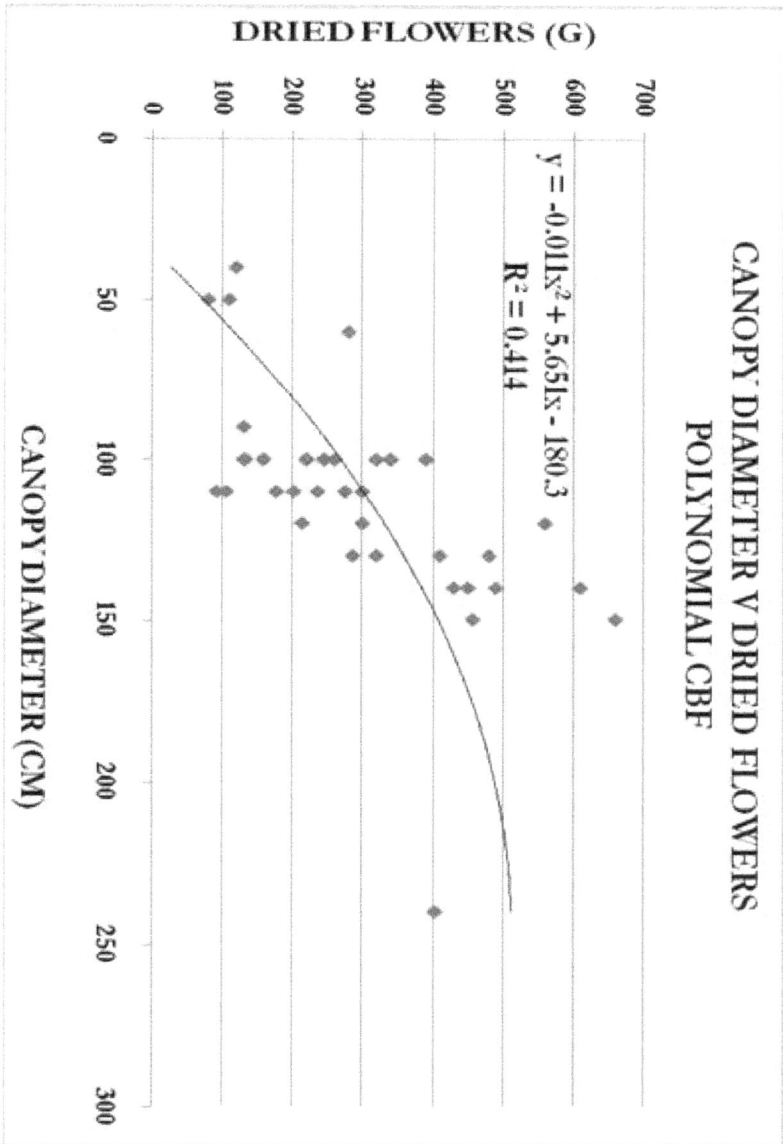

Figure 140. Canopy diameter v dried flowers, polynomial CBF.

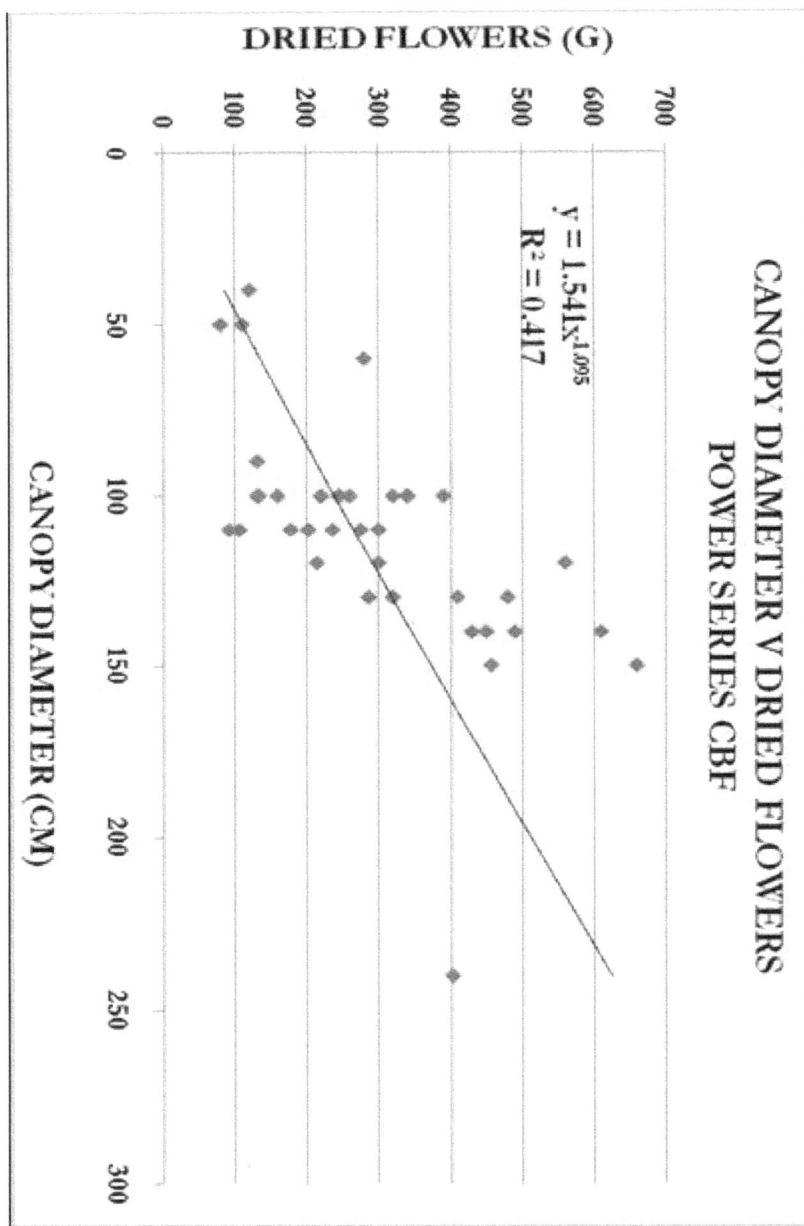

Figure 141. Canopy diameter v dried flowers, power series CBF.

5.　　Male Plants.

In 2006 I took data from a dozen male plants.

NAME	DAYS	HT(CM)	DIA(CM)	HW(G)	DP(G)	WOOD(G)	LEAF(G)	WOOD/DP	LEAF/DP	LEAF/WOOD	DP/HW	WOOD/HW	LEAF/HW
20M-2	34	80	90	1500	170	73	97	0.42941176	0.57058824	1.32876712	0.11333333	0.04866667	0.06466667
I-9	37	160	80	500	96	52	44	0.54166667	0.45833333	0.84615385	0.192	0.104	0.088
I-10	37	130	100	500	110	50	60	0.45454545	0.54545455	1.2	0.22	0.1	0.12
12MUI-1	41	180	100	500	121	53	68	0.43801653	0.56198347	1.28301887	0.242	0.106	0.136
J1WZ5-10	56	200	150	1600	504	275	229	0.54563492	0.45436508	0.83272727	0.315	0.171875	0.143125
I6-5	58	230	110	1400	432	231	201	0.53472222	0.46527778	0.87012987	0.30857143	0.165	0.14357143
J1WZ5-17	58	150	100	900	150	63	82	0.42	0.58666667	1.3015873	0.3	0.126	0.164
I6-3	58	170	100	600	164	83	81	0.50609756	0.49390244	0.97590361	0.27333333	0.13833333	0.135
I2-30	58	160	110	1200	367	187	180	0.50953678	0.49046322	0.96256684	0.30583333	0.15583333	0.15
I6-1	60	220	100	800	256	145	111	0.56640625	0.43359375	0.76551724	0.32	0.18125	0.13875
J1WZ5-8	65	220	130	1400	408	245	163	0.60049020	0.39950980	0.66530612	0.29142857	0.175	0.11642857
H-9	68	160	80	500	196	52	54	0.48955604	0.59043396	1.03846154	0.212	0.104	0.108
NAME	DAYS	HT(CM)	DIA(CM)	HW(G)	DP(G)								

Figure 142. Data for the males, 2006.

	DAYS	HT	DIA	HW	DP	WOOD	LEAF	WOOD/DP	LEAF/DP	LEAF/WOOD	DP/HW	WOOD/HW	LEAF/HW
MAX	89	238	153	190	564	275	123	0.689090	0.5703024	1.3787272	1.12	0.1025	0.1419
MIN	34	8	8	50	96	05	44	0.42	0.3066908	0.16530612	1.11333333	0.4888667	0.6296667
AVG	52.5	121.666667	104.166667	116.666667	263.333333	123.5	170	0.5309163	0.49145101	1.1054447	0.5779475	0.01830986	0.1325042
TOTALS	630	2060	1250	1000	2864	6195	1370	6.3870469	5.9256252	12.071596	3.8635	1.75993833	1.5974563

Figure 143. Totals, averages, minimums and maximums, males 2006.

	DAYS	HT	DIA	HW	DP	WOOD	LEAF
DAYS	1						
HT	0.62016084	1					
DIA	0.32858096	0.50952959	1				
HW	0.13665142	0.19290238	0.6707218	1			
DP	0.45886721	0.61076929	0.8628146	0.84024546	1		
WOOD	0.48700103	0.66381571	0.86183255	0.81675708	0.99287496	1	
LEAF	0.40455353	0.52518418	0.84258205	0.85655903	0.9874348	0.96174123	1

Figure 144. The correlation matrix for the males, 2006.

The test is two-tailed, the degrees of freedom 10, P is less than or equal than 0.05, N = 12, and the critical value is plus or minus 0.5760.

We can graph the harvest weight versus the dried leaf:

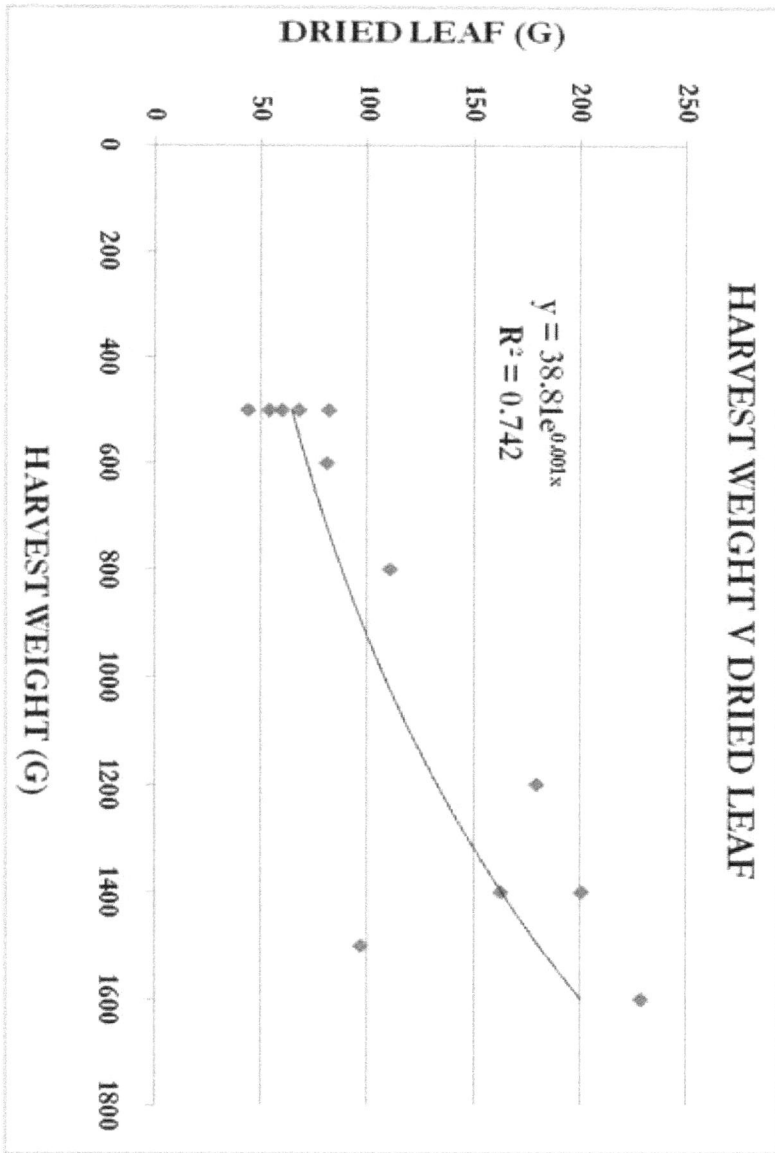

Figure 145. Harvest weight v dried leaf, males 2006, exponential CBF.

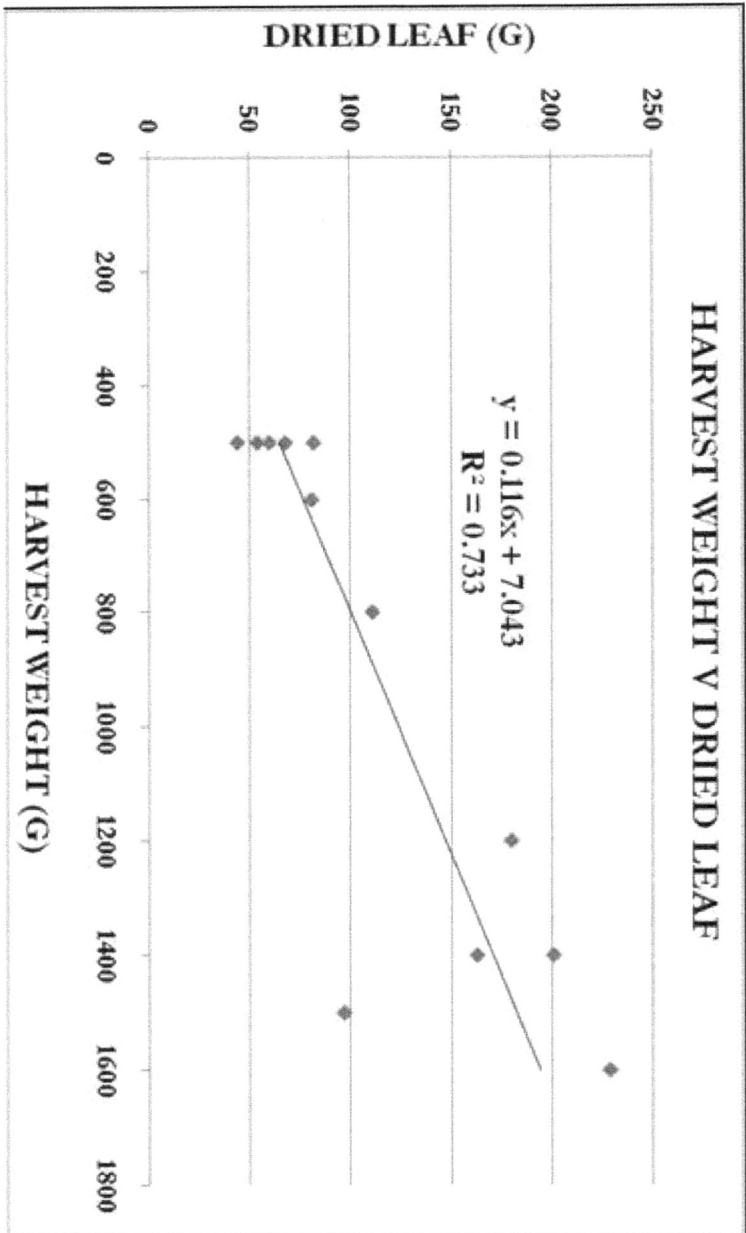

Figure 146. Harvest weight v dried leaf, 2006 males, linear CBF.

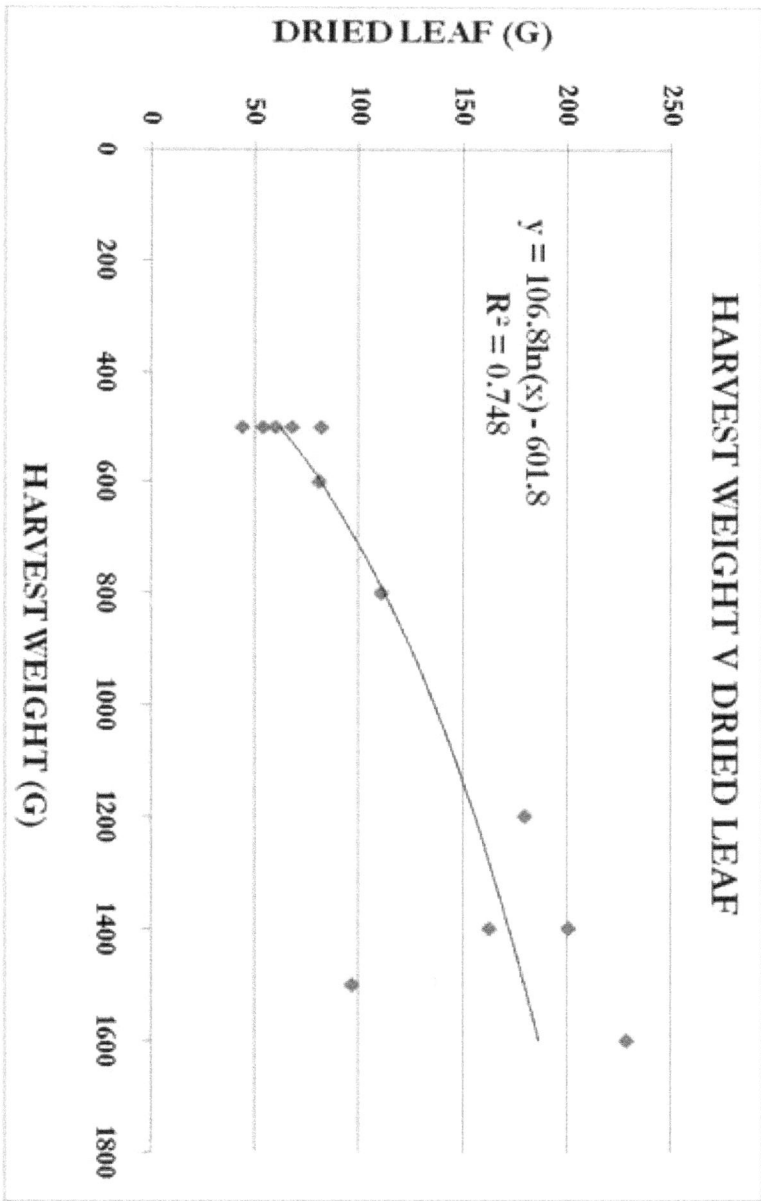

Figure 147. Harvest weight v dried leaf, 2006 males, logarithmic CBF.

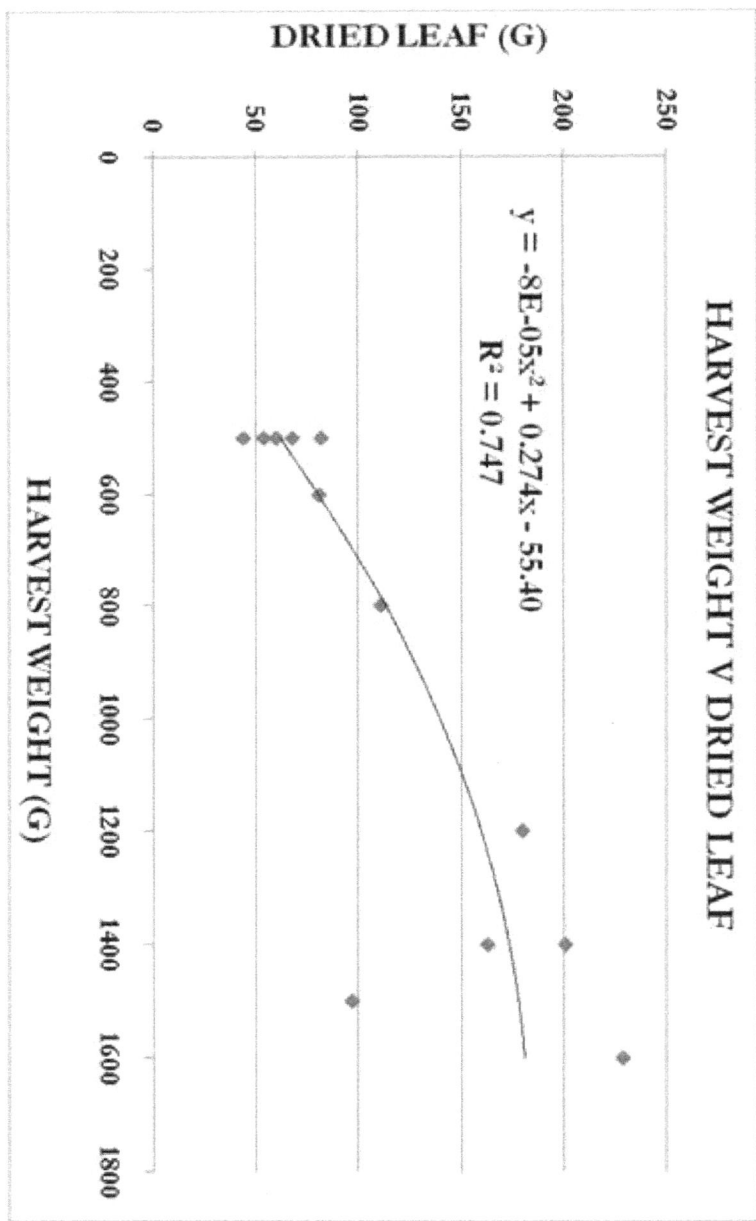

Figure 148. Harvest weight v dried leaf, 2006 males, polynomial CBF.

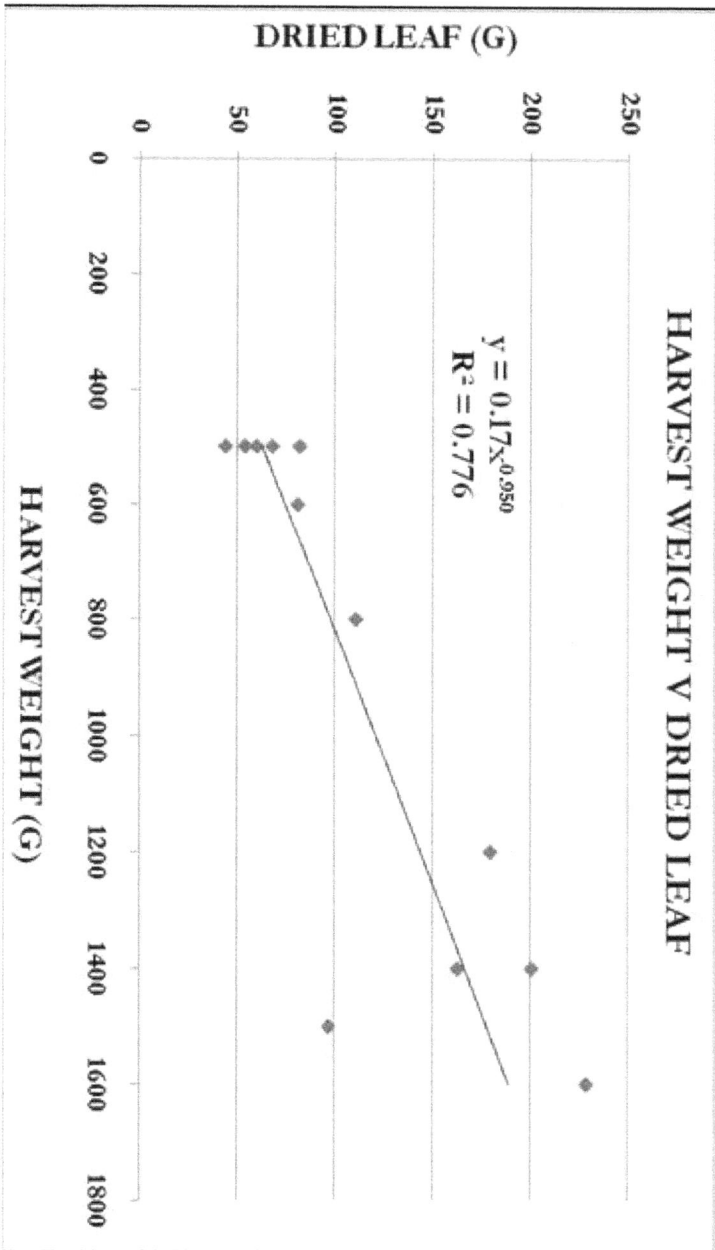

Figure 149. Harvest weight v dried leaf, males 2006, power series CBF.

We can also graph the canopy diameter versus the dried leaf:

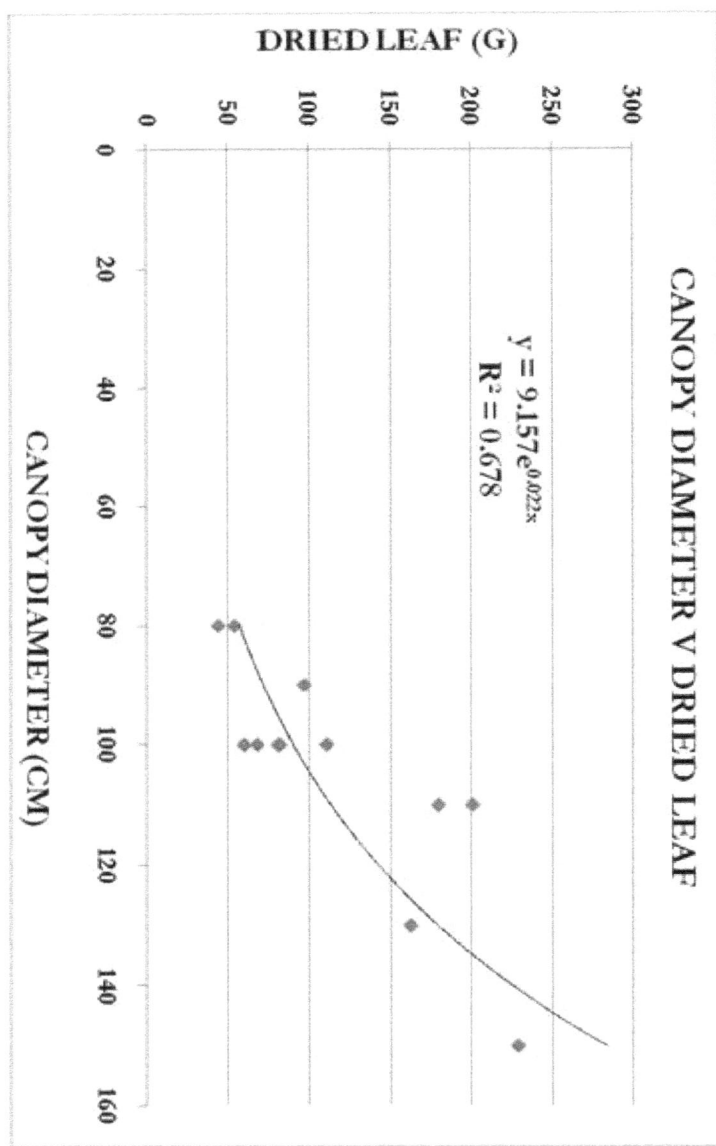

Figure 150. Canopy diameter v dried leaf, 2006 males, exponential CBF.

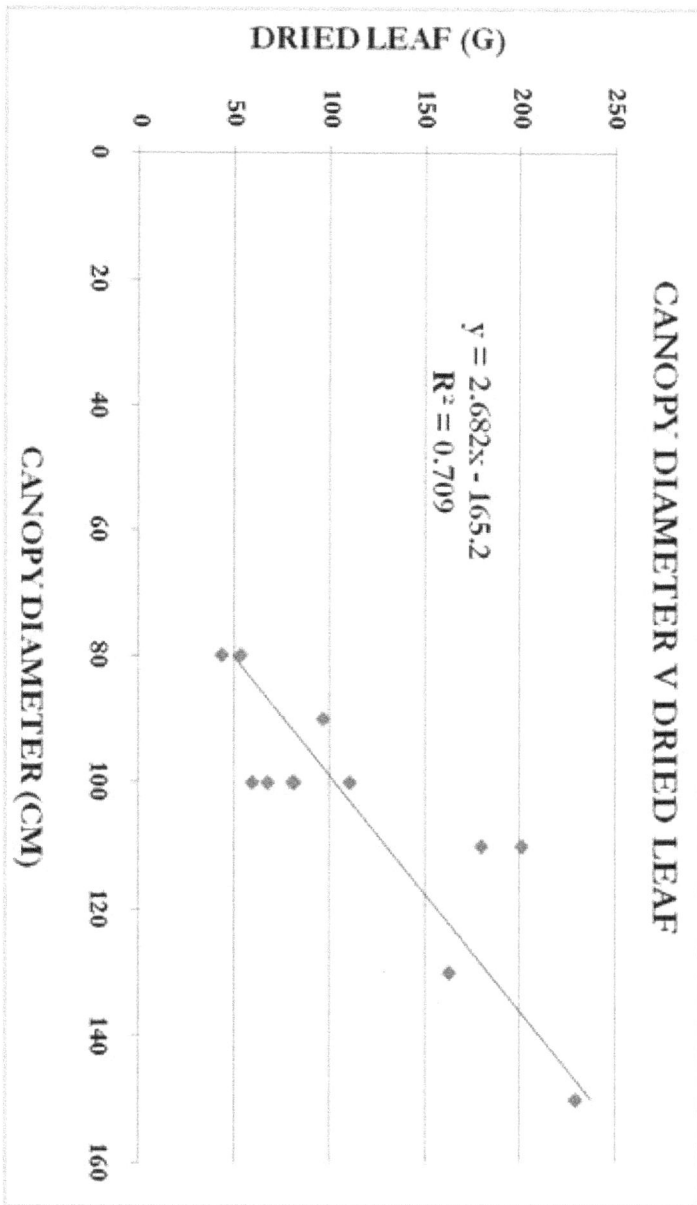

Figure 151. Canopy diameter v dried leaf, 2006 males, linear CBF.

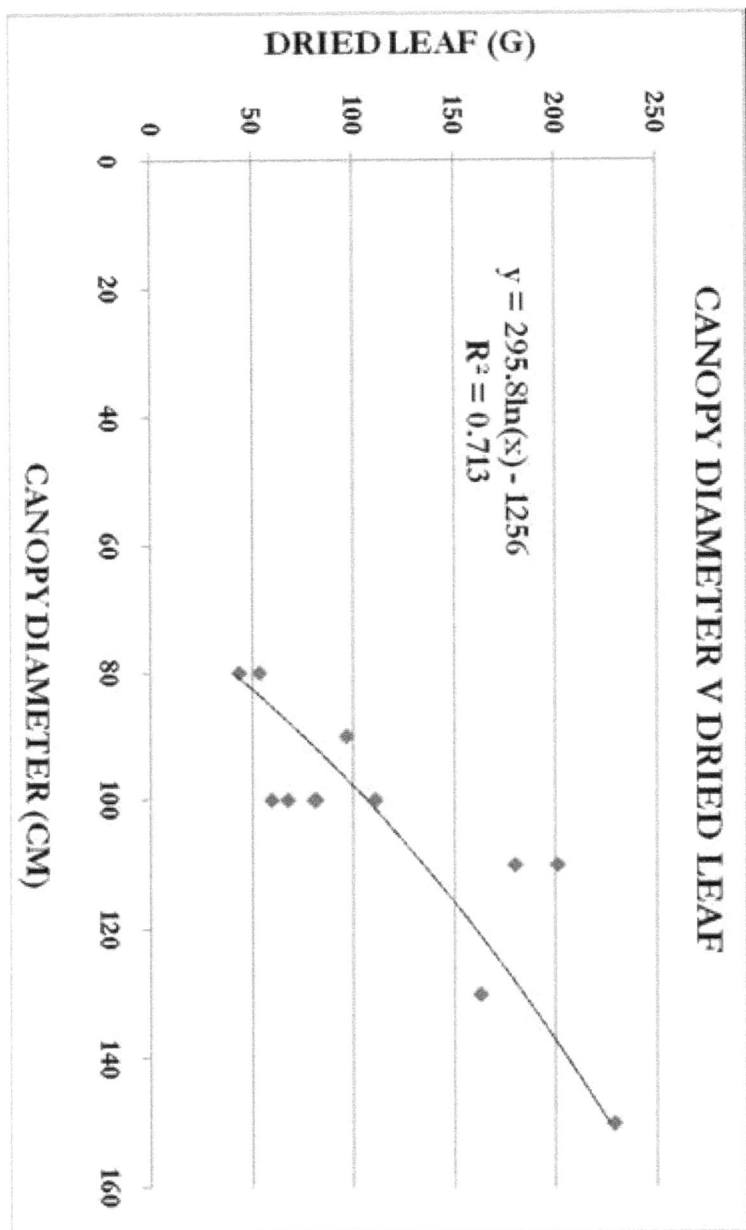

Figure 152. Canopy diameter v dried leaf, 2006 males, logarithmic CBF.

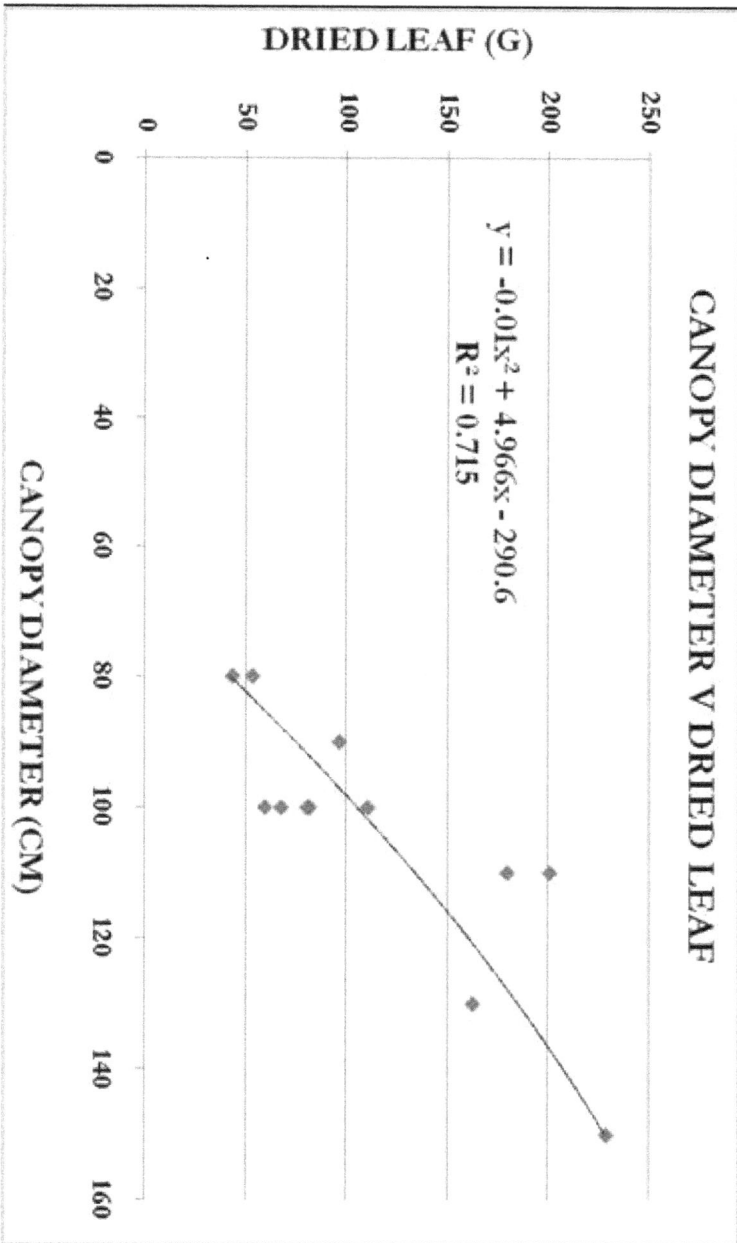

Figure 153. Canopy diameter v dried leaf, 2006 males, polynomial CBF.

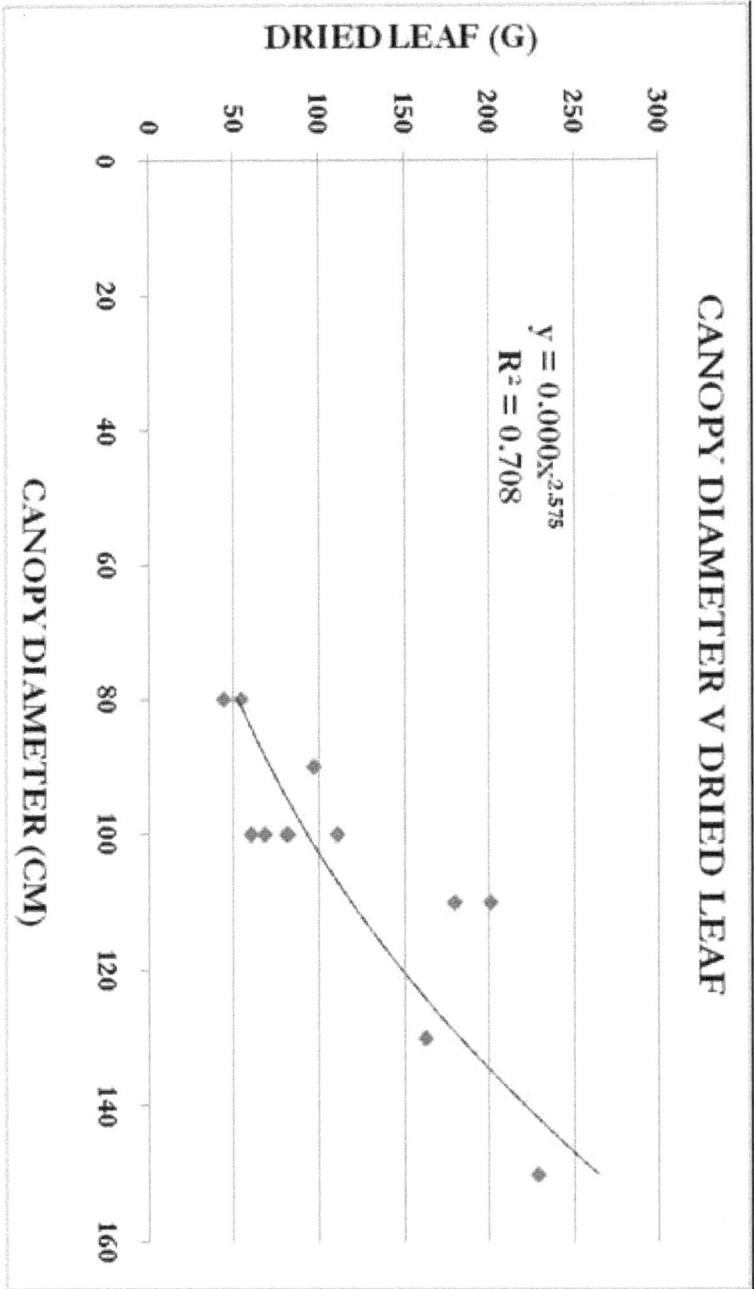

Figure 154. Canopy diameter v dried leaf, 2006 males, power series CBF.

APPENDIX C – THE FIFTH LEVEL

On page nine of *Cannabis Fields* we read: "The estimated yield [leaf] of a male plant in early August ... will be approximately 50% of the weight of [the Leafnbud®] of a female plant of similar age and growth stage." We have to assume that the writer does not mean the weight of the entire plant, either wet or dry, but instead means the weight of the yield [Leafnbud®] of the female plant. No data is presented to substantiate the statement.

On its face this compares male leaf to female Leafnbud®. But in early August, few of the female plants will have developed many flowers. So in essence it compares male leaf to female leaf. Both males and females are still growing in early August.

This is difficult to check. The ARSECA female plants were not sacrificed in early August so there is no baseline to verify this statement. The males were pulled as soon as they exhibited their sex. But some plants in *Cannabis Fields* were measured during this period.

The next problem is to try to identify which of these plants in early August were male or female. The seed data has been zeroed so it is difficult to know. There are two competing statements in *Cannabis Fields* describing their measuring regimen: "Yield measurements were made on 102 plants during the course (page 2) ...." In fact there are 102 plants in the data in Attachment 1. But there is also: "Yield measurements were made on 90 days or older *female* plants (page 1, italics added) ...." This suggests that the DEA did not know which of the plants were male and which female for plants with less than 90 grow days. The best we can assume is that among these younger plants that were measured, half were male and half were female.

What we can do is compare the ARSECA males to the plants in *Cannabis Fields* of similar age and growth stage. This compares plants from two different gardens so caveats apply. Any conclusions will have limited applicability. The 12 ARSECA males have ages between 34 and 68 days. So we could compare these with the 34 plants of *Cannabis Fields* with ages between 30 and 65 days:

357

NUMBER	DAYS	HW(G)	LNB(G)
1	55	11.9	1.4
2	55	57.4	12.1
3	55	72.9	13.5
4	55	12.3	2.1
15	36	4.1	0.9
16	36	14.5	3.2
17	36	13	3.1
18	36	27.9	5.7
19	64	689	116.4
20	65	923.1	126.2
21	65	1040.7	156.5
26	56	103.4	15.3
27	56	153.7	21.1
28	56	239.9	29.6
107.02	30	6.6	1.6
108.02	30	22.2	5.1
109.02	30	166.9	28.3
108.04	64	2691.8	430
107.04	64	459.5	87.8
106.04	64	1608.6	239.6
102.02	30	63.6	10.2
103.02	30	77.2	13.1
104.02	30	71.2	14.1
102.04	64	1947.1	334.2
103.04	64	1754.3	277.5
105.04	64	2232	341.7
97.02	30	65.9	12.6
98.09	30	45.9	8.2
99.09	30	16.7	3.4
90.11	65	656.2	97.3
95.11	65	1131.6	162.8
89.11	65	430	68.7
99.11	65	1078.3	172.7
88.11	65	480.1	71.2
NUMBER	DAYS	HW(G)	LNB(G)

Figure 155. Cannabis Fields plants less than or equal to 65 grow days.

	DAYS	HW(G)	LNB(G)
TOTALS	1705	18369.5	2887.2
AVG	50.147059	540.27941	84.917647
MIN	30	4.1	0.9
MAX	65	2691.8	430

Figure 156. Totals, averages, minimums and maximums for plants from Cannabis Fields with less than or equal to 65 grow days.

	DAYS	HW(G)	LNB(G)
DAYS	1		
HW(G)	0.6410055	1	
LNB(G)	0.6299288	0.9974879	1

Figure 157. The correlation matrix for the 34 plants from Cannabis Fields with less than or equal to 65 grow days.

The test is two-tailed, the degrees of freedom 32, the number of plants is 34, P is less than or equal to 0.05, and the critical value is plus or minus 0.5760. So all the values in the correlation matrix are higher than the level one might expect from chance.

We can also run the x-y scattergraphs:

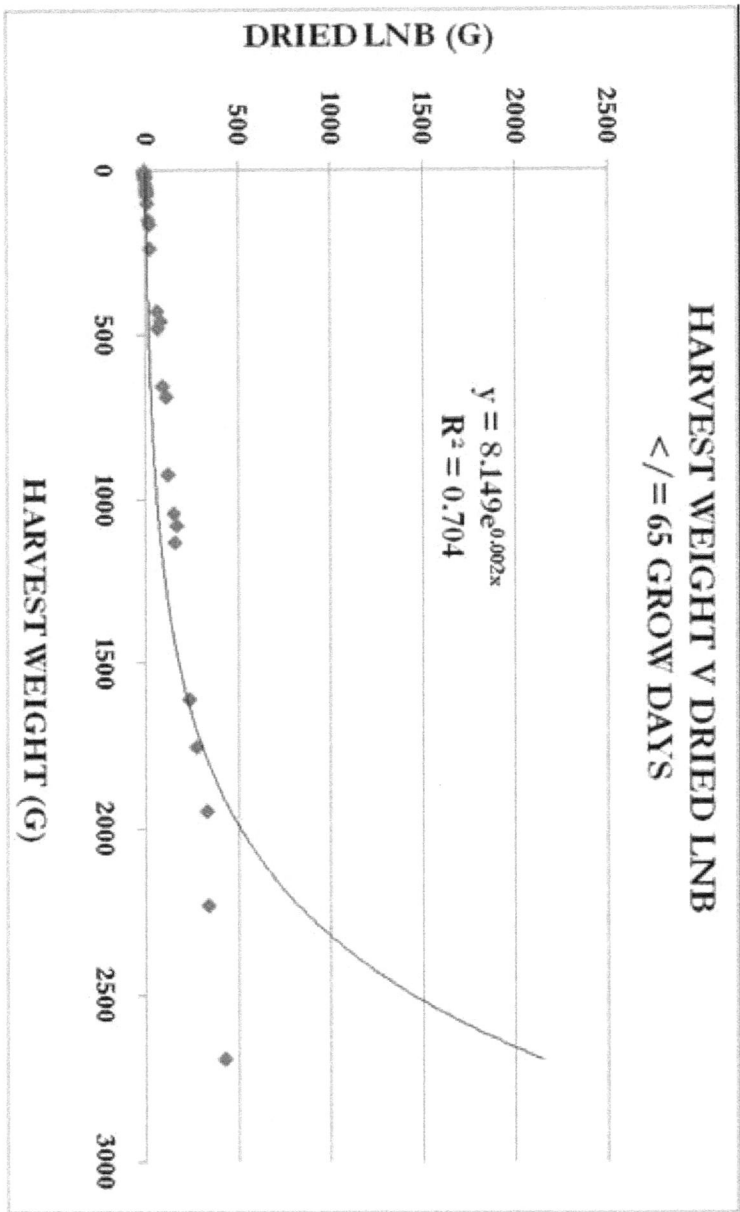

Figure 158. Harvest weight versus dried Leafnbud® for the 34 plants of Cannabis Fields with less than or equal to 65 grow days, exponential CBF.

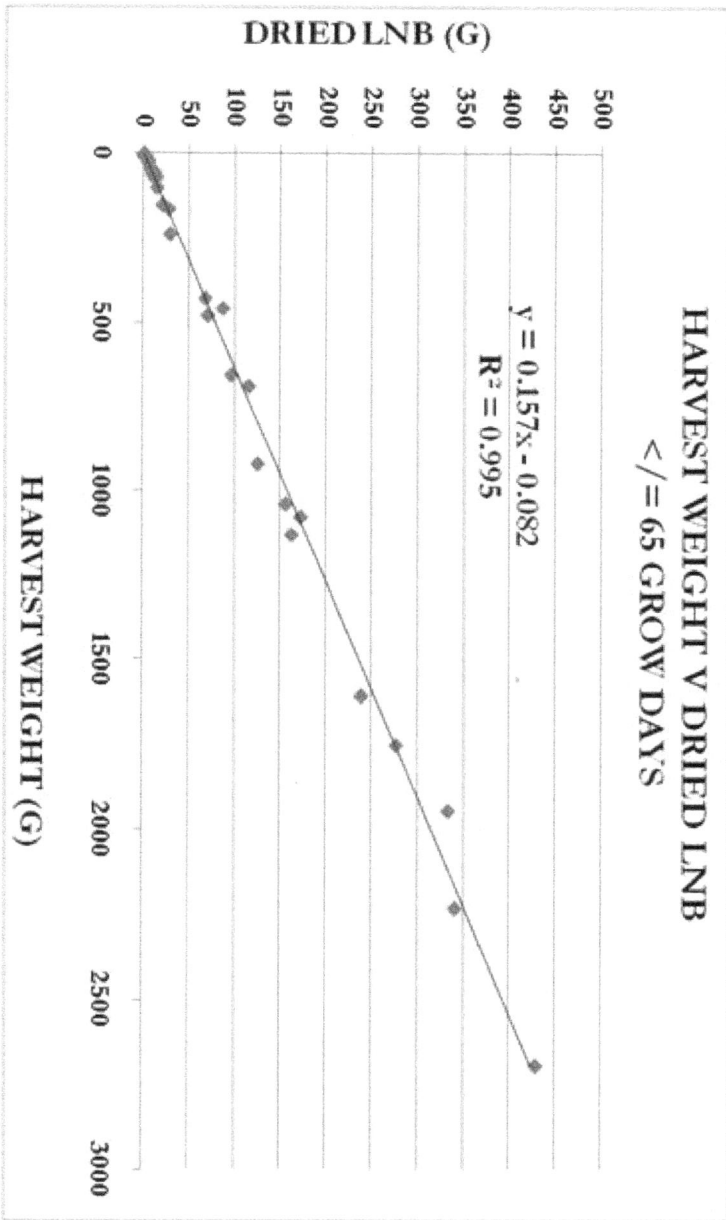

Figure 159. Harvest weight versus dried Leafnbud® for the 34 plants of Cannabis Fields with less than or equal to 65 grow days, linear CBF.

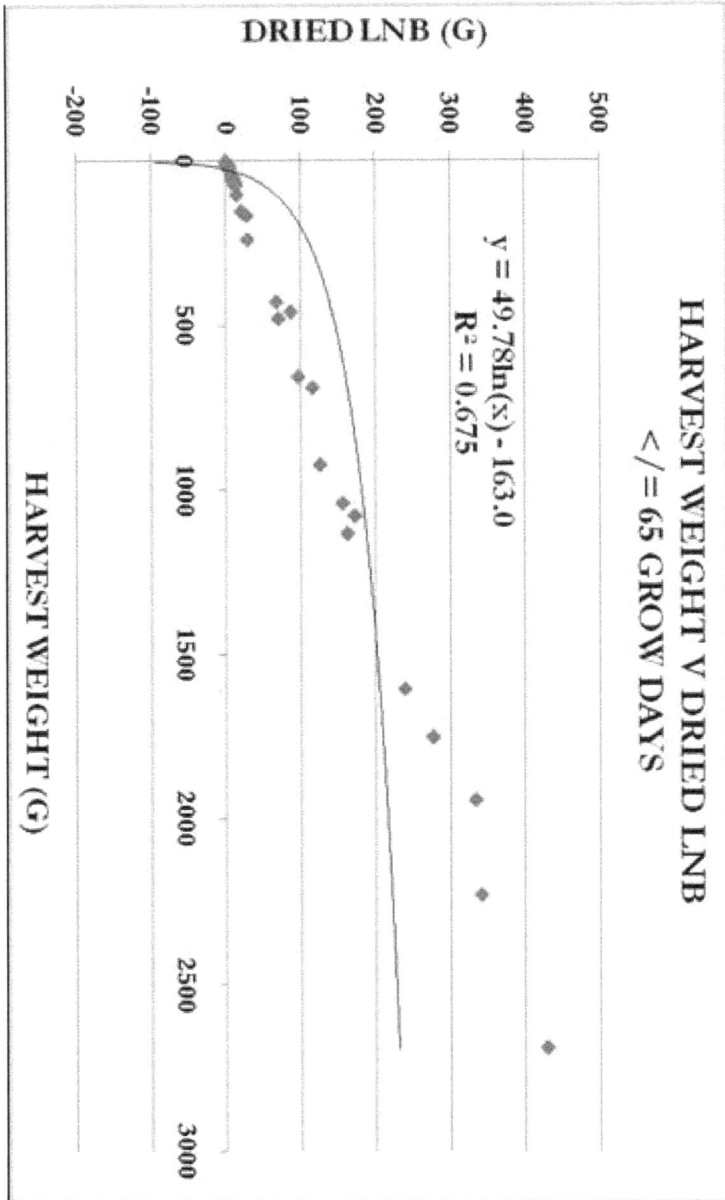

Figure 160. Harvest weight versus dried Leafnbud® for the 34 plants of Cannabis Fields with less than or equal to 65 grow days, logarithmic CBF.

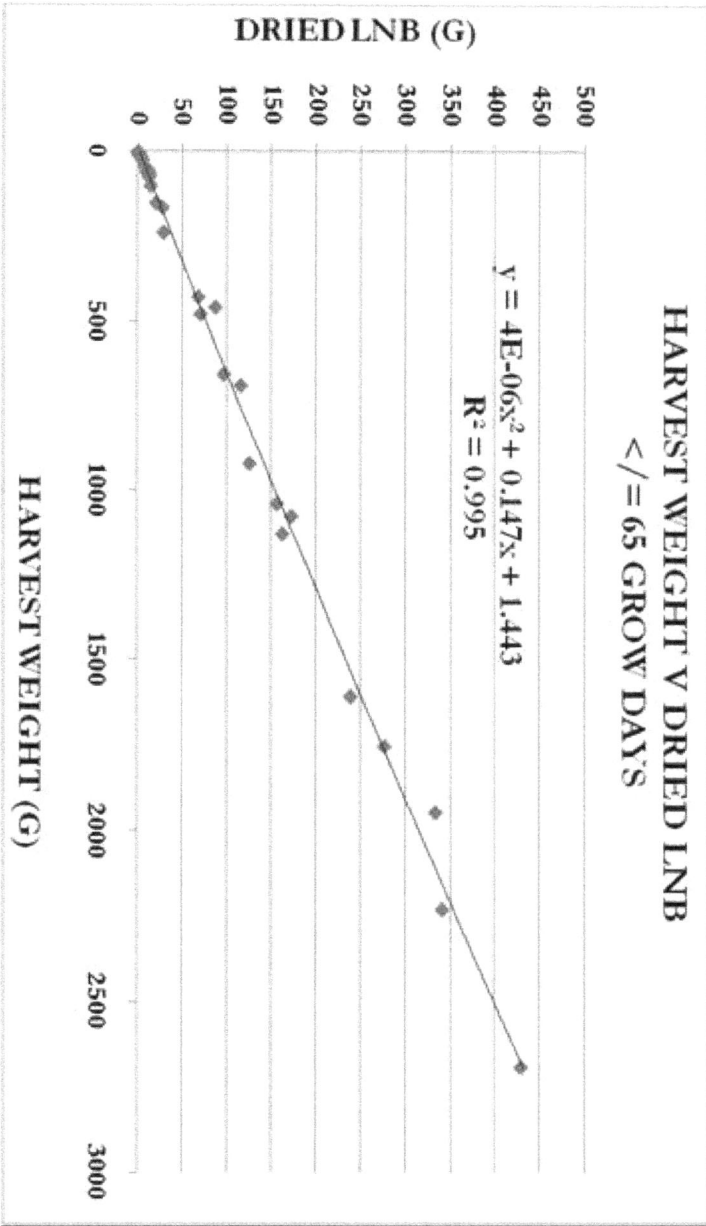

Figure 161. Harvest weight versus dried Leafnbud® for the 34 plants of Cannabis Fields with less than or equal to 65 grow days, polynomial CBF.

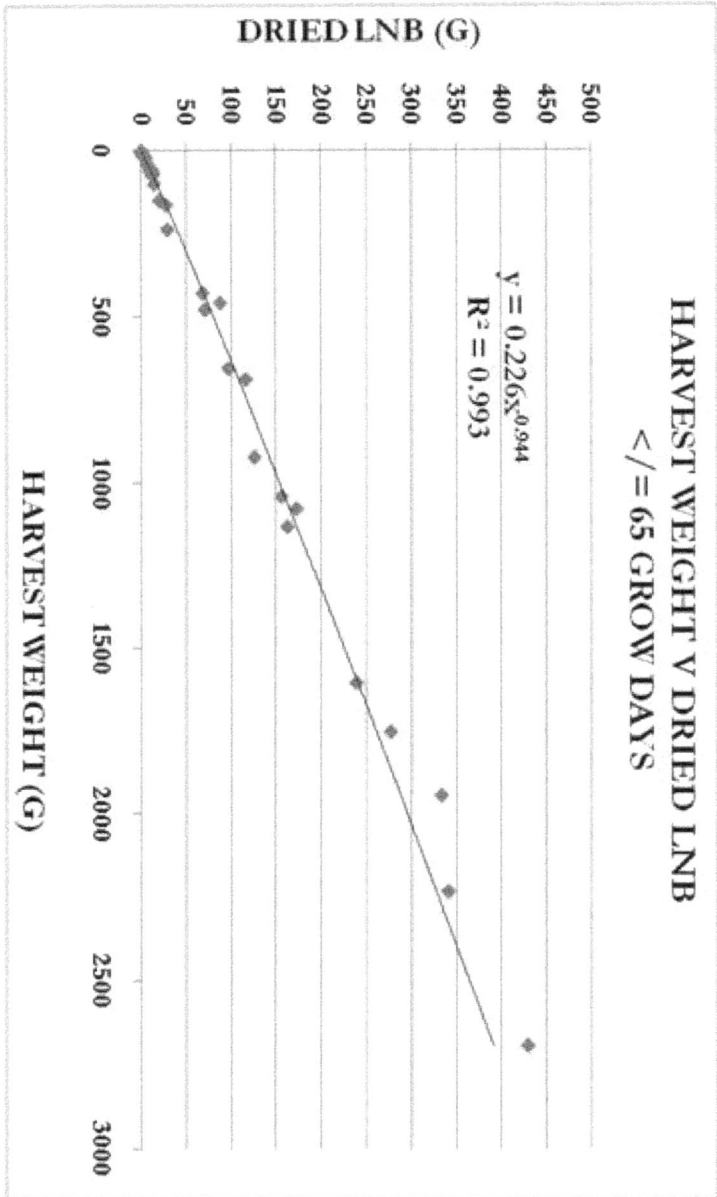

Figure 162. Harvest weight versus dried Leafnbud® for the 34 plants of Cannabis Fields with less than or equal to 65 grow days, power series CBF.

The linear curve of best fit provides an excellent R-squared and is easy to use.

The average weight of the dried Leafnbud® of the 34 *Cannabis Fields* plants of uncertain sex that had grow days between 30 and 65 was 84.92 grams. The average weight of the dried leaf from the 12 ARSECA plants that had grow days between 34 and 68 was 114.16 grams. So the ARSECA males had 134% of the weight of these plants of similar age and growth stage from *Cannabis Fields*, not the 50% reported on page nine.

Does this make any sense? It does when you notice that in general the male plants grow much faster than the female plants. (Males tend to grow faster than females in human populations as well.) Only later do the females catch up and put on weight, normally when they flower. From the standpoint of evolution this would be beneficial since the males need gravity or the wind to spread their pollen over the smaller in height females.

We can also compare the ARSECA males to the mature females, both in the ARSECA and DEA gardens using the linear curves of best fit. The harvest weights of the 2006 males together was 11 kilos, divided by 12 gives 916.67 grams. Plugged into the DEA formula Y = .110X + 72.84 gives 173.67 grams for an expected weight of dried Leafnbud®. Plugged into the ARSECA formula Y = .112X + 33.34 gives 136 grams expected in dried flowers. The actual average weight of the dried leaf from the 2006 males was 114.16 grams. This is 65.73% of the expected DEA dried Leafnbud® for a mature female and 83.94% of the expected weight of the dried flowers for an ARSECA mature female. This obviously compares apples and oranges but it does give us some small sense of how males compare to females, albeit vegetative males to flowering females of the same average harvest weight.

6.   Separation.   In 2001, 2004 and 2006
I took data on the separation of the plant into its dried leaf, flowers
and stalk/branches. Most of the data was gathered from plants that
matured early. Plants that weighed at harvest less than 0.5 kilo were
excluded.

a.   2001 Plant Separation.   The   ten   plants   from
2001 were primarily sativa. Here is the separation data from 2001:

NAME	HT(CM)	HW(G)	WOOD(G)	LEAF(G)	FL(G)
ESP GRN	270	3600	140	215	235
ESP ALTA	250	1600	54	66	200
ESP ALTIS	320	3600	130	212	390
B02	190	600	14	26	40
BUSH	170	500	15	17	60
RFXSK	230	900	16	52	97
ESPXL	250	1100	40	56	120
NOTOZ	180	1700	140	84	150
BF99B	140	1000	20	46	120
REF98C	170	800	72	82	160

Figure 163. Data for the 2001 separation.

Here are the totals, averages, minimums and maximums:

	HT(CM)	HW(G)	WOOD(G)	LEAF(G)	FL(G)
TOTALS	2170	15400	641	856	1572
AVG	217	1540	64.1	85.6	157.2
MIN	140	500	14	17	40
MAX	320	3600	140	215	390

Figure 164. 2001 separation totals, averages, minimums and maximums.

APPENDIX C – THE FIFTH LEVEL

Here are eleven calculated numbers for the ten separated 2001 plants where DP stands for dried plant, HW is the harvest weight, W is the wood (stalk and branches), L is the leaf, and FL the flowers:

DP	W/DP	L/DP	FL/DP	DP/HW	W/HW	L/HW	FL/HW	L/W	FL/W	FL/L
590	0.2372881	0.3644068	0.3983051	0.1638889	0.0388889	0.0597222	0.0652778	1.5357143	1.6785714	1.0930233
320	0.16875	0.20625	0.625	0.2	0.03375	0.04125	0.125	1.2222222	3.7037037	3.030303
732	0.1775956	0.2896175	0.5327869	0.2033333	0.0361111	0.0588889	0.1083333	1.6307692	3	1.8396226
80	0.175	0.325	0.5	0.1333333	0.0233333	0.0433333	0.0666667	1.8571429	2.8571429	1.5384615
92	0.1630435	0.1847826	0.6521739	0.184	0.03	0.034	0.12	1.1333333	4	3.5294118
165	0.0969697	0.3151515	0.5878788	0.1833333	0.0177778	0.0577778	0.1077778	3.25	6.0625	1.8653846
216	0.1851852	0.2592593	0.5555556	0.1963636	0.0363636	0.0509091	0.1090909	1.4	3	2.1428571
374	0.3743316	0.2245989	0.4010695	0.22	0.0823529	0.0494118	0.0882353	0.6	1.0714286	1.7857143
186	0.1075269	0.2473118	0.6451613	0.186	0.02	0.046	0.12	2.3	6	2.6086957
314	0.2292994	0.2611465	0.5095541	0.3925	0.09	0.1025	0.2	1.1388889	2.2222222	1.9512195

Figure 165. Eleven numbers calculated for the ten separated 2001 females.

And this is the correlation matrix for the 2001 females and the associated values:

	HT(CM)	HW(G)	WOOD(G)	LEAF(G)	FL(G)
HT(CM)	1				
HW(G)	0.7676135	1			
WOOD(G)	0.479492	0.8316187	1		
LEAF(G)	0.7281	0.971769	0.8408517	1	
FL(G)	0.7517082	0.8849246	0.7477683	0.8862546	1
N = 10	DF = 8	P<0.05	2-TAIL	CV+/-.6319	

Figure 166. Correlation matrix for the ten 2001 females.

The total dry plant sums to 3069 grams, which divided by the the number of plants (10) gives 306.9. The ratio of average dry stalk and branch to average dry plant is 64.1 divided by 306.9, or .2088628. The ratio of the average leaf to the average dry plant is 85.6/306.9, or .2789182. The average flower to the average dry plant is 157.2/306.9, or .5122189. We can draw the following pie chart of the dried component parts of an average dry plant of these ten sativas from 2001, percentages rounded to two places:

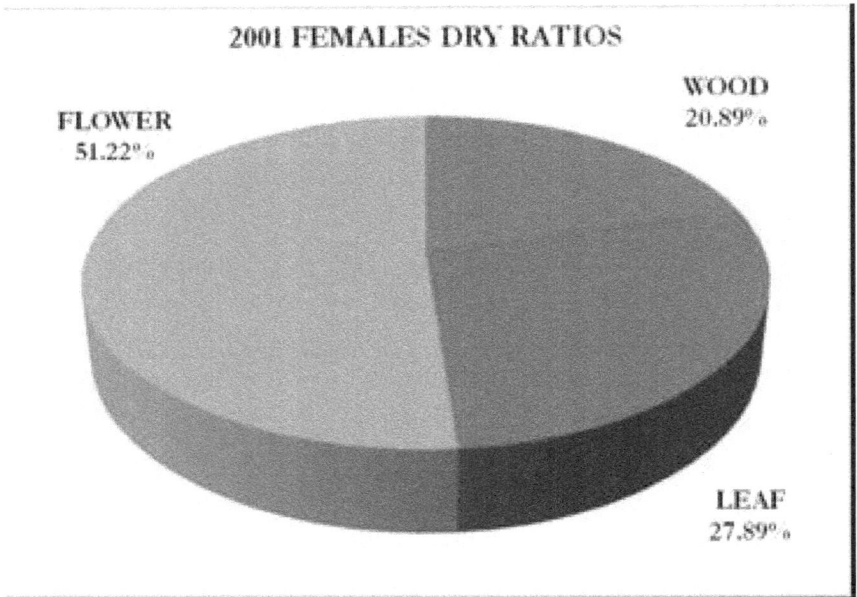

Figure 167. 2001 Female Dry Ratios.

A few caveats apply. The plants were lightly field trimmed, meaning that during the harvest season some of the shade leaves were removed as they aged. Several of the plants were quite small, transplanted to the ARSECA garden later than the others as replacements for males that had been pulled.

b.   2004 Plant Separation. In 2004 I took data from 25 plants and their separated wood, leaf and flowers. Here is the 2004 separation data:

NAME	HT(CM)	HW(G)	WOOD(G)	LEAF(G)	FL(G)
MM73	170	4300	400	60	560
MM72	150	2400	230	20	300
MANO6	200	3300	360	20	430
TUSK23	200	2500	250	50	410
TUSK22	160	3600	310	40	480
MANO5	160	2900	280	50	450
LUI52	150	3900	350	80	610
TUSK24	160	1600	280	20	300
HLND13	190	2700	300	30	480
HBALLS2	190	2900	370	50	320
RH19	170	1700	270	10	220
RH17	160	2000	220	20	320
NUV26	150	3400	340	100	560
NUV27	120	500	50	20	80
BE155	190	1300	100	55	220
B2002109	130	800	40	20	110
COL47	260	2200	320	100	260
SPAK	200	5000	340	20	490
BLKHD48	180	4000	390	50	660
SWTH	140	2500	160	20	340
LUI54	160	2000	130	40	390
DB128	200	1700	240	100	280
COL45	230	3300	160	120	457
B2002111	160	1000	50	44	159
B2002112	170	1700	68	30	120
NAME	HT(CM)	HW(G)	WOOD(G)	LEAF(G)	FL(G)

Figure 168. 2004 plant separation data.

Here are eleven numbers calculated from the 2004 data:

DP(G)	W/DP	L/DP	FL/DP	DP/HW	W/HW	L/HW	FL/HW	L/W	FL/W	FL/L
1020	0.3921569	0.0588235	0.5490196	0.2372093	0.0930233	0.0139535	0.1302326	0.15	1.4	9.3333333
550	0.4181818	0.3636.36	0.5454545	0.2291667	0.0958333	0.0083333	0.125	0.0869565	1.3043478	15
810	0.4444444	0.0246914	0.5306642	0.2454545	0.1090909	0.0060606	0.130303	0.0555556	1.1944444	21.5
710	0.3521127	0.0704225	0.5774648	0.284	0.1	0.02	0.164	0.2	1.64	8.2
830	0.373494	0.0481928	0.5783133	0.2305556	0.0861111	0.0111111	0.1333333	0.1290323	1.5483871	12
780	0.3589744	0.0641026	0.5769231	0.2689655	0.0965517	0.0172414	0.1551724	0.1785714	1.6071429	9
1040	0.3365385	0.0769231	0.5865385	0.2666667	0.0897436	0.0205128	0.1564103	0.2285714	1.7428571	7.625
600	0.4666667	0.0333333	0.5	0.375	0.175	0.0125	0.1875	0.0714286	1.0714286	15
810	0.3703704	0.037037	0.5925926	0.3	0.111111	0.011111	0.1777778	0.1	1.6	16
740	0.5	0.0675676	0.4324324	0.2551724	0.1275862	0.0172414	0.1103448	0.1351351	0.8648649	6.4
500	0.54	0.02	0.44	0.2941176	0.1588235	0.0058824	0.1294118	0.037037	0.8148148	22
560	0.3928571	0.0357143	0.5714286	0.28	0.11	0.01	0.16	0.0909091	1.4545455	16
1000	0.34	0.1	0.56	0.2941176	0.1	0.0294118	0.1647059	0.2941176	1.6470588	5.6
150	0.3333333	0.1333333	0.5333333	0.3	0.1	0.04	0.16	0.4	1.6	4
375	0.2666667	0.1466667	0.5866667	0.2884615	0.0769231	0.0423077	0.1692308	0.55	2.2	4
170	0.2352941	0.1176471	0.6470588	0.2125	0.05	0.025	0.1375	0.5	2.75	5.5
680	0.4705882	0.1470588	0.3823529	0.3090909	0.1454545	0.0454545	0.1818182	0.3125	0.8125	2.6
850	0.4	0.0235294	0.5764706	0.17	0.068	0.004	0.098	0.0588235	1.4411765	24.5
1100	0.3545455	0.0454545	0.6	0.275	0.0975	0.0125	0.165	0.1282051	1.6923077	13.2
520	0.3076923	0.0384615	0.6538462	0.208	0.064	0.008	0.136	0.125	2.125	17
560	0.2321429	0.0714286	0.6964286	0.28	0.065	0.02	0.195	0.3076923	3	9.75
620	0.3870968	0.1612903	0.4516129	0.3647059	0.1411765	0.0588235	0.1647059	0.4166667	1.1666667	2.8
737	0.2170963	0.1628223	0.6200814	0.2233333	0.0484848	0.0363636	0.1384848	0.75	2.85625	3.8083333
253	0.1976285	0.173913	0.6284585	0.253	0.05	0.044	0.159	0.88	3.18	3.6136364
218	0.3119266	0.1376147	0.5504587	0.1282353	0.04	0.0176471	0.0705882	0.4411765	1.7647059	4
DP(G)	W/DP	L/DP	FL/DP	DP/HW	W/HW	L/HW	FL/HW	L/W	FL/W	FL/L

Figure 169. Eleven numbers calculated for the plants separated in 2004.

Here are totals, averages, minimums and maximums and the correlation matrix for the 25 plants separated from 2004:

	HT(CM)	HW(G)	WOOD(G)	LEAF(G)	FL(G)	DP(G)
TOTALS	4350	63200	6008	1169	9006	16183
AVG	174	2528	240.32	46.76	360.24	647.32
MIN	120	500	40	10	80	150
MAX	260	5000	400	120	660	1100

	HT(CM)	HW(G)	WOOD(G)	LEAF(G)	FL(G)
HT(CM)	1				
HW(G)	0.2821431	1			
WOOD(G)	0.3437318	0.790128	1		
LEAF(G)	0.5167118	0.2433065	0.2037304	1	
FL(G)	0.1782885	0.8919054	0.7731786	0.3346536	1

N = 25	DF = 23	P<0.05	CV+/-.3961	2 TAIL

Figure 170. Totals, averages, minimums, maximums and the correlation matrix from 25 plants separated in 2004.

These plants were mostly indica and were seriously field trimmed during the harvest season, meaning almost all the shade leaves were clipped before the plant was harvested. This was done primarily because the shade leaves for the indicas are much broader than those for the sativas. As the plant dries upside down the indica shade leaves tend to close up around the drying flowers. This makes the plant more difficult to dry and later to separate. The second reason was to provide more air flow around the plants as they matured in the field. Clipping the large shade leaves while the plant is still in the field helps prevent molds and aids in pest control.

We can draw a pie chart to represent the proportions of the weights of the wood, leaf and flower to the weight of the dry plant:

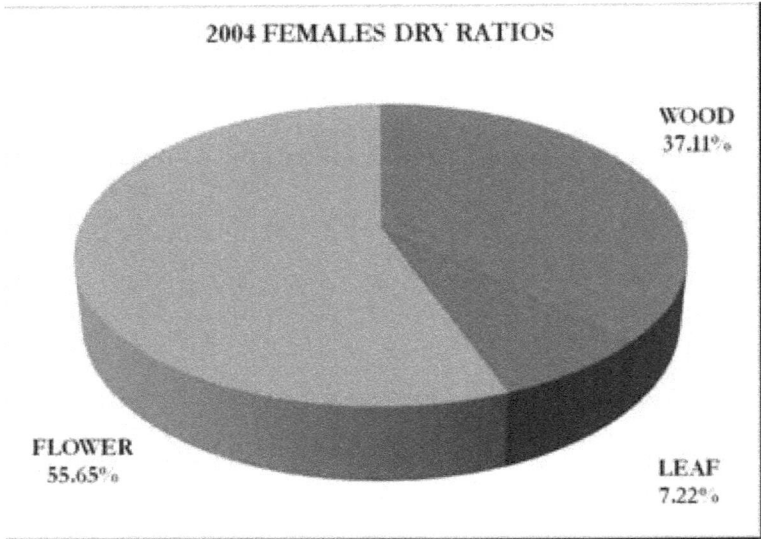

Figure 171. 2004 Females Dry Ratios.

The percentage of leaf is smaller in these plants than that of the plants from 2001, 7.22% compared to 27.89% respectively. Naturally, this distorts the other ratios as well, since the total for the dry plants was calculated, not measured. We can speculate that if the plants had not been seriously field trimmed of their shade leaves that the percentages of flower and wood would be quite a bit smaller. But how much smaller is impossible to determine.

The average flower to wood ratio for the ten 2001 plants was 157.2/64.1 or 2.452418, 2.45 rounded to two places. The average flower to wood ratio for the twenty-five 2004 plants was 360.24/240.32 or 1.4990013, 1.50 rounded to two places. This compares to a Leafnbud®/Wood ratio for the 17 seeded plants from the DEA plantations of 15425.2/17179.3, or .8978945, which is .90 rounded to two places. The same ratio for the 21 so-called sinsemilla plants from the DEA plantation cannot be used since the seed data was simply added to the stalk and branch.

c.   2006 Plant Separation.   I   also   took   separation
data from eleven plants in 2006. The same caveats apply. The data:

NAME	HT(CM)	HW(G)	WOOD(G)	LEAF(G)	FL(G)
SHZAD	110	600	110	39	131
C3	110	700	83	22	131
PSK1	120	1400	188	21	300
C2	120	1500	202	5	275
DBLFN5	120	700	53	22	106
J2-1	200	1000	101	45	133
DHAZE	120	1700	219	147	286
J216B	230	1000	237	51	92
PSK2	120	1400	124	119	202
HNYMN1	120	1300	121	118	177
J226	230	1400	200	91	214
NAME	HT(CM)	HW(G)	WOOD(G)	LEAF(G)	FL(G)

Figure 172. 2006 Separation Data.

	HT(CM)	HW(G)	WOOD(G)	LEAF(G)	FL(G)	DP(G)
TOTALS	1600	12700	1638	680	2047	4365
AVG	145.45455	1154.5455	148.90909	61.818182	186.09091	396.81818
MIN	110	600	53	5	92	181
MAX	230	1700	237	147	300	652

	HT(CM)	HW(G)	WOOD(G)	LEAF(G)	FL(G)
HT(CM)	1				
HW(G)	0.0426404	1			
WOOD(G)	0.4155389	0.6823649	1		
LEAF(G)	0.0551325	0.5497849	0.234342	1	
FL(G)	-0.285997	0.8505331	0.5422735	0.2359489	1

N = 11	DF = 9	P<0.05	CV+/-.5529	2 TAIL

Figure 173. Totals, etc. and Correlation Matrix, 2006.

The plants in 2006 were a mix: sativas, mothers and clones. Here are eleven calculated values:

DP(G)	W/DP	L/DP	FL/DP	DP/HW	W/HW	L/HW	FL/HW	L/W	FL/W	FL/L
280	0.3928571	0.1392857	0.4678571	0.4666667	0.1833333	0.065	0.2183333	0.3545455	1.1909091	3.3589744
236	0.3516949	0.0932203	0.5550847	0.3371429	0.1185714	0.0314286	0.1871429	0.2650602	1.5783133	5.9545455
509	0.3693517	0.0412574	0.589391	0.3635714	0.1342857	0.015	0.2142857	0.1117021	1.5957447	14.285714
482	0.4190871	0.0103734	0.5705394	0.3213333	0.1346667	0.0033333	0.1833333	0.0247525	1.3613861	55
181	0.2928177	0.121547	0.5856354	0.2585714	0.0757143	0.0314286	0.1514286	0.4150943	2	4.8181818
279	0.3620072	0.1612903	0.4767025	0.279	0.101	0.045	0.133	0.4455446	1.3168317	2.9555556
652	0.3358896	0.2254601	0.4386503	0.3835294	0.1288235	0.0864706	0.1682353	0.6712329	1.3059361	1.9455782
380	0.6236842	0.1342105	0.2421053	0.38	0.237	0.051	0.092	0.2151899	0.3881857	1.8039216
445	0.2786517	0.2674157	0.4539326	0.3178571	0.0885714	0.085	0.1442857	0.9596774	1.6290323	1.697479
416	0.2908654	0.2836538	0.4254808	0.32	0.0930769	0.0907692	0.1361538	0.9752066	1.4628099	1.5
505	0.3960396	0.180198	0.4237624	0.3607143	0.1428571	0.065	0.1528571	0.455	1.07	2.3516484
DP(G)	W/DP	L/DP	FL/DP	DP/HW	W/HW	L/HW	FL/HW	L/W	FL/W	FL/L

Figure 174. Eleven numbers calculated for the 2006 plants.

APPENDIX C – THE FIFTH LEVEL

At this point we can draw a pie chart of the average ratios:

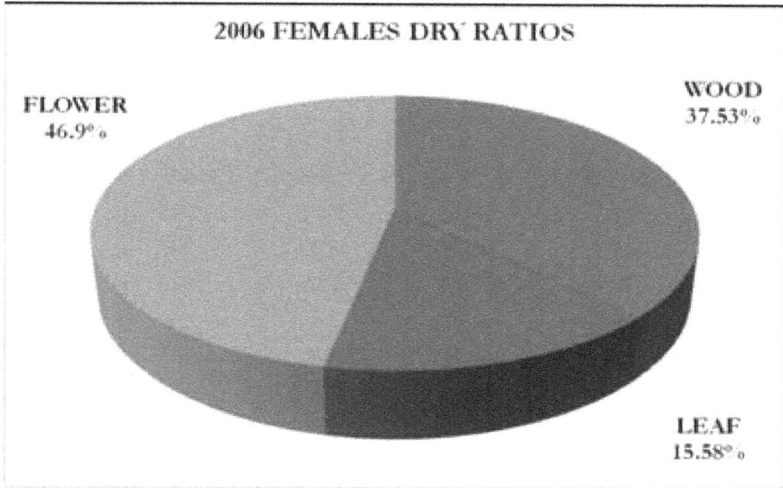

Figure 175. 2006 Dry Ratios.

These plants were not as heavily field trimmed as the plants in 2004 but some field trimming is apparent. Again, the percentages of the wood and the flowers will decline if the percentage of leaf reflected all of the original leaf that was on the plant before it was harvested.

d. **All Plant Separation.** We can combine all of
the separation data together:

NAME	HT(CM)	HW(G)	WOOD(G)	LEAF(G)	FL(G)
ESP GRN	270	3600	140	215	235
ESP ALTA	250	1600	54	66	200
ESP ALTIS	320	3600	130	212	390
B02	190	600	14	26	40
BUSH	170	500	15	17	60
RFXSK	230	900	16	52	97
ESPXL	250	1100	40	56	120
NOTOZ	180	1700	140	84	150
BF99B	140	1000	20	46	120
REF98C	170	800	72	82	160
MM73	170	4300	400	60	560
MM72	150	2400	230	20	300
MANO6	200	3300	360	20	430
TUSK23	200	2500	250	50	410
TUSK22	160	3600	310	40	480
MANO5	160	2900	280	50	450
LUI52	150	3900	350	80	610
TUSK24	160	1600	280	20	300
HLND13	190	2700	300	30	480
HBALLS2	190	2900	370	50	320
RH19	170	1700	270	10	220
RH17	160	2000	220	20	320
NUV26	150	3400	340	100	560

Figure 176. All separation data, page one.

NAME	HT(CM)	HW(G)	WOOD(G)	LEAF(G)	FL(G)
NUV27	120	500	50	20	80
BE155	190	1300	100	55	220
B2002109	130	800	40	20	110
COL47	260	2200	320	100	260
SPAK	200	5000	340	20	490
BLKHD48	180	4000	390	50	660
SWTH	140	2500	160	20	340
LUI54	160	2000	130	40	390
DB128	200	1700	240	100	280
COL45	230	3300	160	120	457
B2002111	160	1000	50	44	159
B2002112	170	1700	68	30	120
SHZAD	110	600	110	39	131
C3	110	700	83	22	131
PSK1	120	1400	188	21	300
C2	120	1500	202	5	275
DBLFN5	120	700	53	22	106
J2-1	200	1000	101	45	133
DHAZE	120	1700	219	147	286
J216B	230	1000	237	51	92
PSK2	120	1400	124	119	202
HNYMN1	120	1300	121	118	177
J226	230	1400	200	91	214

Figure 177. All separation data, page two.

Here are eleven calculated numbers for all the separated plants:

DP(G)	W/DP	L/DP	FL/DP	DP/HW	W/HW	L/HW	FL/HW	L/W	FL/W	FL/L
590	0.2372881	0.3644068	0.3983051	0.1638889	0.0388889	0.0597222	0.0652778	1.5357143	1.6785714	1.0930233
320	0.16875	0.20625	0.625	0.2	0.03375	0.04125	0.125	1.2222222	3.7037037	3.030303
732	0.1775956	0.2896175	0.5327869	0.2033333	0.0361111	0.0588889	0.1083333	1.6307692	3	1.8396226
80	0.175	0.325	0.5	0.1333333	0.0233333	0.0433333	0.0666667	1.8571429	2.8571429	1.5384615
92	0.1630435	0.1847826	0.6521739	0.184	0.03	0.034	0.12	1.1333333	4	3.5294118
165	0.0969697	0.3151515	0.5878788	0.1833333	0.0177778	0.0577778	0.1077778	3.25	6.0625	1.8653846
216	0.1851852	0.2592593	0.5555556	0.1963636	0.0363636	0.0509091	0.1090909	1.4	3	2.1428571
374	0.3743316	0.2245989	0.4010695	0.22	0.0823529	0.0494118	0.0882353	0.6	1.0714286	1.7857143
186	0.1075269	0.2473118	0.6451613	0.186	0.02	0.046	0.12	2.3	6	2.6086957
314	0.2292994	0.2611465	0.5095541	0.3925	0.09	0.1025	0.2	1.1388889	2.2222222	1.9512195
1020	0.3921569	0.0588235	0.5490196	0.2372093	0.0930233	0.0139535	0.1302326	0.15	1.4	9.3333333
550	0.4181818	0.0363636	0.5454545	0.2291667	0.0958333	0.0083333	0.125	0.0869565	1.3043478	15
810	0.4444444	0.0246914	0.5308642	0.2454545	0.1090909	0.0060606	0.130303	0.0555556	1.1944444	21.5
710	0.3521127	0.0704225	0.5774648	0.284	0.1	0.02	0.164	0.2	1.64	8.2
830	0.373494	0.0481928	0.5783133	0.2305556	0.0861111	0.0111111	0.1333333	0.1290323	1.5483871	12
780	0.3589744	0.0641026	0.5769231	0.2689655	0.0965517	0.0172414	0.1551724	0.1785714	1.6071429	9
1040	0.3365385	0.0769231	0.5865385	0.2666667	0.0897436	0.0205128	0.1564103	0.2285714	1.7428571	7.625
600	0.4666667	0.0333333	0.5	0.375	0.175	0.0125	0.1875	0.0714286	1.0714286	15
810	0.3703704	0.037037	0.5925926	0.3	0.1111111	0.0111111	0.1777778	0.1	1.6	16
740	0.5	0.0675676	0.4324324	0.2551724	0.1275862	0.0172414	0.1103448	0.1351351	0.8648649	6.4
500	0.54	0.02	0.44	0.2941176	0.1588235	0.0058824	0.1294118	0.037037	0.8148148	22
560	0.3928571	0.0357143	0.5714286	0.28	0.11	0.01	0.16	0.0909091	1.4345455	16
1000	0.34	0.1	0.56	0.2941176	0.1	0.0294118	0.1647059	0.2941176	1.6470588	5.6
150	0.3333333	0.1333333	0.5333333	0.3	0.1	0.04	0.16	0.4	1.6	4
375	0.2666667	0.1466667	0.5866667	0.2884615	0.0769231	0.0423077	0.1692308	0.55	2.2	4
170	0.2352941	0.1176471	0.6470588	0.2125	0.05	0.025	0.1375	0.5	2.75	5.5
680	0.4705882	0.1470588	0.3823529	0.3090909	0.1454545	0.0454545	0.1181818	0.3125	0.8125	2.6
850	0.4	0.0235294	0.5764706	0.17	0.068	0.004	0.098	0.0588235	1.4411765	24.5
1100	0.3545455	0.0454545	0.6	0.275	0.0975	0.0125	0.165	0.1282051	1.6923077	13.2
520	0.3076923	0.0384615	0.6538462	0.208	0.064	0.008	0.136	0.125	2.125	17
560	0.2321429	0.0714286	0.6964286	0.28	0.065	0.02	0.195	0.3076923	3	9.75
620	0.3870968	0.1612903	0.4516129	0.3647059	0.1411765	0.0588235	0.1647059	0.4166667	1.1666667	2.8
737	0.2170963	0.1628223	0.6200814	0.2233333	0.0484848	0.0363636	0.1384848	0.75	2.85625	3.8083333
253	0.1976285	0.173913	0.6284585	0.23	0.05	0.044	0.159	0.88	3.18	3.6136364
218	0.3119266	0.1376147	0.5504587	0.1282353	0.04	0.0176471	0.0705882	0.4411765	1.7647059	4
280	0.3928571	0.1392857	0.4678571	0.4666667	0.1833333	0.065	0.2183333	0.3545455	1.1909091	3.3589744
236	0.3516949	0.0932203	0.5550847	0.3371429	0.1185714	0.0314286	0.1871429	0.2650602	1.5783133	5.9545455
509	0.3693517	0.0412574	0.589391	0.3635714	0.1342857	0.015	0.2142857	0.1117021	1.5957447	14.285714
482	0.4190871	0.0103734	0.5705394	0.3213333	0.1346667	0.0033333	0.1833333	0.0247525	1.3613861	55
181	0.2928177	0.121547	0.5856354	0.2585714	0.0757143	0.0314286	0.1514286	0.4150943	2	4.8181818
279	0.3620072	0.1612903	0.4767025	0.279	0.101	0.045	0.133	0.4455446	1.3168317	2.9555556
652	0.3358896	0.2254601	0.4386503	0.3835294	0.1288235	0.0864706	0.1682353	0.6712329	1.3059361	1.9455782
380	0.6236842	0.1342105	0.2421053	0.38	0.237	0.051	0.092	0.2151899	0.3881857	1.8039216
445	0.2786517	0.2674157	0.4539326	0.3178571	0.0885714	0.085	0.1442857	0.9596774	1.6290323	1.697479
416	0.2908654	0.2836538	0.4254808	0.32	0.0930769	0.0907692	0.1361538	0.9752066	1.4628099	1.5
505	0.3960396	0.180198	0.4237624	0.3607143	0.1428571	0.065	0.1528571	0.455	1.07	2.3516484
DP(G)	W/DP	L/DP	FL/DP	DP/HW	W/HW	L/HW	FL/HW	L/W	FL/W	FL/L

Figure 178. Eleven calculated numbers, all plants separated.

Here are the totals, averages, minimums, maximums and the correlation matrix and associated constraints:

	HT(CM)	HW(G)	WOOD(G)	LEAF(G)	FL(G)	DP(G)
TOTALS	8120	91300	8287	2705	12625	23617
AVG	176.52174	1984.7826	180.15217	58.804348	274.45652	513.41304
MIN	110	500	14	5	40	80
MAX	320	5000	400	215	660	1100

	HT(CM)	HW(G)	WOOD(G)	LEAF(G)	FL(G)
HT(CM)	1				
HW(G)	0.3040039	1			
WOOD(G)	0.0586988	0.7668545	1		
LEAF(G)	0.4861421	0.2816676	0.0112413	1	
FL(G)	0.0761289	0.8919436	0.8219945	0.1300825	1

N = 46	DF = 44	P<.05	2 TAIL	CV+/-.2907	

Figure 179. All separation data totals, averages, minimums, and maximums and correlation matrix.

The number of plants is 46, the degrees of freedom 44, P is less than or equal to 0.05, the test is two-tailed, and the critical value is plus or minus 0.2907.

Because the ARSECA plants were (mostly) field trimmed, any ratios of one part to another or to totals for the dry plant cannot be applied to other plants from other gardens. But it's clear the variation in the percentages was large from one plant to another. The DEA grew basically one variety, a seedy Mexican ditchweed. This doesn't indicate the very real variations that occur in real world plants from real world gardens. In the face of such variation, one should take care when trying to generalize. This also calls into question the utility of any canopy estimates of Leafnbud® since they depend on these ratios.

7.   Losses.   Though it is easy to
pretend that a gardener can reap a given amount of dried flowers in
theory, in practice there are always losses along the way. These losses
are usually not taken into account. There are at least five different
kinds: trimming, moving, mold, insects and theft.

To try to get some estimate of what the losses due to the
trimming process, I weighed five dry plants and then separated them
into wood, leaf and flowers. I then summed the weights of the
separated parts and compared the results. Here is the data:

NAME	DP(G)	CALDP(G)	WOOD(G)	LEAF(G)	FL(G)
16B	156	155	35	45	75
3D	366	355	70	41	244
UP4	100	95	17	23	55
UP5	186	174	32	37	105
TS	639	600	339	90	171

	DP(G)	CALDP(G)	WOOD(G)	LEAF(G)	FL(G)
TOTALS	1447	1379	493	236	650
AVG	289.4	275.8	98.6	47.2	130
MIN	100	95	17	23	55
MAX	639	600	339	90	244

Figure 180. Data for handling losses, 2006.

The range of handling losses ranged from a low of 0.64% to a
high of 6.10%. The average ratio between the actual weight of the
hanging dry plant to the calculated weight (that summed from the
wood, leaf and flower) for these five plants was $1447/1379 =
0.9530062$, meaning an average loss of 4.69938, or 4.70% rounded to
two places.

Beyond this there are losses, sometimes quite large, due to
molds. A plant with mold cannot be smoked. The entire plant must
often be discarded, a tragedy. Insects, especially worms, damage the

flowers and also make them unsmokable. Simply moving a dry plant from the drying room to the trimming table leaves a small amount on the drying room floor. Finally, there is simple theft, usually by the friends of the grower who have come over to help and feel they are entitled to help themselves, which mostly they are. I don't have any firm numbers to describe these.

8.   Discussion. Beyond the legal, ethical and philosophical problems inherent in any drug war, and the obvious advantages of licensing, taxing and regulating all drugs, any attempt to estimate the ratio of dried flowers to harvest weight has its own complications. Do we use the average, the maximum or the minimum as our best guess? This will depend on the context in which these numbers will be used. If the standard is beyond any reasonable doubt, it seems obvious that the minimum quantity would protect the rights of the largest number of defendants.

The methods used to grow plants at ARSECA are idiosyncratic. How this data is applicable to non-organic gardens is problematic. There was a large variety in the seeds. The plants were left in the ground until very late. Similarly, the data collection was erratic. The tools used were homemade and crude. Biases exist toward plants maturing early in the season and plants with weights greater than half a kilo.

The statistical analysis gives limited results. The r-squared for the curves of best fit for the harvest weight to dried flowers are decent but not strong, again probably due to the extreme variety of plants. There was a good match between the linear curves of best fit for the ARSECA dried flowers versus that for the DEA Leafnbud® for the mature plants without the anomalies. If only large house brand plants are cherry-picked, it is certainly possible to arrive at a pound of dried flowers on average over a small number of these plants. But the average over all plants over several seasons does not indicate this. The plants had much help and were grown under the direction of a master grower so even a quarter kilo may be out of reach for inexperienced growers. Canopy diameter generally was a poor predictor variable for the weight of dried flowers. The male plants in early August in the ARSECA garden were larger, not smaller than plants of similar age and growth stage in the DEA plantation. But males tend to grow faster than females during this period. Separation percentages of wood, leaf and flower to dry plant show a huge range of values, from variety to variety, plant to plant and year to year. These numbers are difficult to use to generalize to other plants in other gardens because the ARSECA plants (many of them) were trimmed of their shade leaves in the field, some lightly and others seriously. Losses due to handling alone can approach five percent. This does not take into account the losses due to molds, pests and theft. In the end we can say that the magic ratio of dried flowers to freshly harvested plant varies from four percent to twenty-two percent with an average of eleven.

The application of detailed field measurements and mathematical analysis techniques has shown that the weight of the dried flowers of a cannabis plant can be estimated from the harvest weight but not particularly accurately. This ratio will change depending on a large number of factors, especially variety and growing methods. Continued field observations at home gardening locations, both domestic and foreign, may provide some opportunity to further validate or invalidate the relationships reported. Development of cannabis dried flower estimation methodologies is essential for understanding how to arrive at a magic number so we can more accurately weigh witches.

Figures

FIGURES AND TABLES

FIGURES AND TABLES

FIGURES AND TABLES

FIGURES AND TABLES

FIGURES AND TABLES

Tables

Bibliography

Baloch, A. W., et al. "Optimum Plant Density for High Yield in Rice (*Oryza sativa* L.)," *Asian Journal of Plant Sciences*, Volume 1, Number 1: 2002.

Bodin, J. <u>De la Démonomanie des Sorciers</u>, l. iv, ch. v. Paris: Chez Jacques du Puys Librairie Juré, 1580.

Bozorgi, Hamid Reza et al. "Effect of Plant Density on Yield and Yield Components of Rice," *World Applied Sciences Journal*, 12 (11): 2011.

Branagh, Kenneth, dir. *The Magic Flute*. Produced by Pierre-Olivier Bardet and Simon Moseley, distributed by Les Films du Losange, Revolver Entertainment, (2006), imdb.com.

Bupkis Mnemonic, et al. "Estimation of Usable Biomass in a Field of Outdoor Cultivated *Cannabis Sativa* L. plants," *IACM 6th Conference on Cannabinoids in Medicine and 5th European Workshop on Cannabinoid Research* (2011), //www.bonn2011.org.

Burr, George L., ed. <u>Translations and Reprints from the Original Sources of European History</u>, vol. III, no. 4. Philadelphia, PA: Department of History of the University of Pennsylvania, 1912.

Chadha, Gurinder. *Bend it Like Beckham*. Produced by Gurinder Chadha and Deepak Nayare, distributed by Fox Searchlight Pictures (2002), imdb.com.

Chapstick, Supra et al. "Biomass Field Studies of Field Cultivated Cannabis sativa L. Plants," *Planta Medica* 78: 2012.

"Critical Values for Pearson's Correlation Coefficient," //capone.mtsu.edu/dkfuller/tables/correlationtable.pdf.

DEA. *Cannabis Fields*, 1992.

Deng, Jianming et al. "Models and tests of optimal density and maximal yield for crop plants," *PNAS*, www.pnas.org.

Encyclopaedia Britannica, 11th ed., vol. XXVIII, Vetch to Zymotic Diseases. NY: The Encyclopaedia Britannica Company, 1911.

Escohotado, Antonio. *La historia general de las drogas*. Madrid: Espasa Forum, 1998.

"**F**acilities," www.olemizzsports.com.

Faulkner, William. Absalom, Absalom! New York: Random House, 1936.

Gilliam, Terry and Terry Jones, dirs. *Monty Python and the Holy Grail*. Produced by Mark Forstater and Michael White, distributed by EMI Films/Rainbow Releasing/Cinema 5 Distributing (1975), imdb.com.

Hooper, Tom, dir. *Les Misérables*. Produced by Tim Bevan, et al., distributed by Universal Pictures (2012), imdb.com.

Hosseini, N. Majnoun et al. "Effect of Plant Population Density on Yield and Yield Components of Eight Isolines of cv. Clark (*Glycine max* L.)," *J. Agric. Sci. Technol.*, Vol. 3: 2001.

Kgasago, Hans. "Effect of planting dates and densities on yield and yield components of short and ultra-short growth period maize (*Zea mays* L.)," Department of Plant Production and Soil Science, University of Praetoria, 2006.

Konrad, Chris. *Cannabis Fields and Postage*, page 9, saveacownow.org.

BIBLIOGRAPHY

Krugman, Paul. "Who Should We Listen To?" *The Conscience of a Liberal*, //krugman.blogs.nytimes.com.

Lin, X. Q. et al. "Effect of plant density and nitrogen fertilizer rates on grain yield and nitrogen uptake of hybrid rice (*Oryza sativa* L.)," *Journal of Agricultural Biotechnology and Sustainable Development*, Vol. 1 (2): November 2009.

Naseri, Rahim et al. "Study on effects of different plant density on seed yield, oil and protein content of four canola cultivars in western Iran," *International Journal of Agriculture and Crop Sciences*, vol. 4-2: 2012.

Nik, Mohsen. Moussavi et al. "Effect of plant density on yield and yield components of corn hybrids (*Zea mays*)," *Scientific Research and Essays*, Vol. 6 (22): 7 October 2011.

Rahman, M. M. and M. M. Hossain. "Plant Density Effects on Growth, Yield and Yield Components of Two Soybean Varieties under Equidistant Planting Arrangement," *Asian Journal of Plant Sciences*, Vol. 10 (5): 2011.

Reukema, Donald L. "The Yield and Density Aspect – Does Dense Spacing Really Produce the Most Volume," *Proceedings of the 1966 Annual Meeting of Western Reforestation Coordinating Committee*, Portland, Oregon, 1966.

Robinson, Phil Alden, dir. *Field of Dreams*. Produced by Lawrence and Charles Gordon, distributed by Universal Pictures (1989), from www.imdb.com.

Sagan, Carl. "Carl Sagan on Alien Abduction," *NOVA*, www.pbs.org.

Scott, Sir Walter. <u>Marmion: A Tale of Flodden Field in Six Cantos</u>, ed. Michael Macmillan. London: Macmillan and Company, Ltd., 1899.

Van der Werf, Hayo M. G. "The effect of plant density on light interception in hemp (*Cannabis sativa* L.)," *Journal of the International Hemp Association*, 4(1): 1997.

Wachowski Brothers, dirs. *The Matrix*. Produced by Joel Silver, distributed by Warner Brothers Pictures (1999), from www.imdb.com.
Wright, Carroll D. Joint Documents of the State of Michigan for the year 1889, vol. III, Part I. Lansing, MI: Darius D. Thorp, State Binder and Printer, 1890.

Zarei, Gholamreza et al. "Effect of Planting Density on Yield and Yield Components of Safflower Cultivars in Spring Planting," *World Academy of Science, Engineering and Technology* 60: 2011.

Index

___

www.ingramcontent.com/pod-product-compliance
Lightning Source LLC
Chambersburg PA
CBHW020340100426
42812CB00029B/3197/J

.